LUTHER'S WORKS

American Edition

VOLUME 37

Published by Concordia Publishing House

and Fortress Press in 55 volumes.

General Editors are Jaroslav Pelikan (for vols. 1-30)

and Helmut T. Lehmann (for vols. 31-55)

LUTHER'S WORKS

VOLUME 37

Word and Sacrament

III

EDITED BY

ROBERT H. FISCHER

GENERAL EDITOR

HELMUT T. LEHMANN

FORTRESS PRESS

Library of Congress Catalog Card Number 55-9893

ISBN 0-8006-0337-0

Printed in the United States of America 1–337

GENERAL EDITORS' PREFACE

The first editions of Luther's collected works appeared in the sixteenth century, and so did the first efforts to make him "speak English." In America serious attempts in these directions were made for the first time in the nineteenth century. The Saint Louis edition of Luther was the first endeavor on American soil to publish a collected edition of his works, and the Henkel Press in Newmarket, Virginia, was the first to publish some of Luther's writings in an English translation. During the first decade of the twentieth century, J. N. Lenker produced translations of Luther's sermons and commentaries in thirteen volumes. A few years later the first of the six volumes in the Philadelphia (or Holman) edition of the *Works of Martin Luther* appeared. But a growing recognition of the need for more of Luther's works in English has resulted in this American edition of Luther's works.

The edition is intended primarily for the reader whose knowledge of late medieval Latin and sixteenth-century German is too small to permit him to work with Luther in the original languages. Those who can will continue to read Luther in his original words as these have been assembled in the monumental Weimar edition (*D. Martin Luthers Werke.* Kritische Gesamtausgabe, Weimar, 1883-). Its texts and helps have formed a basis for this edition, though in certain places we have felt constrained to depart from its readings and findings. We have tried throughout to translate Luther as he thought translating should be done. That is, we have striven for faithfulness on the basis of the best lexicographical materials available. But where literal accuracy and clarity have conflicted, it is clarity that we have preferred, so that sometimes paraphrase seemed more faithful than literal fidelity. We have proceeded in a similar way in the matter of Bible versions, translating Luther's translations. Where this could be done by the use of an existing English version—King James, Douay, or Revised Standard—we have done so. Where it could not, we have supplied our own. To indicate this in each specific instance would have been pedantic; to adopt a uniform procedure would have been artificial—especially in view of Luther's own inconsistency in this regard. In each volume the translator will be responsible primarily for matters of text and language, while the responsibility of the editor will extend principally to the historical and theological matters reflected in the introductions and notes.

Although the edition as planned will include fifty-five volumes, Luther's writings are not being translated in their entirety. Nor should they be. As he was the first to insist, much of what he wrote and said was not that important. Thus the edition is a selection of works that have proved their importance for the faith, life, and history of the Christian church. The first thirty volumes contain Luther's expositions of various biblical books, while the remaining volumes include what are usually called his "Reformation writings" and other occasional pieces. The final volume of the set will be an index volume; in addition to an index of quotations, proper names, and topics, and a list of corrections and changes, it will contain a glossary of many of the technical terms that recur in Luther's works and that cannot be defined each time they appear. Obviously Luther cannot be forced into any neat set of rubrics. He can provide his reader with bits of autobiography or with political observations as he expounds a psalm, and he can speak tenderly about the meaning of the faith in the midst of polemics against his opponents. It is the hope of publishers, editors, and translators that through this edition the message of Luther's faith will speak more clearly to the modern church.

J. P.
H. T. L.

CONTENTS

ABBREVIATIONS

ACW – *Ancient Christian Writers,* edited by Johannes Quasten and Joseph C. Plumpe (Westminster, Md., 1949-).

ANF – *The Ante-Nicene Fathers,* edited by Alexander Roberts and James Donaldson (Buffalo and New York, 1885-1896, American reprint of the Edinburgh edition).

Br A – *Luthers Werke für das christliche Haus,* edited by Georg Buchwald *et al.*, 4th edition (Leipzig, 1924).

CL – *Luthers Werke in Auswahl,* edited by Otto Clemen *et al.* (Bonn, 1912-1933; Berlin, 1955-1956).

C. R. – *Huldreich Zwinglis Sämtliche Werke,* vols. 88 ff. of the *Corpus Reformatorum,* edited by Emil Egli, Georg Finsler, *et al.* (Leipzig, 1905-).

FC – *Fathers of the Church,* edited by Ludwig Schopp (New York, 1947-).

LCC – *Library of Christian Classics.* John T. McNeill and Henry P. van Dusen, General Editors. (Philadelphia, 1953-).

LE – *The Precious and Sacred Writings of Martin Luther,* edited by John Nicholas Lenker (Minneapolis, 1904-1909).

LW – American Edition of *Luther's Works* (Philadelphia and St. Louis, 1955-).

LWZ – *The Latin Works of Huldreich Zwingli,* 3 vols., translated and edited by S. M. Jackson, *et al.* (New York, 1912; Philadelphia, 1922, 1929).

MA[3] – *Martin Luther.* Ausgewählte Werke, edited by H. H. Borcherdt and Georg Merz. 3rd edition (München, 1948-)

MPG – *Patrologia, Series Graeca,* 161 vols., edited by J. P. Migne (Paris, 1857-1866).

MPL – *Patrologia, Series Latina,* 221 vols. in 222, edited by J. P. Migne (Paris, 1844-1904).

PE – *Works of Martin Luther* (Philadelphia, 1915-1943).

PNF[1] – *The Nicene and Post-Nicene Fathers of the Christian Church* (First Series), edited by Philip Schaff (New York, 1886-1900).

St. L. – *D. Martin Luthers sämmtliche Schriften,* edited by Johann Georg Walch. Edited and published in modern German, 23 vols. in 25 (St. Louis, 1880-1910).

S-J – *Luther's Correspondence,* 2 vols., edited by Preserved Smith and Charles M. Jacobs (Philadelphia, 1913-1918).

WA – *D. Martin Luthers Werke.* Kritische Gesamtausgabe (Weimar, 1883-).

WA, Br – *D. Martin Luthers Werke.* Briefwechsel (Weimar, 1930-1948).

WA, TR – *D. Martin Luthers Werke.* Tischreden (Weimar, 1912-1921).

WA, DB – *D. Martin Luthers Werke.* Deutsche Bibel (Weimar, 1906-).

INTRODUCTION TO VOLUME 37

When Luther wrote his Reformation treatises of 1520, he was waging a one-front battle for the understanding of the gospel. Once the break with Rome had occurred, however, the task of re-establishing church life on an evangelical basis confronted those who were convinced that Rome was wrong. Many kinds of programs were brought forward. They differed as their proponents differed on their understanding of the gospel. Therefore, as Luther in the 1520's worked to bring to expression in the life of the church his insight into the nature of the Christian faith, he now found himself facing a two-front battle, against Romanists on the right, and against a tide of critics on the left who felt that Luther was not going far enough. In handling this two-front battle, the Luther of the 1520's showed himself a fallible mortal, but also a remarkably constructive churchman and conservative evangelical theologian.

One of the bitterest controversies of church practice and theology centered on the Lord's Supper. Luther's critique of the Roman Catholic sacramental system, *The Babylonian Captivity of the Church,* 1520,[1] had won wide favor. But what view was to replace the old? Karlstadt's peculiar effort to spiritualize the sacrament, though discredited in Wittenberg, won sufficient hearing that Christians at Strassburg late in 1524 requested both Luther and Zwingli for written opinions.[2] Luther further expressed his vigorous opposition to Karlstadt's doctrine of the eucharist in Part II of *Against the Heavenly Prophets,* January, 1525.[3] The Strassburgers, however, were more pleased by Zwingli's reply. He did not accept Karlstadt's exegesis of the words of institution, but he recognized Karlstadt as an ally in the battle against the Roman

[1] *LW* 36, 11 ff.

[2] Luther complied with *Letter to the Christians at Strassburg in Opposition to the Fanatic Spirit. LW* 40, 63 ff.

[3] *LW* 40, 144 ff.

Catholic view. Martin Bucer, the Strassburg leader, was convinced that Zwingli's doctrine was in essence correct.

Meanwhile, the Dutch humanist Cornelis Hoen, or Honius, had circulated a new spiritualizing interpretation of the sacrament. When Hoen's treatise came to Luther's attention in 1521 he instantly rejected Hoen's view, sensing behind it a basically different understanding of the gospel. "The text is too powerfully present," he wrote.[4] It was otherwise with Zwingli, who encountered Hoen's letter probably early in 1524. Zwingli welcomed it and thenceforth made constant use of the following interpretations of Hoen: (1) Contrary to the idolatrous Roman Catholic opinion, the Lord's Supper is in essence a visible reminder to trust Christ's promise (just as a ring is a pledge from a bridegroom to his bride). (2) The key to the words of institution, "This is my body," is John 6, where our Lord made it plain that *faith* is the spiritual eating and drinking of his body and blood; no material *body* of Christ is present in the sacrament. (3) Matt. 24:23 and I Cor. 10:16 also show that the Roman Catholic notion of a bodily presence is absurd. (4) The words therefore must be understood *figuratively:* "This *signifies* (or *represents*) my body." (5) The verb "is" in Scripture is often meant figuratively, e.g. Matt. 11:14, I Cor. 10:4, the "I am" passages in John, and Gen. 41:26, etc. (6) A bodily presence in the Lord's Supper contradicts the Apostles' Creed, in the article of Christ's ascension; he removed his bodily presence for our good, John 16:7. (7) No recourse to "miracle" is justifiable, for the miracles Christ performed were not contrary to sense experience.

Zwingli had already developed his conception of faith, with which Hoen's agreed. What he especially welcomed in Hoen was the simple exegesis of the words of institution. In private discussions Zwingli now completed a conception of the Lord's Supper rigorously purged of Roman Catholic notions. The Supper became essentially a joyful memorial feast of thanksgiving and a mutual witness of faith. Zwingli carried this view into liturgical practice in Zurich, against Romanist opposition, during Holy Week of 1525.

Deep-rooted differences over the Lord's Supper, kept out of focus for a time by the fluid theological situation and by pre-

---

[4] *LW* 40, 68. Hoen's treatise, *A Most Christian Letter,* is translated in Heiko Oberman, *Forerunners of the Reformation* (New York, 1966), pp. 268-276. Original in Ernst Ludwig Enders, *D. Martin Luthers Briefwechsel* (Frankfurt-am-Main, 1884-1932), III, 412 ff., and in *Zwinglis Werke. C. R.* 91, 512 ff.

carious political conditions, finally became clearer and clearer. Late in 1524 Karlstadt visited Switzerland, and published there several sharp treatises, which impressed especially the Swiss "Brethren" (Anabaptists). Continually mounting pressure upon Zwingli both from the Brethren and from Roman Catholic antagonists demanded a clarification of his position.

What touched off the tinder was a letter from Zwingli, dated November 16, 1524, to Matthew Alber,[5] a Lutheran pastor in Reutlingen whom Zwingli did not know personally. Expounding John 6 as "a most excellently fortified and strong battle line," Zwingli declared that the significance of the sacrament is a "spiritual eating," the remembrance of Christ's atoning death. The idea of a bodily eating of Christ is a "most noxious and idolatrous opinion." The words of institution are figurative; "is" can only mean "signifies" here, as it often does in Scripture, and the bread symbolizes Christ's body. I Cor. 10:16 points to the same interpretation: "communion" there means not eating but the church. Therefore, the Lord's Supper is a memorial meal, an oath of allegiance, a sign of unity. "Nor do I believe," Zwingli wrote, "that there ever was a person who believed that he ate Christ bodily and essentially in the sacrament."

It is not necessary to assume that Zwingli was underhandedly launching a grand campaign to discredit Luther. He was undoubtedly sincere in feeling that the Roman Catholic view must be thoroughly eradicated, and that Luther must be—and would be—brought to see the light. Zwingli intended the letter to Alber as a theologians' discussion, and charged Alber to keep it so; if the letter eventually needed printing, Zwingli would see to it. Nevertheless, though Luther was not mentioned by name, the attack on him was unmistakable. Not only the contents, with its tone of warning, but also the spread of the letter angered the Wittenbergers. It seems not to have been sent to Alber immediately, yet it was circulated around southern Germany in many handwritten copies, and finally published by Zwingli in March 1525. As Walther Köhler has shown, it was Zwingli who opened the public controversy, despite his persistent claim that his opponents were the aggressors.

For a considerable time Luther declined to answer the attack

[5] The letter to Alber is printed in *C. R.* 90, 335 ff., and in *St. L.* 17, 1512 ff.

directly, but the current of events began to move more and more swiftly. In the troubled year of 1525, Zwingli's great theological work, the *Commentary on True and False Religion*, appeared in March, and its supplement, *Rearguard*, in August. Both were directed chiefly against Romanism, but both unmistakably linked Luther's doctrine of the Lord's Supper with that of the Romanists. Zwingli's Swabian-born colleague in Basel, John Oecolampadius, in August published his learned *Genuine Exposition of the Words of the Lord, "This is my Body," According to the Most Ancient Authors*, hoping to win the south German cities to the Swiss side. His view of the words of institution differed from Zwingli's in that Oecolampadius found the figure not in the verb "is" but in the noun "body"; the original meaning, he held, was, "This is the *sign of my body*." He and Zwingli recognized each other perfectly, however, as allies against the Romanists and Lutherans. Word came to Wittenberg (only partially accurate) that the leaders in Basel and Zurich were in accord with Karlstadt.

Though Luther still refrained from a direct reply to the challenge, literary skirmishes took place in the late summer and autumn of 1525 as Luther's Wittenberg colleague, John Bugenhagen, wrote against Zwingli, and John Brenz and other Lutheran preachers prepared the *Swabian Syngramma* ("Group Opinion") against Oecolampadius. The Swiss quickly returned fire. Meanwhile, Martin Bucer and his associates in Strassburg, from 1524 on, felt a strong kinship with the Swiss in the doctrine of the Supper, but published eloquent pleas for peace and tolerance among the conflicting opinions. "Freedom of opinion in matters not necessary to salvation," advised Wolfgang Capito.[6] In October the Strassburgers sent an emissary of peace to Wittenberg, Gregory Casel, to urge the cause of unity. Luther replied to Casel the following month with a long letter expressing his sharp disagreement with the Swiss view.[7]

Luther's first public utterance came in January, 1526, with the appearance of his letter to the Reutlingen congregation,[8] admonishing them to resist Karlstadt's and Zwingli's views. In June, 1526, he published his *Preface* to the German edition of the *Swabian*

[6] Quoted in Walther Köhler, *Zwingli und Luther* (2 vols.; Leipzig, 1924; Gütersloh, 1953), I, 216.
[7] *S-J* 2, 346 ff.
[8] *WA* 19, 118 ff.; *St. L.* 17, 1539 ff.

Syngramma, in which he identified Karlstadt, Zwingli, and Oecolampadius as three heads of a new sect.[9] His first independent treatise on the controversy, appearing in early autumn, 1526, *The Sacrament of the Body and Blood of Christ—Against the Fanatics,* was simply a pastoral presentation of his views, edited by friends from three Easter sermons.[10]

During this year, however, the controversy expanded fantastically. Not only various Lutherans and Zwinglians clashed, but also the mediating Strassburgers, and humanists, Roman Catholics, Anabaptists, and several others who do not fit into any of these categories, such as Caspar Schwenkfeld. Wittenberg's relations with Bucer were embittered by the discovery that in publishing translations of John Bugenhagen's *Psalms Commentary* and Luther's *Church Postil,* he had inserted his quasi-Zwinglian doctrine of the Lord's Supper through annotations and prefaces.[11] In July, 1526, meanwhile, Bucer urged Zwingli as the acknowledged spokesman for the party to attack Luther head-on, in a "friendly but earnest" way, treating him as a teachable brother, but rebuking Luther's arrogance and disproving his arguments.[12] Zwingli accepted the advice, and set to work on a long treatise, the *Friendly Exposition of the Eucharist Affair, to Martin Luther,* which was to appear at the Frankfurt spring fair of 1527.[13] Luther, in the meantime, felt provoked to a similar task, particularly by Oecolampadius' treatises against the *Syngramma* and against Luther's *Preface* to it, and by the widespread misinterpretation of his silence. He too decided to have a major treatise ready for the fair. The stage was set for a theological showdown.

The two treatises in this volume are Luther's most comprehensive and profound discussions of the Lord's Supper doctrine. Together with *Against the Heavenly Prophets,* they are of capital importance for his understanding of the Word and of Christology as well. This is strikingly indicated by the explicit reference to both treatises in the Formula of Concord, a half-century later, in

[9] *WA* 19, 457 ff., *St. L.* 20, 577 ff. The *Syngramma* itself is printed in German translation in *St. L.* 20, 522 ff.

[10] *LW* 36, 335 ff. See the Introduction to this treatise for other events of 1526.

[11] Cf. pp. 147 ff.

[12] Quoted in Köhler, *op. cit.,* I, 462.

[13] Cf. pp. 153 f.

the articles on the Lord's Supper and on the Person of Christ. Luther's doctrine of the sacrament is derived from his doctrine of the Word of God, and his doctrine of the written Word is derived from his understanding of Christ, the Incarnate Word. Through the controversy of the 1520's Luther clarified his understanding and expression of all three doctrines, hand in hand.

Much the same can be said of Zwingli. Criticisms of his position and his tactics, however, are easy to raise. Aside from disagreements over his doctrine itself, these criticisms have centered on his personal position in the controversy, his manner and tactics, and his political involvement. Zwingli felt a great need to prove his independence from Luther. Though he acknowledged Luther's heroic service in overthrowing the yoke of Rome, Zwingli time and again related the development of the controversy, claiming that he had acquired his understanding of the gospel before Luther's name became famous. This claim is debatable; it seems to be partly true and partly less than true. Moreover, he insisted that he had learned from Hoen in 1524 only an exegetical explanation for a view acquired long before. In reality, though he had shared the widespread Erasmian emphasis on the spiritual eating of faith in connection with the sacrament, he did not abandon transubstantiation until 1523. When he clarified his Lord's Supper conception in 1524, having become convinced that his view alone was right and alone capable of opposing Roman Catholicism, he drew the Lutheran doctrine under his censure. His manner and tactics also aggravated the Lutheran party. He worked aggressively to spread his doctrine in the towns of uncommitted southwest Germany; the Lutherans felt not only that these towns were more or less committed to their care, but also that Zwingli and his colleagues resorted to underhanded tactics to win them away. Zwingli, moreover, apparently expected that not only south Germany but also Wittenberg would come around to his view. His urbane manner, his protestation of open-mindedness and desire for concord, and his condescending way of instructing the Lutherans galled them, especially when bitter barbs and boasts occasionally showed through, and actions seemed to betray something else beneath the surface of mildness. Furthermore, Zwingli's political involvement has come under criticism. In those confusing years not only the Wittenberg theologians but also many German

Protestant civil authorities considered Zwingli too closely related with both Karlstadt and the Anabaptists, and they found his political aggressiveness—which later emerged in Zurich's wars with the Roman Catholic Swiss cantons—a second reason for regarding him not only religiously but politically questionable.

In turn, annoyance has been felt, from Zwingli's day on, over Luther's dogmatic "arrogance," his vehement and sometimes crude language, and his political involvement with the princes. The Lord's Supper controversy, however, cannot be understood in terms of such charges and countercharges. It cannot be explained by reference to temperaments or tempers or ambitions, nor to the "dust in the eyes" of both parties, nor to an alleged unreasonableness on one side or the other. The controversy concerned the very nature of the gospel. Of this both the Swiss and the Lutherans were convinced. Both parties by clear intention were fighting by the watchwords *Christ alone! justification by faith alone! the authority of Scripture alone!* Both sides, no matter how each tried to prove the defects of the other's views, passionately believed that the faith by which we are saved is a personal trust in the atoning Savior Jesus Christ. Both insisted that the Scriptures are the only sure tangible seat of authority in the church. Both insisted that Scripture must be interpreted by Scripture, not by external norms. Both Luther and the Swiss were profoundly devoted to the study of the Scriptures. When Zwingli attacked some views of Luther as "absurd," he tried to make it clear that he meant not absurd to human reason primarily, but incompatible with Scripture and the Creed; each of them insisted that the other was misusing reason and importing it into Scripture.

Beneath these similarities of principle, however, lay a deep divergence which showed itself in their respective conceptions of what *faith* is. This divergence in turn is related to basic differences over the person of Christ, the purpose of the sacrament, the interpretation of the spirit-and-flesh contrast, the proper approach to the Scriptures, and the nature of divine revelation and its relation to reason. All of these divergences came to a head in the discussion over the sacrament and the words of institution. The two paragraphs which follow here by no means present a full analysis of the conflicting theologies, but they may indicate the profundity and comprehensiveness of the clash.

Faith is trust in Jesus Christ, said both; it is a purely spiritual relationship. But what does "spiritual" mean? For Zwingli, faith is spiritual in that it is drawn away from created things to the Creator and Savior. It must have no earthly thing for its object. Body and spirit are mutually exclusive. Hence our faith ought not be drawn even to Christ's body, for this too is creaturely and space-bound; it is Christ's divinity alone which saves us. We cannot speak of a "spiritual body," for such an idea is as absurd as "watery fire" or "wooden iron." Nor can the sacrament have been instituted to provide a bodily eating of Christ's body. Such a notion is absurd even to Scripture and the Creed, and even if it were not, it would be useless. The purpose of the sacrament, therefore, is to lift our faith, by remembrance of the breaking of Christ's body for us on the cross, to heaven, where he sits bodily at the right hand of God—or, to express the thought otherwise, as Zwingli did especially in his later writings, to offer us Christ's spiritual presence. Zwingli denies that this conception separates the two natures of Christ in a Nestorian way. It only recognizes, interpreting Scripture by Scripture, that much of the language of the Bible is figurative. Through John 6 we discern the simple and natural sense of Christ's words: offering his disciples bread, a symbol, he says, "This is my body"; by a figure of speech, in which Christ speaks of his human nature but really has in mind the divine, he summons them to partake of his saving divinity by faith. According to this approach, moreover, "nothing about faith is absurd, if only you rightly understand what is proposed for faith to believe."[14] Faith is not forced credulity, negating our senses and our reason, for revelation and reason are harmonious; God, who leads us into light, not darkness, "does not set before us many incomprehensible things" to believe.

At every point Luther vigorously disagreed. For Luther, faith is spiritual in that God the Holy Spirit produces it and nourishes it. Indeed, the biblical antithesis is not so much between the spiritual and the material or earthly or bodily, as between "spirit" —that which is produced by the Spirit and directed toward the Spirit—and "flesh," i.e. fleshliness—that which is produced by and directed toward our selfish selves, or the devil. Because God uses earthly means in and through which to come to us, faith must

[14] *C. R.* 92, 618.

cling to them, not as its objects but as the signs of his potent presence, the points at which he has told us we shall find him. That this is actually the manner of God's revelation we see supremely in Jesus Christ, who is God and man in one person, incarnate on the plane of history. The only Christ we know is this one Jesus, God in human flesh. Therefore his humanity cannot be called useless to our salvation. Indeed, in his exaltation, even Christ's body cannot be considered limited as creaturely bodies are. God's "right hand," to which Christ ascended, according to Scripture means not a location in heaven but the manifestation of God's power; that Christ is at the right hand of God means that wherever God is now at work there the divine-human Christ is at work. Revelation takes place when God enables us to see him thus at work. The sacrament, therefore, was instituted as a means of grace, the feeding of Christ's people—no crass eating, but nonetheless a true partaking of the one Jesus Christ. Such an action cannot be useless, since he commanded it; nor dare it be dismissed as absurd, for it accords perfectly with what we know from Scripture about God's manner of revealing himself. The sacrament, then, is a means through which Christ once more gives himself to us, not something we give to him or do in his and others' presence. To understand "This bread *is* my body" literally by no means implies transubstantiation, or even a materialistic consubstantiation, but simply a "sacramental union," analogous to the union of natures in the person of Christ: not a metaphysical but a religious affirmation that the God-man Jesus Christ has graciously bound his presence to this celebration as a special instance of his self-impartation. As the union of Christ's divinity with his humanity is real, not figurative—though this passes our comprehension—so the promise that he truly unites himself with the bread as we obey his command must be taken at face value. Hence we have no right to read a figurative interpretation into Christ's words of institution, both because Scripture by no means requires it—indeed, forbids it—and because the inner consistency of scriptural faith is not to be found in its comprehensibility but in its focus in Jesus Christ. Faith indeed is not blind credulity. It is unreserved allegiance to Jesus of Nazareth as the Christ, the Son of the living God, whose cross was foolishness and a stumbling-block to the world. So God even yet discloses himself to those who believe, hidden under what reason regards as absurd; even yet he uses the lowly to confound the mighty and leads us into the darkness and even death in order to bring us forth into his marvelous light and his abiding life.

It is an expression of the very heart of Zwingli's faith, then, when he insists that the "spiritual presence" of Christ's divinity in the sacrament is the most that Scripture permits, and that Luther's view is still enmeshed in Romanism. It is an expression of the very heart of Luther's faith when he declares that the "real presence" of the indivisible, living Christ in the sacrament is alone scriptural, and that Zwingli's view is enmeshed in radicalism. For this reason Luther could not agree, either, when Bucer and Zwingli pleaded that since both sides affirmed the necessity and the centrality of the spiritual eating, faith, it was idle to insist upon more. Each side declared the opposing position un-Christian. Luther repeatedly charged that his adversaries were led by an evil spirit, and the Swiss and the Strassburgers repeatedly charged that the Spirit of Christ had forsaken Luther. So the bitter controversy moved inexorably toward its first great climax, the Marburg Colloquy of 1529.

Throughout this quarrel, meanwhile, we must keep firmly in mind its churchly context. We must not regard the controversy as mere theological hairsplitting between two opinionated individuals. Both Luther and Zwingli were constructive churchmen, seeking a renewal of the church life of Europe. If we wish to know Luther's doctrine of the Lord's Supper, we should begin with his constructive churchly writings, such as his liturgies (cf. *LW* 53), his Small and Large Catechisms of 1529, and his sermons. Here, indeed, we shall find not merely the rudiments of his Lord's Supper doctrine but its very heart and essence. We shall find the heart and essence of Zwingli's doctrine of the Supper in similar works where the Zuricher writes as a teacher of the church. The polemical writings of the great controversy are not more truly Luther's and Zwingli's real doctrines; they are rather the elaboration and testing and defense of the doctrine which each proposed for the Christian Church.

Because the literary battle was so intently waged with statement and rebuttal, charge and countercharge, this volume has been annotated with quotations from Luther's adversaries in order to clarify the context of his thoughts. Most of the writings of the Swiss and the Strassburgers on the Lord's Supper are not yet available in English. Indeed, only Zwingli's *Commentary on True and False Religion,* 1525 (*LWZ* 3), and his *Clear Instruction Concerning Christ's Supper,* 1526 (*LCC* 24), are generally accessible; therefore I have quoted from them wherever possible. Where Zwingli's treatises quoted are not available in English, I have cited first from the valuable new critical edition of Zwingli's *Sämtliche Werke* in *Corpus Reformatorum,* volumes 88 ff., rather than the old Schuler-Schulthess edition cited in the copious notes of the Weimar edition. Secondly, since many of the Swiss and Strassburger treatises are found in modern German, along with a detailed historical introduction, in the St. Louis edition of Luther's works, volumes 17 and 20, I have identified references therein.

To several scholars whom I consulted at one or another point in the preparation of this volume, I wish to record my thanks: Dr. Jaroslav Pelikan, Federated Theological Faculty, University of Chicago; Professors George W. Forell and Richard R. Syré, my colleagues at Chicago Lutheran Seminary; Professors Frederick C. Ahrens, Gettysburg College, Lewis W. Spitz, Jr., Stanford University, George Lindbeck, Yale, Quirinus Breen, University of Oregon, Fritz Blanke, Zurich, Ernst Staehelin, Basel, and Dr. Hans Volz of the Weimar Edition Commission.

The most comprehensive study of the controversy is that of Walther Köhler, *Zwingli und Luther,* 2 vols.; Vol. I (Leipzig, 1924) goes to the threshold of the Marburg Colloquy, Vol. II (Gütersloh, 1953) to the Wittenberg Concord, 1536.

In contemporary literature in English the following books are relevant to the controversy: Hermann Sasse, *This Is My Body* (Minneapolis, 1959): a historical study, which includes an English translation of the Marburg discussions; Heinrich Bornkamm, *Luther's World of Thought* (St. Louis, 1958); Regin Prenter, *Spiritus Creator* (Philadelphia, 1953); Yngve Brilioth, *Eucharistic Faith and Practice* (New York, 1956); E. G. Schwiebert, *Luther and His Times* (St. Louis, 1950); Jaroslav Pelikan, *Luther the Expositor* (St. Louis, 1959), a companion volume to *LW* 1-30.

R. H. F.

LUTHER'S WORKS

VOLUME 37

THAT THESE WORDS OF CHRIST, "THIS IS MY BODY," ETC., STILL STAND FIRM AGAINST THE FANATICS

1527

Translated by Robert H. Fischer

INTRODUCTION

What Luther had written on the Lord's Supper issue in 1526 had been intended more as an explanation of his disagreement with the Swiss than as a polemic. Luther had said, "These fanatics do not disturb me, and are not worthy that one should fight with them."[1] Eventually, however, he realized that he had to write against them directly. No longer could he remain undisturbed. The doctrines of Karlstadt and the Swiss were spread by so many writings that the "fanatical" view of the sacrament, Luther wrote, "rages like a plague and grows stronger and stronger."[2]

More than two dozen published writings had directly or indirectly attacked Luther's view of the Lord's Supper between late 1524 and early 1527.[3] In his treatise, *That These Words of Christ, "This Is My Body," Still Stand Firm,* Luther alludes to eleven of these, and it is certain that he was acquainted with at least three more.

As a result of these writings, Luther discovered, the "foolish masses" were ridiculing the sacrament. Even former supporters like Theobald Billican and Urban Rhegius defected to the Swiss side. By August, 1526, it was clear to Luther that he had to publish a polemical treatise of his own. Friends and foes alike were exerting pressure. Oecolampadius declared in print that the Spirit of God must have forsaken Luther, or the latter would not keep silence. Landgrave Philip of Hesse threatened to read nothing more from Luther unless he wrote against the new error of Zwingli and Oecolampadius. Both Melanchthon and Nicolas Gerbel, Luther's friend in Strassburg, urged him to write.

Luther now accepted the challenge. Whether his adversaries mocked his conception as absurd, or only treated the topic of controversy as an indifferent matter, Luther felt that the gospel itself was at stake. More and more he became convinced that

---

[1] *LW* 36, 346.
[2] *WA*, Br 4, 123 ff. (letters of October, 1526).
[3] A list of these writings is given at the end of this Introduction, pp. 8 ff.

the devil himself had caused the whole commotion. Accordingly, though Luther by now was aware that Zwingli and Oecolampadius were the most formidable of these rivals, he treated his opposition as a totality, and directed his attack against the "spirit" he believed controlled his adversaries rather than against them as individuals. One result of this procedure, however, was that Luther tended to hold all of them responsible for anything expressed by one.

Luther concentrated on the writing of his treatise from early January, 1527, to mid-March. The virtually complete manuscript, still extant, shows the care with which Luther wrote, retouched, and more than once revised the work. He succeeded in having it published in time for the Frankfurt spring fair, at which two of Zwingli's treatises also appeared.

Luther's treatise opens with the assertion that the Lord's Supper controversy has been caused by the devil, who has taken possession of the fanatics (pp. 13-23). The quarrel is over the words of institution, and there is no middle ground between the opposing parties (pp. 23-46). Claiming to take his stand on the simple words themselves, Luther declares it is Zwingli's responsibility to prove that they *must* be figurative. Now he proceeds to Zwingli's basic arguments, that Christ's ascension and John 6:63 contradict the presence of Christ in the Supper (pp. 46-78). To the argument from the ascension, Luther replies that this proves no contradiction. Reason cannot disprove Christ's presence. God's right hand does not mean a location in space, but God's effective presence. God can cause a created thing to be present by other modes than the local one. To the retort that the sacrament would be unnecessary if Christ were available everywhere, Luther replies that though God is everywhere, he is not everywhere for us! We are to find him where he bids us seek him.[4] Following the naïve realism of the early fathers, Luther asserts that the partaking of Christ's body, far from being useless, brings abiding benefit not only to our souls but also to our bodies.

Next, Luther argues that the Swiss misinterpret John 6:63 (pp. 78-104). "The flesh is of no avail" cannot apply to Christ's flesh

[4] Cf. *The Sacrament of the Body and Blood of Christ—Against the Fanatics. LW* 36, 342.

without destroying the Incarnation. In a sacrament two things are necessary: the Word and the physical element or act. This does not eliminate faith, but precisely requires it; the mouth eats for the heart, and the heart understands the significance of the act for the mouth. Thus Luther is led to discuss the biblical meaning of "spirit" and "flesh" (pp. 89 ff.). "Spiritual is nothing else than what is done in us and by us through the Spirit and faith, whether the object with which we are dealing is physical or spiritual. Thus spirit consists in the use, not in the object."[5] Luther therefore lays down the rule that where Scripture contrasts flesh with spirit, it cannot refer to Christ's flesh, but refers to fleshliness, or the fleshly mind (p. 95).

Finally, Luther deals with Oecolampadius' arguments from the church fathers (pp. 104-124), and with a variety of details in the Swiss argument (pp. 124-147), recurring to his contention that the way God works with men is to convey to us his Word in "outward things" (pp. 135 ff.). Luther calls upon the Zwinglians to keep to the main point: the proof that a bodily presence of Christ in the sacrament is an absurdity (pp. 144 ff.). At the end Luther denounces Bucer's rascality in inserting the Zwinglian doctrine into his published translations of Bugenhagen's *Psalms Commentary* and Luther's own *Church Postil* (pp. 147-150). This is a proof, Luther declares, that the adversaries' pleas for moderation and peace are deceitful.

Though Luther later disparaged his book as "verbose and not very learned,"[6] he was encouraged that "it has helped many," "has snatched many from their [the Sacrament-blasphemers'] jaws and confirmed and strengthened many more in the truth."[7] Luther's friends applauded the work. His adversaries detested it, and immediately planned their rebuttals. Luther on his part had written before the completion of "*This Is My Body*" that he had a plan for a further treatise, should one prove necessary.[8] So the controversy dragged on.

The text of the treatise, both Luther's manuscript and the printed edition with annotations, is found in *WA* 23, 64-283; in

[5] See p. 92. [6] *WA*, Br 4, 212.
[7] *S-J* 2, 398, and *WA* 23, 379.
[8] *WA*, Br 4, 175.

modernized German in *Br A* 4, 335-480, and in *St. L.* 20, 762-893 (printed version alone).

A list of published writings attacking Luther's view of the Lord's Supper includes the following:

Ulrich [Huldreich] Zwingli:

Letter to Matthew Alber, published in 1525. Cf. p. xiii, above. *C. R.* 90, 335 ff.; *St. L.* 17, 1512 ff.

Commentary on True and False Religion, 1525. *LWZ* 3, 43 ff.; *C. R.* 90, 628 ff.; *St. L.* 20, 441 ff.

Rearguard or Supplement[9] *Concerning the Eucharist*, 1525. *C. R.* 91, 458 ff.

Reply to the Letter of John Bugenhagen of Pomerania, 1525. *C. R.* 91, 558 ff.; *St. L.* 20, 506 ff.

A Clear Instruction Concerning Christ's Supper, 1526. *LCC* 24, 185 ff.; *C. R.* 91, 789 ff. Zwingli's first treatise on the subject in German.

Reply to the Letters of Theobald Billican and Urban Rhegius, 1526. *C. R.* 91, 893 ff. Rhegius of Augsburg had published an exchange of letters between Billican of Nördlingen and himself. Within a few months Zwingli published this reply to them both.

First Brief Answer Concerning Eck's Seven Theses, 1526. *C. R.* 92, 177 ff. John Eck had challenged Zwingli to a debate, which was arranged at Baden, Switzerland, in the summer of 1526. The Zurich Town Council did not allow Zwingli to attend, but he answered Eck in writing. To Eck's first thesis, that the true body and blood of Christ are present in the sacrament of the altar, Zwingli replied, "This article is un-Christian, for it clearly conflicts with God's Word and with the articles of our true, ancient, Christian Creed" (*C. R.* 92, 182). Written in German.

Brief Reply to a Rather Long Letter of a Certain Friend [Jacob Edlibach] . . . in which the Question of the Eucharist Is Treated, 1526. *C. R.* 92, 342 ff.

Declaration on Original Sin, 1526. *LCC* 24, 129 ff.; *C. R.* 92, 369 ff.

---

[9] *Coronis* literally means a flourish of the pen signifying the end of a writing.

Answer to Strauss' Pamphlet Concerning Christ's Supper, January, 1527. *C. R.* 92, 464 ff.; *St. L.* 20, 1494 ff. Jacob Strauss was a vigorous Roman Catholic opponent of Zwingli in Zurich.

John Oecolampadius:

Genuine Exposition of the Words of the Lord, "This Is My Body," According to the Most Ancient Authors, 1525.

Apologetics: Two Sermons on the Dignity of the Eucharist; Reply to Theobald Billican . . .; Antisyngramma, to the Swabian Clergymen, 1526. Billican had written a refutation of Oecolampadius in December, 1525; the *Swabian Syngramma* had been published in January, 1526. The reply to Billican, in German translation, appears in *St. L.* 20, 634 ff.

Reply to Willibald Pirkheimer on the Subject of the Eucharist, 1526. Pirkheimer, the great Nürnberg humanist, had written a rebuttal of Oecolampadius earlier in the same year.

Reasonable Answer to Dr. Martin Luther's Instruction Concerning the Sacrament, Together with a Brief Summary Against the Treatise of Certain Preachers in Swabia Regarding the Words of the Lord's Supper, 1526. *St. L.* 20, 582 ff. A lengthy rebuttal, in German, of Luther's German *Preface* to the *Swabian Syngramma* (1526); the second part is a brief excerpt from the *Antisyngramma.*

Wolfgang Capito:

What One Should Think and Answer Concerning the Dissension Between Martin Luther and Andreas Karlstadt, late 1524. *St. L.* 20, 340 ff. A brief German pamphlet.

Martin Bucer:

Apology, Whereby He Simply Renders Account of his Faith and of the Doctrine Concerning Christ's Supper Which Both He and Other Strassburg Clergymen Profess, and Without Rancor Wards off the Slanders Directed Against him by a Certain Letter of John Brenz, Clergyman of Hall, Issued, It Is Believed, Without the Knowledge of the Author, 1526.

The Psalter, Well Translated out of the Holy Tongue into German. An Exposition of the Psalter, Very Clear and Useful, by John Bugenhagen of Pomerania, Translated from Latin into German, Emended at Several Points by Himself, 1526. Bucer inserted the Swiss doctrine of the Supper into Bugenhagen's commentary. The latter published a vehement protest.

Fourth Volume of Expositions of the Epistles and Gospels . . . by Martin Luther, 1526. Luther had been pleased by Bucer's first three volumes of translations into Latin of his *Church Postil.* In the fourth volume, however, Bucer inserted the Swiss doctrine of the Supper. Luther protested bitterly in a letter to the printer, John Herwagen of Strassburg (*S-J* 2, 377 ff.).

Preface to the Fourth Volume of Luther's Postil, Containing a Summary of the Doctrine of Christ. Letter by the Same Author [Bucer], *Expounding the Passage of I Corinthians 10 [9:24–10:5], With a Few Annotations on Certain Expressions of Luther. Letter of Martin Luther to John Herwagen Complaining of the Above. Martin Bucer's Reply to This, Also Amends to Bugenhagen Concerning the Version of the Psalter,* 1527. Bucer's *Preface* appears in German translation in *St. L.* 17, 1584 ff. In March, 1527, Bucer republished his additions to Luther's *Postil,* defending himself against Luther's and Bugenhagen's reproaches, and rebuking their wrath. Luther appears to have been informed of Bucer's intentions prior to the publication.

Leo Jud:

Opinion of the Learned Erasmus of Rotterdam and of Dr. Luther Concerning the Supper of our Lord Jesus Christ, 1526. This German pamphlet, issued under the pseudonym Ludovicus Leopoldi, claimed that both Erasmus and Luther really taught the Swiss doctrine. Both were enraged.

John Landtsperger:

Answer to the Learned Dr. John Bugenhagen of Pomerania . . . to the Letter Which He Sent to the Learned Dr. Hess, Teacher in Breslau, Concerning the Sacrament, 1525. The author, a former Carmelite of Augsburg, used the pseudonym Konrad Ryss.

Brief Summary Concerning the Old and New Papists, 1526. Another German pamphlet, appearing anonymously.

In his own name, Landtsperger addressed a lengthy letter late in 1526 to the town and university officials at Wittenberg, which he published in the spring of 1527 under the title, *A Fraternal Supplication and Admonition to the Rector and All the Members of the University of Wittenberg.*

Konrad Sam:

A Fine and True German Statement for the Common Man, Whether the Body of Jesus Christ Is to be Honored in Heaven at the Right Hand of God and Sought in the Spirit, Or to be Hoped for on Earth, Essentially in the Bread, 1526. The pamphlet appeared anonymously.

John Schnewil:

Against Uncharitable Condemnation . . ., 1526. A tract directed particularly against Zwingli's Roman Catholic opponent, Jacob Strauss.

Eitelhans Langenmantel:

A Brief Indication How Dr. Martin Luther Has Published Several Writings on the Sacrament, Which However Directly Contradict One Another. . . . A pamphlet, appearing early in 1527, by an Anabaptist patrician of Augsburg.

Valentine Krautwald:

Comparison and Agreement of the Words of the Lord's Supper, on the Body and Blood of Christ, with the Sixth Chapter of John the Evangelist. Also: A Consideration of the Word of God, Whether It Is in the Bread of the Eucharist and the Water of Baptism. In *Corpus Schwenckfeldianorum,* ed. C. D. Hartranft (Leipzig, 1911), 2, 391-408. Two short Latin treatises by the colleague of Caspar Schwenkfeld, presumably published in 1526.

On the Lord's Supper and the Words of the Supper. Two Letters. In *Corpus Schwenckfeldianorum,* 2, 422-438. Latin writings, apparently published in 1526.

This list, indeed, does not include the many treatises of Karlstadt, or the unpublished treatises and letters of Schwenkfeld and Krautwald (cf. p. 40, n. 64).

THAT THESE WORDS OF CHRIST, "THIS IS MY BODY," ETC., STILL STAND FIRM AGAINST THE FANATICS

How very true is the proverb that the devil is master of a thousand arts! This he proves beyond question in all the stratagems by which he rules his world, as in outward, palpable deeds of guile, intrigues, wickedness, sins, murder, destruction, etc. But especially and supremely does he demonstrate his craftiness in spiritual, inward matters which concern the glory of God and conscience. How he can slither and squirm, twist and turn in all directions, and hinder and thwart us on all sides, that no one may be saved and persevere in the Christian truth. As an example of the devil's work let us take the history of Christianity (I shall not mention the ancient fathers and the Jews). In the beginning of the gospel, when God's Word was preached by the apostles purely and clearly, and no human commandments but simply the holy Scriptures were set forth, it seemed as if there would never be any trouble, since holy Scripture was the empress among the Christians.

But what could the devil not do? He finally permitted the Scriptures to be the sole authority, and allowed no pharisaical, Jewish commandments or laws concerning works to prevail any longer. But he also had some of his followers in the Christians' schools, and through them he stealthily sneaked and crept into the holy Scriptures. Once he had wormed his way in and had things under control, he burst out on all sides, creating a real brawl over Scripture and producing many sects, heresies, and factions among Christians. Since every faction claimed Scripture for itself and interpreted it according to its own understanding, the result was that Scripture began to lose its worth, and eventually even acquired the reputation of being a heretics' book[1] and the source of all heresy, since all heretics seek the aid of Scripture. Thus the devil was able to wrest from the Christians their weapons, armor, and fortress (i.e. Scripture), so that it not only became feeble and ineffective against him, but even had to fight against the Christians themselves. He got Christians to become suspicious of it, as if it were plain poison against which they had to defend themselves. Tell me, wasn't that a clever scheme of the devil?

Once Scripture had become like a broken net and no one would be restrained by it, but everyone made a hole in it wherever it pleased him to poke his snout, and followed his own opinions, interpreting and twisting Scripture any way he pleased, the Christians knew no other way to cope with these problems than to call many councils. In these they issued many outward laws and ordinances alongside Scripture, in order to keep the people together in the face of these divisions. As a result of this undertaking (though they meant well), arose the sayings that the Scriptures were not sufficient, that we also needed the laws and the interpretations of the councils and the fathers, and that the Holy Spirit did not reveal everything to the apostles but reserved certain things for the fathers. Out of this finally developed the papacy, in which there is no authority but man-made laws and interpretations according to the "chamber of the holy father's heart." [2]

When the devil saw this he jeered and thought: now I have won! Scripture lies prostrate, the fortress is destroyed, the weapons are beaten down. In their place they now weave walls of straw and make weapons of hay, i.e. they intend now to array themselves against me with man-made laws.[3] Ah, this is serious! What shall I do? I shall not fight against this, but pitch in and help them

[1] The Bible gained a reputation as a heretics' book while the church was engaged in suppressing the Waldensians and Cathari who claimed the Bible in support of their views. The Council of Toulouse in 1229 forbade laymen to be in possession of the Old and New Testament Scriptures. *Br A* 4, 343, n. 1.

[2] *Scrinium pectoris.* Cf. *An Open Letter to the Christian Nobility* (1520). *LW* 44, 202, n. 215; *Misuse of the Mass* (1521). *LW* 36, 205, n. 65: "According to a decree of Boniface VIII (1294-1303), the Roman pontiff has all laws in 'the chamber of his heart.'" *Licet Romanum Pontifex, Decretalium Bonifacii VIII*, lib. i, tit. II: *de constitutionibus*, cap. 1. Aemilius Friedberg (ed.), *Corpus Iuris Canonici* (Graz, 1955), II, col. 937.

[3] Cf. the Romanists' three "walls of straw and paper." *An Open Letter to the Christian Nobility. LW* 44, 127.

build so that they remain nicely united, and help them gather enough straw and hay. It serves my purpose well that they should neglect the Word and not dispute over the Scriptures, but that at this very point they should be at peace and believe what the councils and the fathers say. But within this peace and unity I shall stir up many another controversy and quarrel, so that the pope will contend against emperor and kings, bishops against princes and lords, scholars against scholars, clerics against clerics, and everyone against the other, for the sake of temporal honor, possessions, and pleasure, yet leaving untouched their unity of belief in the holy fathers. The fools! What can they expect to accomplish with quarrels over the Scriptures and the things of God they do not understand? It is better for them to quarrel over honor, kingdoms, principalities, property, pleasure, and bodily needs, which they do understand, and meanwhile remain faithful Christians united in the glossed faith of the fathers, i.e. a flimsy faith.[4]

This is the way the plot worked out for the fathers: Since they contrived to have the Scriptures without quarreling and dissension, they thereby became the cause of men's turning wholly and completely away from the Scriptures to mere human drivel. Then, of course, dissension and contention over the Scriptures necessarily ceased, which is a divine quarrel wherein God contends with the devil, as St. Paul says in Ephesians 6 [:12], "We have to contend not against flesh and blood, but against spiritual wickedness in the air." But in place of this, there has broken out human dissension over temporal honor and goods on earth, yet there remain a united blindness and ignorance of the Scriptures and a loss of the true Christian faith, i.e. a united obedience to the glosses of the fathers and to the holy see at Rome. Isn't this also a piece of devilish craftiness? No matter what play we make, he is a master and an expert at the game.

Now in our day, having seen that Scripture was utterly neglected[5] and the devil was making captives and fools of us by

---

[4] A play on words: *glosen glauben . . . losen glauben.* "Glosses" are brief comments or explanations, e.g. on verses of Scripture, cf. pp. 342 ff.; Luther complains that men's glosses distort and eventually displace the Word itself.
[5] *Unter der banck lag,* i.e. lay under the bench.

the mere straw and hay of man-made laws, we have tried by God's grace to offer some help in the matter. With immense and bitter effort indeed we have brought the Scriptures to the fore again and released the people from man-made laws, freed ourselves and escaped the devil, although he stubbornly resisted and still continues to do so. However, even though he has had to let us go, he does not forget his tricks. He has secretly sown his seed among us so that they may take hold of our teachings and words, not to aid and assist us in fostering the Scriptures, but, while we were leading in the fight against human drivel, to fall upon our host from the rear, incite rebellion and raise an uproar against us, in order that caught between two enemies, we may be more easily destroyed. This is what I call throwing quicksilver into the pond! [6]

However, he does not leave the matter there, but quick as a flash goes to work on the sacraments, although in this respect he has already torn at least ten rips and loopholes in the Scriptures. I have never read of a more shameful heresy, which from the outset has gathered to itself so many heads, so many factions and dissensions, although on the main point, the persecution of Christ, they are united. But he will keep on and attack still other articles of faith, as he already declares with flashing eyes that baptism, original sin, and Christ are nothing.[7] Once more there will arise a brawl over the Scriptures, and such dissension and so many factions that we may well say with St. Paul, "The mystery of lawlessness is already at work" [II Thess. 2:7], just as he also saw that many more factions would arise after him.

[6] A German superstition said that a pond or well would be ruined if quicksilver were thrown into it. Luther implies that, figuratively speaking, the water supply of his followers would thus be cut off. *WA* 23, 285.

[7] On *baptism:* Zwingli: "In baptism we receive a token that we are to fashion our lives according to the rule of Christ." *Commentary on True and False Religion,* 1525. *LWZ* 3, 184. Oecolampadius: "Outward baptism . . . signifies that we are inwardly born and washed from the filth of sin. Neither the Holy Spirit nor the grace . . . is bound to the water." *Reasonable Answer,* 1526. *St. L.* 20, 612. On *original sin:* Zwingli: "The original contamination is a disease, not a sin, because sin implies guilt. . . . To be born a slave is a wretched condition, but it is not a fault [*culpa*] nor a crime in him who is so born." *Declaration Regarding Original Sin,* 1526. *LWZ* 2, 5. On *Christ:* See not only Zwingli's conviction that the noble pagans are among the saved (*Original Sin, LWZ* 2, 12; cf. *Exposition of the Faith,* 1531. *LCC* 24, 275) but also Luther's entire argument that the Swiss doctrine of the Supper rejects Christ, e.g. pp. 53, 150.

If the world lasts much longer, men will, as the ancients did, once more turn to human schemes on account of this dissension, and again issue laws and regulations to keep the people in the unity of the faith. Their success will be the same as it was in the past.

In short, the devil is too clever and too mighty for us. He resists and hinders us at every point. When we wish to deal with Scripture, he stirs up so much dissension and quarreling over it that we lose our interest in it and become reluctant to trust it. We must forever be scuffling and wrestling with him. If we wish to stand upon the councils and counsels of men, we lose the Scriptures altogether and remain in the devil's possession body and soul.[8] He is Satan, and Satan is his name, i.e. an adversary.[9] He must obstruct and cause misfortune; he cannot do otherwise. Moreover, he is the prince and god of this world,[10] so that he has sufficient power to do so. Since he is able and determined to do all this, we must not imagine that we shall have peace from him. He takes no vacation and he does not sleep. Choose, then, whether you prefer to wrestle with the devil or whether you prefer to belong to him. If you consent to be his, you will receive his guarantee to leave you in peace with the Scriptures. If you refuse to be his, defend yourself, go at him! He will not pass you by; he will create such dissension and sectarianism over the Scriptures that you will not know where Scriptures, faith, Christ, and you yourself stand.

Woe betide all our teachers and authors, who go their merry way and spew forth whatever is uppermost in their minds,[11] and do not first turn a thought over ten times to be sure it is right in the sight of God! These think the devil is away for a while in Babylon, or asleep at their side like a dog on a cushion. They do not consider that he is round about them with all his venomous flaming darts[12] which he puts into them,[13] such superlatively

---

[8] *Mit haut und har,* literally, with skin and hair.
[9] Cf. I Pet. 5:8. The Hebrew word *Satan* means "adversary"
[10] Cf. John 12:31, II Cor. 4:4, etc.
[11] *Alles, was yhn yns maul fellet.*
[12] Cf. Eph. 6:16.
[13] *Die er eingiebt,* which has the double meaning of "putting into" and "inspiring with."

beautiful thoughts adorned with Scripture that they are unaware of what is happening. Here no admonition, no warnings, no threats are of any avail. The devil is master of a thousand arts. If God does not defend and help us, all our actions and counsels are nothing. No matter which way you look at it, the devil is the prince of this world. He who does not know this, let him try and see. I have had some experience in this matter. But no one will believe me until he experiences it also.

It is precisely the same devil who now assails us through the fanatics[14] by blaspheming the holy and venerable sacrament of our Lord Jesus Christ, out of which they would like to make mere bread and wine as a symbol or memorial sign of Christians, in whatever way their dream or fancy dictates. They will not grant that the Lord's body and blood are present, even though the plain, clear words stand right there: "Eat, this is my body." Yet those words still stand firm and invulnerable against them. Now, I dealt with this subject carefully in my attack against Karlstadt,[15] in such a way that anyone who did not take pleasure in erring could find guidance against this specter of the devil. But my dear fanatics despise me so haughtily that they do not consider me worthy of a careful answer. It is enough for them to look at my

---

[14] Originally Luther referred to men like Thomas Münzer, Nikolaus Storch, Gabriel Zwilling, and Andreas Karlstadt as fanatics. The disturbances created by them compelled Luther to return from the Wartburg to Wittenberg where he restored order through the preaching of his well-known "Invocavit Sermons" in 1522 (*LW* 51, 69-100). Having directed a further broadside at Karlstadt and the fanatics in 1525 (see note 15), he now also described Zwingli as a *Schwärmer.* Zwingli was sensitive to the charge of being a *Schwärmer.* "You call us fanatics. I don't really understand what 'fanatic' means." If it means fool, Zwingli concedes, he like all men is fond of Lady Folly. But if it means *praestigiator* (juggler, impostor) or *fanaticus* (irrational or mad person), "let's see who are really the madder." He concludes that Luther is a "fanatic, fool, bumpkin, yes a devil, murderer, and corrupter of souls who blasphemes the holy and venerable sacrament of our Lord Jesus Christ." *That These Words . . . Will Always Retain Their Ancient, Single Meaning. Ulrich Zwingli's Christian Answer,* 1527. *C. R.* 92, 831; *St. L.* 20, 1139. "Friend, don't you know what *schwirmen, schwermen, schwarmen* means?" *Ibid. C. R.* 92, 936; *St. L.* 20, 1201. *Schwärmen* or *schwarmen* means "to swarm," as of bees, also "to rave"; Zwingli explained *schwirmen* as "to hallucinate." *Ibid.* C. R. 92, 916; St. L. 20, 1189, n. 9.

[15] Formerly a university colleague of Luther, Andreas Bodenstein von Karlstadt was the chief target of the treatise, *Against the Heavenly Prophets,* 1524-1525. *LW* 40, 79-223.

book and turn up their noses at it and say, "It lacks Spirit." What good is it now for me to write a great deal? They scorn my book, and if they just babble a few words about it, without touching a single argument correctly, they consider it refuted. They rest their case simply upon the production of many books and the soiling of much paper.

One of the reasons I have hesitated until now to write further against them is that I have sensed such arrogance and contempt beneath their celebrated humility. Secondly, their fanaticism is such sheer, empty prattle that it amazes me how these fine, erudite people ever got entangled with it. They proceed, moreover, with such a timorous, tremulous conscience, that it appears to me they wish the beer were back again in the keg.[16] Had they not started the affair, I believe, they would have let well enough alone.

I see in this affair nothing else than the wrath of God, who gives the devil free rein to produce crude, clumsy errors and thick darkness to punish our shameful ingratitude for having treated the holy gospel as so wretchedly despicable and worthless —to make us, as St. Paul says, "believe what is false, since we have not received the love of truth" [II Thess. 2:10 f.]. This fanaticism, moreover, lacks nothing but being new. For we Germans are the kind of fellows who pounce upon anything new and cling to it like fools, and if anyone restrains us, he only makes us more crazy for it; but if no one restrains us, we will soon on our own become fed up and bored with it, and soon chase after something else that is new. Thus the devil has the advantage that no teaching or fancy so clumsy can arise but he can find disciples for it, and the clumsier the more quickly.

But "God's word alone endures forever" [Isa. 40:8]; errors always spring up by its side and pass away again. For this reason I am not worried that this fanaticism will last long. It is much too crude and impudent, and it does not attack obscure and uncertain Scripture but clear, plain Scripture, as we shall hear. So I shall once more set myself against the devil and his fanatics, not for their sake, but for the sake of the weak and simple. For I have no hope that the teachers of a heresy or fanaticism will be con-

[16] I.e. if they had not opened the keg, the trouble would never have started.

verted. Indeed, if that were possible, so much has already been written that they would have been converted. It has never been reported that an author of false doctrine was converted. For this sin is too great, because it blasphemes God's Word and sins against the Holy Spirit.[17] Therefore God lets it become hardened, with the result, according to the word of Isaiah 6 [9 f.], "With seeing eyes you shall not see and with hearing ears you shall not hear, for this people's heart is hardened."

Christ converted no high priest, but their disciples were converted, such as Nicodemus, Joseph, Paul,[18] and the like. The ancient prophets converted no false prophets. Paul, too, was not able to convert false apostles, but laid down the teaching: "When one has been admonished twice or three times, avoid him and dismiss him as a perverted man" [Titus 3:10]. So too the holy doctors have never converted an arch-heretic; not because they had not sufficiently opposed and confuted all the heretics' errors with the truth, but their hearts were obsessed with their own fancies, and they fared the same way as the person who looks through a colored glass: place before him whatever color you will, he sees no other color than that of his glass. The fault is not that you have placed the wrong color before him but that his glass has a different color, as the same passage in Isaiah [6:9] also puts it, "You shall see," he says, "and yet not see." What is this but to say: It will appear before your eyes quite clearly enough for you to see, and others will see it, but you will not. This is the reason, says John 12 [:40], that one cannot convert such people. The proffered truth does not do it. God must take away the colored glass; this we cannot do.

Even if I too can convert no arch-fanatic, yet I shall leave nothing undone, God willing, to place the truth clearly and plainly before their eyes and win away some of their disciples, or at least to strengthen the simple and weak and protect them from the fanatics' poison. Even if I do not succeed in this (from which may God protect me), at any rate I will have made my testimony before God and all the world, and declared that I have nothing to do with these blasphemers of the sacrament and fanatics, nor

[17] Cf. Mark 3:29.
[18] Cf. Matt. 26:57 ff., John 3:1 ff., John 19:38, Acts 9:1 ff.

have I ever had, nor will I ever have, God willing; and I shall wash my hands of all the blood of those souls whom they steal, murder, and seduce from Christ with their poison. I am innocent of it, and have done my part. On my own account, of course, I dare not write against them. But their own writings are my strength. When I read these they fill me with strength and joy, because I see that though the devil rages so bitterly against God's Word, yet God permits him no more than to spew out feeble, stale, rotten obscenities, so that I must say, "You would like to, but you can't!" Now, in return, to spite the devil I shall on this occasion take up only the single saying of Christ, "This is my body," and show how the fanatics have mutilated it down to the present time. Most especially, since they are so slippery and fickle, twisting and turning in a thousand secret corners, I would plead with them in God's name to take their stand on this one passage and to give me a real answer. The other passages I shall save for another time.

I would like to request them, in all kindness, not to become angry that I condemn their doctrine and ascribe it to the devil. I cannot do otherwise or call it otherwise than I believe in my heart. Since they regard us as "un-Christians" whom the Spirit of God has forsaken,[19] they really ought to be forbearing too, in view of all their vaunted spirit, and demonstrate in deeds this forbearance with which they spatter so many books full. For there is no end or limit of boasting in their writings what holy martyrs they are, how much they suffer,[20] how meek and forbearing they

[19] Oecolampadius: "If the real, true Spirit of God has not forsaken you now. . . ." *Reasonable Answer. St. L.* 20, 599. He frequently applied Gal. 4:9 to his adversaries: "They turn back from Christ to the [weak and beggarly] elements." *Apologetics,* 1526, M 7 f. Zwingli wrote on April 5, 1525, that his adversaries in the Lord's Supper controversy "are not led by the same spirit." *C. R.* 95, 317. Bucer: "Let Luther acknowledge that he is being led by a spirit far different from that of Christ." *Preface,* 1527. *St. L.* 17, 1601. Luther and his party are frequently admonished to pray for God's Spirit (cf. Bucer, *ibid.*), which the Swiss and Strassburgers claim has been revealed to them. Oecolampadius, *Apologetics,* H 4; Bucer, *Apology,* 1526, 35). See Luther's Letter to Spalatin, March 27, 1526, in *S-J* 2, 365 ff. *WA,* Br 4, 41 f.

[20] Bucer wrote how Oecolampadius and Zwingli had to "bear daily the burden of persecutions" and be "maligned by the most scurrilous names." *Apology,* 7. Oecolampadius applied Matt. 5:11 to his own party: "Blessed are you when men revile you and persecute you. . . ." *Apologetics,* N 1.

are,[21] how they seek the glory of Christ alone.[22] Yet they are always crying and complaining meanwhile how the servants of Christ are vilified, and how offense thus is given to the common people.[23] And they wish that men forthwith would praise them, saying, "Pure spirit, pure spirit you are; pure truth, pure truth you teach!" then they would be forbearing. Besides, we godless and unforbearing "un-Christians" must put up with having these holy and moderate teachers revile us as idolaters and having our God called the baked God, the edible and potable God, the bread-God, the wine-God, and ourselves called God-forsaken Christians and such names.[24] This altogether venomous, devilish abuse and slander exceeds all bounds. Now a person would rather be upbraided for being full of devils than have a "baked God." Yet we must not be praised for our forbearance or moderation in putting up with this. *Our* servants of Christ will not be vilified by it, nor our people offended. We must call it pure praise and progress, joy and gladness, when they revile us! But if one looks sideways at them or displeases them—oh, that is hindering the glory of Christ, defaming the servants of Christ, offending the whole world; there you have suffering, there you have forbearance, there you have all the martyrs' crowns in a single heap! And even when they are not chided openly, they torture a casually written word and wring from it a complaint over their suffering, dragging the subject in by the ears, as Oecolampadius does against Pirkheimer of Nürnberg,[25] in order that they may praise their forbearance.

---

[21] Zwingli: "We have always stated our position with moderation and reserve in order not to give an example of self-assertion in the church of God." *Clear Instruction on Christ's Supper,* 1526. *LCC* 24, 237. Cf. n. 25, below.

[22] Oecolampadius and Bucer, cited in *WA* 23, 286.

[23] Bucer, cf. *WA* 23, 287.

[24] Zwingli compared "worshiping the consecrated bread" with the worship of the golden calf at Dan (I Kings 12:28 f.). *Letter to Matthew Alber,* published 1525. *C. R.* 90, 342; *St. L.* 17, 1520. He ridiculed the Lutherans' "edible, impanated, baked, roasted, ground-up God." *Reply to Urban Rhegius. C. R.* 91, 934. Oecolampadius defended the epithet, "eaters of God's flesh and drinkers of God's blood," in *Reasonable Answer. St. L.* 20, 588. Cf. Luther's letter to Gregory Casel, November, 1525. S-J 2, 346 ff.

[25] See the Introduction. To Pirkheimer's relatively mild refutation of the Swiss position, Oecolampadius had replied with a lengthy defense, and though he would "gladly condone these great injuries for Christ's sake," he had used very strong epithets against Pirkheimer's person and action. *Reply to Pirkheimer,* 1526. *WA* 23, 286 f.

A person simply dare not speak with them without their raising a howl and a moan, doubtless because of their great forbearance and holiness.

Since we "un-Christians" and unforbearing heathen, I say, must suffer such horrible slander and shameful vilification from them, they, as the holy Christians, in turn should suffer something too, even though they are unwilling to suffer as much as we. For they have to remember that in our conscience and faith we take God's Word just as seriously as they do in their faith, since we too wish to be saved and come to God. We too hope that we shall do as much as they in this matter, and more than they. Thus St. Paul says, "We are not contending against flesh and blood . . ." [Eph. 6:12]. Therefore I do not fix my attention as much upon them, as upon him who speaks through them—the devil, I mean—just as they regard me as full of devils.[26] Yet we are glad to be refuse and offscouring[27] so they may rule, if only we remain free to confess our faith and to shun and condemn what is not of our faith. Now then, let us proceed to the subject at hand.

In the first place, we begin at the point where they write, produce books, and admonish that these subjects ought not be the occasion for rending Christian unity, love, and peace.[28] It is a minor matter, say they, and an insignificant quarrel, for the sake of which Christian love should not be obstructed. They chide us for being so stubborn and obstinate about it and for creating disunity. Now, see here, my dear man, what should I say? We are in the same situation as the sheep that came to the watering place to drink with the wolf.[29] The wolf went upstream, the sheep down-

---

[26] E.g. Oecolampadius, cited in *WA* 23, 287.

[27] Cf. I Cor. 4:13.

[28] At the end of his *Genuine Exposition*, 1525, Oecolampadius urged that the most necessary thing of all is love, which dreads nothing so much as disunity. More particularly Luther must have been thinking of Bucer's *Apology*, which repeatedly deplored the controversy and urged concord. According to Bucer, in Strassburg people are urged not to pry into what really exists in the bread of the Eucharist, lest contention be aroused; in the supreme interest of love, each is permitted his own interpretation; the subject belongs to those things which concern only "externals and symbols of the faith," and are "not necessary for salvation and for propagating the glory of Christ." Cited in *WA* 23, 287-288.

[29] A fable of Aesop. Luther published a collection of Aesop's fables in 1530. *WA* 50, 440 ff.

stream to the water. Then the wolf chided the sheep for making the water muddy. The sheep said, "How can I be making it muddy for you? You are upstream, and you are making it muddy for me." In short, the sheep was forced to admit that he had made the water muddy for the wolf! So too with my fanatics: they have kindled this fire, as they themselves with all lordliness boast as a blessing, and now they would like to shove off the blame for disunity upon us.[30] Who ordered Dr. Karlstadt to start it? Who ordered Zwingli and Oecolampadius to write? Haven't they done it on their own accord? We would have been, and would still be, glad for peace, yet they were unwilling; now the blame is ours, of course!

I earnestly wish, however, that even if these fanatics refuse to fear God, they would at least feel a little abashed before the people and not write such shameless lies. They say there should be peace, but they themselves do not cease to increase strife, as everyone sees and hears; and the more it continues the more they rejoice. Again, they say it is a minor matter, yet there is no topic that they so diligently promote and cultivate and espouse; all other topics lie dormant. Here they become martyrs and saints. Anyone who does not share their fanaticism is no Christian and can accomplish nothing in the Scriptures and in matters of the Spirit. Great and magnificent wisdom this is, when anyone can say, "Bread and wine!" With this wisdom the Holy Spirit alone now operates![31] In reality what is going on here is simply that on top of everything the damnable devil is mocking us through them, as if to say, "I intend to cause all kinds of mischief and dissension in deeds, and then to wipe my mouth and say in words, 'I seek and desire love and unity!' "—as the Psalter also says, "They speak peace with their neighbors, while mischief is in their hearts" [Ps. 28:3].

Well, since they are so completely wicked as to mock the whole

---

30 Luther's colleague, the Swabian preacher John Brenz, had accused the Swiss and Strassburgers of starting a fire and denying the Lutherans the right to put it out. Bucer replied that their only fire was that which Christ desired—a salutary rebuke. *Apology*, 35.

31 Particularly Oecolampadius had made strong claims of spiritual understanding and of the guidance of the Holy Spirit; Bucer had used similar expressions more frequently but also more mildly. Citations in *WA* 23, 288.

world, I shall add a Lutheran warning and say: Cursed be such love and unity in the abyss of hell, because such unity not only divides the Christian Church wretchedly, but in true devilish fashion even mocks it and pokes fun at it for its wretchedness. Now I do not mean to judge so harshly as to hold that they do this out of malice. But I think they are blinded by Satan, and perhaps they have developed a conscience that bites them, saying, "Truly we have caused a great offense and kindled a great fire, now we must paste and putty up the affair with words, and claim indulgence because it is not an important matter. And even if we lose the argument, let us declare in advance that we have not lost anything important, but have committed only a minor offense, and as we say of singers when they make a mistake, 'They only farrowed a piglet.' "

No, gentlemen, none of this peace and love for me! If I were to strangle someone's father and mother, wife and child, and try to choke him too, and then say, "Keep the peace, dear friend, we wish to love one another, the matter is not so important that we should be divided over it!" what should he say to me? O how he should love me! Thus the fanatics strangle Christ my Lord, and God the Father in his words, and my mother the church too, along with my brethren; moreover, they would have me dead too, and then they would say I should be at peace, for they would like to cultivate love in their relations with me. But I intend to expose the fanatics here, that everyone may see what kind of spirit is in them, so that their adherents may realize whom they are believing and following.

It is perfectly clear, of course, that we are at odds concerning the words of Christ in the Supper. And it is well known on both sides that these are Christ's or God's words. That is one thing. So we say, on our part, that according to the words Christ's true body and blood are present when he says, "Take, eat; this is my body." If our belief and teaching go wrong here, tell us, what are we doing? We are lying to God, and proclaiming that he did not say this but said the opposite. Then we are assuredly blasphemers and liars against the Holy Spirit, betrayers of Christ, and murderers and seducers of the world.

Our adversary says that mere bread and wine are present, not the body and blood of the Lord. If they believe and teach wrongly here, then they blaspheme God and are giving the lie to the Holy Spirit, betray Christ, and seduce the world. One side must be of the devil, and God's enemy. There is no middle ground. Now let every faithful Christian see whether this is a minor matter, as they say, or whether God's Word is to be trifled with. Here you have the fanatics and their spirit. I have often said, no ungodly man can have a high regard for God's Word. These fanatics demonstrate forthrightly that they regard the words and works of Christ as nothing but human prattle, like the opinions of academic hairsplitters, which ought fairly to yield to love and unity. But a faithful Christian knows clearly that God's Word concerns God's glory, the Spirit, Christ, grace, everlasting life, death, sin, and all things. These, however, are not minor matters! You see, this is how they seek God's glory, as they boast everywhere.

Neither does it help them to assert that at all other points they have a high and noble regard for God's words and the entire gospel, except in this matter. My friend, God's Word is God's Word; this point does not require much haggling! When one blasphemously gives the lie to God in a single word, or says it is a minor matter if God is blasphemed or called a liar, one blasphemes the entire God and makes light of all blasphemy. There is only one God who does not permit himself to be divided, praised at one place and chided at another, glorified in one word and scorned in another. The Jews believe the Old Testament, but because they do not believe Christ, it does them no good. You see, the circumcision of Abraham [Gen. 17:10 ff.] is now an old dead thing and no longer necessary or useful. But if I were to say that God did not command it in its time, it would do me no good even if I believed the gospel. So St. James asserts, "Whoever offends in one point is guilty in all respects."[32] He possibly heard the apostles say that all the words of God must be believed or none, although he applies their interpretation to the works of the law.

[32] Quoting the last half of Jas. 2:10, Luther in some respects follows the Greek and Vulgate text in his rendering. The RSV reads, "For whoever keeps the whole law but fails in one point has become guilty of all of it."

Why is it any wonder, then, if fickle fanatics juggle and play the clown with the words of the Supper according to their fancy, since at this point they are convicted of belittling God's words and concerns, and making them secondary to human love? Just as if God must yield to men, and let the authority of his Word depend on whether men are at one or at odds over it. How can one believe that these fanatics teach rightly and well, when they are clearly found to be entertaining such devilish ideas and advising things which make for the despising, blaspheming, and disgrace of God and our eternal death and destruction, and who yet think they have acted wisely and presented a salutary Christian teaching?

But we poor sinners, who are altogether devoid of Spirit, have this to say out of the holy gospel against these holy Christians, "He who loves father and mother, wife and child, house and home, or even his own soul more than me is not worthy of me" [Matt. 10:37]. And again, "I have not come to bring peace on earth, but a sword" [Matt. 10:34]. And Paul, "What accord has Christ with Belial?" [II Cor. 6:15]. If we are to practice Christian unity with them and extend Christian love to them, we must also love and be satisfied with, or at least tolerate, their doctrine and behavior. Let anyone do that if he wishes. Not I. For Christian unity consists in the Spirit, when we are of one faith, one mind, one heart, Ephesians 4 [:3 ff.]. This, however, we will gladly do: in civil matters we are glad to be one with them, i.e. to maintain outward, temporal peace. But in spiritual matters, as long as we have breath, we intend to shun, condemn, and censure them, as idolaters,[33] corrupters of God's Word, blasphemers, and liars; and meanwhile, to endure from them, as from enemies, their persecution and schism as far and as long as God endures them; and to pray for them, and admonish them to stop. But to acquiesce in, keep silence over, or approve their blaspheming, this we shall not and cannot do.

All these things I have exposed in order to show how the devil can disguise himself under false humility, peace, and for-

[33] Luther's manuscript here reads *ketzer*—"heretics"; the printed version, probably revised by Luther himself, reads *götzer*. So also on p. 32. On Luther's use of the two terms, see *WA* 23, 289.

bearance, for the warning of all who do not humble themselves from the heart, that they should beware both of the devil and of themselves. For God allows himself to be neither deceived nor mocked.[34] He would rather take an ass and condemn great prophets through her mouth, as he did Balaam [Num. 22:28 ff.]. Therefore, to these fanatics and spirits who offer us such a peace, we may well say as Christ said to his betrayer, Judas, in the garden, "O Judas, would you betray the Son of man with a kiss?" [Luke 22:48]. Yes indeed, a Judas' peace and a traitor's kiss it is when they would be friendly to us and get us to the point of watching in silence while they ravage with fire and sword, by which they bring so many souls into the everlasting fire of hell, all the while wishing it to be regarded as a minor matter and of no consequence. God warns us against these spirits by allowing them to come into the open and betray themselves and reveal how they traffic in lies and falsehoods. And if this stratagem does not shock or warn men, let them go; they want to be lost! The Holy Spirit offers no such stratagems through his poor sinners as the devil does here through his great[35] saints.

Now, to come to grips with the subject, let us take up the saying of Christ, which Matthew and Mark[36] record: "He took bread, and gave thanks, and broke it, and gave it to his disciples and said, 'Take, eat; this is my body which is given for you.'" As I have said, I wish at this time to take up this saying alone, in defiance of the devil and all his spirits, in order to prove that this single text is strong and mighty enough to stand against all their rotten, empty prattle. The other texts will come to their right in their own good time. Now, here stands the text, stating clearly and lucidly that Christ gives his body to eat when he distributes

---

[34] Cf. Gal. 6:7.

[35] The word "great," appearing in Luther's handwritten manuscript, seems to have been omitted inadvertently in the text prepared by the printer. Cf. *WA* 23, 86, 290.

[36] Matt. 26:26, Mark 14:22. "Which is given for you," however, appears in Luke 22:19 (in some texts, including the one Luther used), and in a related form in I Cor. 11:24. There are other minor variations also, which Luther examines when he analyzes the four texts individually in *Confession Concerning Christ's Supper*, pp. 307 ff. The conflated text above, however, was the one used in public worship and instruction: *Formula Missae*, 1523, and *Deutsche Messe*, 1526 (*LW* 53, 27 f., 80 f.); Small Catechism, VI, 4, and Large Catechism, V, 3. Cf. also *LW* 36, 37, n. 84, 319.

the bread. On this we take our stand, and we also believe and teach that in the Supper we eat and take to ourselves Christ's body truly and physically. But how this takes place or how he is in the bread, we do not know and are not meant to know. God's Word we should believe without setting bounds or measure to it. The bread we see with our eyes, but we hear with our ears that Christ's body is present.

Against this saying they have up to now brought forth nothing in their many writings that has even plausibility behind it, not to mention a reasoned argument. I let them boast and show off and even boldly swear by God's judgment and wrath how sure of the matter they are and how they have grasped the truth.[37] But these are just words, with which they would dearly love to conceal and cover over their uncertain conscience so that no one may notice how their heart shakes and quakes within like a reed swayed by the wind [Matt. 11:7], because of the great uncertainty of their fancies and delusions. I too dare take an oath that this saying of Christ, "This is my body," sticks in their hearts like an everlasting splinter from which they can never be free, except by being so completely callous as to feel nothing any longer, Ephesians 4 [18 f.]. I know, of course, what bad consciences do when they begin to make themselves aprons from fig leaves to try and hide themselves [Gen. 3:7]. Since they misinterpret God's Word and follow their own fancy, it is easy also to judge their heart by the Scriptures, which teach us that the wicked has no rest: "His heart is like a wave of the sea, which cannot rest," Isaiah 57 [:20].

This is clearly proved by the anxious tone of their writings.[38] Here they boast, there they complain; here they beg for peace, there they crave instruction; here they shy away from offense, there they seek the glory of Christ. There is so much of this unnecessary mending and patching that they seldom get around to the subject, and write precious little about it. And when they have to come to it, they tread as lightly as if they were actually

[37] Zwingli: "Either the Creed must be shattered or our teaching is true." *Clear Instruction. LCC* 24, 238. Zwingli's oaths in *Commentary:* "by thunder," *LWZ* 3, 239; "by Almighty God," "by heaven," 250; "I call God to witness," 248. Another favorite was "by Hercules."

[38] Several citations from Oecolampadius in *WA* 23, 290; cf. Zwingli, *Commentary. LWZ* 3, 216 ff., 252 f.

walking on eggs, and afterward slip away as if the devil were after them, fearful that they may break their neck with every letter. When they have safely escaped, they wipe away their sweat and anxiety, and thank God for the truth; and there follows so great a teaching and praise of the spiritual eating of the body of Christ and of his remembrance—over which no one contends with them; we knew about these things just as well as they, and before them!—that it is clear they do not know what they are saying, or how they should go about bamboozling the people. My friend, a sure conscience, which is certain about the matter, does not hem and haw so; it speaks out distinctly and boldly, since it is altogether confident. Therefore, let no one believe their swearing and boasting. They are assuredly lying.

But listen, I ask you, how they remove our interpretation from this saying of Christ and bring in their own. They say, "The word 'is' must mean the same as the word 'represents,'" as Zwingli writes;[39] and the expression "my body" must mean the same as the expression "sign of my body," as Oecolampadius writes.[40] So Christ's word and meaning according to Zwingli's text would read, "Take, eat; this represents my body," or according to Oecolampadius' text, "Take and eat; this is a sign of my body." Ah, they are so certain about this meaning and they stand so firm in their hearts—like a reed that the wind blows to and fro,[41] as has been pointed out.[42] Then at once they boast that we have no passage from Scripture which says that Christ's body is in the Supper. Next they humble themselves again, would like to be instructed, and offer to follow if we can prove with Scripture that Christ's body is present.[43]

This certainly is an extraordinary situation! It is just as if I denied that God had created the heavens and the earth, and asserted with Aristotle and Pliny and other heathen that the world

---

[39] This view was first expressed in Zwingli's *Letter to Matthew Alber*, November, 1524, published 1525. *C. R.* 90, 345; *St. L.* 17, 1522.

[40] This view was first expressed in Oecolampadius' *Genuine Exposition*, 1525, 8.

[41] Cf. Matt. 11:7.

[42] Cf. p. 29.

[43] Oecolampadius, *Reply to Pirkheimer*, f 5. Cited in *WA* 23, 290. Zwingli, *Commentary*. *LWZ* 3, 217 f.; *Clear Instruction*. *LCC* 24, 222.

existed from eternity,[44] but someone came and held Moses under my nose, Genesis 1 [:1], "In the beginning God created the heavens and the earth"; I would try to make the text read: "God" now should mean the same as "cuckoo," "created" the same as "ate," and "the heavens and the earth" the same as "the hedge sparrow, feathers and all." The word of Moses thus would read according to Luther's text, "In the beginning the cuckoo ate the hedge sparrow, feathers and all,"[45] and could not possibly mean, "In the beginning God created the heavens and the earth." What a marvelous art this would be—one with which rascals are quite familiar! Or, if I denied that the Son of God had become man, and someone confronted me with John 1 [:14], "The Word became flesh," suppose I were to say: Let "Word" mean "a gambrel" and "flesh" "a mallet," and thus the text must now read, "The gambrel became a mallet." And if my conscience tried to reproach me, saying, "You take a good deal of liberty with your interpretation, Sir Martin, but—but—" etc., I would press until I became red in the face, and say, "Keep quiet, you traitor with your 'but,' I don't want the people to notice that I have such a bad conscience!" Then I would boast and clap my hands, saying, "The Christians have no Scripture which proves that God's Word became flesh." But I would also turn around and, bowing low in humility, offer gladly to be instructed, if they would show me with the Scripture that I have just finished twisting around. Ah, what a rumpus I would stir up among Jews and Christians, in the New and the Old Testaments, if such brazenness were allowed me!

If you ask, "What devil would allow you to do such a thing?" the answer is, "What devil other than the one who allows Zwingli and Oecolampadius to do it? I wouldn't know anyone else, either!" Whoever read in the Scriptures that "body" means the same as "sign of the body," and "is" means the same as "represents"? Indeed, what language in all the world has ever expressed itself so? It is only the arrogance and frivolous wickedness of the very devil, who, mocking us through these fanatics in these important matters, pretends he is willing to be shown with Scripture—

[44] On the eternal existence of the world, cf. Aristotle, *Physics*, I, 9 (192a), *On the Heavens*, I, 3 (270a); and Pliny, *Natural History*, II, 1.
[45] On Luther's use of current notions about the cuckoo, see *WA* 23, 291, 293.

provided that he first eliminates the Scripture or twists it to his own fancy. Just as if I were to rob a man of his weapons with crafty words and give him in exchange sham weapons made of paper, exactly like his own, and then proceeded to defy him to strike me with them or defend himself against me. Now this would be a valiant hero! He would be spit upon and pelted out of the village with dung, if he were really in earnest, or there would simply be hearty laughter as at carnival time, if he were jesting. This is just the way these fanatics treat us also. They wish first of all to change the natural words and meanings of the Scriptures into their own words and meanings; then they boast that we do not have Scripture, in order that the devil may make a laughingstock of us, or rather, may safely strangle us as defenseless enemies. Against all this, however, just one word serves exceedingly well: No! So they stand like butter in the sun.

Here let the judge between us be not alone Christians but also heathen, Turks, Tartars, Jews, idolaters, and the whole world: whose responsibility is it to prove his text? Should it be the Luther who asserts that Moses says, "In the beginning the cuckoo ate the hedge sparrow," or the person who asserts that Moses says, "In the beginning God created the heavens and the earth"? I hope the decision would be that Luther ought to prove his text, since in no language does "God" mean the same as "cuckoo." Well, away creeps Luther to the cross, grieved that he cannot prove that "God" means "cuckoo." For anyone who ventures to interpret words in the Scriptures any other way than what they say, is under obligation to prove this contention out of the text of the very same passage or by an article of faith. But who will enable the fanatics to prove that "body" is the equivalent of "sign of the body," and "is" the equivalent of "represents"? No one has brought them to this point up to now. They rant and rave, "Where is your Scripture? Where is your Scripture?"[46] and press us to prove that the gospel says, "This is my body," though the whole world reads it and must read it. That it also says, however, "This represents my body," or, "This is a sign of my body"—O that is so certain that

[46] Several examples are given in *WA* 23, 292.

they defy God's judgment over it, even though no man has ever read this in the gospel, nor ever will!

God knows, with these crude illustrations I do not wish to offend Zwingli, nor especially Oecolampadius, to whom God has given many gifts, above many other men. Indeed, I am heartily sorry for the man. By such words I look not upon them but only upon the insolent, sarcastic devil who has so deceived and misled them that in return I now find satisfaction to the glory of God, by mocking him again for these clumsy follies of his. For he shall and must be subject to God's Word. This year, please God, I shall see to it that the fanatics' devil, who now hinders me from getting other important work done, comes out into the open. God grant that he may lay a rod to his own backside and wake up a sleeping dog.[47] Amen! For I write these things in order that our people may have answers for the fanatics when they ask so sarcastically where it is written in Scripture that "bread" is Christ's body, and stupidly pretend that they have never read it. Should one ask them in return where it is written in Scripture that "body" means "sign of the body"? Up the flue, that's where! That is where their Bible is!

The sum and substance of all this is that we have on our side the clear, distinct Scripture which reads, "Take, eat; this is my body," and we are not under obligation nor will we be pressed to cite Scripture beyond this text—though we could do so abundantly. On the contrary, they should produce Scripture which reads, "This represents my body," or, "This is a sign of my body." We are unwilling this time to pay the devil the compliment of citing more Scripture than this verse, "This is my body." For even if we put on all the glasses in the world, we would find none of the evangelists writing, "Take, eat; this is a sign of my body," or, "This represents my body." But what we clearly find without the aid of any glasses, so that even young children can read it, is, "Take, eat; this is my body."

Therefore we beg the fanatics not to demand from us a proof of this text, "This is my body." This is something they might ask

[47] In these words Luther expresses the hope that the fanatics' devil will punish himself and bring misfortune to himself through being bitten by the dog he has awakened from a deep sleep. See *Br A* 4, 362, n. 1.

seven-year-old boys who are learning to spell these words in school, where they have the Bible in Greek, Latin, and German. But what they ought to have done was to show us a Bible in which was written, "This is a sign of my body." If they could not do this, they should bridle their mouths and lower their plumes for a while, until they succeeded in producing such a Bible or at least proving with good reasons that this text should be made to read this way. Else they should keep still and not boast, "Where is your Scripture? Where is your Scripture?" unless they scream these words to themselves—as they ought—and not to us. For they are acting against their own conscience.

Here someone sneers at me with sovereign contempt, "Ah, my dear Luther, how easily will they furnish reasons for you and prove their cuckoo!" Honestly, I am just as eager to hear them, believe me, as they are ready to do this. Well, start piping and don't spoil the dance; but let us know whether we are supposed to step or skip. It is against the sneering devil that I am saying these things, not against flesh and blood [Eph. 6:12].

In the first place, it is certain that Zwingli and Oecolampadius agree in their understanding of the text, even though their words differ. For Zwingli's expression, "This represents my body," is exactly the same as Oecolampadius' "This is a sign of my body." The German language and all other languages concede that it is the same to say "laughing represents or signifies joy," and "laughing is a sign of joy"; there is no question or doubt that "to represent or signify" [48] and "to be a sign" are the same thing. But since the point at issue here is whether the word "is" necessarily means the same in Scripture as the word "represents," Zwingli is obliged to prove this from Scripture. If he does not do this, his argument is mere dung. Similarly, Oecolampadius is under obligation to prove from Scripture that the word "body" necessarily means the same as the word "sign of the body." If he doesn't, he too is dung, and our text remains firm as a rock—"This is my body."

Indeed, to show how far they miss the truth: not only are they under obligation to prove from Scripture that "body" is the

[48] *Bedeuten* (*significare*) is translated here by both words. Luther also uses *deuten* frequently in this sense. Cf. p. 36, n. 54.

same as "sign of the body," and that "is" is the same as "represent or signify," but one thing more: even though they should produce such an example in one passage of Scripture (which, however, is impossible), they are still under obligation to prove that it is necessarily so here in the Supper as well, that "body" is "sign of the body." It would not help them at all, even if the entire Scriptures showed nothing but signs of the body in other passages, if they did not show it also at this passage on the Supper. Our present quarrel is not primarily whether somewhere in the Scriptures "body" means "sign of the body," but whether in this text of the Supper it has this meaning. Consciences want to be certain and sure on this point. Therefore, even if you proved that, for example, from Moses,[49] "body" is the same as "sign of the body," consciences are not satisfied. They just mumble and say, "Yes, my friend, who knows whether it therefore may mean the same in the Supper, too?" We must be assured of this also through God's Word, otherwise the words remain firm for us and hold us captive with the clear, distinct text, "This is my body."

Oh, how the devil's pants stink here! How keenly he senses that he is under this obligation, and how reluctant he is to carry it out! For we demand both of these things,[50] and we challenge him in both. For this reason, too, the fanatics shrink from this obligation more than any devil has ever shrunk from the cross.[51] Moreover, it is too much to hope that they will stand still and look you in the eye or hear what they are asked. All they do is take to their heels and rush past. No one will attack this subject. Our pastor John Bugenhagen once challenged Zwingli in writing[52] to prove that in the Supper "is" meant the same as "represent." Would you believe it, when he ought to have answered him, Zwingli sang him instead a ditty about his great sufferings, and meanwhile inquired whether it meant this in other passages

[49] "Moses" refers to the first five books of the Bible.

[50] Luther demands corroboration from the Scriptures in general and specifically with reference to the Lord's Supper.

[51] It was an age-old idea that devils could be put to flight by the sign of the cross; cf. *Large Catechism*, Second Commandment, 74. T. G. Tappert *et al.* (eds.), *Book of Concord* (Philadelphia: Muhlenberg Press, 1959), p. 374.

[52] *Letter Against the New Error Concerning the Sacrament*, 1525. *St. L.* 20, 501.

of Scripture, but found none! That it necessarily meant this in the Supper, however, he did not dare to suggest without exposing himself as a hopeless fool.[53]

This is the way he proves his silly "representation" concept:[54] St. Paul says in I Corinthians 10 [:4], "The rock was Christ," i.e. the rock represents Christ; therefore, the same should apply here also: "This is my body" means, "This represents my body." Again, Moses, in Exodus 12 [:11], "Eat the lamb in haste, for it is the Lord's passover," i.e. it represents the Lord's passover; therefore, here too, "This is my body" equally must mean, "This represents my body."[55]

I ask Zwingli now: Since St. Paul doesn't say, "The rock represents Christ," but, "The rock was Christ," how can you prove thereby that there is a representation or metaphor in the Supper, which is not even in Paul? Through him you try to prove your metaphor, but just as you dreamed it up in the Supper, so you imagine it in Paul also. Similarly, Moses says not, "Eat in haste, it represents the Lord's passover," but, "Eat in haste, it is the Lord's passover." Thus Zwingli is obliged to prove the propriety of his metaphor in Paul and Moses just as much as in the Supper, for the metaphor is apparent at no point. Such an argument, boys are taught in school, is called "begging the question," or "proving the uncertain by the uncertain," but these exalted spirits have not learned this yet. What will Zwingli say on these threadbare subjects? His error, of course, he cannot admit, for that would be disgraceful. He would much prefer to say that he is full of Spirit and must suffer many things, and keep up his boasting until we

---

[53] A highly partisan and misleading interpretation of Zwingli's *Reply to Bugenhagen's Letter,* 1525. *C. R.* 91, 558 ff.; *St. L.* 20, 506 ff.

[54] *Deuteley* is rendered in this volume sometimes by "metaphor" but more often by this derisive expression. Zwingli complained of Luther's mockery: "He makes out of my *düten düteley* . . .; if one conquers by turning good words into sarcastic ones, then Luther has won hands down, for he knows this trick so well that undoubtedly no one will outdo him." *Christian Answer. C. R.* 92, 865; *St. L.* 20, 1158. ". . . No *düteley* here, as he graciously says." *Ibid. C. R.* 92, 879; *St. L.* 20, 1168. Luther similarly ridicules Oecolampadius' concept that "body" means "*sign* of the body" as *zeicheley.*

[55] Zwingli treats these passages in *Rearguard,* 1525. *C. R.* 91, 473, 483 ff., and *Reply to Billican and Rhegius,* 1526. *C. R.* 91, 920 ff., 935 f. Cf. Oecolampadius, *Genuine Exposition,* B 8, C 2, and *Reasonable Answer. St. L.* 20, 610 f.

believe, to oblige him, that there is a metaphor in Paul and Moses even if no one sees it there.

Now, let me make this assumption: even if it were true that there is a metaphor in Paul and Moses, and we obligingly believed him, what does he accomplish? But let us see what a marvelous, masterful conclusion he draws. Paul says, "The rock was Christ," i.e. the rock represents Christ; here too, therefore, when Christ says, "This is my body," it must be the same as, "This represents my body." My friend, let us draw some conclusions, too, according to this wonderful method. All right, I shall prove, using the Zwinglian method, that Sarah, the holy mother of the Jews, remained a virgin, as follows: Luke writes[56] that Mary remained a virgin, therefore Sarah also must have remained a virgin. Isn't this fine syllogizing and good deduction? Again, I shall prove that Pilate is an apostle of Christ, as follows: The evangelist Matthew [10:2] writes that Peter is Christ's apostle, therefore this man Pilate must also be Christ's apostle. And so on; whatever I please shall and must be deduced as an article of faith by such a method. "Yes," you say, "but this is not right; you must prove in each particular instance, that Sarah is a virgin and Pilate an apostle." Why? If Zwingli does not need to prove that there is a metaphor in the Supper, as long as there is one in a single passage in Paul or Moses, it is enough. Schoolboys know that "no deduction can be drawn from pure particulars and even less from negatives." Nevertheless it is the supreme art of our spirits in these sacred articles of faith to concoct these arguments out of particulars, without Scripture.

We must realize, of course, that this is sheer, arrogant mockery on the part of the devil, who in great self-confidence plays the fool with us and makes sport of us with this rotten metaphor-play and clown's play. How else, without the influence of Satan, could such learned men possibly be so blind and pride themselves so haughtily on empty dreams, and advertise them in the world as the strongest of all grounds of faith? No, it is not human to have such gross, thick darkness. So Zwingli with his metaphor

[56] Cf. Luke 1:34 f. Luther and Zwingli both retained the age-old tradition that Mary remained "ever virgin."

lies in the ash heap, just as Dr. Karlstadt before him fell with his *touto.*[57] For Zwingli can prove neither point, viz. that there is a metaphor in any single passage of Scripture, much less that it is necessarily in the Supper. He does not prove either, though he is under obligation to prove both.

The metaphor is quickly taken away from him in Paul and Moses, because Paul says, "They drank from the spiritual rock, and the Rock was Christ" [I Cor. 10:4]. Here St. Paul himself shows that he speaks of a spiritual rock. Now the spiritual rock does not represent Christ, but the rock was Christ himself among the Jews, just as our rock now does not represent but is nothing else but Christ. All this the preachers in Swabia,[58] and I too, have adequately established some time ago against Dr. Karlstadt.[59] But these lofty spirits disregard our Scripture, skip over it and fuss over it a little, and we have an adequate reply. Similarly, when Moses says, "Eat in haste, it is the Lord's passover" [Exod. 12:11], Zwingli cannot prove that "passover" represents the paschal lamb. The rejoinder is quickly made, "Eat in haste, it is the Lord's passover" means, as we say in German, "Eat meat, it's Sunday; drink water, it's Friday."[60] In this instance no man will force me to admit that meat represents Sunday or water represents Friday. So also here, "Eat in haste, for it is the Lord's passover," i.e. this is the day when the Lord walked in Egypt.

There is no proof of representation, either, in all the other passages which they quote. For example, where Christ says, "I am the true vine" [John 15:1], he speaks of the true spiritual vine, which he also *was,* not which *represents* him. How should it read: "I represent the true vine," or, "I am represented by the true vine"? Who then is the true vine, apart from any representation? Again, "I am the shepherd" [John 10:11], "I am the door" [John 10:7], "I am the resurrection and the life" [John 11:25], and all the others. All these sayings are expressed and understood in terms

[57] On Karlstadt, cf. *Against the Heavenly Prophets. LW* 40, 159 ff.

[58] Authors of the *Swabian Syngramma,* 1525; cf. *St. L.* 20, 537 f.

[59] Luther may be confusing his discussion of Matt. 16:18 f. with Karlstadt in *Against the Heavenly Prophets* (*LW* 40, 190) with his discussion of I Cor. 10:4 in *Adoration of the Sacrament,* 1523, directed against the Bohemian and Moravian Waldensians (*LW* 36, 280 ff.).

[60] Sunday a feast day, Friday a fast day.

of being, not of representing. They will never convincingly show a representation there; it is sheer imagination and self-conceit on their part. Moreover, as I have said, even if they discovered certain metaphors, still they cannot prove thereby that it is so in the Supper, and all the toil and care they have expended is merely lost effort. They give me this much credit, however, that in the case of Karlstadt I demolished his *touto,* and that his was not a sound argument.[61] But if I were to judge between Karlstadt and Zwingli, I would say that Dr. Karlstadt's *touto* served this error better than Zwingli's metaphor which, however, has absolutely nothing in it that can disguise the error, because it tries to prove its case purely by unknown, uncertain, and particular propositions—which to every rational mind is ridiculous and ludicrous.

Dr. Oecolampadius also would like to lend a helping hand to that concept of metaphor. When the preachers in Swabia demolished it with an irrefutable treatise, so that he himself could not deny that Paul speaks of the spiritual rock, and no metaphor was there, he still did not honor the truth but grumbled a little against it and said that Paul in this expression was visualizing and thinking of the material[62] rock which represented Christ.[63] As if we were asking here what Paul was visualizing or thinking of, rather than whether there is a metaphor in Paul's words! We know very well that the material rock represented Christ, and hence Christ is in name and reality a spiritual rock. This they did not need to teach us. But whether there is a metaphor in Paul's words, as Zwingli dreams—here they keep silence and nimbly rush past the question; and true to their nature they let us ask about God and answer us about their cuckoo, and then boast that no one is producing any Scripture against them. Indeed, if it makes sense that one does not have to answer when Scripture is produced, but may jabber of something else instead, then no one is

[61] Oecolampadius, *Reasonable Answer.* St. L. 20, 587. For other Swiss opinions of Karlstadt's position, cf. Zwingli, *Commentary.* *LWZ* 3, 221; other citations in *WA* 23, 294.

[62] *Leiblich* is translated variously in this volume: "bodily," "corporeal," "physical," "material."

[63] *Swabian Syngramma.* *St. L.* 20, 538. Oecolampadius, *Apologetics,* L iii; cf. *Reasonable Answer.* *St. L.* 20, 610.

producing any Scripture against them, even if a world full of Scripture were brought up against them!

Now Dr. Oecolampadius also ought to prove his "sign of the body" from Scripture. Our Scripture states, "Take, eat; this is my body," not, "This is a sign of my body." It is also impossible for him to produce one passage of Scripture where "body" is the same as "sign of the body," not to mention his obligation to prove it in the case of the Supper. Indeed, as far as proof is concerned, he lies as deep in the ash heap as Karlstadt and Zwingli. Yet they refuse to do God even the honor of admitting that this is true, but boast that no Scripture is brought up against them. However, if they were not such frivolous despisers of the Scriptures, one clear saying from the Scriptures would move them as profoundly as if the whole world were full of Scripture—which it actually is. For as I see it, every single passage makes the world too narrow. They flutter past, however, and think, "This is only a man's word." Small wonder that no Scripture constrains them!

Even if Oecolampadius holds the opinion that nothing but bread and wine are present, still he cannot on that account conclude with certainty that "body" necessarily means "sign of the body." That is, his argument is not convincing, since one may well interpret the word "body" in other ways than as "sign of the body," and his interpretation can be neither certain nor unambiguous as it should in order to be convincing. There are many other people who share his opinion yet accept neither the concept of representation nor the concept of sign. Karlstadt lets "body" remain body, and bases his position on the *touto*. Others torture the text thus: "Take and eat; my body, given for you, is this," viz. a spiritual food.[64] These also let "body" be body, and yet are

[64] The view of the Silesians Caspar Schwenkfeld and Valentine Krautwald. The former, a nobleman, had veered away from Luther in 1525 and had won the support of Krautwald, a learned canon at Liegnitz. He sent a letter of Krautwald to Luther in October, 1525 (*WA*, Br 3, 631 ff.; *Corpus Schwenckfeldianorum*, 2, 194-209), and brought several other treatises when he visited Wittenberg in December, 1525 (cf. *S-J* 2, 361, 367, 371; *Corpus Schwenckfeldianorum*, 2, 235-282). While Luther was writing *"This Is My Body,"* he received a lengthy unpublished treatise by Schwenkfeld, *Ground and Cause of the Error and Controversy Concerning the Lord's Supper*, February (?), 1527 (*Corpus Schwenckfeldianorum*, 2, 445-580); Luther attacked it in *Confession*, pp. 288 ff., below.

one in faith with him. Others crucify the sacred words thus: "Take and eat; that which is given for you is my body." [65] So many factions and heads does this single sect have already, though they agree on the main point! [66] Yet the Holy Spirit must be in all of them, as they are always boasting everywhere; and in order to point out proofs and arguments, he must not only speak diversely, but even be self-contradictory and at variance with himself. But he clearly confesses thereby that one errs as much as the other, since none of them holds the Scripture as it reads, and no one can prove that it is to be understood in any other way than as it reads.

Yes, if raving like a fanatic were a sound method, I would rave here as well as they, and maintain that only bread and wine are present. And on the other hand, I would think up something entirely new against them all, and agree with no one and proclaim my own notion in the following manner. In this sacred text, "This is my body," Dr. Karlstadt tortures the word "this," Zwingli tortures the word "is," Oecolampadius tortures the word "body." The others torture the whole text and transpose the word "this," setting it at the end and saying, "Take, eat; my body, which is given for you, is this." Some torture the text halfway and set the word "this" in the middle, saying, "Take, eat; what is given for you, this is my body." Others torture the text thus: "This is my body in remembrance of me," i.e. here my body must be not the natural one, but only a memorial of my body, so that the text may read, "Take, eat; this is a memorial of my body, which is given for you." [67]

---

[65] The view of "Konrad Ryss," apparently a pseudonym for John Landtsperger, a former Carmelite of Augsburg, who in 1527 came to Switzerland, took part in the Bern Disputation, 1528, and settled there, dying apparently in 1529. Cf. *WA* 19, 459, n. 1 and *WA*, Br 4, 43, 44, n. 14.

[66] In a passage especially instructive for Zwingli's conception of church unity (*Reply to Billican. C. R.* 91, 901 ff., cf. 918), Zwingli accused the Lutherans of disunity despite their claim to stand simply upon the plain words of Scripture, for some said the bread "*is* Christ's body," others "*under* the bread is Christ's body," and still others "*in* the bread"—which Zwingli claimed to be sheer contradiction. Meanwhile he boasted, "What discord will anyone truly find among us?" There are verbal differences, he conceded, but "the same opinion on the main point."

[67] Perhaps Luther is thinking of Oecolampadius here, cf. *Apologetics*, K iii, as cited in *WA* 23, 294; in inserting several lines into his manuscript as an afterthought, Luther may have overlooked his previous mention of Oeco-

Besides all these there is the seventh group, who say, "This is no article of faith, therefore we should not quarrel over it; let whoever will believe what he will." [68] These even tread this article under foot. Now the Holy Spirit is here in them all, and no one wants to err in these contradictory proofs and text arrangements; yet only one reading of the text can be correct. See how clumsily the devil makes fools of us! Well, since there is nothing left in the text to torture but the word "my," I shall draw this through the fanatics' flax comb, in order not to leave a single bone of the text whole and untortured, for I wish to leave nothing more for anyone to rave about. But I want to be the best fanatic, and neither disarrange nor corrupt the text, nor interpret a single word in the Scriptures other than the way it reads but let each one stand just as it is written, so Oecolampadius may see that "body" does not of necessity mean "sign of the body."

Expressed most simply, my fanaticism is this: since Christ said, "Take, eat; this is my body, which is given for you," let this be his meaning: "In the Old Testament Moses commanded the people to sacrifice the body of an irrational beast, viz. the paschal lamb, but I shall give you another body for the passover feast, viz. the bread, in order to make it easy for everyone to have it, since you Christians must be poor, and in order that my remembrance alone be set forth." That the bread may be Christ's body both in name and in reality, however, I shall prove from Scripture better than Oecolampadius proves his "sign of the body." For the Scriptures say that all things are God's in name and in reality as for example in Moses[69] he calls the land of the Jews his land, and our good works his works, our word his word. Again, in Hosea [2:8] he says of the Jews, "They took my gold, my silver, my grain, my oil, my wine, and gave it to their Baal." And Paul in I Co-

---

lampadius. On the other hand, he may be referring to the obscure "Peter Aloctus" of Cologne, mentioned as the "sixth head" of the sect in S-J 2, 368, cf. *WA*, Br 4, 43.

[68] Especially the Strassburgers, cf. Capito, *Proper Attitude*, 1524. *St. L.* 20, 349 f.; Bucer, *Defense and Explanation*, 1524. *St. L.* 20, 408 f. In December, 1525, Luther had said there were three factions on the question of the sacrament (S-J 2, 361); in March, 1526, and in his *Preface to the Swabian Syngramma*, six (S-J 2, 367; *WA* 19, 458-459); here he lists seven, and in the *Confession*, 1528, he claims there are "nearly ten," p. 165.

[69] Cf. Lev. 25:23; Exod. 34:10 (cf. Isa. 26:12); Num. 23:5; Deut. 18:18 ff.

rinthians 15 [:38, 40] assures me that every material thing is called *corpus* or body, since he says, "God gives to each kind of seed its own body, and the celestial bodies are of another kind."

From this I can easily and elegantly rave that Christ's meaning is as follows: This bread in the Supper is his body, which he made as God who makes all bodies and calls them his bodies; moreover, he ordains this to be his body with the intention that it should be his body in a new manner, viz. to be eaten in remembrance of him. Thus the bread should be called his body for two reasons, first on account of the creation, secondly on account of the ordinance, in opposition to Moses and the body of the paschal lamb in the Old Testament, in which he calls the same bread his body, i.e. a body for his use. Just as I call a knife "my iron," or a coat "my cloth," on account of their use, although not I but God alone made them in respect to their substance, and not I but the smith or tailor made them in respect to their form. So too, Christ can easily call the bread his body, since he has made and now uses this body for his own purpose.

It helps my cause that St. Paul says, "Take, eat; this is my body, which is broken for you" [I Cor. 11:24], which according to the Greek language can be understood thus: which is broken or divided or given among you, as the Scriptures call breaking bread "sharing bread."[70] Similarly the words about the cup may well read in Greek and Hebrew, "This is the cup, a new testament, which is poured out among you" [Luke 22:20], as one pours wine out of a tankard for the guests. Oh, I would make a still more brilliant display here, if I had as much audacity and leisure as my friends the fanatics!

If you say, however, that in the words concerning the cup it is written, "a cup in my blood" [Luke 22:20], but that the wine may not be called Christ's blood, I answer: Yes indeed, there is no need of *touto* or metaphor or sign here. But I wish to cite Scripture to show that red wine is called blood in the Scriptures, Genesis 49 [:11], "He washes his vesture in the blood of grapes," i.e. in red wine. And Deuteronomy 32 [:14], "That they might

70 Cf. I Cor. 10:16, Mark 8:19, Isa. 58:7. While Luther is correct in saying that in special constructions "breaking" means sharing, he is not correct in saying that *huper* in I Cor. 11:24 can mean "among you."

drink the good blood of the grape." Now if red wine is blood, but Christ has used the wine of this same land, which is red; and if all wine is his wine, since he made it and now uses it here for his Supper, then he must be understood thus: Moses sacrificed much animal blood, and much red wine for drink offerings, but why are all these objects needed by the poor in the New Testament? This red wine, which in another sense is my blood of the grape, shall now be also my blood among you, in place of all the blood and wine which Moses used for his sacrifices. Indeed, in German also one may call a red wine "blood," as for example, "How well the blood looks in the glass!" So the philosophers speak also, calling wine "the blood of the earth." [71] Now as Christ says, in John 4 [:34], that his food is to do his Father's will, although this only resembles food, so also he may call his red wine and the blood of the earth "his blood," because the wine resembles blood, especially because the Scriptures call red wine the "blood of the grape." I challenge Oecolampadius to derive his "sign of the body" out of Scripture in this way!

Yes, Sir Martin (you say), you play the fanatic pretty well, but what will you do with the other words that Christ[72] adds: "Which is given for you and poured out for the forgiveness of sins"?—though bread and wine are of no use for the forgiveness of sins, even if they are broken and distributed at table. Answer: Ah, my friend, do you expect to catch a fanatic with the Scriptures? I would be ashamed to be called a fanatic if I could not answer that! I would at least open my snout and bluster, "You offer only conjectures, notions, and illustrations!" If that didn't help, I would lace up my pants and leap over the subject till my ribs cracked and I became limp, and then say, "Aha, he has not shown me any Scripture." Whoever cannot do this should be thrown out of the fanatics' brotherhood and guild, for this is our fanatics' supreme method and last resource. Now don't watch me too closely, either, to see which way I shall hop and flop like a fanatic.

Bread and wine are eaten and drunk for the forgiveness of sins; that is, because Christ ordained them to be eaten and drunk

---

[71] Pliny, *Natural History*, XIV, 5.

[72] Luther's rendering of the words of institution represents a harmony of Luke 22:19 f. and Matt. 26:28. Cf. p. 28, n. 36.

in order to keep his remembrance, it is proper to call this an eating and drinking of the forgiveness of sins, since in connection with it we should remember that forgiveness and do as he says afterward, "Do this in remembrance of me." Just as one drinks wine to seal a sale, to show that it was a fair and just transaction which should be kept in remembrance and honored.[73]

Have I played the fanatic just about enough? Aren't the words of Christ now just about tortured to death? Actually, I have done the job a little too well, better than befits a fanatic. Dear Christians, at least give me credit for mocking the damnable devil so, for he mocks us. My wretched fanatics are still too inexperienced to be able to despise good insights and thoughts. Therefore they think, when they dream something up, it is forthwith the Holy Spirit.[74] Oh, how many fine insights I have had into the Scriptures which I have had to let go, whereas, if a fanatic had had them, all the printeries in the world would have been too few for him. And I can well believe that if these fanatical thoughts of mine had occurred to one of them, probably neither Karlstadt, Zwingli, Oecolampadius, nor the others would now be of any account. Nevertheless, all this is fanaticism, and Christ's words remain firm: "This is my body, which is given for you."

O how my Oecolampadius would exult if he could produce a Scripture passage in which "body" might mean "sign of the body," as I have demonstrated like a fool that bread and wine may be called Christ's body and blood. How gladly would he let the matter rest if "body" might be called "sign of the body," although he could not prove that it should and must be so called, as he is under obligation to do. But he cannot; God has stepped in and prevented him. It must stand as his own dream, and be labeled Oecolampadius' silly sign-concept.[75] A faithful Christian, however who listens in on our fanaticism and sees how we play dice with the sacred words of Christ, each according to his own fancy, would surely say, "Oh, you are rascals, the whole lot of you, treating God's Word as stuff and nonsense; I shall hold to the simple text."

Perhaps they will reproach me, however, for consigning

[73] Cf. Zwingli, *Commentary*. LWZ 3, 181.
[74] On Zwingli's dream concerning Exod. 12:11, see p. 52, n. 85.
[75] *Zeichelei und geuchelei.*

Oecolampadius' sign-concept so utterly to the devil, and will profess that even if he cannot prove the word "sign of the body" from Scripture, yet there are plenty of Scripture passages which force the conclusion that only bread and wine must be present. Answer: Where then, my fair love? Suppose they say: The Scriptures contradict themselves, and no one can reconcile them unless he believes that mere bread and wine are present in the Supper.[76] Answer: What Scripture? Suppose they say: Oh, where the article of faith is established that Christ ascended to heaven and sits on the right hand of God in his glory. Again, eating flesh is of no avail, John 6 [:63], "The flesh is of no avail." So, if flesh and blood are in the Supper, Christ could not be sitting at the right hand of God in his glory, and he would be giving us something to eat which is of no use for salvation. Therefore name any Scripture you will, it must make of Christ's body a "sign of the body," and this must be the text in the Supper! [77]

Who would have expected such lofty wisdom from the fanatics? Here you see the best single argument that they have. Suppose now that I ask them whether they have learned this from the Scriptures, and can prove that these two scriptural passages, viz. that Christ is seated in heaven and that his body is in the Supper, are contradictory; or again, that the flesh is of no avail and that Christ's body is eaten in the Supper; and, where all this is supposed to be written. They will answer me, "You must love us along with the Scriptures; you must believe us. We are certain of it without Scripture, and more certain than if the Scriptures said it."

I reply: How is this? Oh, you fool, open your eyes! Don't you see that heaven, where Christ is seated in his glory, is high above, and the earth where his Supper is observed is here, far below? How can a body be seated so high in glory and at the same time be here below, allowing itself to be profaned and taken by hands, mouth, and belly, as if it were a fried sausage? Would

---

[76] Cf. Oecolampadius, *Reply to Pirkheimer*, C. 1. See *WA* 23, 296.
[77] Oecolampadius had emphasized the Ascension in *Reasonable Answer*. *St. L.* 20, 591, 594; Zwingli had emphasized John 6:63 in his *Letter to Alber*. *C. R.* 90, 340 f.; *St. L.* 17, 1518 f.; and *Commentary*. *LWZ* 3, 212 ff. Zwingli put the two arguments together in *Clear Instruction*. *LCC* 24, 199 ff.

this be consistent with the majesty of God and the glory of heaven? Ah, this is more than certain! [78]

Thank you, good gentlemen! I did not know that in articles of faith it was entirely unnecessary to inquire into God's Word, but only to open our physical eyes and judge according to them, by the standards of reason, what is to be believed. Now I understand what is meant by "faith is the conviction of things not seen" [Heb. 11:1]. In the new interpretation of these spirits it means: "Faith must believe no more and no farther than one's eyes and fingers point out to him and the reason can measure. Now anyone who asks too many questions becomes unwelcome, but I must ask some more, that I may become still more clever. How do we become certain, good gentlemen, that a body may not through the power of God be at the same time in heaven and in the Supper, since the power of God has neither measure nor number, and does things which no mind can comprehend but must simply be believed? When he says, "This is my body," how shall I calm my heart and convince it that God has no means or power to do what his Word says? And perhaps, even if a body is not now visibly present at several places, he may well know of other ways by which he might render a body invisibly present, indeed, even visibly, in many places at the same time. If he could do this, would you not have deceived us woefully by saying No before you knew for sure? Have you also proof from the Scriptures that they do not concede this possibility to the omnipotence of God?

Friend, don't confuse us with the Scriptures; it is not the fanatics' practice to rely upon the Scriptures. But you ought to produce Scripture that God does and can do such things. All right, here is my Scripture: What God says, he can do, Romans 4 [:21], and with God no word is impossible, Luke 1 [:37]. Since he says here, then, "This is my body," he certainly can and does make it so. Now you in turn are obliged to prove that he does not and cannot do it. For that is your sovereign argument with which you would dislodge these words. This is the right place for blows, and we stand on the right field of combat. If you do not prove that it is impossible, then we unhorse you and run you

---

78 Cf. Oecolampadius, *Genuine Exposition*, E 3 and *passim*. See *WA* 23, 296.

through with the words, "This is my body"; God says it, God does it. *En garde,* you precious horsemen! Now is the time!

Here perhaps they may say: We can prove it very well. Once we climbed up to heaven secretly, just at midnight, when God was most soundly asleep. We had a lantern and a master key with us, broke into his most secret chamber, and unlocked all his chests and strongboxes in which his power lay. We took gold scales so that we could weigh our loot accurately and be sure to hit it just right. But we found no power that can enable a body to be at the same time in heaven and in the Supper. Therefore it is certain that "body" must mean "sign of the body." May God repay you, Satan, you damnable wretch, for the shameful and cocksure way you ridicule us! But my ridicule in turn will tickle you, too, what do you bet?

There lies the celebrated argument, now, that they slobber about the most, above all others, and on which they rely and insist most stubbornly, when they say that the two Scripture passages are contradictory: Christ is seated in heaven, and his body is in the Supper, though they do not prove it. But they do prove clearly that these two passages and their reason are contradictory. This, however, it would not have been necessary to prove; I could have told them just as well. What you say, that Scripture is contradictory, matters not at all. Who asks what you say? I would laud and honor them, however, if they would prove their assertion with Scripture or in some other way. But they must leave this undone, in order that this text may remain firm, "This is my body."

If we establish that Oecolampadius can neither prove this assertion of his nor indicate how the Scriptures are contradictory in the sight of God—which, to be sure, he can never do—then the whole argument has been won and we have established everything. For if it turns out that we retain the words, "This is my body," i.e. that Christ's body is present in the Supper, then the saying in John 6 [:63], "The flesh is of no avail," will harmonize perfectly well. Miracles aplenty will then take place, the sacraments will not be mere symbols,[79] and their whole swarm which is so big will scatter and fly away like dust before the wind. For

[79] Zwingli, *Letter to Alber.* C. R. 90, 331; *St. L.* 17, 1528; cf. also citations from Bucer and Oecolampadius in *WA* 23, 297.

it will not be necessary to relegate Christ's body and blood to the status of a useless or insignificant thing. Of this I am sure.

However, if we should judge the articles of our faith and the Scriptures according to our reason and our eyes, as Oecolampadius does here, then indeed every point in the Scriptures is in opposition to the other. For the text that Mary is a virgin and mother [Luke 1:27, 31] is opposed to the texts, "Be fruitful and multiply," and "I will make for man a helper fit for him" [Gen. 1:28, 2:18]. If I should deny for that reason that she was a virgin, and exclaim, "The Scriptures are contradictory," someone would fairly answer me, "Yes, for you and your reason they are contradictory; but how are they contradictory before God? Tell me that!" So I would be in the same position as Oecolampadius is here.

Again, that Christ is God is contrary to the text, "God created man" [Gen. 1:27]. Go on now and say, "He is not God, because divinity and humanity are more opposed to each other than heaven and earth; and the person, Christ, cannot be at the same time in the Godhead and in humanity." Let your reason be that these texts are contradictory. Then someone will answer you, "Yes, you say so, and in your eyes they are contradictory, but show me that they are also contradictory in God's sight!"

So too, that Christ's body is both in heaven and in the Supper is a contradiction, says Oecolampadius, and so it is in his eyes. Yes, but no one asked him to teach us his say-so, and what appears to him to be thus and so, but what God says and how it is in God's eyes. There he lies helpless, yet he must do as we have said if he wishes to make his teaching certain and sure. Here let them answer, here let us see how they will crack their heads. But they do not do it. They will grumble something foolish and pipe a different tune, in order to keep men from noticing how they are being forced into a tight spot.

Compare them now, these fanatics and corrupters of the Scriptures. Karlstadt produced his *touto*,[80] which turned out to be untenable. Then Zwingli came and tried to improve the matter with his metaphor, which was even less tenable. Next comes Oecolampadius with his "sign of the body," as the best idea of

[80] See also p. 38, n. 57.

all, and it proves least tenable of all. So his argument runs: "I, Oecolampadius, say that the Scriptures in this case are contradictory." Now isn't this a fine, delicate basis of faith, when a man can say, "Although God's Word stands there and says, 'This is my body,' nevertheless because I cannot comprehend or believe it, and it appears to me to contradict Scripture, it is therefore not true and must have another meaning, regardless of how clearly God's Word stands there." This is Oecolampadius' "spirit" and his celebrated "truth,"[81] that human fancy and unbelief shall prevail over God's Word and form the basis of our faith. Who could not do the same thing in all other articles of faith as well? How profoundly can Satan mislead such people? Hence this argument of Oecolampadius is overthrown with a single word: No! These texts are not contradictory; a man may say so and imagine so, but not prove it. Thus all his elaborate system lies in the slop.

Now do you demand Scripture from us, dear fanatics? Here it is: "Take, eat, this is my body." Torment yourselves for now with this text; later you shall have more. Oh, how sure you were, not thinking that you could ever be challenged or confronted with this saying! For you had not only crucified it but also buried it and set guards around the grave so that it was utterly impotent. But now it has risen from the dead and will die no more, and casts you, its enemies, under its feet and makes you its footstool.[82] What deceived the good Oecolampadius is the fact that scriptural texts which are contradictory must be reconciled, and one passage must receive an interpretation which will accord with another; for it is certain that the Scriptures cannot be at variance with themselves. But he did not notice and consider that he would be the one who alleged this variance in the Scriptures and who ought to prove it. He simply asserted it and proclaimed it as if it were already sealed and delivered. This is where he stumbled and fell.

If they would stop and think, however, and take care to speak nothing but God's words, as St. Peter teaches [I Pet. 4:11], and

---

[81] Oecolampadius: "Unconquered stands the truth. . . ." *Reply to Pirkheimer*, *a* 4.

[82] Allusions to Matt. 27:66, Rom. 6:9, Ps. 110:1, all of which also figured exegetically in the controversy.

if they would leave their own assertions and assumptions at home, they would not create so much misfortune. This saying, "The Scriptures are not self-contradictory," would not have misled Oecolampadius, for it is grounded in God's Word that God does not lie nor does his Word deceive.[83] But this addition to his word, "I, Oecolampadius, say that the Scriptures here are contradictory," brings him into such toil and sweat that he denies, twists, reinterprets, and tortures the Word of God any way he pleases. Lord God, how easily such a horrible downfall takes place, and still we are sure and fearless on this slippery path!

But I shall put my finger still more accurately upon their real argument which leads them to such an error, and I shall stake my body and soul, which I would not gladly lose, that I shall not fail in my purpose. Poor sinner that I am, I too know a little about the Spirit, and a great deal about the old rogue who rages in us—I mean, the flesh. This one factor moves them above all others: that according to reason it is altogether absurd to believe that we should eat and drink Christ's body and blood physically in the Supper. And I know for certain that if they should win, their ultimate exultation would be, "Yes, I was perfectly sure that it could not be right: it just never made sense to me that Christ's body and blood should be treated in this way!" as they are now whispering secretly among themselves, and as the foolish masses are prattling openly. But they would like to conceal this, for they are ashamed to admit it. They know very well that it is worthless talk, but they are pleased to see the foolish masses blurt it out, and they say and write nothing against it.

It is shameful, however, that they have not enough decency and honesty to admit openly what they really wish in their hearts and what they would like to have and see and hear but allege instead that the Scriptures constrain them—which they know is not true, for they seize the Scriptures with guile and malice in order to use them as a cloak before the people, and under the guise of Scripture they spread their poison among the people.

Although they conceal all this with great diligence, still the old rogue peeks out and exposes himself to view clearly enough.

[83] Cf. Titus 1:2, Ps. 33:4.

Zwingli as much as confesses that he has never believed it his whole life long, and I have no doubt that he believes nothing at all. Indeed, what is more, he places himself upon the judgment seat and judges the heart and spirit of all men, declaring that no man has ever believed this.[84] If this is not too rash, it certainly is rash enough, and besides, it is not true, as I know only too well. Now from this confession it is to be observed that he does not draw this notion from the Scriptures, which he discovered only long afterward, as his book, *Rearguard,* in particular, and others prove. Long before he ever found these Scriptures he had these beliefs, and only now does he run and hunt up Scripture and force it to suit his notion.[85] Before Dr. Karlstadt started writing, he too said a long time ago to a certain person, "My friend, you will not persuade me that God is in the bread and wine." So, by the power of God, they are caught off guard.

In the same way when Oecolampadius[86] skips over the Scriptures confronting him, God help us, how gaily he leaps and dances with his notion, asking: What purpose does it serve? Why didn't the disciples worship the bread? Why does Scripture indicate no miracle here? How does it help if Christ is invisibly present? Why must Christians believe such a difficult thing? What sense does it make that the King of glory permits such wicked fellows to trifle with him? In particular, however, it is his blasphemous words that portray his heart best, when he calls our God a baked

---

[84] "Nor do I believe there ever was a person who believed that he ate Christ bodily and essentially in the sacrament. . . ." *Letter to Alber.* *C. R.* 90, 350; *St. L.* 17, 1526. Cf. *Rearguard.* *C. R.* 91, 493; *Clear Instruction.* *LCC* 24, 199.

[85] Perhaps Luther had in mind the fact that Zwingli wrote his treatise, *Rearguard,* 1525, as an afterthought to reinforce his *Commentary on True and False Religion.* Even more, he must have been thinking of Zwingli's claim in *Rearguard* that while his view on the Lord's Supper had been fixed for years, he had only recently acquired new biblical support besides the metaphorical arguments, viz. the insight through a dream that the passover, Exod. 12:11, provided a proof of his position. *C. R.* 91, 483 f. "Others" doubtless means Zwingli's *Reply to Bugenhagen,* 1525 (*C. R.* 91, 558 f.; *St. L.* 20, 507 f.), where the concept of trope and the interpretation of "is" as "represent" appear. Incidentally, Walther Köhler has shown that Zwingli did not fix his view of the sacrament until 1523-1524. *Zwingli und Luther* (1924), I, chap. 1; cf. Hermann Sasse, *This Is My Body* (Minneapolis: Augsburg Publishing House. 1959), pp. 120-130.

[86] A number of supporting citations from *Genuine Exposition, Apologetics,* and *Reply to Pirkheimer* are given in *WA* 23, 298.

God, a bread-God, a meat-God, and many, many other names.[87] Who can possibly fail to understand now what they think in their hearts? If the Scriptures moved them, they would surely have done with such obscenities and deal with Scriptures.

This is the rancor and hatred of natural reason, which wants nothing to do with this article and therefore spits and vomits against it, and then tries to wrap itself in Scripture so that it may avoid being recognized. Not a single article of faith would remain if I followed the rancor of reason. I too could use this spitting and vomiting against it, to show the blasphemers that spitting is not simply an art of the Holy Spirit. I can say of God: Of what use is it that he is man? Why must one believe such a difficult thing?[88] Why don't the apostles worship him in the Supper? What sense does it make that this Divine Majesty permits himself to be crucified by wicked fellows? Oh, what a meat-God! Oh, what a bloody God! Oh, what a dead God! And so forth.

With this rancor, however, my dear fanatics prepare the way for the virtual denial of Christ, God, and everything. In part, already, they have made a start at believing nothing at all.[89] They follow the fancy of reason, which they expect to lead them aright. But this scoffing only serves the purpose of stirring up the foolish masses, who do not trouble themselves with Scriptures. They themselves know perfectly well that all their heathenish vomiting proves nothing against this article, or if it disproves this one, it also disproves all articles. For God's Word is always folly to reason, I Corinthians 1 [:18]. Therefore they would keep silent about all this if they were really in earnest about the Scriptures and did not have hearts full of sheer rancor and unbelief which had to spill out of their mouths. More on this subject later.

---

[87] Cf. p. 22, n. 24. *LW* 36, 336, n. 2; 344.

[88] To Zwingli, Luther's view thrusts upon people assertions which are not only difficult but impossible to believe, and force the senses to rebellion. *Commentary*. *LWZ* 3, 212 ff. "Why, pray, do we burden pious hearts with words of this kind, which no intellect can comprehend?" *Ibid.*, 250. Cf. his dictum at the Marburg Colloquy, 1529: "It is not true that God puts before us many incomprehensible things." Sasse, *This Is My Body*, p. 241.

[89] Perhaps Luther was thinking of such a statement as that of Zwingli: "Almost everything the Hebrews, Christ, Paul, and the apostles said, I call a trope." *Reply to Bugenhagen*. *C. R.* 91, 575; *St. L.* 20, 519. Cf. p. 16, n. 7.

Again, when Oecolampadius in his first book plays nasty tricks and defames the sayings of the fathers, he has to admit that he has not derived his notion from the fathers' writings, for they speak so mightily that they very frequently extort the admission from him, "This appears to be against us."[90] My friend, what else is this than to say, "The fathers strongly imply something else; I cannot derive my argument from their writings, but must work hard to twist their nose around to my sense"? But anyone who must work so hard to twist and force these sayings around to his position admits forthwith that they yield not his position but rather the very opposite, and he is importing and reading his own thoughts into them. What advantage his nose-twisting of the fathers brings him, however, we shall see later.

The amazing thing, meanwhile, is that of all the fathers, as many as you can name, not one has ever spoken about the sacrament as these fanatics do. None of them uses such an expression as, "It is simply bread and wine," or, "Christ's body and blood are not present." Yet since this subject is so frequently discussed by them, it is impossible that they should not at some time have let slip such an expression as, "It is simply bread," or, "Not that the body of Christ is physically present," or the like, since they are greatly concerned not to mislead the people; actually, they simply proceed to speak as if no one doubted that Christ's body and blood are present. Certainly among so many fathers and so many writings a negative argument should have turned up at least once, as happens in other articles; but actually they all stand uniformly and consistently on the affirmative side. Our fanatics however can speak of virtually nothing but the negative. In short: Oecolampadius has derived his view neither from the Scriptures nor from the fathers, but he sweats and toils to import it into both.

This should be quite enough to answer the fanatics. For since we prove and establish that the saying of Christ, "This is my body," still stands firm, and that their best arguments are worthless, and bare and devoid of all proof, then surely all the other texts concerning Christ's Supper also stand firm. For I have

[90] A half dozen citations are given in *WA* 23, 299, from *Genuine Exposition*, where Oecolampadius acknowledged difficulties in quotations from Hilary, Cyprian, and Irenaeus.

taken up the least and simplest of them, just to challenge the impotent, unsound, feeble prattle of the fanatics. So I treated this subject not without care also in my book against the heavenly prophets,[91] and up to now no fanatic has refuted that book for me. I maintain, however, that they scorn it and do not read it, or if they do read it, they curl their lips and pass it by, on account of their great humility and fulness of all wisdom and holiness.

However, in order to strengthen our people, I shall go on and show that the fanatics' reasons and arguments are worthless, and shall prove to the point of superfluity that it is contrary neither to Scripture nor to the articles of faith for Christ's body to be at the same time in heaven and in the Supper. I shall do this even though I do not owe it to the fanatics; rather, they are under obligation to prove that it is contrary to Scripture, and they cannot do it, as we have said. If I have proved this, however, then the words, "This is my body," should be allowed to stand and remain just as they read. That I should show visibly with eyes and finger that Christ's body is at the same time in heaven and at table, as the fanatics ask of us,[92] of course I cannot do. He who is unwilling to believe the words of God need not demand anything further from me. So I do enough if I prove that it is not contrary to God's Word, but consistent with Scripture.

In the first place, we take up the article that Christ sits at the right hand of God, which the fanatics maintain makes it impossible for Christ's body also to be in the Supper. Now if we ask how they interpret God's "right hand" where Christ sits, I suppose they will dream up for us, as one does for the children, an imaginary heaven in which a golden throne stands, and Christ sits beside the Father in a cowl and golden crown, the way artists paint it. For if they did not have such childish, fleshly ideas of the right hand of God, they surely would not allow the idea of Christ's bodily presence in the Supper to vex them so or castigate themselves so with the saying of Augustine (whom in other

---

[91] Part II. *LW* 40, 144 ff.

[92] Oecolampadius: "The nature of a body is to be in one place. A body which can be at the same time in many places will not be regarded as a true body. A body has location, unless it can be shown otherwise from Scripture." *Reasonable Answer*. *St. L.* 20, 603.

respects they do not believe at all, nor anyone else), "Christ must be bodily in one place, but his truth is everywhere."[93]

From these childish ideas it must follow further that they also bind God himself to one place in heaven, on the same golden throne, since apart from Christ there is no God, and where Christ is there is the Godhead in all its fulness, as Paul says, "In him the whole Godhead dwells bodily" [Col. 2:9], and John 6 [14:9 f.], "Have I been with you so long, and yet you do not know me, Philip? He who has seen me has seen the Father. Do you not believe that the Father is in me and I am in the Father?" From this it follows still further that we and all creatures also sit on the same throne of God—perhaps as the lice and fleas in his cowl!—since Paul says, Acts 17 [:28], "We are his offspring, and in him we live and move and have our being."

We ask them further: Where is the Scripture which limits the right hand of God in this fashion to one place? Suppose they say: God help us, don't we produce texts enough? Are you blind? Don't you see how our books are full of texts from the Scriptures? Indeed, I see very well that you are worthless spouters, that you produce an enormous amount of prattle where it is not necessary, as for example about spiritual eating, Christ's sitting in heaven, remembrance of him in the Supper, and the like, about which no one is questioning you. This is your cuckoo letting himself be heard; here you are full of Scripture. But where it is necessary you pass by, dumb as a clod, indulging in the dream that the entire Scriptures are in harmony with your notion. As Solomon says in Ecclesiastes 5 [:3], it is the way of the world that "what lies on one's mind, one dreams about"—one can't get it out of one's mind. And Virgil, "Lovers fashion dreams of their own."[94]

Why do you not ponder and learn first whether it is or is not Scripture that God's right hand is a specific place, because the

---

93 In *Genuine Exposition,* C 6, Oecolampadius had quoted from Canon Law (*Decretum of Gratian,* Part III, *de Consecratione,* dist. II, c. 44, c. 1. *Corpus Iuris Canonici,* I, col. 1330) without citing Augustine. The Decretum reads: "The body in which he arose must [*oportet*] be in one place"; Augustine's text (*Gospel of John, Tractate 30,* 1. *PNF*[1] 7, 186) reads *potest,* but the context justifies the *PNF* translation, "can be only in one place."

94 Charles Anthon (ed.), Virgil's *Bucolica Ecloga* (New York: Harpers, 1852), 8, 108. In quoting, "*qui amant, ipsi sibi somnia fingunt,*" Luther omitted *ipsi.*

Scriptures speak quite abundantly of the right hand of God? But you erect such a great and risky fanaticism upon your empty dream and then boast that you produce much Scripture; and because you enjoy so much joining in this dance, it seems to you that heaven is full of fiddles.[95] As they say, the person who likes to dance is easy to pipe to.[96] Thus, since it pleases you that Christ is in heaven and not in the Supper, you let St. Augustine's saying persuade you so easily to affirm that God's right hand is a place in heaven—you who otherwise are so stubborn, wise, and inflexible about the sayings of all the fathers that if all of them together unanimously constrain you to a Yes, you will still make a No out of it. Yet you think no one should notice why you produce a great deal of Scripture on unnecessary topics, while on the necessary topics you produce not a tittle but only your own dreams.

The Scriptures teach us, however, that the right hand of God is not a specific place in which a body must or may be, such as on a golden throne, but is the almighty power of God, which at one and the same time can be nowhere and yet must be everywhere. It cannot be at any one place, I say. For if it were at some specific place, it would have to be there in a circumscribed and determinate manner, as everything which is at one place must be at that place determinately and measurably, so that it cannot meanwhile be at any other place. But the power of God cannot be so determined and measured, for it is uncircumscribed and immeasurable, beyond and above all that is or may be.

On the other hand, it must be essentially present[97] at all places, even in the tiniest tree leaf. The reason is this: It is God who creates, effects, and preserves all things through his almighty

[95] Cf. the proverb, *Der Himmel hängt nicht alles voll Geigen* in Karl Friedrich Wilhelm Wander, *Deutsches Sprichwörter Lexikon* (5 vols.; Leipzig, 1867-1880), II, 646.

[96] Cf. the proverb, *Dem ist leicht zu pfeifen, der Lust zu tanzen hat. Ibid.*, III, 1260. Cf. also *Luthers Sprichwörter-sammlung* in WA 51, 649, 678.

[97] *Wesentlich und gegenwertig. Wesentlich*, "essentially" or "substantially," means for Luther "in essence" in the ancient philosophical sense, cf. *Against Latomus. LW* 32, 202; it does not have the modern connotation of "for all practical purposes." The editors of *Zwingli Hauptschriften*, meanwhile, usually annotate Zwingli's *wesenlich* with *dinglich*, "real" in the legal sense. *Gegenwertig* means both "in the present time" and "here." Cf. p. 61, n. 102, p. 121, n. 201; and p. 52, n. 84, p. 127, n. 216, p. 234.

power and right hand, as our Creed confesses. For he dispatches no officials or angels when he creates or preserves something, but all this is the work of his divine power itself. If he is to create or preserve it, however, he must be present and must make and preserve his creation both in its innermost and outermost aspects.

Therefore, indeed, he himself must be present in every single creature in its innermost and outermost being, on all sides, through and through, below and above, before and behind, so that nothing can be more truly present and within all creatures than God himself with his power. For it is he who makes the skin and it is he who makes the bones; it is he who makes the hair on the skin, and it is he who makes the marrow in the bones; it is he who makes every bit of the hair, it is he who makes every bit of the marrow. Indeed, he must make everything, both the parts and the whole. Surely, then, his hand which makes all this must be present; that cannot be lacking.

At this point the passage of Isaiah 66 [:2] derived from Genesis 1, undeniably applies: "Has not my hand made all these things?" Psalm 139 [:7-10]: "Whither shall I go from thy Spirit? Or whither shall I flee from thy presence? If I ascend to heaven, thou art there! If I make my bed in hell, thou art there! If I take the wings of the morning dawn (and these are certainly great wings, as great as half the world) and dwell in the uttermost parts of the sea, even there thy hand shall hold me."

Why should I say a great deal? The Scriptures ascribe all miracles and works of God to his right hand, e.g. Acts 4 [5:31], Christ is exalted by the right hand of God; Psalm 118 [:15 f.], "The right hand of God does wonders, the right hand of the Lord exalts me." In Acts 17 [:27 f.] Paul says, "God is not far from each one of us, for in him we live and move and have our being." And Romans 11 [:36], "From him and through him and to him are all things." And Jeremiah 23 [:23 f.], "Am I not[98] a God at hand, and not a God afar off? Do I not fill heaven and earth?" Isaiah 66 [:1], "Heaven is my throne and the earth is my footstool." He does not say, "A part of heaven is my throne, a part or spot of the earth is my footstool," but, "Whatever and wherever

[98] Jeremiah's text does not contain the negative here.

heaven is, there is my throne, whether heaven is beneath, above, or beside the earth. And whatever and wherever earth is, whether at the bottom of the sea, in the grave of the dead, or at the middle of the earth, there is my footstool." Come and tell me now, where are his head, arm, breast, body, if with his feet he fills the earth and with his legs he fills heaven? He reaches out ever so far over and beyond the world, above heaven and earth.

What can Isaiah intend with this saying but, as St. Hilary[99] also says on this subject, that God in his essence is present everywhere, in and through the whole creation in all its parts and in all places, and so the world is full of God and he fills it all, yet he is not limited or circumscribed by it, but is at the same time beyond and above the whole creation? All this is an infinitely incomprehensible thing, yet these are articles of our faith, clearly and powerfully attested in the Scriptures. In comparison with this it is a trivial matter that Christ's body and blood are at the same time in heaven and in the Supper. And if the fanatics began to approach this point with their reason and their eyes, they would quickly fall headlong and say that it is nothing and (as it is the great virtue of the ungodly to say), "There is no God," Psalm 14 [:1].

For how can reason tolerate it that the Divine Majesty is so small as to be present in essence in a kernel, on a kernel, above a kernel, throughout a kernel, inside and outside—and, even though it is one single Majesty, can nevertheless be completely and entirely present in every individual thing, countless in number though they be? For he certainly makes every single kernel in particular, in all its parts, on the inside and throughout, so his power must be present there throughout, in and on the kernel. But now, his power is one and simple and is not divided, as if he made the husk of the kernel with his fingers and the pith of the kernel with his feet. Thus the entire divine power must be present throughout, in and on the kernel. For he alone makes it all. On the other hand, the same Majesty is so great that neither this world nor even a thousand worlds could embrace it and say, "See, there it is!"

[99] Hilary of Poitiers, *On the Trinity*, I, 6. *MPL* 10, 29; *FC* 25, 7 f.; cf. *Tractate on Psalm 118*, XIX, 8. *MPL* 9, 629.

Here, now, let the fanatics answer me. Body, of course, has still another relation with other bodies; they may fit together, as for example bread is a body, wine is a body, Christ's flesh is a body. Here one body may be in another, as I can be in the open air, and in a garment or a house, as money can be in a purse, or wine in a cask or tankard. But here, where we are dealing not with body but spirit—indeed, who knows what this is[100] that we call God? He is above body, above spirit, above everything man can say or hear or think: how at one and the same time can such a being be completely and entirely present in every single body, every creature and object everywhere, and on the other hand, must and can be nowhere, beyond and above all creatures and objects, as our Creed and the Scriptures confess both truths about God? Here reason must conclude without further ado: Oh, surely this is utter nonsense and can be nothing but nonsense. Now if he has found the way whereby his own divine nature can be wholly and entirely in all creatures and in every single individual being, more deeply, more inwardly, more present than the creature is to itself, and yet on the other hand may and can be circumscribed nowhere and in no being, so that he actually embraces all things and is in all, but no one being circumscribes him and is in him —should not this same God also know some way whereby his body could be wholly and completely present in many places at the same time, and yet none of these places could be where he is? Ah, we miserable children of men, who judge God and his doings according to our own imagination, and think of him as a cobbler or a day laborer!

Yes, they say, of course we believe that God's power is everywhere. But it is not necessary on that account for his divine nature or his right hand to be everywhere. Answer: I believe also, of course, that at the bottom of your hearts you believe nothing either about God or about God's power. I am certain, moreover, that you will, of course, leap over all these irrefutable Scripture passages which I am adducing and expounding here, and that you will curl your lips and say, "Humph! He speaks of kernels and tree leaves, but he produces no Scripture." For this is what you are accustomed to do. And then you jabber something about your

[100] I.e. something beyond our comprehension.

forbearance or babble about irrelevant matters, and that must serve as Scripture. We know, however, that God's power, arm, hand, nature, face, Spirit, wisdom, etc., are all one thing; for apart from the creation there is nothing but the one simple Deity himself. And thus, if before the creation of the universe there doubtless existed the power and hand of God, God's nature itself, then it did not become something else after the creation of the universe. Indeed, he makes and does nothing except through his Word, Genesis 1, John 1,[101] i.e. his power. And his power is not an ax, hatchet, saw, or file with which he works, but is himself. Then if his power and Spirit are present everywhere and in all things to the innermost and outermost degree, through and through, as it must be if he is to make and preserve all things everywhere, then his divine right hand, nature, and majesty must also be everywhere. He must surely be present if he makes and preserves them.

For good measure I shall also prove this with an example and story from Scripture. It is our belief, of course, as the Scriptures teach us, that our Lord Jesus Christ is in essence and by nature true God, and "in him the fulness of the Godhead dwells bodily," as St. Paul says in Colossians 2 [:9]. Thus, apart from Christ there is simply no God or Godhead at all, as he himself also says in John 16 [14:9 f.], "Philip, he who has seen me has seen the Father. Do you not believe that the Father is in me and I am in him?" All right, Christ walks on earth, and the entire Godhead is in him in person and in essence on earth. Now tell me: How can it be true at one and the same time that God is entirely present, personally and essentially,[102] in Christ on earth in his mother's womb, yes, in the crib, in the temple, in the wilderness, in cities, in houses, in the garden, in the field, on the cross, in the grave, etc., yet nonetheless also in heaven in the Father's bosom?[103] If this is true and undeniably consistent with the faith

101 Cf. Gen. 1:3, 6, 9, etc.; John 1:3, 10.

102 *Personlich gegewertig, wesenlich. Personlich* means "in person" in the ancient Christological sense; it does not have the modern connotation of "personality." Cf. *Augsburg Confession*, I, 4.

103 Zwingli: "Hilary did not have the idea that in the Lord's bread is eaten the body of Christ which hung upon the cross, or wailed in the manger, as our friends say." *Commentary. LWZ* 3, 245, cf. 252 and *Clear Instruction. LCC* 24, 189.

that the Godhead itself is essentially and personally present in Christ on earth in so many places, and yet at the same time in heaven with the Father, it follows that he is everywhere at the same time, and essentially and personally fills heaven and earth and everything with his own nature and majesty, in accordance with the Scriptures, Jeremiah 22 [23:23 f.], "I fill heaven and earth, and am a God near at hand," and Psalm 139 [:7], "Whither shall I flee from thy presence?"

Moreover, when Christ, the Son of God, was to be conceived in his mother's womb and become incarnate, he certainly had to be already present in essence and in person in the Virgin's womb, and had to assume humanity there. For the Godhead is immutable in itself and cannot pass from one place to another as creatures do. Therefore he did not climb down from heaven as on a ladder or descend as by a rope, but was already in the Virgin's womb in essence and in person, as he was also in all other places, everywhere, according to the nature and character and power of divinity. If he is in a certain place, then, such as the Virgin's womb, in his essence and in his own person, and at the same time present with his Father, as our Creed requires, he is certainly also present everywhere in this way. For there can be no reason why he should be able to be in the Virgin's womb and not also be present everywhere in the same way.

Yet in Christ there is something different, higher and greater than in all other creatures. For in him God not only is present in his essence as in all others, but also dwells bodily in him in such a way that one person is man and God. Although I can say of all creatures, "There is God, or God is in it," I cannot say, "This is God himself." But of Christ faith[104] asserts not only that God is in him but that Christ is God himself. Anyone who kills a man may be called a murderer of a being who belongs to God and in whom God is present, but he who kills Christ has killed God's Son, indeed, God and the Lord of glory himself. Now, that God not only is in him but also dwells in him in such a way that God and man are one person—this is the mighty work and wonder of God, which makes all reason foolish, and which faith alone must cling to unless all is to be lost.

[104] *Der Glaube* can mean "faith" and "the Creed."

Therefore we are speaking now of the first question alone, how God himself is personally present in all things, without which presence even God could not have become man nor one person made of divinity and humanity. For, as we have said, he had to be present first in his mother's womb, as he is in himself in the Godhead. O Lord God, where are they who believe all this? What will happen if reason comes in here with its swarm of fanatics? Fanaticism over the sacrament will then become much more attractive compared with these beliefs. Very well then: God abides, and so do his own.

It has been shown convincingly enough by now that the right hand of God is not a particular place where Christ's body is seated, as the fanatics dream, but is the power of God himself. For God's right hand of course cannot be a creature but must be something above and apart from all creatures, for there is no one and nothing other than God himself who is in all things everywhere. Therefore this also must be true, that God's right hand is in all things everywhere, as we have heard. I truly believe that we do not bypass the Scriptures here like the fanatics, or discuss things other than those which are pertinent to the subject, but that we have firmly established and determined from the clear and correct ground of Scripture and the articles of faith that the right hand of God is everywhere. They, however—the fanatics—lose the point and fail to maintain their position when they say it is a particular place, supporting their carnal ideas from Augustine.[105]

Now let us come to grips with them. They admit that Christ is at the right hand of God, and thereby claim to have won the point that he is not in the Supper. This is indeed the fearful sword of the giant Goliath of which they boast. But what if we should take this same sword away from you and lop off your head with it, and with precisely the same text by which you claimed to prove that Christ's body must not be present in the Supper, should prove that it must be there? You would regard this deed of David as no mean feat, would you not?[106] Very well then: Take notice and listen to us. Christ's body is at the right hand of God; that is granted. The right hand of God, how-

[105] Cf. p. 56, n. 93. [106] Cf. I Sam. 17:4, 50 f.

ever, is everywhere, as you must grant from our previous demonstration. Therefore it surely is present also in the bread and wine at table. Now where the right hand of God is, there Christ's body and blood must be, for the right hand of God is not divisible into many parts but a single, simple entity. So too, the article of the Creed does not say that Christ is at one part, such as a little finger or fingernail of the right hand of God, but it says without qualification, "at the right hand of God," that wherever and whatever God's right hand is in reality and in name, there is Christ, the Son of man.

This is also the intention of Christ wherever he confesses in the gospel that all things have been delivered to him by the Father [Luke 10:22] and all things put under his feet, Psalm 8 [:6]. That is, he is at the right hand of God, which means nothing else than that even as a man he is over all things, has all things under him, and rules over all. Therefore he must also be near at hand, in and about all things, and have all things in his hands. For nothing is delivered to him or put under his feet according to his divinity, since he himself made all things at the beginning and preserves them. But to sit at God's right hand is the same as to rule and have power over all things. If he is to have power and rule, surely he must also be present there in his essence through the right hand of God which is everywhere.

Now what is the result? Just this: even if Christ had never spoken or set forth these words at the Supper, "This is my body," still the words, "Christ sits at the right hand of God," would require that his body and blood may be there as well as at all other places, and that although there need be no transubstantiation or transformation of the bread into his body,[107] it can well be present nonetheless, just as the right hand of God is not necessarily transformed into all things even though it is surely present and in them. How this takes place, however, is not for us to know; we are to believe it, since the Scriptures and the articles of faith so irrefutably confirm it.

---

[107] Since 1520 (cf. *Babylonian Captivity*. *LW* 36, 28 ff.) Luther had rejected transubstantiation, but Zwingli repeatedly insisted that transubstantiation was still the logical outcome of Luther's teaching, e.g. *Clear Instruction. LCC* 24, 191 ff.

We poor sinners, indeed, are not so foolish as to believe that Christ's body is in the bread in a crude visible manner, like bread in a basket or wine in a cup, a belief with which the fanatics would like to saddle us,[108] to amuse themselves with our folly. But we believe precisely that his body is present, as his words say and indicate: "This is my body." When the fathers and we occasionally say, "Christ's body is in the bread," we do so quite simply because by our faith we wish to confess that Christ's body is present. Otherwise we may well allow it to be said that it is in the bread, it is the bread, it is where the bread is, or whatever you wish.[109] Over words we do not wish to argue, just so the meaning is retained that it is not mere bread that we eat in Christ's Supper, but the body of Christ.

Moreover, the fanatics should consider that God has more ways by which to have one object in another than this crude mode which they set forth, as wine is in a cask, bread in a box, or money in a pocket. "Levi was in the loins of Abraham," says the writer to the Hebrews [7:10], as the Scriptures describe all children as in their fathers' loins or from their loins. Again, all colors and lights and everything that men see are said to "be in their eyes," so that even heaven and earth may be in one's eye. Again, everything that stands before a mirror is in it. Again, trees and all fruits are in the kernel or seed. Again, all things are in our hearts, even God himself, and this indeed is a greater wonder

[108] Luther had opened himself to this charge by writing, e.g., "Heaven and earth are his sack; as wheat fills the sack, so he fills all things." *The Sacrament of the Body and Blood of Christ—Against the Fanatics*, 1526. *LW* 36, 343. Cf. Oecolampadius: "If Christ is in the bread, then wherever the bread is placed or carried, it will be necessary for the body also to be carried to the same place, for it is bread; and one will be at liberty to play with it, so that it will be borne up and down, forward and backward in the bread, according to the whim of the administrant." *Reply to Pirkheimer, d* 1. He also derided the idea that Christ is "enclosed in the loaves and falling crumbs on many altars," or that the bread is a "wrapping" for Christ's flesh. *Genuine Exposition*, E 7, A *v*. Konrad Sam: "Do you mean that one eats Christ in the bread, just as when one ices an almond with sugar?" *A Fine Statement*, 1526, B 1. See *WA* 23, 302.

[109] Zwingli: "If you take 'is' substantively [i.e., in the sense of existence], the papists have already won, and the bread must be the flesh. But when they say that 'under' or 'in' this bread the flesh of Christ is eaten, they altogether take away this word 'is' which alone would establish that the bread is his body, or that the body is eaten here." *Reply to Billican*. *C.R.* 91, 901.

than all others. Who will doubt, then, that God has many more modes which he does not tell us about, where one thing is in another, or two things are present at the same time in one place?

But it is just as great a wonder that many bodies are in one place, as that one body is in many places. He who can bring about the one can bring about the other also. Now we have clear Scripture that Christ came to his disciples through the closed door, and out of his grave, even through the sealed stone.[110] Whether he entered through the window or the door, his body and that through which his body passed must have been at one and the same time in one place, both intact and unchanged. The evangelist says not that they saw him enter, but, "He appeared or stood in their midst" [Luke 24:36], which sounds as if he had been there already, hidden, and now revealed himself, as he also did to Mary Magdalene at the grave [John 20:14], and with all to whom he appeared. And in Acts 8 [7:55 f.] he appeared to St. Stephen in the town hall standing at the right hand of God. And in Acts 22 [:17 f.] he appeared to St. Paul in the temple. Again, in Matthew 17 [:5] the Father appeared in the clouds upon Mt. Tabor, and in Luke 3 [:22], too, the Father came in his voice and the Holy Spirit in the form of a dove. These and similar appearances which were granted to the prophets, apostles, and saints many, many times, show indeed that both God and Christ are not far away but near, and it is only a matter of revealing themselves; they do not move up and down or back and forth, for God is immutable, and Christ also sits at the right hand of God and does not move hither and yon.

So too, Christ says in John 3 [:13], "No one has ascended into heaven but he who descended from heaven, the Son of man who is in heaven," whereby he shows indeed that his body is at the same time in heaven and on earth, yes, even at the ends of the earth. For by his glorification he did not become another person, but before as well as after was present everywhere. Yet Oecolampadius imagines he has won a great point over Willibald

[110] John 20:19, 26, says simply that while the doors were shut, Jesus came and stood among the disciples. The gospels do not say explicitly that at the resurrection Jesus emerged through the stone, but only that an angel came and rolled it back, Matt. 28:2.

Pirkheimer of Nürnberg, claiming he does not know how great a sin it is for Pirkheimer to interpret this text as referring to the humanity of Christ.[111] If I were Pirkheimer, however, I would send Oecolampadius some spectacles and ask him to count the letters; perhaps it would help to keep them from stepping so lightly over the texts of Scripture and substituting for them their own dreams in the books they have scribbled for us.

But what is the meaning of "Son of man—descended—ascended"? He speaks so clearly about the Son of man, as the one who came down among us and ascended again. Now of course it is certain that Christ did not come down or ascend according to his divinity, but according to his humanity. If Oecolampadius indeed wished to boast so haughtily, he should first prove that this text refers to Christ according to his divinity, and teach the meaning of descending and ascending, and expound the text carefully and cogently. But that is not necessary for us fanatics. It is enough if we rave like fanatics, and this will instantly be called pure Scripture. However, since many teachers have expounded the descent from heaven, I shall forego such an explanation until I hear my fanatics express themselves. I cannot write everything all at once.

By this kind of talk perhaps I shall now attract other fanatics who would like to trip me up, arguing: If Christ's body is everywhere, ah, then I shall eat and drink him in all the taverns, from all kinds of bowls, glasses, and tankards! Then there is no difference between my table and the Lord's table. Oh, how we will chew him up! Such shameful pigs are we dreadful Germans for the most part that we have neither restraint nor reason, and if we hear something about God we pay as much attention as if it were a buffoon's fairy tale. Just now a story against the sacrament is circulating among the masses who have been misled by the teaching of the fanatics, that one should rather die than write and send out a sermon among them, for when they hear that it is all nonsense, they immediately want to do a mess on it and wipe their behinds on it. The civil government ought to punish such blasphemers. It is an offense against the law and an act of

[111] *Reply to Pirkheimer, f 7.*

insolence, since they know nothing about what they are saying but speak blasphemy anyway. God knows, I write about such difficult matters with great reluctance, for it is destined to reach such dogs and pigs.[112] But what am I to do about it? The fanatics must bear the responsibility for pushing me to it.

Listen now, you pig, dog, or fanatic, whatever kind of unreasonable ass you are: Even if Christ's body is everywhere, you do not therefore immediately eat or drink or touch him;[113] nor do I talk with you about such things in this manner, either; go back to your pigpen and your filth. I said above that the right hand of God is everywhere, but at the same time nowhere and uncircumscribed, above and apart from all creatures. There is a difference between his being present and your touching. He is free and unbound wherever he is, and he does not have to stand there like a rogue set in a pillory, or his neck in irons.

See, the bright rays of the sun are so near you that they pierce into your eyes or your skin so that you feel it, yet you are unable to grasp them and put them into a box, even if you should try forever. Prevent them from shining in through the window—this you can do, but catch and grasp them you cannot. So too with Christ: although he is everywhere, he does not permit himself to be so caught and grasped; he can easily shell himself, so that you get the shell but not the kernel. Why? Because it is one thing if God is present, and another if he is present for you. He is there for you when he adds his Word and binds himself, saying, "Here you are to find me." Now when you have the Word, you can grasp and have him with certainty and say, "Here I have thee, according to thy Word." Just as I say of the right hand of God: although this is everywhere, as we may not deny, still because it is also nowhere, as has been said, you can actually grasp it nowhere, unless for your benefit it binds

---

[112] See Matt. 7:6: "Do not give dogs what is holy; and do not throw your pearls before swine. . . ."

[113] Zwingli: ". . . visible and tangible flesh." *Commentary*. *LWZ* 3, 209. Leo Jud: "Then if I eat cheese and drink water, I also eat and drink his flesh and blood." *Opinion of the Learned Erasmus and Doctor Luther*, 1526, B 1. See *WA* 23, 302. The Swiss constantly argued that a body is perceptible, and that Christ suffered perceptibly, therefore if his body is present in the Supper, it must be there perceptibly. Cf. Zwingli, *Clear Instruction*. *LCC* 24, 190 ff.

itself to you and summons you to a definite place. This God's right hand does, however, when it enters into the humanity of Christ and dwells there. There you surely find it, otherwise you will run back and forth throughout all creation, groping here and groping there yet never finding, even though it is actually there; for it is not there for you.

So too, since Christ's humanity is at the right hand of God, and also is in all and above all things according to the nature of the divine right hand, you will not eat or drink him like the cabbage and soup on your table, unless he wills it. He also now exceeds any grasp, and you will not catch him by groping about, even though he is in your bread, unless he binds himself to you and summons you to a particular table by his Word, and he himself gives meaning to the bread for you, by his Word, bidding you to eat him. This he does in the Supper, saying, "This is my body," as if to say, "At home you may eat bread also, where I am indeed sufficiently near at hand too; but this is the true *touto,*[114] the 'This is my body': when you eat this, you eat my body, and nowhere else. Why? Because I wish to attach myself here with my Word, in order that you may not have to buzz about, trying to seek me in all the places where I am; this would be too much for you, and you would also be too puny to apprehend me in these places without the help of my Word."

O how very few there are even among the most learned who have ever pondered this article concerning Christ so profoundly, or have ever believed it is so utterly incomprehensible that God should be man and man should be God! But there stands the Scripture, and faith holds it to be certain truth. If it is true, then, we have here overthrown one of the fanatics' best arguments, viz. that for Christ's body to be at the same time in heaven and in the Supper is not a contradiction, but consistent with Scripture and the Creed. And it is grounded actually in the first article, where we say, "I believe in God the Father almighty, maker of heaven and earth." Precisely this article shields and sustains our interpretation of the Supper, as we have heard. Not that I wished hereby to measure and span God's power with measuring rods,

[114] Cf. p. 38, n. 57.

as the fanatics do, as if he had not many other ways than I have demonstrated by which to maintain a body in many places—for I believe his words, that he can do more than all the angels may conceive—but I have indicated one of these modes, to stop the fanatics' mouths and vindicate our faith.

However, since they go as far as to boast that their opinion is the certain truth—"most certain, most certain truth" it must be called[115]—they are really under obligation to prove that Christ's body may not be in heaven and the Supper, and that such articles are contradictory, and that the right hand of God is a specific place. For if their boast is true, that they have the truth with certainty, they must also be certain that the right hand of God is a special place, and still more certain that one body may not be in heaven and the Supper, and that such articles are contradictory. Their boast, however, I challenge them to make good with proof, as they should and ought. If they do it, I shall recant and join their side; but against this I am fortified. I warn them, however, to produce clearer Scripture and better arguments than they have done up to now. For I say to them in advance, they will have watchmen, and if I live and God helps me, I shall tell them forthrightly where they miss the mark.

Now Oecolampadius wants it known how greatly he seeks Christ's glory when he vents his sarcasm against Pirkheimer, saying that it must be truly a fine King of glory who would permit his body to be tossed to and fro upon the altar even by ungodly knaves, etc.[116] The purpose which these and similar words serve is that if a saint of Münzer's stripe[117] should read it, he'd say that he would do a mess on the King of glory and show him his backside: "What kind of glory of Christ do you call it, that his body is in the Supper?" Here I answer: According to Oecolampadius' wisdom, it is true, Christ has no other glory than to sit at the right hand of God on a velvet cushion and let the angels sing and fiddle and ring bells and play before him, and to be unconcerned

---

[115] Citations of Bucer, Oecolampadius, and Zwingli in *WA* 23, 303.

[116] Cf. p. 65, n. 108.

[117] Thomas Münzer, the brilliant and erratic spiritualist, was the object of Luther's polemic in *Letter . . . Concerning the Rebellious Spirit,* 1524. *LW* 40, 49 ff., and other writings. A revolutionary leader in the Peasants' War, he was captured and executed in 1525.

with the problem of the Supper.[118] But according to the faith of us poor sinners and fools, his glory is manifold, when his body and blood are present in the Supper: first, in that he makes fools of the learned and clever fanatics and permits them to become offended and hardened over his words and works, which he so foolishly speaks and performs that they cannot bring themselves to believe, as St. Paul says in I Corinthians 1 [:23], "We preach Christ, a stumbling-block to Jews and folly to Gentiles," and again [1:25], "The foolishness of God is wiser than men." Now, this is surely a great glory of the divine wisdom, and in the midst of us fools he is a glorious, praiseworthy God, who can catch the wise with mere folly and make their wisdom foolish so that they must be blind where they would like to be most wise. Such wisdom and glory no other king can wield, as St. Paul says in I Corinthians 2 [1:20], "Has not God made foolish the wisdom of the world?" To reduce wisdom to folly and shame is no mean glory and virtue!

In the second place, it is a glory and praise of his inexpressible grace and mercy that he concerns himself so profoundly with us poor sinners and shows us such gracious love and goodness, not content to be everywhere in and around, above and beside us, but even giving us his own body as nourishment, in order that with such a pledge he may assure and promise us that our body too shall live forever, because it partakes here on earth of an everlasting and living food. Now, we poor fools hold that glory appears when someone shows his virtue, mercy, and goodness to others. For anyone to permit himself to be glorified and served by others is a mean sort of glory, not a divine glory. Therefore one might do well to take the fanatics to school to learn what glory means.

Here the fanatics really come out into the open and show what kind of spirit they have. Knowing that they do not have Scripture on their side, they pounce upon this idea and try to confirm their error through the glory of Christ, get all excited in vain, and argue: It is not glorious but shameful for Christ to be in the Supper, therefore he surely is not there and cannot be

118 "I know today a more glorious Christ than one who permits himself to be touched or carnally eaten. . . ." *Apologetics,* H 8. *WA* 23, 303.

there, for Christ must be glorious.[119] Now if I ask them, "Who says it is not glorious?" they answer, "We do!" If I ask further, "Who are you? How do you know this? and, How do you prove it?" "Ho!" they retort, "isn't it enough that we say so? You always have to be answered with Scripture!"

Ha! You ought to be ashamed of yourselves to the bottom of your hearts that you have made such a display of this subject, and yet have failed to prove a single bit of it! Meanwhile, you do not see that if your conclusion were good and convincing, I also would brag and boast that the Son of God was not born of a woman, as the heathen bragged against SS. Cyprian and Augustine.[120] Why? Because it is not glorious for God to be born from the frail body of a human. Again, it is not glorious for Christ to be led by the devil out of the wilderness to [the pinnacle of] the temple and the high mountain, therefore it did not happen. Again, it is not glorious that he was crucified, therefore it did not take place!

Ah, Lord God, are these the high and mighty spirits? Will the people be led by such flimsy, worthless prattle away from the clear, definite words of God, "This is my body"? Why, this would make God's glory an altogether worldly and carnal thing, just as it would be inglorious for a worldly king to be hanged or crucified. But the glory of our God is precisely that for our sakes he comes down to the very depths, into human flesh, into the bread, into our mouth, our heart, our bosom; moreover, for our sakes he allows himself to be treated ingloriously both on the cross and on the altar, as St. Paul says, in I Corinthians 11 [:27], that some eat the bread in an unworthy manner.

Yet though he unceasingly permits his Word, his works, and all that he has to be persecuted, blasphemed, profaned, and misused before his divine eyes, he is nevertheless seated in his glory. If I had not read it in their books, I would never have believed that they would try to establish this article with such fools' tales. But through God's wrath they are blind, and they do not earnestly desire to instruct consciences and give them certainty, but only

[119] So at length in *Apologetics,* C iiii ff. See *WA* 23, 303; cf. p. 47, n. 78, and n. 118, above.

[120] What Luther is quoting from Cyprian is not apparent; in regard to Augustine, cf. *Faith and the Creed,* IV, 9. *MPL* 38, 105 f.; *FC* 27, 325 f.

to confuse and astonish the foolish masses so that they will listen to their cuckoo and marvel at it. As I have said, this is the way the devil mocks us.

But since we poor sinners must be abused as having profaned and blasphemed Christ with our belief and teaching that Christ's body is in the Supper, let us now hear how they glorify and honor him. First they take from him and deny to him the love, grace, and goodness that he wishes his body to be bodily our food in the Supper. In place of this they allot to him a seat at a special, single location, like a bird in its bower.[121] Isn't this to regard Christ as a child or a fool, from whom one can take a gulden and give him back a metal slug or a twig of aspen leaves, persuading him that it is more valuable than the gulden? In short, our belief is that all the works of God are glorious, as the 111th Psalm says [v. 3], "His work is praise and beauty," [122] i.e. whatever God does is praiseworthy and excellent. God can do nothing inglorious or hateful. But this excellence is not every man's knowledge; it is spiritual.

Out of exactly the same lofty spirit they also lay their foundation upon such a firm rock as this: "Yes," they say, "since this work is so great a miracle—that Christ's body is at the same time in heaven and in the Supper—why don't the apostles and evangelists praise it as a miraculous work, as they do with other miracles?" [123] Answer: What do you expect? He who does not have Scripture must have his own ideas; he who has no mortar must build his wall with mud. Now who can answer this choice objection? One might say: Perhaps the apostles and evangelists were so poor that they could not grow enough cinnabar or brazil-

---

[121] E.g. Zwingli: "This word 'until' [i.e. until Christ's return, Ps. 110:1] binds him to the right hand of God until the predetermined day, so that we may easily understand that he will never be anywhere else than at the right hand of God until the judgment is completed. . . ." *Reply to Billican. C.R.* 91, 907.

[122] Text in Latin: *Confessio et decor opus eius.* The Vulgate text reads *magnificentia* instead of *decor.*

[123] Oecolampadius: "If they [the apostles] did not marvel, they did not regard this in the way you do." *Reply to Pirkheimer, e* 5; cf. *Genuine Exposition,* B iii. *WA* 23, 303. Zwingli: "The second point is the perfect calm of the disciples. They were not at all excited or perturbed." *Clear Instruction. LCC* 24, 227. "Do we read that any one of the apostles worshiped the Supper when Christ was instituting this commemoration of himself?" *Commentary. LWZ* 3, 239.

wood with which to paint a little red printer's index sign with the caption, "Here is a miracle." Our fanatics would like Christ and his disciples to be summarily obliged, whenever describing a miraculous work of Christ, to add a caption that it is a miraculous work. Otherwise, they would contend that it is neither a work wrought, nor miraculous, but simply nothing. Now since Christ says, "This is my body," and does not add, "This is a great miracle," it is nothing when he says, "This is my body." This is almost as nasty a little trick as Dr. Karlstadt trotted in with his period and his capital letters,[124] but this too was supposed to become a rock upon which Christendom would stand or else fall and sink to the bottom altogether.

Reasonable and conscientious men see clearly here that it is a shame to spread such drivel among the people, and it does not deserve an answer. Nonetheless, the people pounce upon it, cling to it, and treat it as pure Scripture and truth in opposition to these words that are so clear, simple, and lucid, "This is my body." Not that they can regard it as truth in their conscience, but they dearly wish it were the truth. But we should give thanks to God the merciful Father for so reducing the fanatics to shame in their own cleverness that they themselves must announce how they traffic in lies and dreams. Thus he warns us that it is sheer devil's delusion and mockery, in order that each man may guard himself from such fanatics; but that if anyone refuses to heed the warning, he will be so much the more grievously damned. So we believe, now, that all the words and works of Christ are sheer wonders, wherefore Isaiah 9 [:6] calls his name "Wonderful." But we accord the evangelists and the apostles the freedom which events they wish to describe as miraculous works and which they do not.[125]

They have one argument, however, which I regard as the strongest of all; they are in earnest about it too, and I believe it is true. It is this: such articles, they say, are burdensome to people. For it is difficult to believe that a body is at the same time

[124] Karlstadt, *Dialogue,* 1524. *St. L.* 20, 2321; cf. Luther's *Against the Heavenly Prophets. LW* 40, 158 ff.

[125] For an understanding of the point Luther is making one must take into account that *wunder* is variously translated as "miracle," "wonder," or "marvel."

in heaven and in the Supper.[126] So I praise my fanatics that for once they candidly confess the real reason that impels them. They might well have kept quiet about the other reasons and dispensed with so much writing long ago. This single one by itself most assuredly would have sufficed to demonstrate their faith. For out of this argument spring all their other arguments, and they would not have labored so much with the others if this one had not constrained them.

Now you have it! If anything is difficult for a person to believe, let him believe and declare that it is not true, and it is certainly not true, as this argument proves and demonstrates! On these grounds it is certainly not true that Christ is God and man. For it is difficult, yes, impossible to believe—with the exception of the saints, to whom it is not only easy but also joy and gladness, yes, life and salvation, to believe all the words and works of God; but these do not concern us.

Here we have caught the fanatics in their own admission that they hate the sacrament and feel spite, aversion, repugnance, and loathing in their hearts toward it; and this is why they rave so against it. Ah, they ought to be a bit more cautious, leaving such notions in their pens, but God does not will it. The Greeks say, "A liar should have a good memory."[127] So says Hilary, "An ungodly man cannot be prudent."[128] The devil always sets his seal on his works in this way, and leaves his stench behind. Why? Ah, there's no fighting against God's wisdom; he is bound to win.

[126] Zwingli: "That the symbolic bread is the flesh of Christ is so abhorrent to the mind of all believers that no one of us has every truly believed it. . . . This idea of mangling the flesh the mind so rejects that one would not dare to chew, but would spit it out of one's mouth." *Rearguard*. *C. R.* 91, 493. "Peter said that those who bind burdens hard to bear upon the brethren were tempting God [Acts 15:10]. Hence those who lead the simple masses around by the nose, making them think they eat flesh here, not only tempt God, but thrust burdens on men's minds which no intellect can bear." *Brief Reply . . . to a Rather Long Letter of a Certain Friend*, 1526. *C. R.* 92, 355. Oecolampadius derided the idea as "difficult to believe, confirmed by no sure miracle," "requiring a mutation of the universal order of nature," "vain and void of utility." *Reply to Pirkheimer, e* 5, *f* 6; *Genuine Exposition*, D 5. Cf. p. 53, n. 88.

[127] The saying is found in Quintilian, *Institutio oratorica*, IV, 2, 91. (J. S. Watson [ed.], *Institutes of Oratory* [2 vols.; London, 1892], I, 292) and is cited by Jerome (*MPL* 23, 267) and Erasmus (*Adagia* II, III, 74). No source in Greek literature includes this proverb.

[128] *On the Trinity*, V, 26. *FC* 25, 155, very loosely quoted here.

They have still more arguments: Since we do not read that the apostles did reverence to the sacrament or adored it, but sat at table as for other meals, it is concluded that the apostles did not believe that Christ's body was present; therefore it is certainly nothing but bread.[129] A very precious and strong argument is this! From it I shall also draw some further conclusions: the apostles sat at table during the Supper, and did not adore Christ whom they saw sitting there bodily, and did him no reverence, therefore I conclude that they did not believe that he sat there; therefore it is certainly not true that Christ sat at the table during the Supper. Mary and Joseph did not adore Christ when he was born; so it is certain that Christ was not there, but Mary bore a monstrosity.[130]

Such faith must have such proofs; on such pillars such a church must stand! Should the apostles adore the sacrament, which they did not see, and not adore Christ, whom they did see? "But they should have dreaded it." [131] Yes, if they had been fanatics! But they cling to Christ with unreserved love, believing his Word without any dread at all. This is what love is accustomed to do, as St. Paul says in I Corinthians 13 [:7] that it believes all things and regards nothing impossible, especially what it hears from its beloved. It clings more to his words than to that which the words say. Mary Magdalene at the grave thought she would take Jesus away by herself, so ardent was the love in her heart [John 20:15].

My foolish little fanatics, however, measure the apostles' hearts by their own hearts, which are full of loathing and hatred against the sacrament, thinking, "We despise and loathe the sacrament, and we cannot believe in it or honor it. Therefore the apostles also had just as little desire and love for Christ's Word, and would have dreaded it if Christ's body had been present." Well, I can put up with it when the devil mocks us with such nonsense, for I believe that he mocks himself more than us.

One thing more. Yes, they say, the works and wonders which Christ did were visible, such as when he made wine out of water,

---

[129] Cf. p. 73, n. 123.

[130] *Mondkind*, a miscarriage in the form of a shapeless lump of flesh.

[131] Oecolampadius, *Genuine Exposition*, B 1. See *WA* 23, 304; Zwingli *Letter to Alber*. *C. R.* 92, 350 f.; *St. L.* 17, 1527.

made the blind see and the deaf hear, and so forth. But since the miracle here is not visible, surely Christ's body is not present.[132] Get a patch, dear fellows, get a patch! The fur needs it badly; the skin and the hair are all worn out! Such notions as these must always pass for pure Scripture and nothing but the truth among such people: "Now I hold it to be true that whatever miraculous sign is not visible is nothing at all, and never took place." Christ, the Son of God, was conceived by the Holy Spirit in the womb of Mary, the greatest of all God's miracles. But this was not visible to human eyes, therefore it certainly is not true! The Godhead dwells in Christ on earth and to all eternity; but this is not plainly visible, therefore it is not true! What will they do here to their chief argument and cornerstone: Christ sits at the right hand of God? This is not plainly visible; is it therefore not true? But perhaps it is no miracle to them that Christ sits at the right hand of God, but an ordinary thing, as when a teacher sits in his chair!

If these are to pass for good arguments and reasons which ought to teach us certain truth, prove our beliefs, and assure consciences, then we are in a bad way indeed. If someone brought me such books with no title or name and I did not know that they were such learned and excellent men, I would certainly have thought they had been done by some gypsy or vagabond in order to mock us Christians. There is no evidence, at any rate, that despite good intentions and a devout spirit they were misled through spiritual blindness, as happened with the heretics, but it appears to be sheer wilfulness which wants to play the buffoon with God's Word. It ought not be possible, of course, that such rotten, feeble, insipid drivel should seriously influence a single man in his right mind, even if he were a Turk or a Jew, let alone a Christian. But the great spite and aversion they bear against

132 Zwingli: "When, I ask, did Christ ever perform a miracle which no man recognized with his senses, no man experienced? . . . We sense that the bread and wine are bread and wine, nor has any sense ever experienced it otherwise, yet do we impose a miracle upon everyone's faith?" *Reply to Billican. C. R.* 91, 908 f.; cf. *Clear Instruction. LCC* 24, 190 f., 195 f. In his letter to John Herwagen, September, 1526, Luther quotes Bucer as writing: "The miracles of Christ were of such a nature that when he said, 'This is it,' the senses could immediately perceive that it was so. Therefore the body of Christ must be visible in the sacrament or it is not in the sacrament." *S-J* 2, 379.

the holy sacrament, and the passionate fondness which they have for their own idiosyncrasy, make them so rash as to think that everything they may take hold of, even a straw, is a spear and a sword. And they delude themselves into thinking that they strike a thousand dead with every stroke. Their idiosyncrasy brings grief to us all; may God ward it off. Amen!

Hence our rock and our simple, clear text still stands firm: "This is my body." It has submitted to storming by stubble and chaff, but these have been scattered and routed by a little breeze.

Now we shall attack their second cornerstone and a second chief argument. For although they have, along with the first argument which we have now overthrown, many other flimsy arguments besides those we have mentioned, I shall pass over these now, and in connection with the second cornerstone I shall treat some of them, lest I too become a fanatic over such flimsy, rotten buffoonery. For I certainly hate this drivel, because these are not passages of Scripture by which one might usefully treat some aspects of spiritual doctrine, but I am forced to enter my objections, and meanwhile waste time and neglect better things. But this is the way Satan must act, always causing unhappiness and trouble.

Now their second chief argument is the saying of John 6 [:63], "Flesh is of no avail," which Oecolampadius boasts of as his iron wall.[133] In truth, he needs a good one! But if all which is difficult to believe is false, as they say, it is certainly false also that this is his wall of iron. For I believe it with great difficulty; it appears to me to be of paper, though it may perhaps have an iron color.

In the first place, when they are under obligation to prove with Scripture that "flesh" in this passage must mean Christ's

---

[133] We cannot trace Oecolampadius' early reference to John 6:63 as an "iron wall," though in his *Second Reasonable Answer*, chap. 8, June, 1527, he mentions having used the expression. In *Genuine Exposition*, 1525, he had called the verse "an angel armed with a fiery sword," cf. Ernst Staehelin, *Das theologische Lebenswerk Johannes Oekolampads* (Leipzig, 1939), p. 281. The *Swabian Syngramma* spoke of the collapse of Oecolampadius' "arguments of iron and bronze" in regard to I Cor. 10:4 and Exod. 12:11. *St. L.* 20, 540. Zwingli called John 6:63 a "bronze wall" [cf. Jer. 1:18, 15:20], the most "effective armor," "indestructible adamant," *Commentary*. *LWZ* 3, 212, 248; "the best-equipped, strongest battleline." *Letter to Alber*. *C. R.* 90, 337; *St. L.* 17, 1514.

body—for this above all is the heart of the matter and is what we are asking them about—they behave according to form: they glide over it, assert and declare it as if it were certain, like knights who had won a valiant victory, and say, "Oh, we regard it as sure truth." Dear Lord God! Who asked you about your notion? Who wants you to tell what you regard as certain? How often now have you heard that these two terms, "possible" and "necessary"—"may" and "must"—are further apart than heaven and earth? Children and laymen of all languages are well aware of that. You are being asked whether what you teach must be so, and you answer: It may be so! Yes, Judas may be godly, so it is an excellent deduction: therefore Judas must be godly; Pilate may become a Christian, therefore Pilate must become a Christian!

Here also, when you ought to prove that "flesh" necessarily means Christ's body in this passage, you are altogether speechless; but when you are under obligation to speak and tell us it must mean Christ's body, then you gush and gabble. Indeed, it might also mean a pork roast, if assigning meaning is up to me and gabble and gush are the rule. For one can irrefutably testify against you that as often as Christ speaks in the Scriptures of his flesh or body, he adds the word "my," saying, "my flesh," "my body," as he says in the same chapter, John 6, "My flesh is food indeed." Again, "He who eats my flesh," etc. Again, "Unless you eat the flesh of the Son of man," etc. [vv. 55, 56, 53].

Now, however, since he does not say here, "My flesh is of no avail," but simply, "Flesh is of no avail," you really find yourself in trouble and distress because you must prove it means Christ's flesh here. There is a very great difference between Christ's flesh and ordinary flesh. When we ask you point-blank and challenge you, "Who commanded you to alter and emend the text, and make 'my flesh' out of 'flesh'?" you must become speechless. Again you are unable to prove it, yet you assume it and insist on it as if it were proved with absolute certainty. So the argument lies prostrate; it is unproved and it will remain forever unproved. This is Oecolampadius' iron wall.

Yes, they say, the context of the saying shows that "flesh" here means Christ's body. Where? Oh, the word which Christ speaks, "Flesh is of no avail"; he does not say, "Fleshly mind or interpretation is of no avail," [134] as you flesh-eaters[135] say. Besides, the word "of no avail," in Greek *ōphelei* [or Latin], *conducit, prodest,* means properly that which is of no use, of no good, or which profits nothing. Had Christ wished to understand here by "flesh" a fleshly mind, and not his own flesh, he would have had to say, "Flesh perceives or understands nothing." But since he actually says, "Flesh does not help," of course he must be speaking of his own flesh which indeed understands a great deal, but does not help anyone by being eaten.

You see, I was perfectly certain that you would answer something different from what you were being asked, and pass by when you were hailed. You ought to prove that "flesh" here means Christ's body; so you prove and teach us that *percipere* and *conducere,* to perceive and to avail or be useful, are two different words.[136] But who requested or asked you for that? All this we know perfectly well, and the *Vocabularius ex quo* or the *Gemma*[137] would also have taught it to us without the aid of these great spirits and experts.

It still remains unproved that "flesh" here means Christ's body. For supposing that not the *percipere* (to perceive) but *conducere* (to avail) stands here, how does this help you? Couldn't Christ say, "Flesh is of no avail," i.e all that flesh understands, perceives, wishes, says, does, leaves undone, has, experiences, in short, flesh and all that flesh is—this is of no avail? And if I wish to condemn the fleshly mind, I am not obliged to say, "The fleshly mind perceives nothing"; indeed, it is a much stronger condemnation if I say, "The fleshly mind is of no avail." Now it doesn't matter very much to us whether "flesh" here means precisely fleshly mind; we are satisfied that it means flesh. But flesh em-

---

[134] Zwingli, *Commentary.* *LWZ* 3, 200 ff.; *Clear Instruction.* *LCC* 24, 209 ff., 199 ff. Oecolampadius, *Reasonable Answer.* *St. L.* 20, 608 f.; *Apologetics. St. L.* 20, 698 ff. Luther had challenged Karlstadt on the same point in *Against the Heavenly Prophets.* *LW* 40, 203 ff.

[135] A common epithet on the Swiss side, cf. p. 22, n. 24. *Fleisch* means both "flesh" and "meat"; the implication is that the Lutherans are not only "meat-eaters" but also cannibals. *Commentary.* *LWZ* 3, 216.

[136] Bucer contrasted *conducit* with *percipit, intelligit* in *Apology,* 20. See *WA* 23, 305.

[137] These were the titles of Latin-German dictionaries. Cf. P. T. Starnes, *Renaissance Dictionaries* (Austin, Texas, 1954).

braces all that is in the flesh: mind, reason, will, words, works, etc., as has just been said. All this is of no avail. And this word *ōphelei,* "is useful" or "avails," comes nowhere near requiring or proving that "flesh" here must be understood of Christ's body, since it can perfectly well be understood of ordinary flesh, as I have here proved. Now what has become of the iron wall? Where is the certain truth?

Thus the iron wall has been blown down by one little word: "my." For since it does not read, "My flesh is of no avail," but simply, "Flesh is of no avail," we have in the first place established that it may not be understood of Christ's body. Since he himself does not further say, "My flesh," it is forbidden to emend his words and add anything to them; and their meaning is certain and sure, if we do not understand them as referring to his flesh.

Secondly, they cannot prove with a single letter that "flesh" here means Christ's flesh. For if we conceded to them without proof that "flesh" here is the equivalent of "my flesh," who would thereafter prevent it from meaning "Christ's flesh" at every point where simply "flesh" occurs in the Scriptures? Immediately all the ancient heresies such as the Manichaeans, Valentinians,[138] *et al.,* who say that Christ did not have natural flesh and blood and was not real man, would come swarming in in droves, because they saw that such evil things were said about the flesh in the Scriptures. Indeed, such bumblebees also are buzzing around Zwingli's head and stinging him when he writes against Dr. Eck at Baden,[139] "If Christ's flesh is eaten, nothing but flesh comes of it, because all that is born of the flesh is flesh" [John 3:6], as we shall hear. Ugh! what shameful fools and monkeys the devil would make of

---

[138] The Swiss were associating the Lutherans with these heresies. Manichaeism, a third century heresy or rival religion, and second century Valentinian Gnosticism both insisted that the material world and the flesh are evil, and therefore Christ could not have had a true body or shared true manhood. Both heresies are mentioned in the Augsburg Confession, Art. I. See also pp. 99, 115.

[139] *Brief Answer to Eck's Seven Theses,* 1526. *C. R.* 92, 182; cf. *Letter to Alber. C. R.* 90, 339; *St. L.* 17, 1517; Oecolampadius, *Genuine Exposition,* E 6. John Eck, Luther's opponent, had challenged Zwingli to a disputation, which took place in Baden, Switzerland, in 1526, but the Zurich Town Council forbade Zwingli to attend. Zwingli answered Eck in writing. Cf. Myconius' *Life of Zwingli* in *LWZ* 1, 16 f.; John T. McNeill, *History and Character of Calvinism* (New York: Oxford University Press, 1954), pp. 60 ff.

us, that on account of such empty prattle we should deny these clear, manifest words, "This is my body," and allege that the Scriptures are contradictory and force us to this position! But our ingratitude well deserves this.

Although by now this argument and iron wall has been sufficiently battered down, nevertheless since their bragging and boasting know no bounds, we shall expose their folly still more clearly. We too would like to rave like fanatics and concede that "flesh" here means Christ's flesh, as they jabber. Not that it is really so—but we would like to play the fool and go along with this carnival mummery, so that men may see what comes of it. Let us assume now that the iron wall stands firm, that Christ's flesh is of no avail.

Now I ask: When the Virgin Mary was bodily pregnant with the Son of God and carried Jesus Christ our Lord nine months in her womb, and then as a mother brought him bodily into the world, as our Creed and the Gospels say, did she also carry and bear Christ's flesh bodily in and through her flesh? As a fanatic I simply do not believe it. Why? Because Christ's flesh, bodily conceived, borne, and handled, is of no avail. If it is of no avail, then nothing took place, as our argument declares, "Christ's flesh is of no avail." Therefore nothing is there. For if his flesh is not present in the sacrament for the reason that flesh is of no avail,[140] neither is it in his mother's womb, precisely for the same reason that it is of no avail. The reasoning is the same in both instances.

Again, the angels announced to the shepherds, and the shepherds found it so, that Christ lay in the manger in bodily form and present with his flesh [Luke 2:8 ff.]. But who wants to believe that that is true? Even if Christ, and all the angels with him, said, "There lies my body in the manger," nonetheless we say, "No, for flesh is of no avail, therefore thy body cannot be present physically, but the swaddling cloths and the manger represent thy body, because for flesh to be of no avail and to be absent are one and the same thing."

Again, Simeon took him up in his arms bodily when his parents brought him bodily into the temple [Luke 2:22 ff.]. But

140 The word order of the handwritten manuscript, reproduced in *WA* 23, 172, rather than the printed text is the basis of the translation of this sentence.

all this is a big pack of lies and contrary to the glory of Christ, because flesh is of no avail, i.e. it cannot be bodily present. This is our position, with it we remain, and further, it is our iron wall!

Again, Christ permitted himself to be baptized in the Jordan; he walked in the wilderness and in the towns and upon the sea[141] —and all this bodily. All this is a fiction! Why? Oh, flesh is of no avail, i.e. Christ's bodily presence is not there, as was said.

Again, Christ sat at table bodily at the Supper, and also spoke with his disciples physically, and they with him; and physically washed their feet [John 13:1 ff.]. Yes, that is what they say! But it is a lie and blasphemes the glory of God, for flesh is of no avail, therefore he certainly was not bodily present, but only spiritually.

You say: Stop, for God's sake, you will buzz yourself to death. In this way you would even buzz Christ right out of the garden, the cross, and his whole passion, saying that none of these things happened bodily, because of course he had to be bodily present in them all and yet his flesh is of no avail if it is bodily there.

Yes, my friend, I shall also buzz him away from the right hand of God, on which our entire interest focuses, and prove that he is not there. For flesh is of no avail. Now although his flesh is seated at the right hand of God, it is still the same flesh of Christ, for it did not become a different flesh at the right hand of God. If it is the same flesh, it is of no avail there either. If it is of no avail, then it is not there either, but is nothing at all, and its fate is the same in this passage as in the Supper.

Indeed, what is more, I shall prove that Christ's body is not spiritually in their hearts either,[142] which however is the height of their prattle. For, as I have said, flesh is of no avail; but flesh is and remains flesh whether in the stomach, bread, the cross.

[141] Cf. Luke 5:16, 9:6; Matt. 14:25.

[142] Zwingli consistently taught that Christ himself is the spiritual food of the soul [John 6:27 ff.], e.g. *Commentary. LWZ* 3, 200 ff.; but in the earlier phase of the controversy he preferred to emphasize that the sacrament is the symbol of the body of Christ, which is not present here; to "eat Christ's body spiritually" means simply to come to Christ in faith. *Commentary. LWZ* 3, 212, 214, 250; *Clear Instruction. LCC* 24, 216, 229, 237 f. Eventually he was willing to say that Christ is in the sacrament, but invisibly, as he is in the hearts of believers invisibly, not bodily, e.g. *Rejoinder and Rebuttal*, 1527. *C. R.* 92, 789; *St. L.* 20, 1119.

heaven, spirit, and wherever you will. The places do not change it: wine, grain, money, cloth remain exactly what they are, even if they change places a thousand times a day. Should not Christ's flesh also remain the same flesh whether in heaven, spirit, manger, mother, or wherever you will? If it is present there bodily, as it must be, it is of no avail. If it is of no avail, it is not there but is nothing at all.

Now you see what a mighty swarm of fanatics the saying can stir up: "Flesh is of no avail." It makes heaven and earth too narrow for Christ's body and hounds him straight out of heaven and out of the Spirit, though the fanatics had spirited him thither as to a mighty fortress secured with genuine iron walls, to keep him well protected from dishonorable handling by knaves at the altar. Actually, this passage is the strongest argument of all, and a real iron wall—yes, for us to use against them! They could have brought forth nothing more strongly opposed to themselves than just this saying, of which they boast most of all. So it goes with us poor sinners and thoughtless, defenseless servants of the baked bread-God;[143] those who wish to slay us bring us plenty of weapons with which to slay them and defend ourselves.

Here perhaps they will answer: We do not say that Christ's flesh is of no avail whatsoever, but only when one eats it physically; otherwise, if one eats it spiritually, i.e. if one believes that it was delivered into death for us, etc., it avails according to the word of Christ, John 6 [:55], "My flesh is food indeed."[144] I thank them for the good instruction; but the fact still remains, it is not thereby proved that Christ speaks of the physical eating of his body. For he says not, "To eat my flesh physically is of no avail," but simply, "Flesh is of no avail." Therefore such instruction does not help the matter at all; it shall and must be proved that he speaks of physical eating. This you will never do.

---

[143] Cf. p. 22, n. 24.

[144] Bucer interprets Christ as saying in John 6: "If faith and hence my spirit are lacking, you will not receive life, and the eating of my flesh will be of no avail. I have been speaking of that spiritual and life-giving eating of myself." *Apology*, 18. Meanwhile, Zwingli: "The flesh of Christ profits very greatly, aye, immeasurably, in every way, but . . . by being slain, not eaten. Slain it has saved us from death, but eaten [physically] it is of no avail at all." *Commentary*. *LWZ* 3, 209; cf. 202 ff. and *Clear Instruction*. *LCC* 24, 199 ff.

Even if you proved it—which you cannot do—I would like to hear exactly why Christ's flesh is of no avail when it is physically eaten, and not also when it is physically conceived and born, laid in the manger, taken up in one's arms, seated at table at the Supper, hanging upon the cross, etc.[145] All these are outward modes and uses of his flesh as truly as when he is physically eaten. Is it better when it is in his mother's womb than when it is in the bread and in the mouth? If it is of no avail here, it can be of no avail there either; if it avails there, it must also avail here. For nothing more can be made out of this than that Christ's body is dealt with physically and outwardly, whether it is eaten or conceived, born or carried, seen or heard. Nowhere in sight is the spiritual eating which avails, but only the physical using or handling, to speak in your terms. Who will teach me here? Is no one at home? Oh, well, then the previous instruction also is of no avail and does not help me at all. And I must continue to maintain what I have said, that Christ's flesh either must avail in the Supper or must be of no avail whatsoever whether in heaven or in the spirit.

Once again I ask: What if I eat Christ's flesh physically in the Supper in such a way that I also eat it spiritually at the same time; would you not concede then that Christ's flesh in the Supper avails very much? "But how can this be?" you say. Precisely thus: I shall eat his body with the bread physically, and yet at the same time believe in my heart that this is the body which was given for me for the forgiveness of sins, as the words read, "This is my body, which was given for you"—which you yourselves call the spiritual eating. Now if the spiritual eating is there, the physical eating cannot be harmful but must also be useful on account of the spiritual eating. Ho! now answer me; I am in desperate need of instruction here.

Yes, you say, we separate the spiritual eating from the

---

145 Zwingli: "Christ is our salvation by virtue of that part of his nature by which he came down from heaven, not of that by which he was born of an immaculate virgin, though he had to suffer and die by this part; but unless he who died had also been God he could not have been salvation for the whole world. . . ." *Commentary*. *LWZ* 3, 204 f.; cf. *Clear Instruction*. *LCC* 24, 212 ff.

physical or bodily.[146] God's thanks to you for this! Are you of such a stripe, such upright, honest people, that you thus defame and slander us poor, innocent sinners throughout the world with shameless lies in so many books? Is this your new talent and lofty spirit which the blinded Luther cannot grasp? When have you ever heard from us that we eat Christ's Supper, or teach that it should be eaten, in such a way that there is only an outward, physical eating of the body of Christ? Have we not taught in many books that in the Supper two things are to be kept in mind? One, which is the supreme and most necessary point, consisting of the words, "Take, eat, this is my body," etc.; the other is the sacrament or physical eating of the body of Christ.[147] Now, of course no one can drive these words through the throat into the stomach, but he must take them to heart through the ears. But what does he take to heart through these words? Nothing else than what they say, viz., "the body which was given for us," which is the spiritual eating. We have said, further, that if anyone physically eats the sacrament without these words or without this spiritual eating, it is not only of no avail to him, but even harmful, as Paul says [I Cor. 11:27], "Whoever eats the bread in an unworthy manner will be guilty of profaning the body of the Lord."

Therefore you did not need to teach us that physical eating is of no avail. We actually go further and say that physical eating is even poisonous and deadly. But thereby it is not proved

---

[146] Bucer wrote that his party emphasized the spiritual presence of Christ and the eating by faith, and "cared nothing about the fleshly eating." *Apology*, 24. Oecolampadius: "We exhort to faith . . . rather than to the eating of bread." *Reply to Pirkheimer*, c 2. Cf. Zwingli, *Commentary*. *LWZ* 3, 202 ff.

[147] Cf. *Adoration of the Sacrament*, 1523. *LW* 36, 277 ff., 295 ff. Luther's earlier discussions of the Lord's Supper emphasized such distinctions as promise (objective gift) and faith (subjective appropriation), cf. *Babylonian Captivity*. *LW* 36, 38 ff. This distinction remained important, cf. *The Sacrament—Against the Fanatics*, 1526. *LW* 36, 335. But more and more, under pressure of the fanatical spiritualizing of the believer's reception of Christ's body and blood, especially from 1525 on, cf. *Against the Heavenly Prophets*, Part II. *LW* 40, 175 ff., Luther also emphasized simple obedience to the command to eat and drink in the Lord's Supper. Note the dual emphasis in the word "sacrament:" here Luther contrasts "sacrament" with the words of institution; in *LW* 36, 335, he contrasted "sacrament" (as the given "object of faith") with inward faith.

that Christ's body is not there. Indeed, it rather proves that he is there. If he were not there, the physical eating would be harmless and useful; but now since it is of no avail and even harmful, it must surely be present and be eaten. Thereby it is not proved, either, that Christ's saying pertains to the Supper, "Flesh is of no avail." Thus your dream consists entirely of sheer lies and slanders. The mouth, which eats Christ's flesh physically, obviously does not know what it eats or what the heart eats therein. For the mouth this would not even be at all useful, for it cannot grasp or comprehend the words. But the heart knows well what the mouth eats, for it grasps the words and eats spiritually what the mouth eats physically. But since the mouth is the heart's member, it also must ultimately live in eternity on account of the heart, which lives eternally through the Word, because here it also eats physically the same eternal food which its heart eats spiritually at the same time.

So we request, dear sirs, that if you wish to rave against the Lutherans or new papists,[148] as you slanderously call us, you should at least refrain from lies, and impute to us in word or print nothing but what we really teach. For what you have falsely asserted about us in the past is not what we teach, as you have now heard. Or, if you wish indeed to write against us, then write and prove that the Lutherans are such idolaters that they teach there is no Word of God in the Supper, but only the body of Christ in the bread; again, that they have no heart or soul with which to grasp these words and eat, but only a mouth with which they eat the body of Christ. If you prove that, I shall concede that your writing is altogether right and firmly established. It is against such people that your fanaticism is directed, no one else. For example, if (let us say) mice or pigs ate the sacrament, of course it would be of no avail to them.

But leave us the words in the Supper and grant that we have souls; and we shall quite frankly ask what devil commanded you to sever the Word from the body of Christ in the Supper, likewise

[148] Karlstadt had written a treatise *Against the Old and New Papistic Masses*, 1524. John Landtsperger's contribution to the present controversy mentioned the epithet in its title: *A Brief Account of the Old and New Papists* . . ., 1526. Others on the Swiss side also used it.

to separate the heart from the mouth in us, and to push the physical eating alone into Supper and rip the spiritual eating out of it. For although the ungodly practice this separation and severing in the Supper to their own damnation and eat only the body of Christ without the Word, with the mouth but without the heart, only physically and not spiritually, this is not the way Christ instituted the Supper. He joined both together, the Word and his body, to be eaten spiritually with the heart and physically with the mouth. Now, of course, misuse by the ungodly cannot and must not break or alter God's ordinance and institution.

From all this we conclude irrefutably that the iron wall of Oecolampadius, or the saying, "Flesh is of no avail," cannot pertain to the Supper at all. As we have heard, a spiritual eating is instituted in the Supper by Christ alongside the physical, for in it there is God's Word which says to the heart, "Take, this is my body," which the stomach or mouth cannot grasp or eat physically. Although the ungodly and the papists and fanatics disregard these words and so miss the spiritual eating, nevertheless Christians hit it right with their faith.

Consequently, less than nothing is said with the words, "Flesh is of no avail, therefore it is not there." In this way I too could easily prove that there is no God nor creation, if only I set aside God's Word as they do in the case of the Supper. Set aside the word, "God created the heavens and the earth" [Gen. 1:1], and I would like to see who would have a God or of what use he would be. Set aside the word, "Christ, God's Son, is our Savior," and I would like to see who would have Christ, or to whom he would be of any use. Bodily, of course, we have him, for God and Christ would be near at hand even if he did not cause a word of all this to be preached. But whom would this benefit? To whom would it be of any use? No man would be able to know that he was anything. If he is of no avail or use, of course, neither is he anything at all, as the iron wall concludes that that which is of no avail is nothing.

So too, if God's Word had not said that the heavens and the earth are his creation, to whom would they be of any use or of what benefit would they be? To the stomach, of course, they are physically useful, but not to the soul. If they are of no avail, then they are nothing under any circumstances. But if God's Word is added, the heart uses that Word and partakes spiritually of precisely that in the Word of which the body makes use and partakes outwardly and physically. Ah, why should I waste many words? The old rogue, the devil, has so blinded the fanatics that they do not know what they are saying themselves. They prattle a great deal about spiritual eating, but know neither what spiritual nor what physical eating is. Therefore we intend to speak a little about this subject here for the instruction of those who need it, in order to expose the fanatics' foolishness still further and show up the sneering devil.

In the first place, the term "spiritual eating, drinking, or handling" is not to be used when that which one eats, drinks, or handles is spirit or a spiritual object. For then Christ's flesh could not be spiritually eaten or drunk, since Christ's flesh, wherever it may be—in a spiritual or in a material or physical object, visibly or invisibly—is by nature true, physical flesh which one can grasp, feel, see, and hear, which was born of a woman and died on the cross. Rather, it is called "spiritual" because it comes from the Spirit, and needs to be and must be partaken of by us in a spiritual way. "The object is not always spiritual but its use must be spiritual."[149] This we must prove with examples.

When the Virgin Mary conceived and bore Christ, Christ was certainly a real, physical, visible man and not only a spiritual being; yet she conceived and bore him spiritually also. How? In this way: She believed the word of the angel that she would conceive in her womb and bear a son. With the same belief in the angel's word she conceived and bore Christ spiritually in her heart at the same time as she conceived and bore him physically in her womb. If she had not conceived Christ spiritually in her heart, she would never have conceived him physically. God could have made Christ's body from her body in her sleep, without her knowing it. as he made Eve from Adam, but then she would not have been his mother, just as Adam was not Eve's mother.

Now what did she conceive in her heart? Nothing else than what the angel's words declare, viz., "You shall conceive the Son of God" [cf. Luke 1:31]. Since she grasped the word and through

[149] This sentence is in Latin in the original text.

faith became pregnant with it in her heart, she also became physically pregnant with that which the word in her heart said to her. Her womb knows not what it conceives, for it does not understand the angel's word, but her heart surely understands what the womb conceives. Thus she is doubly pregnant, spiritually and physically, and yet with a single fruit. The physical conception would have been of no avail to her if it had taken place without the spiritual conception. Here you see that the spiritual conception does not require the fruit to be a spiritual object. Indeed, the fruit is physical, and yet there is a spiritual conception along with the physical.

Again, the shepherds saw the infant Lord physically in the manger, as did the noble[150] Simeon, also in the temple [Luke 2:8 ff., 2:22 ff.]. But the seeing would not have helped them at all had there not been also a spiritual seeing. Now who gave them this spiritual seeing? Without doubt it was not the sight of the babe but the word of the angel which directed them to Bethlehem to behold the Savior, and the answer of the Holy Spirit who had inspired the noble Simeon, that he should see the Christ of the Lord before he died. By the same word there arose in their hearts a spiritual seeing, i.e. faith, with which they now came to look upon the babe spiritually as the Savior, and then also with the physical eyes. Now, he is a single babe, a single Savior, and yet he is looked upon in two ways: spiritually through the Word, physically through the act of sight. But the physical eyes do not know what they see. They see the Savior, of course, but cannot understand that he is the Savior; for they cannot comprehend the Word. But the heart knows well what the eyes see, for it understands the Word and knows that the eyes see the true Savior. Here the object is physical, and yet there is a spiritual seeing along with the physical.

Again, the woman with a hemorrhage certainly touched no spiritual thing when she touched the hem of Christ's garment, but the material garment of Christ. Nevertheless, it was a spiritual

---

150 In the original the text reads, *herr Simeon*. It has not been possible to document this usage of *herr* in any of Luther's writings. Presumably the appellation, *herr*, in this context, is parallel to that applied in medieval and reformation times to clergy who had oversight over certain services in cathedral churches.

touching of this garment in her heart when she said to herself, "If I only touch the hem of his garment, I shall be made well" [Matt. 9:21]. You see, these words and this faith in her heart are a spiritual touching. Of course, her hand could not grasp the word which her heart spoke, "Touch," and it did not know what it touched, but her heart knew well that her hand touched the Savior's garment. But whence came this knowledge? Not from the touching but from the word, "This is the Savior." Now what did her heart touch spiritually here? Nothing else than this very same material garment which the hand touched physically. The material garment is one, yet there are two kinds of touch, a spiritual and a physical kind.

Abraham was given the land of Canaan by God. Now, the land is a material thing, yet there is also a spiritual taking possession of this land. For Abraham took possession of it spiritually by his faith when his heart said, "I believe and accept it." But whence came this possessing? Without doubt not from the land, of which he never possessed a single foot, but from the word which God spoke, "To you and your descendants I will give this land" [Gen. 12:7]. When his children took possession of it bodily, their body or hand of course did not know what they were taking, for the body does not understand God's Word, but Abraham's heart knew very well and saw what his children's bodies took. Now, they take possession bodily in no other way than Abraham had first taken it spiritually through faith in God's Word.

And when he begot his son Isaac of Sarah, his son was indeed a physical human, yet there were also two kinds of begetting, spiritual and physical. For Abraham first begot Isaac spiritually through his faith when his heart said, "I believe that I shall beget Isaac." But whence came this begetting? Not from his body or from Sarah, but from the word, "Sarah shall bear you a son" [Gen. 18:10]. Now when he begot his son physically, his body certainly did not know what it did, for it could not understand the Word. But his heart knew very well what his body did, for the heart understood the word very well and knew that his body had begotten Isaac, whom he had begotten first through God's Word in faith. Now there is only one bodily Isaac, whom his heart begot spiritually through faith and his body begot physically through the physical act, as St. Paul highly praises this faith of Abraham in Romans 4 [:13 ff.].

Thus, all that our body does outwardly and physically, if God's Word is added to it and it is done through faith, is in reality and in name done spiritually. Nothing can be so material, fleshly, or outward, but it becomes spiritual when it is done in the Word and in faith. "Spiritual" is nothing else than what is done in us and by us through the Spirit and faith, whether the object with which we are dealing is physical or spiritual. Thus, "Spirit consists in the use, not in the object,"[151] be it seeing, hearing, speaking, touching, begetting, bearing, eating, drinking, or anything else. For if a person serves his neighbor and does it physically, it is of no avail to him, for flesh is of no avail. But if he does it spiritually, i.e. if his heart does it out of faith in God's Word, it is life and salvation. Now, only one kind of bodily object is there—his neighbor, with whom he is dealing—but two kinds of action. The body does not know what it does, but lets itself be directed like an animal. But the heart knows very well what the body does. Whence? Not from the neighbor but from the Word of God which says, "Love your neighbor" [Lev. 19:18].

For so God does with us when he sets before us two things: his work and his Word. The body is to do the work, the soul is to grasp the Word. If the work were presented without the Word, it would help no one. For example, if he had let Christ be born of Mary without the Word, the work would have been of no avail to her, for she would have known nothing of it, and would not even have recognized it. Again, if he had let Christ die and rise again, and had let this deed remain hidden and not be proclaimed through the Word, whom would it help? How is it helpful even now for those before whose eyes he is brought physically,[152] yet who do not accept the Word in their hearts? Now, since our body must deal physically with such works and yet cannot understand the Word and, on the other hand, since the soul cannot come forth and deal physically with the work, God divides the matter according to the two aspects and gives the Word for the soul and the work for the body, in order that they both may be saved,

[151] This clause is in Latin in the original text.
[152] I.e. in the Lord's Supper.

and partake of the single grace under two modes, to each its proper part.

Now tell me who are the real Capernaites here! Oecolampadius rebukes us for being Capernaites[153] because we eat Christ's flesh physically in the Supper. I say, however, that the fanatics are the real Capernaites, for the Capernaites also divided the work from the Word and fastened on the physical eating of flesh, just as our fanatics do. They excise and set aside the words in which the spiritual eating consists, and meanwhile gape and gawk at the physical eating, like fools who look someone in the face and stare with fixed eyes, so that they cannot perceive the words clearly confronting them, "Take, eat, this is my body." So the Capernaites would do.

We, however, certainly cannot be Capernaites, for we maintain both the physical and the spiritual eating. The mouth eats the body of Christ physically, for it cannot grasp or eat the words, nor does it know what it is eating. As far as taste is concerned the mouth surely seems to be eating something other than Christ's body. But the heart grasps the words in faith and eats spiritually precisely the same body as the mouth eats physically, for the heart sees very well what the uncomprehending mouth eats physically. But how does it see this? Not by looking at the bread or at the mouth's eating, but at the word which is there, "Eat, this is my body." Yet there is only one body of Christ, which both mouth and heart eat, each in its own mode and manner. The heart cannot eat it physically nor can the mouth eat it spiritually. So God arranges that the mouth eats physically for the heart and the heart eats spiritually for the mouth, and thus both are satisfied and saved by one and the same food. Even the uncomprehending body does not know that it is eating a food by which it will live forever. For the body does not feel it, but dies and decays as if it had eaten some other kind of food, like an irrational animal. But the soul sees and clearly understands that the body will live eternally because it has partaken of an eternal

[153] "They are Capernaites, who promise themselves a fleshly table, as if the flesh of Christ were contained in the bread." *Genuine Exposition*, A 6, etc. *WA* 23, 308. Derivation of this epithet is the fact that Christ's discourse in John 6 took place at Capernaum, cf. John 6:24.

food which will not leave it to decay in the grave and turn to dust.

Yes, they say, when Mary conceived and bore her child, she also saw him physically, and the shepherds and Simeon saw him, and all the others saw everything which they believed.[154] What can one say? If I have heard you correctly, you soft, tender fruit, you would like to teach your God how he shall offer himself physically to you. Perhaps you would also like to become Mary, his mother, and Simeon, and not be content with the mode which he presents to you. As you will; go your way and make one of your own, and you will soon see what comes of it. But we trust our God, who has willed to be born of Mary spiritually and physically but not to be eaten and drunk by her physically or spiritually. By the shepherds and Simeon he wanted to be seen spiritually and physically but not born and not eaten. So, according to his good pleasure, he has permitted himself to be physically and spiritually handled, seen, heard, born, suckled, carried, touched, and the like by whomever he willed. But here in the Lord's Supper he wants to be neither born nor seen nor heard nor touched by us but only eaten and drunk, both physically and spiritually. Accordingly, by this eating we obtain just as much and arrive at the same point as they with their bearing, seeing, hearing, etc.; and he is just as near to us physically as he was to them, except that it had to be by another mode in order that he might be equally near everywhere in the world, which would not have been possible were he to appear visibly. Moreover, he has not denied to us even the seeing, but promised it, except that it is deferred and reserved until the Last Day, in order that faith may have room and we may not attain to salvation here in this miserable life. What more should he do?

I hope now that all this has made it perfectly clear what "spiritual" means. Surely "spiritual" must mean what the Spirit does and what comes from the Spirit, just as "fleshly" is what flesh does and what comes from the flesh, as Paul says in Romans 8 [:5], "Those who are of the flesh are fleshly minded, but those who are of the Spirit are spiritually minded." Again [8:13], "If by the Spirit you put to death the deeds of the flesh you will live."

[154] Luther may have deduced this objection from what Zwingli had said on the visibility of miracles, cf. p. 77.

Here, indeed, you find that even the fruit and works of the Spirit are called "spiritual" because they come from the Spirit, as he also says in Galatians 5 [:22 f.], "The fruit of the Spirit is love, joy, patience," etc. In short, he calls the entire life of Christians spiritual, and he calls them altogether spiritual, in I Corinthians 1 and 2.[155] Thus without doubt he who in faith physically eats Christ's body in the Supper eats spiritually and lives and walks spiritually precisely in the physical eating. Our fanatics, however, are full of fraud and humbug. They think nothing spiritual can be present where there is anything material and physical, and assert that flesh is of no avail. Actually the opposite is true. The Spirit cannot be with us except in material and physical things such as the Word, water, and Christ's body and in his saints on earth. Now have we properly overthrown the iron wall?

Now we should like to consider the saying of Christ, "Flesh is of no avail" [John 6:63], and see whether we can handle it better than the fanatics. Our position is that where the two words, "flesh" and "spirit," are placed in opposition to one another in the Scriptures, flesh cannot mean Christ's body but always means the old flesh which is born of the flesh, John 3 [:6]: "That which is born of the flesh is flesh." For why should the Scriptures contrast them if they are compatible with each other? Now Christ's body and flesh certainly are quite compatible with the Spirit; indeed, he is the Spirit's dwelling place bodily, and through him the Spirit comes into all others. The first witness is Moses, Genesis 6 [:3]: "My spirit shall not be judge among men forever, for they are flesh." Again, Isaiah 40, "All flesh is grass, but the spirit blows upon the grass and it withers."[156] And Christ in John 3 [:6]: "That which is born of the flesh is flesh, and that which is born of the Spirit is spirit." But much more fully, St. Paul in Romans 8 contrasts spirit and flesh practically throughout the entire chapter; and Galatians 5 [:17]: "These two, spirit and flesh, are opposed to each other," etc. I suppose this is familiar to everyone who reads the New Testament. If anyone does not believe it, let him just read; he will find that where flesh and spirit are placed in

---

[155] No verse in I Corinthians 1 precisely corresponds to this sentence, but cf. 1:2, 7, 30, and 2:12, 15.

[156] Luther paraphrases Isa. 40:6 f.

opposition to one another, flesh is certainly condemned as something sinful, as the enemy and adversary of God. Then it will not be necessary to cite all the passages here.

Since it is true and incontrovertible, then, that where flesh is placed in opposition to spirit, it does not mean Christ's body but the old Adam born of the flesh, it is certain that this verse also, John 6 [:63], "Flesh is of no avail," cannot be understood of Christ's body, because Christ in this passage contrasts flesh with spirit. For so his words clearly read, "It is the spirit that gives life, the flesh is of no avail; the words that I have spoken to you are spirit and life." Here you see manifestly that he distinguishes flesh from the Spirit and sets it in opposition to the Spirit. For he certainly teaches that life and spirit are in his words and not in the flesh; but in regard to the flesh he concedes that it is of no avail. How could it avail, if neither life nor spirit is in it? If no life or spirit is in it, then there must be nothing but death and sin in it. What heretic has ever been so utterly depraved, with the exception of the Jews, as to maintain this of Christ's flesh? Now let the fanatics test themselves at this point. Let us see what they can do. They have boasted that it is an iron wall and the certain truth. If they can make good their boast, I shall pay attention.

We have seen now that in this passage "flesh" cannot mean Christ's body but surely means the old Adam. It is opposed to the Spirit, or at any rate is without spirit and is not spirit—which means the same thing as opposed to spirit. I hope, therefore, that we poor sinners have not too widely missed the mark when we have interpreted "flesh" to mean fleshly understanding. For in the flesh, which is not spirit, there are of course the highest and best of faculties: the intellect, senses, will, heart, and mind. If flesh is of no avail, then its senses, intellect, will, and all its actions and its powers are of no avail, and Christ's meaning in this passage must be: "My dear disciples, who murmur and become offended at my words, you do not understand me rightly. You seize upon the work—the physical eating of flesh—and you interpret it as chewing it with the teeth and digesting it in the body, like meat from the butcher shop. That is a fleshly, deadly interpretation. This flesh I do not give you to eat in that way. There must be spirit here, not flesh. My words must be understood spiritually, of the spiritual flesh. All my words are spirit; therefore both flesh and eating and everything that I tell you are spirit and are to be understood and used spiritually. For the spirit gives life, flesh is of no avail," etc.

The fanatics, then, stubbornly presume to take their stand upon this text, "Flesh is of no avail," and they boast loudly about it. Inevitably the text in their hands is altogether obscure and indefinite, but it is quite definite on our side, so that it is directly opposed to them. In any case, then, they must also pardon us if we take our stand firmly and stubbornly on the text, "This is my body," which is so completely lucid, definite, and clear that it can be made obscure and indefinite by no ingenuity or force, and upon it all sorts of fanaticism will come to grief. For we do not yet see the Scriptures of which they boast and assert that they run counter to this passage and on account of which we should not rely on it so stubbornly. What we do see is that their blind imagination sees through a painted glass and indulges itself in the fancy that the Scriptures run counter to this text at several places. On the contrary, they harmonize with it and resist this fanaticism.

But Zwingli above all is a clumsy carpenter and hacks rough chips when he writes to Baden,[157] " 'That which is born of the flesh is flesh,' John 3 [:6]. If Christ's flesh is eaten, nothing but flesh comes of it. Fie and shame on him who says so! But it would follow from Eck's interpretation." These are his words. I say that you fanatics are brazen, impudent fellows. To be sure, before men you display your great humility, meekness, and forbearance; but before God and his Word you are altogether mad and foolish.

Now see what a beautiful conclusion emerges: "That which is born of the flesh is flesh, therefore where Christ's flesh is eaten, nothing but flesh can come of it." The passage in John 3 [:6] speaks of the birth and nature of the flesh, so he applies it to fleshly eating—so completely does this spirit hold the Scriptures in his power.

---

[157] *Brief Answer to Eck's Seven Theses.* C. R. 92, 182. Cf. p. 81, n. 139.

I maintain that Zwingli speaks here of natural flesh coming into being, just as bread and meat upon being eaten become flesh and blood in the eater; and he holds that if Christ's flesh were eaten, it would have to be digested and become flesh and blood like other foods. He says that this is granted and asserted by the saying in John 3 [:6], "That which is born of the flesh is flesh." Go harmonize yourself down the stairs! [158] But if his meaning is that he who eats Christ's flesh becomes flesh or fleshly and not spiritual, it harmonizes still more nicely, and may accordingly yield the conclusion: He who eats bread becomes bread, and he who eats sausage becomes a sausage, and he who drinks wine becomes wine! So it would be a miracle if wolves did not eventually bear sheep or actually turn into sheep, because they eat so many of them. Well, such drivel we shall ignore.

We cannot tolerate the blasphemy, however, when these fanatics try to weave and merge Christ's flesh into this saying also: "That which is born of the flesh is flesh." Their meaning is simply that Christ's flesh is born of flesh. Thereby they show how nicely they read and understand the sixth chapter of John. Old Satan drives them to believe these things and to speak with such rashness and obstinacy. How would it be possible for them to think well at all of Christ's flesh when they insist that it is born of flesh and is flesh? For then they must surely proceed a step further and say that his flesh is of no avail; they cannot prevent it.

We poor sinners and servants of the "baked God," however, say this: Christ's flesh belongs with the saying, "That which is born of the Spirit is spirit." For his flesh was born not of flesh but of the Holy Spirit, as even children and the whole world confess in the Creed: "I believe in Jesus Christ our Lord, who was conceived by the Holy Spirit." And the angel said to Joseph in his sleep, Matthew 2 [1:20], "Do not fear to take Mary your wife, for that which is conceived in her is of the Holy Spirit."

And in Luke 1 [:34 f.], when Mary asks the angel how it could be that she would have a child, since she knew no man, Gabriel says, "The Holy Spirit will come upon you, and the power

---

[158] *Reime dich wol die treppen hinab.* Though this saying is not to be found in any collection of German proverbs, it means: an interpretation, because it is untenable, must fall. *Br A* 4, 428, n. 5.

of the Most High will overshadow you; therefore the holy child which shall be born of you shall be called the Son of the Most High." Here you see clearly that Christ's body is born of the Spirit and is holy, therefore he must certainly be not flesh but spirit, according to the saying of Christ, "That which is born of the Spirit is spirit." Of no other man, however, do the Scriptures speak in this manner. Not that I present these passages for the sake of the fanatics—for they would scowl at them and skip right over them, as their virtue and lofty spirit are accustomed to do—but I wish by means of them to strengthen and comfort us poor Capernaites and flesh-eaters against their pompous devil. For if their fanaticism continues, that Christ's flesh is of no avail, soon Marcion,[159] Mani, and Valentinus will come teaching that Christ had no real body but an apparition of a body, because it is not compatible for Christ's body to be of no avail and yet for him to have a real body.

From these passages now we learn what spirit or spiritual, flesh or fleshly are: we do not call "flesh" that which can be seen by the eyes or touched by the fingers, as the fanatics do when they call Christ's body useless flesh; but, as I have said above, all is spirit, spiritual, and an object of the Spirit, in reality and in name, which comes from the Holy Spirit, be it as physical or material, outward or visible as it may; on the other hand, all is flesh and fleshly which comes from the natural power of the flesh, without spirit, be it as inward and invisible as it may. For St. Paul in Romans 8 [:5] calls even the fleshly mind "flesh," and in Galatians 5 [:19 ff.] enumerates among the "works of the flesh" even "heresy, enmity, envy," etc., which however are entirely inward and entirely invisible.

Now if Christ's flesh is distinguished from all flesh and is solely and pre-eminently a spiritual flesh, born not of the flesh but of the Spirit, then it is also a spiritual food. If it is a spiritual food, it is an eternal food which cannot perish, as Christ himself says in John 6 [:27], "Labor for the food which does not perish, which

[159] Marcion, a second century heretic, like Manichaeus (Mani) and Valentinus (cf. p. 81, n. 138), held that Christ, being spiritual, would have been contaminated had he possessed a real human body. Cf. pp. 110 ff., below. Oecolampadius and Zwingli, meanwhile, accused Luther of Marcionitism, e.g. *Clear Instruction. LCC* 24, 219.

the Son of man will give to you;" and again, "I am the living bread which came down from heaven" [6:51]; again, "If anyone eats of me, he will live for ever" [6:51]. And so, throughout the entire chapter he teaches that his flesh is the true, living, eternal food which gives life and sustains all who eat of it; and he who does not eat of it must die, etc.

Why? For this reason: His flesh is not of flesh, or fleshly, but spiritual; therefore it cannot be consumed, digested, and transformed, for it is imperishable as is all that is of the Spirit, and a food of an entirely different kind from perishable food. Perishable food is transformed into the body which eats it; this food, however, transforms the person who eats it into what it is itself, and makes him like itself, spiritual, alive, and eternal; as Christ says, "This is the bread from heaven, which gives life to the world" [6:33].

Whether Christ's flesh is eaten physically or spiritually, then, it is the same body, the same spiritual flesh, the same imperishable food which in the Supper is eaten physically with the mouth and spiritually with the heart, according to Christ's institution, or eaten spiritually with the heart alone through the Word, as he teaches in John 6 [:63]. For the fact that it is eaten physically with the mouth in the Supper does not prevent it at all from becoming flesh or a fleshly food. On the contrary, whether it enters the mouth or the heart, it is the same body; just as when he walked on earth, he remained the same Christ, whether he came into the hands of the faithful or of the wicked.

Therefore, Zwingli should not conclude, "If Christ's flesh is eaten, nothing but flesh comes of it." This would be quite true if we were speaking of beef or pork, and Capernaites talk this way. But he should conclude, "If Christ's flesh is eaten, nothing but spirit comes of it, for it is a spiritual flesh and does not let itself be transformed, but transforms the person who eats it and gives him the Spirit. Since this poor maggot sack, our body, also has the hope of the resurrection of the dead and of the life everlasting, it must also become spiritual, and digest and consume everything that is fleshly in it. And that is what this spiritual food does: when the body eats it physically, this food digests the body's flesh and transforms it so that it too becomes spiritual, i.e. alive and blessed forever as Paul says in I Corinthians 15 [:44], "The body will rise spiritually."

To give a simple illustration of what takes place in this eating: it is as if a wolf devoured a sheep and the sheep were so powerful a food that it transformed the wolf and turned him into a sheep. So, when we eat Christ's flesh physically and spiritually, the food is so powerful that it transforms us into itself and out of fleshly, sinful, mortal men makes spiritual, holy, living men. This we are already, though in a hidden manner in faith and hope; the fact is not yet manifest, but we shall experience it on the Last Day.[160] And indeed, if they can eat and drink ordinary bread and wine without harm at the same time as they spiritually eat Christ's body and blood, they certainly ought to concede to us that it would be harmless to eat Christ's flesh physically alongside the spiritual eating, since Christ's body is surely as good as bread and wine, as I have written against Dr. Karlstadt.[161] But this matter does not deserve to have such high and mighty spirits read and answer it, so I must let it pass here, too.

Here I shall drop the subject of the two cardinal points and cornerstones of the fanatics, as they put it: "Christ is seated at the right hand of God," and, "Flesh is of no avail," therefore his body cannot be in the Supper. If these two points are overthrown, they have utterly lost their case, as they themselves clearly sense and even admit. I hope, however, that they have been reduced to stubble and dust, and the truth has avenged itself on the devil. From now on there is nothing better he can do than come back with props of straw to shore up his case. So, he who has helped me has still more in reserve than they think. Peace I crave if possible, so I may publish the prophets.[162] But if it is not to be,

---

[160] Cf. p. 71. The idea of the sacrament as a "medicine of immortality" goes back to Ignatius of Antioch in the early second century. Cf. Sasse, *This Is My Body*, pp. 182 ff.

[161] *LW* 40, 203 f.

[162] Though the controversy concerning the Lord's Supper with Karlstadt, Zwingli, and Oecolampadius made demands on Luther since 1525, he desired to devote his time and energy to the translation and interpretation of the Bible. Since 1524 he had been working on the so-called major and minor prophets (*WA*, DB 2, XI-XII). References to the progress he was making and the events distracting him from the work of translating and interpreting the prophets are found for example in his letters to Wenceslaus Link (June

then let come what may. I trust I shall accomplish more with one book than they will with ten. For lies require much babble and prattle; truth can be stated briefly.

They lay pebbles for a foundation, however, and bring up Matthew 24 [:23] just for show: "Then if any one says to you, 'Lo, here, lo, there is the Christ!' do not believe it."[163] This I have answered sufficiently in my book, *Against the Heavenly Prophets*,[164] and my answer has not yet been refuted by them. Similarly, when they say, "If the bread is Christ's body, then the bread was crucified for us," I have also answered this in the same book.[165] These two points come from Dr. Karlstadt, who brought them among others against me. Again, their question, where Christ commanded the eating of his body in the Supper, also comes from Dr. Karlstadt,[166] and is easily answered thus: Put on your glasses, or have a boy spell out these words, "Take, eat, this is my body," and you will find out.

In short, if we conquer in these two principal points, that it is not a contradiction but perfectly congruous to say that Christ sits at the right hand and yet is in the Supper, secondly, that flesh is of no avail and yet that Christ's body is eaten in the Supper, then I shall gladly teach them where Christ commanded his body to be eaten, and where it is written that in the Supper there is forgiveness of sins, consolation of souls, and strengthening of faith.[167] So too, with all their tatters of questions, with which like beggars they are trying to mend and patch themselves, and yet

---

29, 1526), Nicholas Hausmann (October 14, 1526), Michael Stiefel (January 1, 1527) and John Lang (February 4, 1527). *WA*, Br 4, 96; 122; 152; 268.

[163] Oecolampadius, *Genuine Exposition*, K 6 in *WA* 23, 310; cf. Zwingli, *Clear Instruction*. *LCC* 24, 221.

[164] *LW* 40, 219 f.

[165] Zwingli, *Brief Answer to Eck's Seven Theses*. *C. R.* 92, 184. Luther: *LW* 40, 193.

[166] *LW* 40, 198 f. Oecolampadius: "If there is in these words a command and ordinance of God, let the imperative be pointed out." *Reasonable Answer*. *St. L.* 20, 617; further citations in *WA* 23, 310.

[167] Zwingli: "It is clear that the eating of the Eucharist does not take away sins." *Letter to Alber*. *C. R.* 90, 351; *St. L.* 17, 1528. "They are wrong, by the whole width of heaven, who think that sacraments have any cleansing power." *Commentary*. *LWZ* 3, 182. All three points are listed in Zwingli's summary of Luther's errors in *Friendly Rejoinder*. *C. R.* 92, 793; *St. L.* 20. 1122. Cf. Oecolampadius, *Genuine Exposition*, K 4 f. in *WA* 23, 310.

they can never cover their bad conscience or keep it warm with them. In this art I am bold enough to boast that by God's grace I am a master. For if Christ remains mine, everything remains mine; of this I am sure.

Dr. Oecolampadius also pities us and seeks to help us poor people when he complains:[168] If Christ's body were in the bread, we would inevitably be so troubled by many thoughts about the miracle, how Christ's body became bread, that we would surely neglect his remembrance, which however he earnestly commands. Therefore it is better to say there is nothing to it than to be burdened with such troubles. Now really, this is a dangerous business! It ought to give an inept, lazy schoolboy something to figure out, how the cow walked through the door yet had to leave her tail in it, or how an ox could leave his dung on the beam above him. Oh, it is tiresome business to waste time and words over such devil's buffoonery. Just as if Christ had commanded us to investigate how his body is in the bread! In this way I could also say: Christ is not God, for if that were true, we would gain so much food for thought about this great miracle, how the Godhead could become man, that meanwhile we would surely forget the faith. In order that this may not happen, it is better if Christ is not God!

Next the question begins to distress him greatly, whether the bread is nobler than the womb of the Virgin.[169] There is a superabundance of such prattle in their books. In all of them, the best feature by far is their testimony how unquiet, unsure, uncertain a heart they have in these matters, which cannot cease or desist from brooding and searching more and more, since it feels that all it finds will not prove true and sound. Yet because they have seen that I am full of cheerful words, they would like to persuade us with lofty, defiant words that they too are altogether certain in these matters. But words won't do. There must be truth and a sure conscience. A sure conscience does not beg so.

To hold them now to their two principal points, I shall leave

---

[168] Oecolampadius, *Genuine Exposition,* E 2 in *WA* 23, 310.

[169] "The matter of the bread, on account of the most noble flesh of Christ thus substantially united with it, will then be nobler than the flesh of the eater, indeed, even nobler than the womb of the Virgin." *Reply to Pirkheimer, d* 1 in *WA* 23, 310.

aside all their other prattle and confine myself to these that I have mentioned. For I know these spirits well; I have had many of them to deal with. I know how slippery they are, how they flutter this way and that, just looking for an excuse for prattling even where there is none, if only to avoid having to stand still and answer the real main points about which they are being insistently asked. For they think an answer has been given if they produce a book and write on it the word *Answer*.[170]

Finally, we shall also deal with one or two of the fathers' sayings to see how Dr. Oecolampadius handles them.[171] To be sure, they regard St. Augustine as their own, for he often uses the words mystery, sacrament, sign, invisible, intelligible. But Oecolampadius can deduce nothing from this, despite his boast that he has the definite truth. For although St. Augustine often says that the bread in the Supper is a sacrament and sign of the body of Christ, Oecolampadius has not yet established thereby that mere bread and not Christ's body is present, because one can say that Christ's body is invisibly present under a visible sign, as the same St. Augustine says, "The sacrament is a visible form of an invisible grace."[172]

Here St. Augustine explains in his own words what he means by the terms, sacrament, sign, invisible, intelligible—something altogether different from the way Oecolampadius interprets them. St. Augustine does not say that a sacrament is a figure or sign of something future or absent, like the stories of the Old Testament, but a form of something present and yet invisible. Since we have

---

[170] See in the Introduction how many of the Swiss party's treatises were entitled *Answer* or *Reply*.

[171] Here Luther deals particularly with *Genuine Exposition*, cf. G 2 ff., H 8, K 2 in *WA* 23, 310. For the Swiss interpretation of patristic evidence, see also Zwingli, *Commentary*. *LWZ* 3, 240 ff.; *Clear Instruction*. *LCC* 24, 197 f., 207 ff., 231 ff. In this field Zwingli usually deferred to Oecolampadius. Already in 1524 Luther had commissioned colleagues to gather patristic evidence on the sacrament; cf. *Letter to Nicholas Hausmann*, February 2, 1525. *WA*, *Br* 3, 431.

[172] Quoted in Latin in the text, often referred to by the Reformers as Augustine's, this definition is found in Lombard's *Sentences*, IV, d. 1, c. 2. It is derived from Augustine's thought, e.g. *City of God*, X, 5, *First Catechetical Instruction*, 26, 50, *Epistle 105* (*To the Donatists*), 3, 12, *Questions on the Heptateuch*, III, 84 (on Lev. 21:16). *MPL* 34, 712; *Christian Doctrine*, II, 1.

Augustine himself here explaining his meaning in his own words, we need no other, alien interpretation or explanation.

Now, as often as St. Augustine uses these words, *sacramentum vel signum corporis et sanguinis domini*, "the sacrament of Christ's body and blood,"[173] and the like, he stands firmly on our side against the fanatics, for he means that bread and wine are a visible form of his present, invisible body and blood. It is up to Oecolampadius to prove that St. Augustine uses the word "sacrament" and similar expressions here as a sign of something absent or future, as he dreams up out of his own head, thus ascribing lies and falsehood to St. Augustine. If he does this, we shall yield. We have St. Augustine's own explanation, as we have said. When they now produce several sayings from St. Augustine which make him speak in such a manner, that bread is a sacrament or sign of his body and must be understood invisibly and spiritually, etc., they are doing nothing else than furnishing us with weapons to clout them on the head—as if we were not sufficiently equipped already without them!

But what will they say to the word which St. Augustine writes to Januarius in *Epistle 118*:[174] "It is clear that the first time the disciples received the body and blood of the Lord, they did not receive it fasting. But it pleased the Holy Spirit that in honor of so great a sacrament the Lord's body should enter the mouth of the Christian before any other food"?

Come, now, you fancy interpreters, interpret this saying for us. Here St. Augustine stands and calls the Supper a sacrament, and yet he says that the disciples have received the Lord's body and blood in the sacrament; moreover, that the Lord's body shall enter Christians' mouths before other food, in honor of this great sacrament. What is meant here by "Christians' mouths"? What does this mean: "The Lord's body enters the mouth before other

[173] Luther renders freely the words of Augustine, which read literally, "the sacrament or sign of the Lord's body and blood."

[174] *Epistle 54, To Januarius. MPL* 33, 203; *FC* 12, 258. Between the words "fasting" and "It is clear" Luther omitted Augustine's sentence, "Is the whole church, then, to be unjustly blamed because it [the Lord's Supper] is always received fasting?" Apparently Luther omitted this sentence because it dealt with the question of fasting, which was Augustine's concern, while Luther's attention was focused on the actual reception of Christ's body.

food"? and that this takes place in this sacrament? Is it quite sufficiently clear what Augustine means by the word "sacrament"? Does it mean merely an empty sign of something absent? What is meant by the Lord's body? Does it mean a piece of bread, or does it represent a piece of bread? Here is the point, that Augustine calls it a "sacrament of the body and blood," an outward visible form under which Christ's invisible body and blood are truly present, received, and taken into the mouth physically like other visible, material food.

Again, on *Psalm 33,* St. Augustine says,[175] "Christ was carried in his own hands when he gave his body to the disciples and said, 'This is my body.' Yes, he carried the same body in his hands." Is this saying also obscure?

Here I must briefly address their conscience. For their mouth and pen have sunk so deeply into a No, as the saying goes, that they can no longer return to a Yes. Their conscience, I say, must surely think: "It is true, we interpret and bend St. Augustine and the fathers to our meaning. But the subject certainly resists becoming sure, for this is not a matter of *may* but of *must.* It takes no great wisdom to say, 'This or that may be so understood'; but this is real wisdom when confronted with the demand to prove it *must* be so understood and cannot be otherwise. 'Possible' won't do, 'necessary' will, as the logicians say. Now we boast of the sure truth, but to be honest we do not prove it. And especially since one or two sayings of St. Augustine stand there and assert quite clearly and lucidly that Christ's body is in the sacrament, and that a sacrament is not an empty, simple sign, as we say, therefore it is quite possible that in all his other sayings Augustine uses the word 'sacrament' or 'sign' in this way, and all his sayings do not help us at all." What do you bet, I say, that their conscience must tell them this? For how can they avoid admitting that Christ's body must enter the Christian's mouth through which no food has entered, and that Christ's body must be carried in his hands when he says, "This is my body"?

---

[175] *Exposition* (*Enarratio*) *of Psalm 34* (Vulgate 33), 1. *MPL* 36, 306; *PNF*[1] 8, 73. Introduced by Oecolampadius with the words, "Here it behooves us to undo a certain knot in Augustine." *Genuine Exposition,* A 6 in *WA* 23, 311.

Holy Christendom has, in my judgment, no better teacher after the apostles than St. Augustine. Should this dear and holy teacher be so reviled and defamed by the fanatics as to be regarded as the cloak and support of their poisonous, deceptive teaching? To this I shall answer No as long as I have breath; this does him an injustice. Indeed, it is a good thing to say No to this, because the fanatics interpret his words only according to their own understanding, and yet do not prove their interpretations; still, they boast that they have the clear, pure truth with certainty. Their proof amounts only to this: It could be so understood. When they get this far, they pounce upon it and boast: It *must* be so understood. For he who boasts that he is sure of the truth, as these fanatics do, actually says, "It must be so," yet they slap their own cheeks and brand themselves liars by the fact that they prove no more than that it *may* be so. "It is possible, therefore it is necessary" [176]—school children know how much that argument is worth!

All that interests them is to see if they can make the sayings of Scripture or of the fathers uncertain and bring them into doubt in the minds of the common people. When they have succeeded, they leave it at that. So they immediately boast that they have the truth with certainty, never thinking that they ought to prove their point, just as if they did this to spite us. But what kind of spirit is it who directs his ingenuity only to rendering Scripture passages uncertain and doubtful, and does not on the other hand render them certain and firm again, and thus builds on sand and boasts with certainty that he is making things uncertain—well, this is easy to see. Christ's Spirit it surely is not; he makes sure and certain all that he teaches, as St. Paul extols the *plērophoria*,[177] and in II Corinthians 1 [:19] says, "In Christ Jesus it is not Yes and No, but Yes, Yes."

Now surely Oecolampadius is doing nothing else with the sayings of the fathers than to wrench them out of the sense in which they have been traditionally held, and to render them uncertain. On the other hand, he does nothing to make them certain

---

176 This sentence, like many which express academic maxims, is in Latin in the text.

177 "Conviction," I Thess. 1:5, "full assurance," Col. 2:2 (KJV). Cf. p. 126, n. 214.

and confirm them in his sense. He leaves them dangling and hanging between heaven and earth, with all his followers and adherents. But this is not teaching but misteaching,[178] and to extol this as sure truth is doubly to lie and deceive poor consciences.

Tertullian, the most ancient writer of all after the Apostolic period, in the fourth book against the heretic Marcion, says,[179] "The bread which Christ took and divided among his disciples, he made his body, by saying, 'This is my body,' which is the same as 'form of my body.' A form, however, there could not have been unless there were a real body. An empty thing[180] or void, such as a phantom, is incapable of form. Or did he make the bread an empty thing or a phantom of his body, because he did not have a real body? In that case he must have given bread for us." This saying is supposed to help Oecolampadius maintain that there is nothing but bread in the Supper, and he stands stubbornly upon the word *figura*, since Tertullian explains the words of Christ thus: "This is my body, i.e. *figura* (or form) of my body." Thus Oecolampadius has his grounds for making the word of Christ in the Supper, "my body," read, "sign of my body."

Here once more I must remind them of their duty and responsibility, which they are always and forever forgetting, viz. that they should prove that Tertullian's saying not only may or can but ought and must be understood according to their delusion; if they do not, we rightly brand them as liars and deceivers, because they boast that they are sure of this matter and have the pure truth, and condemn us along with our faith. Now it is impossible for him ever to prove that *figura* here is the same as "sign," as others[181] also have shown him before. With his stubborn streak he forces Tertullian, so that *figura* here must mean "a sign." And yet it cannot mean this. Tertullian will not submit to it, as we shall hear. Since Oecolampadius forces this word in such a way and fails to produce proof, he is already defeated, and Tertullian does not help

178 A play on words: *nicht leren sondern nerren.*

179 *Against Marcion,* IV, 40. *MPL* 2, 491; *ANF* 3, 418. Tertullian, writing in the 190's and thereafter, was not the most ancient post-Apostolic writer, though he was the earliest major theologian to write in Latin.

180 Luther used the word *ein eitel* to translate Ps. 4:2. Tertullian's expression is *vacua res.*

181 E.g. Pirkheimer, *Reply to Oecolampadius,* G 2 ff. in *WA* 23, 311.

him at all. How shall one interpret it differently? Now do you hear what I am asking? You must produce proof; it is your responsibility to speak, and mine to listen. See how he stands speechless!

We are not at this moment discussing whether Tertullian and other teachers teach rightly or wrongly. For we wish to build our faith not upon men's but upon God's Word, the one rock. Not that we despise them, for they have surely had as good an intention as we can ever have, and they have offered their work for our benefit. But what we are discussing is whether the fanatics use the sayings of the fathers rightly, or whether they deal in lies, and we must see what the fathers really said. Now there is Tertullian who says that Christ made the bread in the Supper his body, according to the words, "This is my body." Here is no obscure or ambiguous word, for to make bread into body is distinct, clear, lucid speaking. This Oecolampadius ignores and overlooks, for it is on our side.

But that which follows, "This is the same as *figura* of my body," Oecolampadius claims as favoring him. But *figura* is an obscure and ambiguous word. Of course, he would like to interpret it to mean a parable,[182] type, or interpretative sign, just as one describes the stories in the Old Testament as figures of the New, as Adam is called a figure or type of Christ, or as a bride is called a type or figure of the Church.[183] But *figura* in the Latin language does not mean that kind of type; the word *figura* is misused in such an instance. Oecolampadius accepts this misuse most gladly, for it serves him well. But he ought to prove that his use is correct, yet he cannot. We say that Tertullian employs the word *figura* in accordance with proper usage in the Latin language, where it means a form or figure in the mathematical sense—stating whether a thing is long, thick, broad, round, white or black, which one can see, feel, and handle, as we Germans also say about the sacrament that Christ's body is present under the form of the bread and his

---

182 Among the terms used by Luther and his opponents to refer to figurative language, *gleichnis* is the most fluid. Luther uses it frequently in the next treatise, *Confession*. In this volume it has been variously translated: "parable," "illustration," "figure," "type," "likeness," "similarity," "resemblance," "comparison."

183 Cf. Rom. 5:14, Eph. 5:32.

blood under the form of the wine. Exactly that which we call *gestalt*, "form," Tertullian calls in Latin *figura*.

Now if Oecolampadius cannot prove that *figura* here means a type, he is exposed as a falsifier of Tertullian and a deceiver, and his "sign of the body" falls to pieces. But when will he prove it? When the cuckoo becomes a nightingale! What have we here, now, with this mighty boasting about the sayings of the doctors and citing them so falsely and fraudulently, and then bragging that it is the pure truth? Just what I have said: With sheer dreams and indefinite fantasies they are leading consciences astray, and common people are thunderstruck as if something great is there, when actually there is nothing to it. Counterfeiters are burned, but falsifiers of Scripture are called holy teachers!

Now to understand Tertullian's meaning, we must observe that the heretic Marcion,[184] with many other heretics, taught that Christ had not assumed a real, natural body from Mary, but was only a shadow or phantom of a body which could be neither grasped, felt, nor held, just as the devils on occasion appear in various guises, whereas there is nothing, or a mere phantom, before one's eyes.

Against this Marcion, Tertullian[185] fights, maintaining that Christ had a real, natural body, and concluding: That which is only an empty thing, shadow, or phantom cannot have a form, for a phantom has neither color nor thickness nor length nor breadth; it is nothing but an apparition. If it had color, one could grasp it and identify the color; if it had thickness or length, one could break it, lift and carry it, put and lay it down. Again, one can apply no color, thickness, or length to it, upon it, around it, or above it. This is one thing. Now Marcion confesses that Christ's body, i.e. the shadow or phantom of his body, is in the bread. Thereupon Tertullian concludes: How could Christ's body be in the bread and assume the form of bread if it were not a real, genuine body, since it is impossible for a form to exist where no real body but only a phantom is present?

---

[184] For a discussion of Marcion's teaching concerning the origin of Christ and exhaustive citation of patristic references to Marcion's view, see Adolf von Harnack, *Marcion: Das Evangelium vom fremden Gott* (Leipzig, 1921), pp. 109 ff.

[185] *Against Marcion*, IV, 40. *ANF* 3, 419.

This is the one syllogism or conclusion of Tertullian. This is his meaning when he says, "The bread which Christ took and divided among his disciples he made his body, when he said, 'This is my body,' i.e. the form of my body." The bread, he says, he has made the form of his body in such a way that Christ's body is present under the bread. For there cannot be form without body, as he says later. He had to speak of form, however, for the reason that Christ's body, invisibly present, is seen in no other way than under the form of bread. Indeed, it is no longer the form of bread but it is the form of Christ's body, says Tertullian. But it could have been no form at all, he continues, if it were no real body, for that which is void, such as a phantom, can assume no form. Thus you hear once again that the bread cannot be the form of Christ's body, unless his body was a real body, because a phantom cannot assume a form.

What this conclusion of Tertullian against Marcion establishes, I leave open. It does not concern us here. But this much is perfectly clear: Tertullian's meaning is that Christ's real, natural body is present in the bread of the Supper in such a way that the form of the bread—its thickness, breadth, length, and color—has now become, through his Word, the form, thickness, length, and color of Christ's body, when he says, "This is my body." I certainly add no words of mine here, but refer to Tertullian's own words. And what kind of attack against Marcion would it have been if Tertullian had tried to prove from the Supper that Christ had a real body, while he himself did not believe that Christ's body was present in it? Now, however, he says that there cannot be the form without body; and yet the bread is the form of his body. Certainly, then, Christ's real body must be truly present where its form is, which has been made its form by the Word, out of the bread. This is Tertullian's meaning, I am perfectly sure, and his words are distinct and clear.

The second syllogism or conclusion is: If this were not correct, and Christ had made the bread a phantom of his body (as you might say, Marcion) since he is not supposed to have a real body, then you must say that he gave mere bread for us for the forgiveness of sins, because he says, "This is my body, which is given for you." If nothing but a phantom is present in the bread and the phantom cannot have been given for us, then the bread must have been given for us, because nothing else is there to which the words can refer, "This is my body, given for you." This is what he says: "Or, if he made the bread a phantom of his body, for the reason that he had no real body, then he must have given the bread for us." Here we may understand clearly that Tertullian intends to have in the bread the body which is given for us, lest it should have to be said that bread is given for us. Thereby he proclaims with all possible clarity that the words of Christ, "Take, eat, this is my body, given for you," embrace both bread and body, and that the body is in the bread. This, however, no one would say who held that there was nothing but bread in the sacrament.

From all this it is sufficiently clear, I think, that Tertullian does not understand *figura* here in Oecolampadius' manner as a type or sign, but as a form, and he calls it the form of the body of Christ because Christ's body is in and under it. And he declares distinctly that if Christ's body were not present, it would remain bread and the form of bread that would be given for us. Let Oecolampadius prove his "figure" in this way too. These are mighty strange saints, it seems to me! The holy doctors follow the practice, in expounding the Scriptures, of using lucid and clear passages to clarify the obscure and ambiguous passages. It is also the Holy Spirit's practice to illumine the darkness with light. But our fanatics proceed the other way around: they tear out of a text an obscure, ambiguous word which pleases their fancy, ignore the context, and then run around trying to use it to make a lucid, clear text obscure and ambiguous, and then claim that it is the pure truth. This is the method of the devil, who is a lord of darkness and tries with darkness to extinguish the light.

For example, here in Tertullian Oecolampadius takes the obscure word *figura,* of whose meaning he himself is not certain, and views it incorrectly. This word must now be regarded as the bright sun. Next he runs to the clear words, "This is my body"; these must be merely clouds and darkness. Just so they also regard the obscure sayings, "Flesh is of no avail," and, "Christ is seated at the right hand of God," as sun, and try thereby to darken the words of the Supper.[186] Not that the Scriptures are obscure; but their imagination is blind and lazy, so that it cannot view the clear words correctly, just as a lazy man does not open his eyes to see the real light but takes a glimmer to be the light.

Another saying Tertullian has in his book, *Against the Jews,* where he treats the passage of Jeremiah 11, "They said, 'Let us put wood on his bread.'"[187] This Tertullian interprets as follows: "Without doubt the wood is put on his body, for so Christ himself expounded it when he called the bread his body, which body the prophet of old had proclaimed as bread."

I do not argue here whether Tertullian introduces the passage of Jeremiah with a correct translation, for in the Hebrew it means, "Let us uproot the tree with the food," i.e. with fruit and all. We are not discussing the translation here, but we are discussing what Tertullian understood this passage to mean. Now it is certain that by "wood" he understands and interprets the cross which Christ bore, and by "bread" his body, and he is speaking about the bread in the Supper, for Christ nowhere else calls bread his body. In John 6 [:35], to be sure, he says he is bread, but does not say that bread is his body. Now, my friend, does anyone who calls the bread in the Supper the body of Christ which was crucified, also confess that nothing but bread is present in it? But Tertullian does just this by saying clearly of the bread, to which Jeremiah referred, that it was crucified and that wood was put upon it, and that the same bread is His body, making the bread and the body identical.

In the same way he also writes against Marcion in the third book,[188] employing the same saying of Jeremiah, "Let us put wood on his bread." "Without doubt," says Tertullian, "on his bread means upon his body. For so did God himself expound it even in

186 Cf. Zwingli, *Commentary* (*LWZ* 3, 220) where (also using the figure of sun and darkness) he explains why he does not force John 6:63 into conformity with the words, "This is my body," and make that verse square with the latter, but instead makes the latter fit the former: "First, the things Christ is there discussing are so perfectly clear. . . . Second, faith sees that the true meaning is the one which the words bear upon their face" (viz. a symbolical meaning).

187 *Against the Jews,* 10. *MPL* 2, 629; *ANF* 3, 166; also, *Against Marcion,* IV, 40. Cf. Jer. 11:19 (Douay). Oecolampadius, *Genuine Exposition,* C 7.

188 *Against Marcion,* III, 19. *MPL* 2, 348; *ANF* 3, 337.

your gospel (you Marcionites), when he called his body 'bread,' in order to point out that he has made or given the bread to be the form of his body, which body the prophet of old had referred to the form of bread, a mystery which the Lord himself would by and by interpret." Here Tertullian reiterates that the bread is a figure or form of the body of Christ, and that Christ gave such a form to his body when he said, "This is my body," just as we have heard above in connection with the first passage. So it is perfectly clear that he is speaking here of the bread and the body in the Supper. And he says, *Propheta figuravit corpus eius in panem,* i.e. the prophet long ago ascribed to the body of Christ the form of bread, which Christ afterward did more clearly when he said, "This is my body," and made bread the *figura* of his body.[189]

All these, of course, are the words of Tertullian, that Jeremiah with his prophecy previously adjudged the bread to be the form of the body of Christ, which Christ afterward fulfilled in fact, making the bread be the form of his body. All this must be said of the natural bread, which has a form as it is present in the Supper —not of the spiritual bread of which John 6 speaks. For the latter gives no form to Christ's body, but is Christ himself, as he says, "I am the bread from heaven" [6:41]. Since Tertullian understands, then, that it is the natural bread of which Jeremiah speaks, on which the Jews have put the wood, and says this is Christ's body which was crucified, I think it is convincingly proved that under the form of the bread in the Supper Tertullian confesses Christ's true body, on which the wood of the cross has been put. Let us see what our obscurers and darkeners will try to do in this light!

Indeed, to help them test their obscurantism and prove their erudition, I shall give them as a bonus this saying of Tertullian from his book, *On the Resurrection of the Flesh:*[190] "The flesh is washed, in order that the soul may be cleansed; the flesh is anointed, that the soul may be consecrated to God; the flesh is 'signed,' that the soul may be fortified; the flesh is shaded by the

---

[189] Tertullian's text reads: *Et dedit panem sui corporis figuram.*

[190] *Resurrection of the Flesh,* 8, *MPL* 2, 806; *ANF* 3, 551. Oecolampadius had used this quotation in favor of his own view in *Genuine Exposition,* G 7. "Signed" means with the sign of the cross.

laying on of hands, that the soul may be enlightened in the Spirit; the flesh is fed with the body and blood of Christ, that the soul may fatten upon God."

Now, explain to us here how our flesh can be fed with the body and blood of Christ. Try turning it around, and just as you say in the Supper that bread represents or signifies the body and wine the blood of Christ, so teach us the reverse here, that the body of Christ represents bread and the blood represents water or wine by which the body is fed. But see to it that you make your interpretation sure and prove that it must be so. For we are not satisfied, here or anywhere else, when you only say it may be so.

What kind of spirits and people have we here, who malign the good ancient doctor before the world, to mislead and confuse the common people's consciences with lies and deception, and then boast that it is the pure truth, and thereby blaspheme God the Holy Spirit besides? It would be much better for them frankly to repudiate the holy fathers than to try with such deception and fraud to lure them over to their side and seduce the world under the name of the fathers, to whom before God and the world they are doing an injustice.

Irenaeus also is one of the most ancient doctors. He had to fight the Valentinian heretics who taught that Christ is not God's Son and that there was no resurrection of the flesh. They also held that the body would not be saved, but only the soul, because St. Paul says, "Flesh and blood cannot inherit the kingdom of God" [I Cor. 15:50]. Against this Irenaeus writes that the body also will be saved, and that there is a resurrection of the flesh, as our Creed confesses. Among other things he cites this proof against them: If the body is not to be saved also, why should it be fed with the body and blood of the Lord in the sacrament? If it eats an eternal food there, it will surely live eternally by means of it. But let us hear his own words. In the fourth book, chapter 5,[191] he says, "Just as the bread which is produced from the earth, when it receives the naming of God,[192] is no longer common bread but a sacrament, consisting of two things, an earthly and a heavenly,

[191] *Against Heresies,* IV, 18, 5. *MPG* 7, 1028 f. *ANF* 1, 486.

[192] Irenaeus wrote *ekklēsis tou Theou,* which was rendered in Latin *invocatio Dei.*

so also our bodies, when they receive the sacrament, are no longer corruptible, because they have the hope of the resurrection."

What will the fanatics do here, who boast that Irenaeus is on their side, and claim to be sure about the matter besides? Oecolampadius,[193] of course, wishes to use this saying like a warrior knight against the papists and their transubstantiation, and against Valentinus. But I should like to hear and see the man who could interpret this quotation to the effect that nothing but bread and wine are present in the Supper. There stands Irenaeus, saying that the bread is not ordinary, common bread, inasmuch as it has been named or called by God, but "eucharist," as the ancients spoke of the sacrament. But what can this "naming" be, with which God names the bread? It can be nothing else than the word which he speaks, "This is my body." There, indeed, he names it, and gives it a new name which it did not have before when it was ordinary bread; and he says, "Let this bread, after this naming or word, consist of two things, the one earthly—i.e. bread, which is produced from the earth, as Irenaeus says here—the other heavenly," which must certainly be Christ's body, which is in heaven. What other sort of heavenly thing can be in the sacrament along with the earthly thing, which by God's naming or word is present?

Oecolampadius here makes of the earthly and the heavenly a single thing, viz. the bread which is earthly, inasmuch as it comes from the earth, and also heavenly, because God is thanked and praised for it. Thus is Irenaeus to be twisted and taught to buzz like a fanatic. If one asks: How do we become certain that this is Irenaeus' meaning, or who ever heard that our thanksgiving or words are a heavenly thing? the answer is, "I, Oecolampadius, say so. If this does not satisfy you, you have no spirit." In this way all bread on all tables, when the blessing is pronounced, may properly be called heavenly, for thanksgiving is there. Must we simply believe this and require no proof—but is it sure truth if the fanatics merely say so? Yes, indeed; confounded be anyone who demands further proof! Well, of course, this is simply to leap over Irenaeus and not to answer his words in the least. Yet this must be called not only an answer, but also the sure truth!

---

193 *Genuine Exposition,* G iii in *WA* 23, 313.

But Irenaeus will not tolerate this misinterpretation. For we know that ordinary, common bread remains ordinary, common bread even if Christ and all the apostles recite the blessing over it, and it does not thereby become a heavenly thing; just as Christ in John 6 [:11] distributed the bread among the people and thanked and praised God for it, yet it remained ordinary bread and did not become heavenly.

But Irenaeus says here that on account of the Word of God it is no longer ordinary bread, but along with the earthly bread there is also something heavenly present. It would be shameless presumption if anyone tried to interpret "God's naming" as human thanksgiving, blessing, and praise. Paul, indeed, teaches us in Romans 4 [:17] what God's "naming" or "calling" means when he says, "God names or calls into existence the things that do not exist." So too, Irenaeus speaks here of God's naming or calling, as Moses also testifies in Genesis 1[194] that God through his naming or calling, i.e. through his Word, created all things. Otherwise, you be the expert and tell me what else *vocatio dei* may mean, when God calls, speaks, declares, names.[195] This is his Word, when he says, "This is my body," just as he says in Genesis [1:3], "Let there be light," and there is light. My friend, it is God who names or calls, and what he names immediately comes into existence, as Psalm 33 [:9] says, "He spoke, and it came to be."

There are, then, three aspects in the sacrament according to Irenaeus. The first is *vocatio dei,* God's word or naming, which is there when he says, "This is my body." Through this naming or word, he says, the bread becomes the eucharist or sacrament, so that the bread is now a twofold thing; whereas previously it was ordinary bread and a single thing, altogether earthly, now however it is both earthly and heavenly. What the heavenly aspect is, the fanatics ought to show us if they allege it is not that which is indicated in the naming or God's word when he says, "This is my body." That this naming is our thanksgiving or word, Oecolampadius says boldly, and yet he is just as certain of it as he is of the entire article. Therefore it is a disgusting presumption to

[194] Cf. p. 61, n. 101.
[195] Luther writes in Latin: *Quando deus vocat, dicit, appellat, nominat.*

claim something so brazenly as certain. It must be obvious that it is uncertain and merely their own dream.

Again, Irenaeus says that our bodies even now are no longer corruptible when they receive the sacrament, but have thereby the hope of the resurrection. For we see that the ancient doctors spoke of the sacrament in such a way that it even bestowed upon the body an immortal nature, though hidden in faith and hope until the Last Day. Now, of course, ordinary bread cannot sustain the body eternally or make it incorruptible. For it is a corruptible food, even when Christ himself pronounces thanks over it, as he himself in John 6 [:27] calls the bread which he had distributed among the people a food which perishes. Hence, according to Irenaeus' opinion, there must be present in the sacrament something heavenly, which lives eternally and can and does give eternal life. For he speaks of the physical eating when he says that our bodies receive the sacrament, and that through this same physical eating our bodies are already incorruptible in hope. This, of course, can be nothing but the body of Christ, of which he says in John 6 [:55, 58], "My flesh is food indeed. He who eats my flesh will live forever."

With these matters the fanatics should concern themselves and produce a careful answer, not flutter about and slobber something irrelevant, as Oecolampadius does. For they ought to consider that these matters would move us to make demands of them and not let them get by in any old way. To pass lightly over these matters indicates a haughty heart which despises all men as clods, just as if they should be compelled to be satisfied if a fanatic mutters his little contribution, and straightway accept that as the sure truth. If we are not so learned and holy as they, at least we also have consciences which induce and impel us to seek the truth. So, since they boast that they are sure of the truth, they are under obligation to prove this to us who maintain that their truth is nothing but drifting sand and swirling wind.

Again, Irenaeus says immediately before this, "How can they say that flesh must go to corruption and may not inherit life, if it is nourished with the body and blood of the Lord?" Here we see again that the body is nourished with the body and blood of the

Lord in order that it may live eternally, and not go to corruption as the heretics say. This, indeed, is Irenaeus' expression for bodily eating and food for the body, and yet the same food is held to be the body and blood of the Lord. It won't do to skip over this; neither would it be adequate to say that the body and blood of the Lord here mean bread and wine as signs of Christ's body and blood. For these do not give to the body incorruptible life, concerning which Irenaeus says here against the heretics that they do not grant incorruptible life to the body, even though it eats that food which gives it. It is not enough, moreover, for them to interpret it any way they please; they must prove it and make it certain, as they boast that they are certain.

Again, in the fifth book, chapter 5, he says,[196] "The cup, which is a created thing, he acknowledges as his own body, by which he gives increase to our bodies." Observe, again, that the body of Christ in the cup strengthens our bodies. This, of course, is said concerning physical food beyond all doubt, yet it is the body of Christ, as indeed at the same time the cup is a created thing. Again, shortly thereafter he says,[197] "Now when the mixed cup and the manufactured bread receive the Word of God, they become the sacrament of the body and blood of Christ, through which things the nature of our body grows and subsists. How dare they say, then, that the body is incapable of receiving the gift of God, which is eternal life, if this body is nourished with the body and blood of the Lord, and is his member?" Here we learn that bread and wine receive the Word of God which Irenaeus had earlier called receiving the naming of God, and he clarifies himself by saying that the sacrament is not a sign of the absent body of Christ but is the body of Christ himself, as that by which not only is our body physically fed but also the nature and substance [*wesen*] of our body is nourished, strengthened, and sustained unto eternal life and becomes a member of the body of Christ. I am eager to hear how the fanatics will try not only to parry these and similar

[196] *Against Heresies,* V, 2, 2. *MPG* 7, 1125; *ANF* 1, 528. Probably from haste the quotation has been telescoped; in *Genuine Exposition,* G v, as quoted in *WA* 23, 314, it reads correctly, "The cup . . . he acknowledges as his blood . . .; and the bread . . . as his own body. . . ."

[197] *Against Heresies,* V, 2, 3. *MPG* 7, 1125; *ANF* 1, 528.

sayings but also to harmonize them with their nonsensical interpretation, in such a way as to make it perfectly certain that Irenaeus agrees with them. This barren, indefinite interpreting and word-torturing, such as Oecolampadius practices, we do not believe at all. It must be distinct, clear proof—stronger than ours. If they do this for me, I shall praise them as men who have the very heart of the Holy Spirit.

We should also like to hear St. Hilary, who is another of the ancient doctors and an excellent interpreter of Scripture. He writes against the Arians in book 8, *On the Trinity:*[198] "If the Word has truly become flesh, and we truly receive the Word which became flesh in the Lord's food, how are we to believe that he does not dwell in us by his nature, he who, when he became man, has assumed the nature of our flesh, nevermore to lay it aside, and has mingled the nature of his flesh with his eternal nature in the sacrament of the flesh, of which we become partakers in common?" Here, indeed, Hilary says that in the food of the Lord, i.e. in the sacrament, we truly take the Word who became flesh, or as we might say more directly, the enfleshed Word; and for that reason Christ remains in us naturally, or with his nature and substance, not only spiritually as the fanatics dream. And he calls the sacrament "a sacrament of the flesh distributed among us in common,"[199] indicating that not only bread is distributed among us but also flesh. He says further that in this sacrament Christ mingles together —not only spiritually—the nature of his flesh with his eternal nature. Now what is meant by "the nature of his flesh"? Does it mean bread and wine? or his body in its nature and essence? Let anyone gloss and interpret as he will, just so he makes his gloss certain and shows good reason for interpreting the words of Hilary differently from the way they read. For as they stand, they give us in the sacrament not only Christ's natural flesh but also his eternal divinity.

---

[198] *On the Trinity*, VIII, 13. *MPL* 10, 246; *FC* 25, 285. Cited in *Genuine Exposition*, H ii. Hilary of Poitiers was one of the ablest defenders of the Nicene doctrine in the period when Arianism threatened to engulf it. Arianism, which taught that the Word is not truly divine but rather the most exalted of creatures, is condemned by name in the Augsburg Confession, Art. I.

[199] The Latin text reads: *Sacramentum carnis nobis communicande.*

Shortly thereafter he says,[200] "If we wish to say how Christ is truly and naturally in us, let us learn not to speak so of him, lest we speak like fools and godless men. For Christ says, 'My flesh is food indeed, and my blood is drink indeed. He who eats my flesh and drinks my blood abides in me, and I in him' [John 6:55 f.]. No doubt remains that it is the true body and blood, because both through the Lord's own acknowledgment and through our faith it is truly flesh and truly blood, which, as they are received and drunk by us, bring it about that we are in Christ and Christ in us." It is St. Hilary's whole concern in this same passage to maintain that just as Christ according to his divinity is by nature in the Father and is in essence one with him, so Christ through the sacrament which we eat and drink is by nature and essence in us and we in him. Moreover, he uses the word "naturally"[201] everywhere in this passage in order to demonstrate a natural union of the body of Christ with us, and not only a spiritual one existing in the will and the mind.

Thus Hilary says, "That which we eat and drink effects these things in us"; he does not say, "That which we believe and know spiritually." The true body and the true blood are eaten and drunk. What is meant by "eating and drinking"? It is easy to do as the fanatics do here—make up a gloss and call "mystery," "the Lord's food," "eat," and "drink" whatever they please.[202] This, of course, we also could do as well as they, and not need all their great, masterful skill to do so. However, no one requested this skill from them; but this has been requested: even if they have interpreted and explained the matter with infinite skill, would they also please prove that this explanation is sure and right, in the sense that it must be so and cannot be otherwise? This they have not done even to this day in dealing with any single passage of Scripture. They even disdain to do it, just as if it were not necessary and

---

[200] *On the Trinity,* VIII, 14. *MPL* 10, 247; *FC* 25, 286. Cited in *Genuine Exposition,* H iii; cf. *WA* 23, 314.

[201] The word *natürlich,* here translated "naturally," means "by nature," in the ancient philosophical sense. It is not set in contrast here with "unnaturally" or with "supernaturally"; neither does it have the modern connotation of "obviously." Cf. p. 57, n. 97, p. 61, n. 102.

[202] A thrust at Oecolampadius, cf. *Genuine Exposition,* H iiii ff. Cf. *WA* 23, 314.

they were not under obligation to do it, and as if it were quite enough if they simply say, "God means a cuckoo."[203] If they have to do it, however, they will not write me so many books, I am sure. Their spirit and skill will peter out in time. Interpreting and glossing as one pleases is something everyone can do, without any special spirit.

The holy martyr St. Cyprian, writing to Pope Cornelius how Christians should be strengthened by the sacrament for suffering in time of persecution, says,[204] "Now indeed the 'peace' is necessary not only for the sick but also for the strong; nor is communion—the sacrament—to be granted only to the dying but also to the living, that we may not leave those whom we stir up and exhort to the battle naked and unarmed, but may fortify them with the protection of Christ's blood and body. For since we use the sacrament for the purpose that it may be a safeguard to those who receive it, we must equip those whom we wish to be safe against the adversary with the armor of the Lord's food. For how shall we teach or incite them to shed their blood in confession of his name, if we deny them Christ's blood when they are about to fight? Or how can we make them fit for the cup of martyrdom, if we do not first admit them to drink in the church the cup of the Lord by the right of communion?"

In this saying we see that for Cyprian *communion, eucharist,* and *peace* are one and the same. He speaks of proffering the sacrament to strengthen those who are about to fight; and he asserts distinctly that they receive the Lord's body and blood in this proffering. To be sure, a fanatic here can make of the blood, cup, and sacrament a sign of the blood and a metaphor, forcing Cyprian to say what they wish. But to prove this as well is not necessary for them; it is enough if the spirit says so!

Again, in his *Treatise against the Lapsed* he says:[205] "People coming back from the devil's altars approach our Lord's sacred

---

[203] Cf. p. 31.

[204] *Letter* 53, 2. *MPL* 3, 856; *ANF* 5, 337. The *pax* actually means reconciliation with the church. *ACW* 25, 85. Cornelius (pope 251-252) died as a martyr during the persecutions in the reign of the Emperor Decius. Cyprian, bishop of Carthage, died as a martyr in 258 during a new wave of persecutions which began toward the end of 256 under the Emperor Valerian.

[205] *On the Lapsed,* 15 f. *MPL* 4, 478 f.; *ACW* 25, 25 f. Cf. I Cor. 10:14 ff., 11:27 ff.

body with filthy hands still reeking with the odor of the sacrifice; and still belching from the poisonous food of idols, they want to get at the body of the Lord with a mouth still stinking from their crime and still reeking of their deadly excrement. They scorn all that St. Paul says against this in I Corinthians 10 and 11, but do sacrilege and violence to his body and blood, and their hands and mouth sin more grievously now against their Lord than when they denied him."

Here, you see, Cyprian indicates that they take Christ's body into their mouth and throat, and commit sacrilege against his body with hand and mouth. Now the mouth, of course, cannot eat Christ's body spiritually. A fanatic, however, quickly retorts that the body and blood of Christ here mean bread and wine as signs—and he does not need to prove it. In short, if it is granted that one may alter and reinterpret words so freely without being obliged to prove it, then there is no saying, no single letter in the whole world but will serve the fanatics. If one lets the words stand in their literal meaning, however, according to the rules of language, so that bread means bread and body means body, or else is required to prove another interpretation with sound reasons, then there is no saying nor letter in the whole world which favors the fanatics, and their boast that they have the sure truth is nothing but a lie.

Even the saying of Augustine on Psalm 98,[206] which above all had the greatest plausibility, does not favor them: "You will not eat the body which you see, nor drink the blood which they who crucify me will shed. A mystery[207] have I given you; if you understand it spiritually, it will give you life"; and on John 6:[208]

[206] *Exposition of Psalm* 98 (RSV 99:5), 8. *MPL* 37, 1265; *PNF*¹ 8, 486. Zwingli cites the same quotation, from Gratian's *Decretum*, Pars. III, dist. II, *de Consecratione*, cap. 44. *Corpus Iuris Canonici*, I, col. 1330. *Clear Instruction. LCC* 24, 208.

[207] Luther has rendered Augustine's *sacramentum* here as *geheymnis*—"mystery." *Sacramentum* was the common Latin translation of the New Testament word *mustērion*.

[208] *Gospel of John, Tractate* 25, 12. *MPL* 35, 1602; *PNF*¹ 7, 164, cited in *Genuine Exposition*, F 5, and by Zwingli, *Clear Instruction. LCC* 24, 197 f. It is quoted by Luther in his early treatises, *The Blessed Sacrament of the Holy and True Body of Christ* . . ., 1519. *LW* 35, 45 ff., and *The Babylonian Captivity of the Church*, 1520. *LW* 36, 18. The same thought appears in Augustine's *Sermon 112*, 5. *PNF*¹ 6, 448.

"Why do you make ready your teeth and stomach? Believe, and you have already eaten." Since Augustine speaks of teeth and stomach, his meaning is most certainly directed against the Capernaites and our fanatics, who think that Christ's body is to be bitten and chewed by the teeth and digested by the stomach, like a piece of beef. But this is not what Christians teach, nor do we poor sinners teach so. This they know perfectly well, but they choose to ignore it.

So too, when Augustine says that one will not eat the flesh which one sees, he is also speaking of the manner in which one eats beef, as he himself explains earlier that he speaks against those who thought that Christ would carve to pieces and distribute his body. Indeed, if they wish to hold fast this saying of Augustine, he will completely take away from us Christ's body and flesh, even spiritually. For so he reads, "Not the flesh which you see, not the blood which is shed," just as if one should partake of another blood and flesh than Christ's flesh and blood. Now, of course, we eat no other flesh and blood, even spiritually, than exactly that which men saw and crucified. So St. Augustine here dare not deny or condemn the statement that Christ's body and blood are eaten, as his words read, but rather he condemns the fleshly eating as one eats sausage and bread, chews them with his teeth, and digests them with his stomach.

The fanatics fail completely to "discern" the body of Christ from other flesh, as St. Paul says in I Corinthians 11 [:29]. They speak of it no differently than if it were perishable, digestible, masticable meat, such as one buys in the butcher shop and cooks in the kitchen. Such simpletons are they that they do not see that this flesh is an imperishable, immortal, incorruptible flesh, as the 16th Psalm sings of it, "Thou wilt not let thy holy one see corruption; my flesh also shall rest in hope" [v. 10]. Death indeed tried once, wanting to devour and digest it; but it could not. This flesh tore its stomach and throat into more than a hundred thousand pieces, so that death's teeth fell to pieces and turned to dust, and this flesh remains alive. For this food was too strong for death, and has devoured and digested its devourer. God is in this flesh. It is God's flesh, the Spirit's flesh.[209] It is in God and

[209] The text reads: *Ein Gotts fleisch, Ein geistfleisch.*

God is in it. Therefore it lives and gives life to all who eat it, both to their bodies and to their souls.

If the fanatics had been able to see this little point, they would not have become so foolish as to revile us as flesh-eaters, but would have minded their own business.[210] For they are the real flesh-eaters, because they are dealing in this matter with such fleshly thoughts, believing that Christ's flesh is exactly like any other flesh, utterly useless and perishable. All their pride and boast is that when they twist and wrench the Scriptures and the sayings of the fathers to suit their own bias, they think this is all right and consider the truth surely established thereby. But that is far from the case.

I have written previously against the heavenly prophets,[211] too, asking how it happens that, in their view, bread and wine are useful in the Supper and do not prevent people from remembering Christ's suffering, yet Christ's body and blood are not just as useful or good as bread and wine to enable us to meditate on his suffering. Or why should this follow:[212] "Christ's flesh is of no avail, therefore it is not present," and not this also: Bread and wine are of no avail, therefore they are not present? But here one must rush past and not answer. Yet this is the sum of the matter: The fanatics direct all their teaching and writing and their persistent effort to the end of rendering our text and our faith with respect to this article uncertain and unsettled. If they could succeed in this, they would indulge in the fancy that they had won. But even if they succeeded and made us uncertain and confused, they have not yet made their own belief certain. For they do not prove one letter of the glosses which they propose.

Now what kind of spirit is it that tries to make this side uncertain and confused, and yet cannot make his own certain or secure—indeed, does not even want to and is not interested in making it certain? Surely it is no other spirit than the devil, who takes pleasure in jarring men's hearts everywhere, and permits

---

210 The proverbial saying reads: *Sondern sich selbs bey der nasen genommen.* For the meaning and origin of this form of the proverb see Ernst Thiele, *Luthers Sprichwörter-sammlung* (Weimar: Hermann Böhlaus Nachfolger, 1900), pp. 357 f., No. 394.

211 *LW* 40, 203 f.

212 *LW* 40, 202.

them on no side to be certain and sure, but keeps them dangling and hovering whichever way his wind blows, like an aspen leaf. The Holy Spirit, however, is the sort of teacher who is sure and makes men sure, and does not let them toss and dangle, for "in Christ it is not yes and no, but yes and amen," II Corinthians 1.[213] And St. Paul teaches and confidently asserts a *plērophoria*[214] in Christ, a full, certain, sure understanding, upon which a man can die and risk everything.

I should like to advise these men, however, that they may as well be full-fledged fanatics as half-fanatics, and that since the effort surely should be made with boldness, they should quickly go the whole way and remove these words, "This is my body, given for you," entirely and utterly from the Supper. For the way they believe and regard the Supper, they do not need these words at all. It would be perfectly adequate if they celebrated the Supper with these words: "Christ took bread, gave thanks and broke it, and gave it to his disciples saying, 'Take, eat, do this in remembrance of me.'" For these words suggest quite adequately that one should eat this bread and thereby remember Christ. This is the fanatics' Supper, complete and entire.[215] Why should the useless, unnecessary text remain, "This is my body, given for you," since this idea is sufficiently comprehended in the remembrance of the Lord when it is proclaimed that his body was given for us? For what else is to be remembered than that he was given for us, as St. Paul explains? [I Cor. 11:26]

"O how gladly would we do this, if the words did not stand in all the Gospels!" Oh, there is a good answer to that. You must boldly say, "They were inserted somehow from the margin into the

213 Luther's free rendering of II Cor. 1:19 f.

214 Cf. p. 107, n. 177.

215 If one puts "represents" for "is" in the words of institution, says Zwingli, "This will be the sense: 'Take and eat, for that which I now command you to do will represent or call to your remembrance my body, which now is given for you;' for immediately thereafter he adds, 'Do this in remembrance of me.' See, there is the purpose for which he commands the eating, viz. in remembrance of him. . . . It is to be a sign whereby those who trust in Christ's death and blood witness before the brethren that they have this faith." *Letter to Alber. C. R.* 90, 345; *St. L.* 17, 1522 f. Cf. *Commentary. LWZ* 3, 228; Konrad Sam: "What did he command them to do? Don't you hear? To take bread and eat, and remember him." *A Fine Statement,* A iii; Bucer, *Preface,* B 4, etc. as cited in *WA* 23, 315.

text, but not written by the evangelists themselves." Because your reasoning is this: Whatever appears to you useless and unnecessary is not true, just as Oecolampadius, like a know-it-all, says,[216] "There is no use or need for Christ's body to be in the bread, therefore it is not true." So too, here: It is sheer useless and unnecessary prattle for the words to remain in the Supper, therefore they should not be there, since without them the Supper is quite completely described, instituted, and used, and no further need or use is shown why they must be there; however, if some need were shown, one can easily dream up something to reply against it. Still it is in your heart that these words are superfluous and of no avail, and you dearly wish that they were not there, because they give you a terrible beating.[217]

These are two of Dr. Oecolampadius' shameful, dreadful blasphemies, when he asks of what use or need it is for Christ's body to be in the bread, and, if we do not show him, he will conclude there is nothing to it. Now what shall I say of the outrageous audacity of this hellish Satan? Well then: even if we could not show how it is useful and necessary for Christ's body to be in the bread, should God's Word for that reason be false, or be twisted around according to our notion? A faithful, God-fearing heart does this: it asks first whether it is God's Word. When it hears that it is, it smothers with hands and feet the question why it is useful or necessary. For it says with fear and humility, "My dear God, I am blind; truly I know not what is useful or necessary for me, nor do I wish to know, but I believe and trust that thou dost know best and dost intend the best in thy divine goodness and wisdom. I am satisfied and happy to hear thy simple Word and perceive thy will."

But those who are possessed with devilish arrogance invert this procedure and, by asking why it is useful and necessary, try

---

[216] "What need have we for his body to be in that bread? I do not see what benefit accrues to us from this." *Reply to Pirkheimer, d* 1; further citations in *WA* 23, 315. Cf. Zwingli: Because of John 6:63, "She [the church] will not even brook the question whether the body of Christ is in the sacrament of the eucharist in actual, physical, or essential form." *Commentary. LWZ* 3, 212.

[217] For the variety of idiomatic meanings of *das gebrandte leid* see Jacob and Wilhelm Grimm (eds.), *Deutsches Wörterbuch* (16 vols.; Leipzig: Hirzel, 1854-1954), II, 304 f.

to smother God's Word. They boldly set themselves on the judgment seat, summon God to the bar to give an account of his Word, and ask the poor defendant why he chooses and uses such words, and why it is useful and necessary to do and say these things. If he does not show their use and necessity, they immediately take him away and crucify him as a malefactor, and then boast with the Jews that they have the sure truth and have rendered service to God.[218] Isn't it horrible to hear this? This is where one comes out when one tries to treat God's Word according to men's fancy.

Now, dear sirs, since you have such teachers, be warned herewith to notice what kind of preachers you have. Devil's masks they are, who under a fine pretext and fair words set forth the devil in God's place. Here they reveal that they understand absolutely nothing about God's Word and faith.[219] St. Paul says in Romans 8 [:26], "We do not know what we should pray for." This even the heathen Socrates[220] realized, when he said that we should pray God to give what is good for us, for he knows this best. Our fanatics have the still higher ambition to climb straight past God and prescribe purposes for him, and to know what is useful and needful for us to believe, or they take their stand and presume to say to him, "Thou art a liar!"

If they had any understanding of faith, however, and ever felt a spark of it, they would know that faith's highest single virtue and quality and glory is the willingness not to pry into the benefit or necessity of what one believes. It refuses to encircle God or to demand why, for what purpose, from what necessity he commands or enjoins something, but is perfectly happy to be unwise, to give God the glory and believe his simple Word. Shame on you, you leaders of the blind.[221] that you should not know this, yet spew so many books into the world with such great boasting, whereby you expose before everyone's face your own folly and ignorance!

God commanded Abraham to sacrifice his son Isaac [Gen.

---

218 Cf. John 16:2.

219 Zwingli had written that Luther did not understand what faith is and how it is produced, e.g. *Commentary. LWZ* 3, 182, 212 ff.

220 Xenophon, *Memorabilia Socratis,* I, 3, 2: "And he prayed to the gods, simply to give what is good, as the gods would know best what is good."

221 Cf. Matt. 15:14.

22:2]. Of course, it was deeply hidden from Abraham of what need or use this would be. Had he proceeded to dispute with God, like our fanatics, in an effort to know of what use or need it would be, or had he tried to invert God's words, what sort of blessing would he have obtained? Just the same as Lucifer merited in heaven! [222]

Again, our mother Eve also had God's word that she should not eat of that one tree [Gen. 2:17]. Then the fanatics' false god approached her with exactly this question, saying, "Why has God commanded this?" [Gen. 3:1 ff.]. As if to say: Of what use is it? For what is it necessary? Oh, there's nothing to it; God's word doesn't mean that! And he gave her another interpretation of God's word. So she fell and drew us all down with herself, without exception, just as now he assails us also through these fanatics and draws near crawling upon his serpent's belly:[223] "Why has Christ put his body into the bread? Of what use is it? What is the need? Oh, it's all nonsense; his word does not mean that!" So he comes interpreting his poisonous lies and blasphemies to us as divine knowledge and claiming this as the clear truth. Therefore, St. Paul rightly warns us against this serpent in I Corinthians 10 [II Cor. 11:3], saying, "I am afraid that as the serpent deceived Eve by his cunning, your thoughts will be led astray from the simplicity that is in Christ." Isn't it true that these fanatics seduce us by their cunning from the simple sense of these clear, simple words, "This is my body"?

Well, suppose I grant the possibility that Christ cut his flesh into pieces visibly and physically and gave it to us to eat, as the Capernaites understood it and the fanatics dream;[224] it would not on that account be of no avail, and would not apply to the saying, "Flesh is of no avail." Why? Because we are confronted by the common article of our faith, that Christ's flesh is full of divinity, full of eternal good, life, and salvation, and he who takes a bite of it takes to himself therewith eternal good, life, full salvation,

222 Cf. Isa. 14:12 (KJV).
223 An allusion to Gen. 3:14.
224 Like Karlstadt (cf. *Against the Heavenly Prophets. LW* 40, 208 ff.), the Swiss argued that "broken for you," I Cor. 11:24, represents the crucifixion, and therefore no literal breaking of Christ's body takes place in the Lord's Supper. Zwingli, *Clear Instruction. LCC* 24, 229.

and all that is in this flesh. And if he believed it, he would also have life and salvation from it; but if he did not believe it, this treasure would not help him at all, but would rather harm him.

Now, however, it is impossible that this flesh should be cut into pieces, divided, torn, corrupted, or destroyed. For it is a blessed, divine, incorruptible flesh, as Peter says in Acts 2 [:24], "It was not possible that death should hold this flesh," because the 16th Psalm says, "Thou wilt not let thy holy one see corruption" [v. 10], and John 18 [19:36] quotes from Moses [Exod. 12:46], "Not a bone of him shall be broken." It could at one time suffer and die, but that it should be cut into pieces, divided, broken, chewed, digested, consumed, and destroyed, is not possible. It must be entirely and all at once conceived, born, carried, eaten, and believed; and where it is, it must bring benefit. For there is pure benefit and good in it, except where it is without faith. For without faith nothing brings any benefit, as St. Paul says, [Titus 1:15] "To the impure all things are impure," and in Romans 14 [:23], "Whatever does not proceed from faith is sin."

Consequently, as has been said, it is one of the greatest blasphemies of our time and a truly abominable thing to hear, when Zwingli and Oecolampadius dare to say that Christ's flesh is of no avail if it is eaten physically, even for believers.[225] Just as if the eternal good could not be good, and eternal life could not be life on account of our usage, and would have to change its essence, nature, and character according to whether it was eaten or not eaten by men; or as if it were just an empty flesh with no divinity in it. From this example we can judge with full certainty that the wicked Satan speaks through them, for the Holy Spirit is not so absent-minded as to blaspheme the flesh of Christ shamefully and decry it as a useless flesh, when he himself indwells it and accomplishes perfect good and benefit through it wherever it is, whether in the bread or in heaven or in the heart. Indeed, it cannot be of no avail; that is impossible.

Nor does it help them to boast that they rightly teach and

[225] Zwingli: "The flesh of Christ is of no avail if it is eaten. Therefore, those words of Christ, 'This is my body,' cannot be understood as if through them the flesh of Christ is eaten." *Reply to Billican. C. R.* 91, 898. Oecolampadius: cf. p. 127, n. 216.

praise Christ in other subjects.[226] For he who deliberately denies, blasphemes, and desecrates Christ in one subject or article cannot correctly teach or honor him at any other point; it is sheer hypocrisy and deception, however impressive its appearance. For this is the way it is: one either loses Christ completely, or has him completely. He does not divide himself into pieces; with the whole heart, with the whole soul he wills to be loved and honored. Through these fanatics, however, the devil prepares the way for other heretics who will come and say that Christ is nothing, and has neither flesh nor divinity, as happened in the early days of Christendom. Now if this particular example does not move and convert them, and if it does not help others to guard against them and to detect and avoid their devil, then there is no more help for them; they want to be lost, but it is not my fault; their blood be on their own heads.[227] I have warned them enough.

Although no Christian man desires to know why it is useful to believe that Christ's body is present in the bread, but simply believes the words of God with fear and humility, we should like, nevertheless, to indicate certain benefits, not to instruct the fanatics—for they pay no attention, and are not even interested in learning—but because the devil mocks us through them. First, it is even a benefit that clever, arrogant spirits and reason be blinded and disgraced in order that the proud may stumble and fall and never partake of Christ's Supper; and on the other hand, that the humble may be warned and may arise and alone partake of the Supper, as St. Simeon says [Luke 2:34], "This child is set for the fall and rising of many in Israel." It is useful and good that arrogant, godless blasphemers be so cut off that they should not join in partaking of the holy sacrament, for one should not "throw to the dogs what is holy, nor pearls before swine" [Matt. 7:6]. Now the fanatics believe that nothing but bread and wine are present, hence it is surely so. They have as they believe, and so

---

226 Oecolampadius: "The true preachers must not be vexed [because of the new Lord's Supper doctrine]; for we teach and point to Christ the crucified, and turn men from the elements of this world to the heavenly things" [Col 2:20, 3:2]. *Reasonable Answer. St. L.* 20, 626. Cf. Bucer, *Preface*, E 5 *St. L.* 17, 1602.

227 Cf. Acts 18:6.

they eat nothing but bread and wine, and partake of the Lord's body neither spiritually nor physically. It is very good and useful that our possession should not be scattered among the unworthy but kept holy and pure among the humble alone.

In the second place, as we heard above,[228] Irenaeus and the ancient fathers pointed out the benefit that our body is fed with the body of Christ, in order that our faith and hope may abide and that our body also may live eternally from the same eternal food of the body of Christ which it eats physically. This is a bodily benefit, nevertheless an extraordinarily great one, and it follows from the spiritual benefit. For Christ surely will make even our body eternal, alive, blessed, and glorious, which is a much greater thing than giving us his body to eat for a short time on earth. Therefore he wills to be "in us by nature," says Hilary,[229] in both our soul and body, according to the word in John 6 [:56], "He who eats me abides in me and I in him." If we eat him spiritually through the Word, he abides in us spiritually in our soul; if one eats him physically, he abides in us physically and we in him. As we eat him, he abides in us and we in him. For he is not digested or transformed but ceaselessly he transforms us, our soul into righteousness, our body into immortality. So the ancient fathers spoke of the physical eating.

The third benefit, I hope, will be convincingly proved. For they must grant us that in the Supper we have God's words, namely these: "This is my body, given for you; this is my blood, poured out for you for the forgiveness of sins." So I ask them again whether God's Word is of any avail? If it is of no avail, why does the prophet Isaiah say in chapter 55 [:11], "God's Word shall not return empty, but shall accomplish that which avails"? Why does St. Paul call it in Romans 1 [:16] "the power of God for salvation to every one who has faith"? Why does he call it "the word of life," "the word of grace," "the word of salvation," "the word of wisdom," etc.? [230] Are life, grace, salvation, wisdom, strength, and power mere useless things? If so, what is useful?

---

[228] Cf. pp. 115 ff.
[229] Cf. p. 120, n. 198.
[230] Phil. 2:16, Acts 14:3, 20:32, 13:26, I Cor. 12:8.

Why do these great gentlemen rage so, and ask of what avail Christ's body is in the Supper, just as if it were nothing but a piece of beef, and remove the Word of God from their sight as if we had a Supper without God's Word? Who are the Capernaites and flesh-eaters here? We have God's Word in the Supper: this they must concede to us. But God's Word accomplishes what is good times without number; indeed, it does all things: it produces and strengthens faith, conquers sin, the devil, death, hell, and all evil; it makes us obedient to God, indeed, children and heirs; it glorifies God, it delights all angels and gladdens all creatures. But all this must also be in the Supper, because God's Word is in it.

"Yes," they say, "but we are not asking whether God's Word is of any avail, but what the body of Christ in itself avails in the bread; this, this, Luther—bite yourself with this!" When the mighty spirit asks this question one might lose heart on account of him. But if again I reply, "I will not let anyone separate the body of Christ from the Word," they would hiss and hoot at me. Well, suppose it is as they dream, that Christ's body is alone in the bread and no Word of God is there with it—though this is not possible; let us see what they gain. Why, they will run out of the rain and fall into the water![231] For if Christ's body is present without the outward Word of God, it cannot be present there without the inner, eternal Word which is God himself, John 1 [:1]. For this "Word became flesh" [John 1:14] and is in the flesh.

Now I ask, in turn, whether God himself may also be of some avail? To be sure, when he walked on earth, he availed to the extent that whomever he touched with his flesh, he helped. Through his body, with his physical voice, he called Lazarus from the grave [John 11:43]. He touched the leper and made him clean [Matt. 8:3]. He walked upon the sea, and stretched forth his hand to the sinking Peter and drew him to the land [Matt. 14:31], and all his acts were miracles and good deeds. It is also his character and nature to do good wherever he is. Why should he now be of no avail in the bread, when it is the same flesh,

[231] *So werden sie dem regen entlauffen und yns wasser fallen.* For this proverbial expression see Wander, *Deutsches Sprichwörter Lexikon,* III, 1582.

the same Word, and the same nature, and must be altogether good and useful?

They say,[232] "Yes, but one does not see or feel the usefulness." Good Lord, is this the flaw? To the fanatics, of course, he is of no avail. They would like to grope and feel for something in order to escape having to believe, like the flesh-eaters and Capernaites, who also would like to feel and bite into something. We who believe, however, know that the body does avail for us, wherever it is. If it is in the bread and is physically eaten with faith, it strengthens the soul by virtue of the fact that it believes it is Christ's body which the mouth eats, and so faith clings to the body which is in the bread. Now that which lifts, bears, and binds faith is not useless but salutary. Similarly, the mouth, the throat, the body, which eats Christ's body, will also have its benefit in that it will live forever and arise on the Last Day to eternal salvation. This is the secret power and benefit which flows from the body of Christ in the Supper into our body, for it must be useful, and cannot be present in vain. Therefore it must bestow life and salvation upon our bodies, as is its nature.

This I would want to say if it were possible that Christ's body alone were present in the Supper, without God's Word. This, however, is not the case, for there stand God's words, "This is my body," which grasp, comprehend, and give us physically the body of Christ; therefore the body of Christ must be useful through the Word. Indeed, even if it were true that Christ's flesh were merely a piece of beef, and yet God's Word were there bidding us to eat of it, it would nevertheless be useful on account of the Word. For example, Abraham received the promise of his son Isaac, who, however, was only flesh and a physical child. But Abraham was extolled as righteous by God because he believed he would have his son Isaac, Romans 4 [:22; Gen. 15:6]. Here the fanatics might also ask of what use Isaac was to Abraham's faith, and then they might say, "Isaac was nothing at all; the Spirit must be present, the flesh is of no avail."

And what would be surprising if Isaac—or beef—were useful, if it were embraced and presented in God's Word? Even the devil, death, sin, hell, and all kinds of trouble would be nothing but

[232] Cf. p. 77, n. 132.

benefit and advantage if they were presented to us as embraced in God's Word, and were believed by us. Now, death can be of benefit to me, in body and soul, if I have Christ's word which says, "Whoever loses his life for my sake will find it" [Matt. 16:25]; thus, through the Word, death must incite and strengthen my soul unto the righteousness and obedience of faith, and drive my body into life. If this is so, should not Christ's body, which in itself is pure life and salvation, and full of God, be just as useful to me through the Word as death, sin, and the devil? True, one does not feel and see this. But neither does one feel and see how the devil and death are useful through the Word. Faith feels it, however. My friend, come here and convince us that since death apart from the Word is of no avail but harmful, it must be nothing at all. For this is your argument, that whoever is of no avail is nonexistent, so that Christ's body also must be of no avail to you.

The result of this great and arrogant wisdom by which they scorn God's Word so shamefully, as Oecolampadius does in his blasphemous *Antisyngramma*,[233] is that they do not see the Word of God in the Supper, and simply gape and stare at the physical eating, thinking that the divine Word must set forth nothing but spiritual things and have nothing to do with outward, material things. But this is the seed of Münzer's and Karlstadt's spirit, who also wanted to tolerate nothing outward, until they were utterly drowned in flesh.

God inverts this order, however, and sets before us no word or commandment without including with it something material and outward, and proffering it to us. To Abraham he gave the word including with it his son Isaac [Gen. 15:4 ff.]. To Saul he gave the word including with it the slaying of the Amalekites [I Sam. 15:2 f.]. To Noah he gave the word including with it the rainbow [Gen. 9:8 ff.]. And so on. You find no word of God in the entire Scriptures in which something material and outward is

[233] This reply to the *Swabian Syngramma* was incorporated into Oecolampadius' *Apologetics*, 1526. "The outward word, though it represents, does not occupy the position of teacher; so far is it from being an object of faith, offering blood for us, bestowing upon us peace and the forgiveness of sins, and food and clothing. . . . The words and signs are given to us simply to admonish us to seek the realities, not that we may understand. . . . From words we learn nothing but words." *Apologetics*, O 5, cf. O 1 ff. See *WA* 23, 316.

not contained and presented. If we followed the fanatical spirits, we would have to say that all these material, outward things were of no avail and simply nothing. So too, here in the Supper, included with Christ's body crucified for us we have been given the word that it is present in order to be eaten physically. And this eating was to avail for the forgiveness of sins, as the words state, just as Isaac had to come forth bodily and become Abraham's son, as the words state, and as the rainbow had to appear materially, also as the words state.

But they must concede, these fanatics, that even in their spiritual eating something material is set forth. For Christ's body, even if it is at the right hand of God, is nevertheless a body and an outward, material thing having bone and flesh, which no spirit has—as he himself says in the last chapter of Luke [24:39], "A spirit has not flesh and bones as you see that I have." If they wish to be so much like Münzer, and not tolerate flesh and bone, then they must not eat Christ even spiritually, for they still are eating flesh and bone. What kind of distinction is that? Indeed, why is it any better for them to eat flesh and bone with their soul than to eat it with their mouth? If it is of no avail in the mouth, how can it be of any avail in the soul, since it is the same flesh and bone everywhere? But they want nothing but spirit; and indeed, this is what they do have: the devil, who has neither flesh nor bone.

Of course, on the subject that outward things are of no avail, I wrote carefully against Dr. Karlstadt[234] to explain the proper distinction: outward things apart from God's Word are of no avail, such as the pope's laws. But outward things connected with God's Word are salvation and blessedness, because they inhere in the Word and bind our faith, as I have just said concerning Isaac and the rainbow. Both of these are outward, material things, but since they are connected with the Word, Abraham had to attach his faith to the coming Isaac, who was embraced in God's Word. The devil along with his fanatics, however, so hates the Word that he always seeks to sever it from outward things, but God seeks to keep these unsevered, and connects them to each

[234] *Against the Heavenly Prophets. LW* 40, 146 ff.

other. What we say, that here we have something not merely outward but connected with the word, "This is my body," they do not hear, but rage past it like madmen, crying, "Outward things are of no avail, outward things are of no avail!" And they will not abandon this Münzerish spirit until they have caused trouble just as Münzer did. For since they have the very same spirit, I am afraid they will bring forth the very same fruit; as the tree is, so it bears fruit [Matt. 7:16].

From such a spirit it must follow that civil government is of no avail, being an outward thing, since men are unwilling to hear or see that it is embraced in God's Word and must be believed to be God's ordinance, Romans 13 [:1 ff.]. This belief indeed is not unavailing before God, and therefore this fanatical spirit must remain seditious and murderous. Now see, civil order is an outward thing, yet it binds our faith, and is also an article of faith on account of the word in which it is contained, Romans 13 [:1]: "All authorities that exist everywhere are of God." But this is of no help to fools until they knock their heads against it.

I should like to know, however, where they get the idea that there is a God, that God's Son is man, that one must believe, and all the other articles of our faith, which of course have never occurred to reason. Did they get these ideas from the Spirit before they physically and outwardly heard or read them? Here they must say No, I know full well, for they got them through the material, outward Word and Scripture. Then how can this outward Word, through which the Holy Spirit is given with all his gifts, be of no avail? Oh, in their blind arrogance they think they have Christ at the right hand of God, locked up in a closet, and do not believe that he is present in his Word and in the outward things of which his Word speaks. Therefore, as St. Paul says, "They do not understand either what they are saying or the things about which they make assertions, but wishing to be masters of the Scriptures, they have become vain babblers," I Timothy 1.[235] On another occasion we shall deal with this better and more fully.

Further, they say, "But what is the need for Christ's body to be present in the sacrament? Faith can be strengthened perfectly

[235] Luther quotes I Tim. 1:6 f. freely.

well without it, through the gospel which is preached."[236] This is true—but again we are trying to summon God to trial and shove under his nose the question why he is so concerned—or why we need him—to proffer us this Word and work of his! Is He trying to make fools out of us, as if we ourselves did not know as well as he what we need and he needs? Does he think, even though he is God, that he alone is wise, and is he trying to instruct us who are spiritual? If he has flesh and blood, we have the spirit; so, his flesh is of no avail but our spirit lives. We intend to sing him another song so he will get busy and think over the matter, and speak to us words and show us works we can see as needful. If not, our verdict is that he is a Capernaite, an Atreus, a Thyestes,[237] and a flesh-eater, and we shall see how he defends himself from our charge!

How do you like this spirit? Isn't he humble and reasonable, modest and thoughtful? He certainly leaves his invective and blasphemy back home at Basel,[238] and rebukes Luther excellently, doesn't he, when he scolds thus and snaps at everything![239] Who are the worst rebukers and snappers? Are they those who rebuke both our God and the people? Or those who alone rebuke the seducing spirits? This, to be sure, is to have a log in one's eyes and yet try to correct the speck in another's eye.[240]

---

[236] Oecolampadius: "Moreover, the bodily presence of Christ is not necessary. As our adversaries themselves admit, the soul receives this as often as the Word is preached in the gospel and received with faith. In the hearing of the Word through faith we can receive the body and blood of our Lord." *Reasonable Answer*. *St. L.* 20, 633.

[237] Oecolampadius deemed Luther's view "cruel, and like a Thyestean banquet." *Reply to Pirkheimer, c* 8. The epithet stuck, and recurred frequently in anti-Lutheran polemics. King Atreus of Mycenae, feigning reconciliation with his brother Thyestes, slew three of Thyestes' sons and served them in a banquet to their father. Cf. Aeschylus, *Agamemnon*, ll. 1555 ff.

[238] Oecolampadius had written: "My friend, if you wish to teach, leave your invective back at Wittenberg." *Reasonable Answer. St. L.* 20, 599. In the introduction (*St. L.* 20, 584), he declared that he would ignore Luther's unseemly behavior, and would "not forget the command of Christ, who forbids us to return reviling for reviling" [I Pet. 3:9].

[239] E.g. "Luther, you should not speak so censoriously with us. Well, if all you ever do is to turn your immoderate zeal into a venomous, hateful wrath, and yourself from a spiritual man into a fleshly one, although we patiently keep silence, the spiritually discerning will see clearly who it is that casts the stars down from heaven. They will see clearly who is the scarlet, blood-colored beast, and which heads have two horns" [cf. Rev. 12:3 f., 13:11, Dan. 8:3, 10]. *Reasonable Answer*. *St. L.* 20, 593.

[240] Cf. Matt. 7:3 f.

This is the second abominable blasphemy of Oecolampadius. For he who asks why something which God says and does is necessary surely is trying to elevate himself above God and be wiser and better than God. This is the real spirit of Münzer, who even said he would do a mess on both Christ and the Scriptures if they would not be governed by his spirit.[241] Immediately thereafter came Zwingli, and when he was confronted by the statement that in the Supper we eat Christ's body invisibly, in an ineffable manner, he went and screamed about Christ,[242] "O what a fine light of the world Christ then turns out to be! How well he enlightens us, if we cannot know how his body is eaten there in the bread!" Like Münzer, he is not far from doing a mess on Christ.

A man's heart might burst at such insolent prattle of the hellish devil and his fanatics. They demand to know how Christ's body is in the bread, else it is false to say that he is in it; and yet they cannot know, either, how it occurs that they can open their mouths, move their tongues, hold a pen in their hands, or even more trivial things, not to mention knowing how they see, hear, speak, and live physically. All such things we feel, and we are daily involved in them, yet we do not know how they occur; nevertheless, we wish to know how Christ's body is present in the bread, else we refuse to acknowledge Christ as our light and master!

Now even though it is not our obligation, we too would like to show for good measure why it is necessary for Christ's body to be present in the bread. Briefly, the first need is on God's side. For if it were not so, Christ would be a liar in his words, "Take, eat, this is my body, given for you." Here, you handsome devil, is the need! God is truthful; what he says he can do, and does [Ps. 33:4]. Since he says here, "This is my body," and refers with the word "this" to the bread, as the fanatics admit, his body must

---

[241] Cf. p. 70, n. 117.

[242] In the *Syngramma* the view was expressed that Christ's body is not crushed with the teeth, but is partaken in a certain ineffable manner. *St. L.* 20, 558 f., 565. Zwingli retorted: "O scanty, meager, obscure, secret letters, which lack any norm by which we may judge how Christ's body is eaten here! O Christ our light, why have you not enlightened us here?" ***Reply to Billican.*** *C. R.* 91, 901; cf. ***Clear Instruction.*** *LCC* 24, 219 f.

of necessity be present. The need for God to maintain his glory is an important matter, for he boasts that he is truthful and faithful. Meanwhile, we can readily believe that this need does not greatly concern the spiritual god of the fanatics, for *he* can easily assume that our fleshly and baked God is a liar, as he himself has been from the beginning, and that he does not keep or fulfil his words, as indeed is the case.

The second need is on the side of our faith. Faith in God's Word is necessary for us, because it has been spoken in order that we should believe it, and God wills and demands of us to have faith where his Word is. Now, there stand God's words, which embrace and comprehend the body of Christ, saying that he is present. Therefore as the Word and faith are necessary, so also is the body comprehended in the Word necessary for us, in order that our faith may be correct and consistent with the Word, because the two, Word and body, are not to be separated. And even if the body were separate and apart from the Word, it still would be necessary, because life and salvation are in it.

Of course, it is true that this might well take place apart from the sacrament.[243] It may also take place apart from the body of Christ which is at the right hand of God. Should Christ therefore not be at the right hand of God? Again, it may take place apart from the gospel, for who could hinder God if he had actually willed to redeem us, yet had decided not to have it preached and not to become man? Just as he created heaven and earth, and accomplishes all things continuously even now without outward preaching, and does not on that account become man: would the gospel therefore be nothing? But if it is his will to give salvation to you through the humanity of Christ, through the Word, through the bread in the Supper, who are you, insolent, thankless devil, that you dare to ask why he does not do it in a different way and without these means? Will you prescribe and choose means and measures for God? You ought to leap for joy that he does it in whatever manner he chooses, if only you obtain it. Don't you think I also could ask: Since the gospel and the remembrance of Christ can be had in all preaching, what then is the need of

[243] Oecolampadius: "To receive the spiritual gifts we do not need the Lord's bodily presence at all." *Reasonable Answer*. *St. L.* 20, 603.

celebrating a Supper in addition, and taking bread and wine in it? What is the need for anyone to read the Scriptures for himself? What is the need for anyone to admonish and comfort another individually, since all this can happen in regular public preaching? Aren't these childish, blind thoughts in such important matters? God means to fill the world and give himself to us in many different ways, to help and strengthen us by his Word and works; shall we be so complacent and bored that we hinder him, and tolerate nothing but the way that happens to please us? You are a black, hopeless devil! Enough said for now.

Now that the fanatics think they have won their case, they go and make out of the Supper a symbol,[244] i.e. a sign of remembrance, whereby Christians may be recognized outwardly, as beggars and Jews are recognized by the yellow badge.[245] They regard it simply as a symbol that Christians use among one another, without reference to God, whereby they practice and maintain love for one another. Such things inevitably followed from this spirit, for since they tear God's Word away from the bread and wine, and let nothing remain but eating and drinking, as in taverns, naturally God is not served by it at all, nor is our faith helped; but their observance makes gluttony and gourmandizing out of it. For what does God care about our eating and drinking, as he says in Jeremiah? [cf. 7:21]. What does it help our faith that the belly eats and drinks? It used to be said concerning parish fairs that they were held in order that friends might meet one another and friendships might be strengthened. So too, Christ's Supper here has been made into a parish fair.[246]

If one asks how they prove this, however, the answer comes: Oh, isn't it enough that we say so? As a matter of fact, he who finds the words of God hard to believe in this article is relieved of a great vexation by such prattle. But if we maintain our position that his words are true and Christ's body and blood are present in

---

[244] Cf. p. 48, n. 79.

[245] The prescription that Jews must wear a badge dates from the thirteenth century. The reference to beggars is not clear; perhaps Luther meant to refer "yellow badge" only to the Jews, and to imply that beggars also had their distinguishing emblems.

[246] Zwingli used the idea of a parish fair as a sort of analogy for the purpose of the Lord's Supper. Cf. *Commentary*. *LWZ* 3, 243, 238 ff.

the Supper, they must concede to us that the Supper is something more than a parish fair. But where his Word is torn away from the Supper and mere bread and wine are made of it, then I grant that they may make a parish fair or carnival of it. There is no difference. If they please, they may even make a dance or game of it. We don't care, just so long as we may stay away from their blasphemous and hateful supper.

We know, however, that it is the Lord's Supper, in name and in reality, not the supper of Christians.[247] For the Lord not only instituted it, but also prepares and gives it himself, and is himself cook, butler, food, and drink, as we have demonstrated our belief above. Christ does not say, in commanding and instituting it, "Do this as your summons to mutual recognition and love," but, "Do this in remembrance of me" [Luke 22:19, I Cor. 11:24]. If we are to do it in remembrance of him, then surely it is instituted in his service and in his honor. But with what do we serve him? With eating and drinking? In my opinion, we do it by strengthening our faith and learning to know him, as we have often taught. And no doubt will remain if we insist that his body and blood are present, as the holy fathers also describe these fruits of the Supper.

I hear it said, too, that this error pleases some adherents of the papacy, and that certain persons now hope to prove above all that the mass is a sacrifice, especially since some of the fathers call the sacrament a sacrifice, such as Irenaeus, Cyprian, and Augustine. And since they feel it is un-Christian to sacrifice Christ daily, who sacrificed himself once and neither can nor will be sacrificed again, they seize upon the bread and wine, and since nothing but bread and wine are supposed to be in the sacrament, they think that there is no further danger in regarding the mass as a sacrifice, and that now they may more easily earn a reward, since they supposedly sacrifice only bread and wine.[248]

---

[247] Cf. Zwingli: "The 'Eucharist,' then, or 'Synaxis,' or Lord's Supper, is nothing but the commemoration by which those who firmly believe that by Christ's death and blood they have become reconciled with the Father proclaim this life-bringing death, that is, preach it with praise and thanksgiving." *Commentary*. *LWZ* 3, 237. On *synaxis*, cf. *LW* 35, 50 f.; 36, 352.

[248] Perhaps an inference from such a passage as *Commentary*. *LWZ* 3, 234 ff., where Zwingli argues against a repetition of Christ's sacrifice [Heb. 9:12],

If that were true, it would serve them just right, that God's judgment may remain truthful, of which St. Paul speaks [II Thess. 2:10 f.], "God sends upon them a strong delusion, to make them believe what is false, because they refused to love the truth and so be saved," and Christ in John 5 [:43], "I have come in my Father's name, and you do not receive me; if another comes in his own name, him you will receive." Just so, these gentlemen also persecute and hate the gospel without end, hence they shall adopt fanaticism and falsehoods in its place.

But what if the mass should now disappear precisely for the reason by which you thought to uphold it, and what if you thus lost both gospel and mass through adopting this fanaticism, so that what you had left was neither faith for the soul nor reward for the belly? For if the common people felt that you were offering nothing but bread and wine for their sins in the mass, they would immediately pull back their hand and disavow both sacrifice and reward. For who would be so foolish as to have a piece of bread and a drink of wine given for his soul, especially in the New Testament, since we are redeemed by the precious blood of Christ, not by gold or silver, not by bread or wine? For the fanatics even entertain the hope that with this teaching of theirs they can utterly overthrow the mass along with the pope and all, and establish a great unity and equality among all Christians.

Let anyone who will, and in any way he will, regard the mass as a sacrifice; whether he considers it nothing but bread, or Christ's body, he will have to answer this: It is quite certain that Christ cannot be sacrificed over and above the one single time he sacrificed himself. Such daily sacrificing and the sale of such sacrifices for our sins, as used to be the custom and practice, the papists themselves now see, praise God! is the greatest blasphemy and abomination ever known on earth, and not one of the ancient doctors held, taught, or wrote any such thing. For Irenaeus[249] calls it a sacrifice in the sense that we offer bread and wine, which

---

yet insists that the Supper is essentially our commemorative act, and a sacrifice of believers to God. On the early patristic idea of a eucharistic sacrifice, cf. Sasse, *This Is My Body*, pp. 18 ff., 27 ff.

[249] *Against Heresies*, IV, 17, 5; 18, 1 and 6. *MPG* 7, 1023, 1029; *ANF* 1, 484, 486.

through God's Word becomes the sacrament, solely for the purpose of giving thanks, in order that we may acknowledge thereby how God feeds us, just as it was done in the Old Testament, but never for our sins or to redeem our souls or to propitiate God, as is the case when the papists celebrate mass. Some call it a sacrifice because we remember thus the one sacrifice which Christ once made for us, just as every year we call Easter "the Resurrection" or "Day of resurrection," and say, "Christ is risen today," not that Christ rises every year, but that every year we commemorate the day of his resurrection.[250] In this sense St. Augustine calls the sacrament a sacrifice. But he who refuses to believe may go his way, sacrifice and blaspheme until he is ready to stop; the truth on this topic has sufficiently come to light.

I should like herewith to request and admonish my respected fanatics, in order that we may soon come to the point and bring the discussion to an end, that they agree to pay the truth such deference as to avoid unnecessary details, answer us on the real central issues, and hold their position consistently. For example, to point it out once again: it is not necessary in this matter for them to teach us that Christ is seated at the right hand of God, having left the earth and ascended into heaven, and that our hearts should ascend thither and not cling to earthly things—and a host of other such arguments; for by God's grace we know all these things perfectly well. Rather, what is necessary is to prove convincingly how these two expressions are contradictory: THAT CHRIST'S BODY IS SEATED AT THE RIGHT HAND OF GOD, AND IS AT THE SAME TIME PRESENT IN THE SUPPER; how it may come to pass that God's power could become so weak as to be unable to accomplish this, and how all this may be overthrown by sound argument and clear Scripture. Here is where we should be instructed, here is the real need, to convince us that the words, "This is my body," are dark and obscure[251] and need to be understood otherwise than the way they read. Do you hear, dear gentlemen, what I ask—

[250] Augustine, *Letter 98, To Bishop Boniface*, 9. *MPL* 33, 363; *FC* 18, 137; cited by Zwingli in *Clear Instruction*. *LCC* 24, 234. "Christ is risen today!" was an ancient Easter greeting, and became the title of several medieval hymns, cf. p. 260, n. 161.

[251] Oecolampadius: "That your passage is obscure is obvious." *Reasonable Answer*. *St. L.* 20, 598. Cf. p. 113, n. 186.

where I stand—where I call? Friend, don't pass by and don't look down on me so haughtily, and don't sing some other song for me instead!

Similarly, you need not teach us that flesh is of no avail, and that we must eat, live, and do all things spiritually, and that without spirit nothing avails. This we realize already. We should like to know more, viz. how the saying, "FLESH IS OF NO AVAIL," is contrary to the saying, "CHRIST'S BODY IS IN THE BREAD"; again we should like to be assured that "FLESH IS OF NO AVAIL" is said concerning Christ's body; again, that Christ's body is a perishable, useless, corruptible food, though he himself says in John 6 [:27, 33] that it is an imperishable food which gives life; also, how in the Supper it is a perishable, useless flesh, whereas by nature and character it is an eternal food. Here, here, we cry; listen to us here! Explain, too, why the saying, "If anyone says to you, 'Look, here is the Christ!' or 'Look, there he is!'" [Mark 13:21, cf. Matt. 24:23], must be referred to the sacrament.[252] These and all the other things that you regard as the grounds for your fancy, make certain and clear to us. What you have worked out up to now is all in vain, and nothing is established by it; for you have said a great deal, indeed, but you have undertaken to prove nothing.

Zwingli, it is true, boasted[253] that he would press and squeeze out of the words, "This is my body" the sense, "This is the sign of my body." But there was one who stood by and watched how he worked the wine press, and observed that someone had played a trick on him and had filled the press with nothing but pebbles, painted the color of grapes. So the poor man pressed laboriously, yet nothing would come out, until the whole press, stones and all, collapsed on his head and crushed him. Truly, Christ's words do not submit to much pressing and squeezing. They are pebbles,

[252] Karlstadt had used this passage, *Dialogue. St. L.* 20, 2351; Luther commented on it in *Against the Heavenly Prophets. LW* 40, 219 ff. The Swiss also took up Karlstadt's argument, cf. Zwingli, *Clear Instruction. LCC* 24, 221.

[253] "We grant you that the sense of the Lord's words must be pressed out of these very words ['This is my body,' etc.], but with these presses or machines: 'The flesh is of no avail,' [John 6:63] and 'The Lord said to my lord: Sit at my right hand, until etc.' [Ps. 110:1]. Indeed, we deny that even one real, pure, and unmixed drop can be squeezed out of them unless you press with the weight of these and similar passages." *Reply to Billican. C. R.* 91, 899.

yes, real rocks, which dare not be handled by the godless with impunity, as he says in Matthew 22 [21:44], "He who falls on this stone will be broken to pieces, but when it falls on any one, it will crush him."

So too, if you wish to keep the fathers on your side, as you boast, and not completely disavow them, do not get into such a position that you simply gloss them at will, but press and squeeze their words well to see if they will yield such a meaning. You need not teach us that the sayings of the fathers may be twisted or turned this way or that, but show whether it is certain that they shall and must be so turned. Surely you see that we are perfectly familiar with your brand of wisdom, and have not the slightest desire for your intellectual mastery in the topics that we already know. Yes, we acknowledge and praise you as the finest of all teachers, but what you teach, one can easily understand without needing any faith. For anyone who cannot understand that bread is bread and wine is wine must certainly be a fool. But here is the trouble: you should prove that it is nothing but bread. St. Paul is not so fine a teacher, for he teaches what no man can understand; but his proof is so strong that he compels one to believe. This you do not do, but spend your time speaking about other subjects. But if you must flaunt your wisdom and if you imagine it helps the case, please do this: let the greater part of the talk deal with the main subject. Now I think I have given sufficient admonition as to what you ought to do. But what do you bet that it won't help? For I know this flighty, coy, slippery devil perfectly well.

Your boasting about your holy life and suffering, and your judgment that the Spirit of God has forsaken me,[254] we gladly let pass. Indeed, we poor sinners wish you might be still better than your boast, because we are certain that it is not only harmless but even salutary to us when there are faithful, holy people on earth; while we do not wish them harm, we appreciate them and, indeed, truly need them. But if in the future you wish to boast of your life even more, my request is that you be willing to back up your boast with deeds, and rebuke and correct your

[254] Cf. p. 21, n. 19.

followers for their wickedness,[255] and not approve their doing such great injury and injustice to others, lest your boast have to be regarded as lying and your holy life as hypocrisy.

Martin Bucer is one of the most eminent men among you, and a dear Christian brother and co-worker with Christ among you, who lauds you as saints already in this life.[256] This man translated our pastor John Bugenhagen's *Psalter* into Latin[257]—for by God's grace he has a great talent for language and translating. He has so corrupted this fine book with the poison of your doctrine of the holy sacrament that it is difficult to know what can be done about it, since this book has come into the hands of so many people, and now, under Master John's name and work, precisely the error is being sold which the latter so constantly combats with deed and word. Such a thing you holy people overlook, as if you were pleased with it, and you do not hold him responsible for retraction and restitution, though you know perfectly well how concerned Master John is and how deeply he has been offended by this piece of rascality.

Similarly, the best book I ever wrote, the *Postil*, which even pleases the papists, he has so revised with forewords, inserted words, and qualifying words[258] that under my name this blasphemous, shameful teaching has been spread and disseminated more widely, perhaps, than by all your books. What shall I do? How can I help the situation? I must act as if a dog had bitten me. I

[255] In the first Wittenberg Edition of Luther's works, 1548, a section beginning here and running through this paragraph and the next six was deleted as being too harsh again Bucer. For this deletion Melanchthon was likely responsible, but Sasse indicates that Luther shortly before his death had acknowledged he had spoken against Bucer too strongly. Sasse, *This Is My Body*, p. 319. Nicholas Amsdorf wrote a whole treatise in protest at the omission, and George Rörer wrote several paragraphs about it in the Jena Edition of Luther's works, Vol. 3, (1556). *St. L.* 20, 892 ff. Luther's passage was restored in the second Wittenberg Edition, 1551.

[256] In his *Apology*, A 6 ff., Bucer lauded the "solid piety and perfect saintliness" of Oecolampadius and Zwingli: "Certainly anyone who despises men who teach and do these things despises Christ." In *Preface* he declared that Luther must "either blaspheme the Holy Spirit or adore Christ in them." *St. L.* 17, 1604.

[257] Luther's pen slipped; in 1526 Bucer had translated into German Bugenhagen's Latin *Commentary on the Psalter*, 1524. Perhaps Luther was thinking of Bucer's Latin revision of Luther's German *Postil*, cf. n. 259, below. Bugenhagen published a protest against Bucer's tampering with his treatise.

[258] *Vorreden, unterreden und einreden.*

have denounced it in prefaces,[259] but what does that help? The devil saw clearly that this book was being disseminated everywhere. Therefore he seized it, and loaded and smeared it with his dung. So I, an innocent man, must now be the wagon driver of the devil's manure, whether I will or not. However, we suffer not at all, but walk on a bed of roses, and are revilers and brawlers! They, however, are pure holiness, though meanwhile they practice such venomous tricks and murderous thrusts which won't be healed. Really, if I were a Christian, I should prefer to have my neck cut off than to have someone play such tricks whereby I am forced by means of my book to spread this soul-poison unknowingly and unwillingly.

So enamored are these people and their devil with their error that they even propagate it by means of other men's books, just as if there were too few books by which they may now stun the world. What will happen after my death, when they do this during my life, while I sit here in Wittenberg looking on? Indeed, Martin Bucer would not have needed to teach me his dream and fancy about "the prize" and "the same food."[260] It is not so subtle a thing that I could not also have judged whether it commended itself to me. Besides, if he found fault with my exposition, he knew well enough where to correct me with Bible verses and books of his own, and it would not have been necessary so to disfigure my favorite book and thus inject his poison into men's hearts behind my back. Such things all pass among you for holy, virtuous Christian works. Shame on us intolerant people for protesting against it!

---

[259] In 1525-1526, just when he was coming to espouse the Swiss doctrine of the Lord's Supper, Bucer translated Luther's sermons on the Epistles and Gospels of the church year, the *Church Postil,* 1522 ff., into Latin. Luther was pleased with the earlier volumes of this translation, but in the fourth volume appeared a preface deploring Luther's vehemence and commending Zwingli and Oecolampadius, some notes to correct Luther's eucharistic interpretations, and finally, in a "Letter to the Christian Reader," a detailed criticism of Luther's 1525 sermon on the Epistle for Septuagesima, I Cor. 9:24–10:5 (*Sermons on the Epistles. LE* 8, 99 ff.; *WA* 17^{II}, 132 ff.). Luther sent a sharp letter of protest to the printer, John Herwagen of Strassburg. *S-J* 2, 377 ff., cf. *LW* 40, 332. Bucer defended himself in various writings, including an expanded republication of his *Preface* to the fourth volume of Luther's *Postil,* 1527.

[260] In the "Letter to the Christian Reader" mentioned above, Bucer expounded the words "prize" [I Cor. 9:24] and "the same food" [10:3].

With that this man Bucer is not satisfied. Master Philip Melanchthon must also serve as his target, when Bucer writes[261] unabashedly that Philip may now believe what he will, but that there was a time when he too taught clearly that nothing but bread was present in the Supper. You see, my friend, you see how these holy people besiege us and wish simply to drive and force us blind, spiritless flesh-eaters into their belief, as if their god could not come to his glory and uphold their belief without us Wittenbergers. I will not dwell upon that trick just now, although it deserves it, lest they seize the pretext of our intolerance to get off the subject and laud their own holiness. This is all we ask, that they remove such examples from their midst and not tolerate them, before they so hotly vindicate themselves and wipe their mouths. For it is unbecoming of holy people to display such arch-villainous examples and devilish tricks to their neighbors.

Paul says in Romans 2 [1:32] that not only those who do such things but also those who approve them deserve to die. If it concerned only our life, we poor, unholy, intolerant sinners would gladly keep quiet and endure these things from the great, virtuous saints; but it concerns our doctrine which is set forth by us before other people for the salvation of their souls. They get in ahead of us and befoul, poison, and infect it so that it does more harm through us than through their own books. Against this we surely have to protest a little. Whether people will now see what their vaunted holiness is, I can't help; it is Christ's responsibility, who says by their fruits shall trees be known [Luke 6:44].

Their faction also maligns me with the judgment that because I wrote against the peasants, the Spirit has departed from me, and that having become hardened, I cannot understand the clear truth.[262] Of course, this and other talk about myself I ignore, nor do I boast of my lofty spirit. Of great gifts and graces of my God and the Spirit, however, I do boast, I hope, quite fairly and

---

261 "Whatever may be his opinion now, Philip Melanchthon, that great paragon of erudition, wrote on this passage in his *Annotations on John* [1523], 'Christ is chewed by the Word, and therefore by faith, not by fleshly eating, service, sign, etc.'" *Apology*, 20. *WA* 23, 320.

262 This remark may refer to the sharp words expressed in Zurich over Luther's writings concerning the Peasants' War. Zwingli, *Letter to Vadian*, Oct. 11, 1525. *C. R.* 95, 382.

not without cause. And it does not seem to me so profound to understand that mere bread and wine may be on a table, which even a child and a fool understand perfectly well. I too see them every day in front of me on my table. But you, dear councilors at Basel and Strassburg, and all you who have such sacramentarian sects in your midst—may this talk of theirs give you fair warning not to put bags over your eyes, but to pay close attention to the game. Münzer is dead, but his spirit is not yet eradicated.

For what we are to make of this spirit who in a seditious way still comforts and exonerates the peasants and condemns me for writing against them, is easy to see. The devil does not sleep, but ever continues to spit fire. That is why I said above: This spirit is not good, and means no good through these fanatics, although I think the preachers against whom I write have no malice in mind. But dear God, they are not their own masters; the spirit has blinded and captured them. Therefore they are not to be trusted. For any spirit that does away with Christ's flesh is not of God, says St. John [I John 4:2 f.]. And he adds: Let there be a testing [4:1]. Now this spirit certainly does away with Christ's flesh, because he makes of it a useless, perishable, and altogether common flesh, like beef or veal, as we have heard. Therefore he cannot be honest. I warn, I counsel: Beware, watch out, Satan has come among the children of God!

Here I leave the matter for now, until they return. For the saying, "This is my body," still stands firm against all their fanaticism. This I have now upheld, praise God, with this book. God grant that they may be converted to the truth; and if not, that all they write may become cords with which to entangle themselves and fall into my hands. Amen.

CONFESSION CONCERNING CHRIST'S SUPPER

1528

Translated by Robert H. Fischer

INTRODUCTION

The long treatises of Zwingli and Luther which appeared simultaneously at the Frankfurt spring fair of 1527 brought the eucharist controversy to the boiling point. Zwingli's Latin work, *Friendly Exposition of the Eucharist Affair, to Martin Luther,*[1] his most carefully written treatise on the subject as well as his fullest to date—of approximately the same length as Luther's *"This Is My Body"*—is particularly important for depicting Zwingli's conception of faith and the Scriptures, and his mature view of John 6. It also contains his first extended discussion of Christology in relation to the eucharist, introducing the rhetorical figure alloeosis.[2] It consists chiefly of two parts. In the first and longer part Zwingli attacks Luther's views as expressed in the *Letter to Herwagen,* 1526, *Against the Heavenly Prophets,* 1525, *Adoration of the Sacrament,* 1523, and *The Sacrament—Against the Fanatics,* 1526; in the second, Zwingli analyzes the various scriptural accounts of the words of institution. His main positive emphasis is that *faith* is the true appropriation of Christ; a bodily eating of Christ in the sacrament not only adds nothing, but actually corrupts the purity of faith. A "mental or spiritual presence" of Christ in the sacrament is the most that can be affirmed. A crisp summary lists four errors of Luther: (1) that Christ's body, naturally eaten in the sacrament, strengthens faith; (2) that it also forgives sins; (3) that Christ's body is naturally brought into the sacrament by the reciting of the words of institution; (4) that the gospel is appropriated by the recipient, and the body and blood of Christ bestowed upon him.

A German popularization of this treatise, which Zwingli issued at the same Frankfurt fair, *Friendly Rejoinder and Rebuttal to the Sermon of the Eminent Martin Luther Against the Fanatics . . .,*[3] briefly recapitulates the polemical arguments. End-

---

[1] *C. R.* 92, 562 ff.
[2] Cf. p. 206, n. 63.
[3] *C. R.* 92, 771 ff.; *St. L.* 20, 1104 ff.

ing with the same four-point summary, it urges the reader simply to love God and not worry over theological subtleties: this point was not greatly exalted by the early Christians, for they never made it into an article of faith.

Zwingli no doubt sincerely meant his treatises to be "friendly," as he called for a sense of responsibility before God, an end to the scandal of disunion, and the formation of a common front against Romanism. He wrote, however, in a condescending, schoolmasterish tone, and inserted a number of barbed comments. Much sharper yet was the letter which Zwingli sent to Luther with the two treatises on April 1.[4] This begins by rebuking Luther for his self-contradiction and arrogance, but then appeals for unity against the papists and urges Luther to give up his vain notion of a bodily presence in the sacrament; the most Zwingli can acknowledge is that Christ is present to the believer "by contemplation alone." The Wittenbergers, of course, were only embittered by Zwingli's "raging, foaming and threatening."[5]

The Swiss and the Strassburgers received Luther's treatise, *"This Is My Body,"* with similar anger and contempt. In a letter of May, 1527, to Luther's friend, Andreas Osiander, Zwingli declared that "Luther's whole book consists of lies, slanders, deceit, and distortions," and boasted that he would so answer that not a single soldier out of Luther's great hosts of words would emerge unscathed; within three years Italy, France, Spain, and Germany would come around to the Swiss view.[6] Urged on by the Strassburgers, Oecolampadius and Zwingli produced German treatises, both of which appeared in June: *That Dr. Martin Luther's Misunderstanding of the Everlasting Words, "This Is My Body," Is Untenable. The Second Reasonable Answer of John Oecolampadius,* and *That These Words of Jesus Christ, "This Is My Body Which Is Given For You," Will Forever Retain Their Ancient, Single Meaning, And Martin Luther With His Latest Book Has By No Means Proved or Established His Own and the Pope's View. Ulrich Zwingli's Christian Answer.*[7] Oecolampadius, restating his position

---

[4] *WA*, Br 4, 184 ff.

[5] *S-J* 2, 398.

[6] *C. R.* 96, 129 f. Osiander published the letter with a retort.

[7] Zwingli's treatise in *C. R.* 92, 805 ff.; *St. L.* 20, 1122 ff.

as positively as possible, goes so far as to acknowledge a "sacramental presence" of Christ—to faith alone. Zwingli's rebuttal of Luther is much more bitter and negative. Closely following the sequence of Luther's treatise, Zwingli concentrates on Christ's ascension to the right hand of God, and John 6:63, in order to prove that a real presence of Christ in the sacrament is absurd and useless. He devotes considerable space to the principles of Scripture interpretation and to the two natures of Christ. Zwingli's summary of Luther's errors now numbers six items: (1) that Christ's body is everywhere, like his divinity; (2) that Christ invites us to find him in this sacrament; (3) that Christ's body, physically eaten, forgives sin; (4) that Christ's flesh is a wholly spiritual flesh; (5) that Christ's body, physically eaten, sustains our body until the resurrection; and (6) gives or increases faith.

The year 1527 was one of the most difficult in Luther's life. During the summer he experienced not only the most excruciating spiritual torments, but also so sudden and severe an attack of illness that he expected to die,[8] and his recovery was very slow. In August the plague struck Wittenberg, and when the university moved to Jena, Luther, who remained behind with Bugenhagen, was burdened with extra pastoral duties. In great discomfort his wife was expecting another child in December, and near that time his little son Hans fell ill. Meanwhile other demands were crowding in on Luther: the Elector was demanding his assistance with the church visitation of Saxony, he was trying to proceed with his translation of the Old Testament prophets, he was called to settle a feud between John Agricola and Melanchthon, and he had to write a letter against Karlstadt's latest trouble-making activity. It was not until November that the treatises sent by the Swiss reached him, accompanied by another vitriolic letter from Zwingli, though it is quite possible he had seen Amsdorf's copies shortly before. In December he set to work on a full and final rebuttal, and despite an interruption to write a tract, *Concerning Rebaptism*,[9] he labored on it with such astonishing concentration that he had his "Great Confession" in the press by February, 1528, easily in time for the spring fair.

---

[8] Cf. *S-J* 2, 404 ff.

[9] *LW* 40, 229 ff.

Luther's *Confession Concerning Christ's Supper*, intended to be his last word on the subject, is divided into three parts. In Part I, following the sequence of Zwingli's and Oecolampadius' recent treatises, Luther warns his readers against the fanatics. Against Zwingli (pp. 163-252) Luther deals first with several minor points (pp. 163-206), attacking Zwingli's figurative interpretation of the Bible texts and his contention that Luther's view contradicts both the Creed and Scripture. Though Zwingli, who was self-conscious over his familiarity with classical grammar and rhetoric, had referred in his treatises to more than a dozen kinds of figure of speech, Luther now takes pains to argue that Zwingli's figurative exegesis is even grammatically unsound. Next, Luther comes to grips with Zwingli's two main arguments. In the dispute over the meaning of "the right hand of God" (pp. 207-235), Luther rejects Zwingli's alloeosis concept, and expounds his own view of the union of natures in the person of Christ. Luther summarizes his approach in four points: (1) Jesus Christ is in essence and nature true God and true man in one person; (2) the right hand of God is everywhere; (3) God's Word does not deceive us; (4) objects can be present at a given place in other ways than the "local" mode which Zwingli recognizes.[10] Here Luther develops his doctrine of the ubiquity of Christ's glorified body. He comes near to implying that his literal interpretation of Christ's words of institution rests upon this philosophical theory, but in the last analysis he is saved from this conclusion by his view of the relation between Christian faith and all human explanations of that faith: as it has been finely said, "The believer approached the sacrament in faith—not faith in the ubiquity of the body of Christ but faith in the promising God." [11]

The interpretation of John 6:63 was Zwingli's second main topic. Once more in an important discussion of "spirit" and "flesh" (pp. 235-252), Luther defends himself against alleged errors, and reiterates his rule that Christ's flesh cannot be meant where Scripture places spirit and flesh into contrast.

Next Luther turns to Oecolampadius (pp. 252-288), particularly

---

10 See p. 214.

11 Jaroslav Pelikan, *Luther the Expositor* (companion volume to *LW* 1-30), p. 142 f.

to his *Second Reasonable Answer*, dealing with him more respectfully than with Zwingli, but rejecting his arguments no less decisively. Luther then devotes a few paragraphs to refuting Caspar Schwenkfeld and Valentine Krautwald (pp. 288-294), the Silesians who had proposed another "spiritual" interpretation of the sacrament. He follows with an excursus on "Identical Predication" (pp. 294-303), opposing John Wycliffe, whose support Capito and Zwingli had claimed. Luther attacks the assertion that two substances cannot ever be one substance, arguing chiefly on the basis of the biblical mysteries of the Trinity and the Incarnation, but also on the ground that "logic must first seek the aid of grammar," as a synecdoche unites diverse beings into one entity.

In Part II (pp. 303-360) Luther carefully examines the four biblical texts of the Lord's Supper one by one. Oecolampadius had already done the same in *Apologetics*, and Zwingli likewise in *Friendly Exposition*. Luther concludes that the texts singly and together require a literal rather than a figurative exegesis. A penetrating discussion of I Cor. 11:26 ff. and 10:16 ff. deals with the meaning of "communion" and of worthy and unworthy reception, based once again on the conviction that it is God himself who comes to us in the Supper, not we who approach him, and that when he meets us a decision inevitably is made, for him or against him.

In Part III (pp. 360-372) Luther declares his intention to confess all the articles of his faith in opposition to the sacramentarian heresy and all others, so that neither during his lifetime nor after his death would these people be able to claim that Luther agreed with them. The result is a remarkable little gem, which not only was printed and circulated separately at the instigation of Luther's friends, and even issued with hostile glosses by the Romanist Jerome Dungersheim, but also influenced the formulation of the Schwabach Articles in 1529, and hence in turn the Augsburg Confession. It is modeled on the Apostles' Creed, with a discussion of the foundations of Christian ethics woven into the treatment of the second article, and a discussion of evangelical church practice in opposition to Romanism woven into the third.[12]

[12] Most recently this third part of Luther's treatise was published separately in *MA*[3] 4, 285 ff.

The "Great Confession" remains the most detailed and the most profound of Luther's treatises on the Lord's Supper. In later controversies on the subject it stood forth, as the Weimar editor has dubbed it, as "the shibboleth of the genuine Lutherans."[13] In the Formula of Concord it was quoted more often and more extensively than any other treatise of Luther, and not only on the Lord's Supper but also on the person of Christ.

This treatise was indeed his last published word on the controversy, until under provocation from Schwenkfeld he took up his pen once more in 1544, to indicate in his *Brief Confession on the Holy Sacrament*[14] that he still maintained the same views. He paid no attention to the lengthy and bitter rebuttals by Oecolampadius and Zwingli, which, hastily written for the autumn fair and printed together in one volume, added nothing essentially new to the controversy: *Concerning Dr. Martin Luther's Book Entitled "Confession": Two Answers, by John Oecolampadius and Ulrich Zwingli.*[15] Nor did he take notice of the host of lesser treatises that continued to appear against him.

So the controversy stood at the end of 1528. One important development, however, had taken place. Martin Bucer wrote in a letter to John Comander: "As soon as Luther published his great confession on the holy Supper, I began to realize that he by no means taught a local inclusion of Christ in the bread, or any such conjoining of Christ with the elements, which would be unworthy of Christ either as true man or as reigning in heaven."[16] Bucer "began to ponder a concord," and later in 1528 he published a *Dialogue* as his first cautious step in that direction. He was not converted to Luther's view, but he was becoming convinced of the possibility as well as the urgency of an agreement, and he energetically advised Philip of Hesse to bring about a colloquy between the adversaries. Philip had proposed such a meeting in 1527, but Luther had turned it down. Now Philip renewed his efforts and succeeded in arranging the Marburg Colloquy in October, 1529.

---

[13] *WA* 26, 249.
[14] *WA* 54, 141 ff.
[15] Zwingli's treatise in *St. L.* 20, 1228 ff.; Oecolampadius' in *St. L.* 20, 1378 ff.
[16] Quoted in *WA* 26, 247.

The translation in this volume is based on the printed text, along with extensive fragments of Luther's original manuscript, in *WA* 26, 261-509. In the preparation of the translation the text and notes in *CL* 3, 352-516, *EA* 30, 151-373, and *St. L.* 20, 894-1105 were compared. An English translation of Luther's *Confession Concerning Christ's Supper* appeared in a remarkable little volume entitled *Luther on the Sacraments* (Newmarket, Virginia: Henkel Press, 1853). Two sermons preached on the Second Day of Christmas, 1527 (*WA* 23, 733-741) contain ideas set forth by Luther in the treatise which follows.

CONFESSION CONCERNING CHRIST'S SUPPER

Praise and thanks be to God forever through Jesus Christ our Lord, that the book which I published last year against the fanatics and enemies of the holy sacrament[1] has borne no little fruit. In the first place, many faithful hearts which had been confused and unsettled by the fanatics' worthless words have been set at peace, and now give thanks to God with great joy, as they frankly acknowledge to me in writing. Secondly, I have dealt Satan such a square and solid blow that now he has really become raving mad against me. This is well shown by the spirit's most recent answer[2] against my little book. Published some time ago, it finally reached me at Wittenberg on St. Martin's Day. Perhaps it feared the plague.[3]

God help us, how wrathful these heroes are! Not only do they forget their moderation of which they so dearly love to boast against me, and which they would still like to maintain[4]—though there is no adder so poisonous as they are in these writings—but they smart so keenly with pain and rage that they cannot see what they should reply, or against what. Especially Zwingli's spirit, who stirs in a great deal about images, purgatory, veneration of saints, the keys, original sin,[5] and goodness knows what other crazy new doctrines, for no other purpose than to spew out a lot of words where none are needed, and leap over the points where an answer is needed, as I shall show.

---

[1] I.e. the first treatise in this volume, *That These Words of Christ, "This Is My Body," etc., Still Stand Firm Against the Fanatics*, 1527.

[2] Zwingli's rebuttal, *That These Words of Jesus Christ, "This Is My Body . . .," Will Forever Retain Their Ancient, Single Meaning. . . . Ulrich Zwingli's Christian Answer*, 1527. See the Introduction.

[3] St. Martin's Day was November 11. On the course of the plague in Wittenberg, see Luther's correspondence and other letters from August 2 to November 19, 1527, in *S-J* 2, 409 ff.

[4] *Christian Answer. C. R.* 92, 810; *St. L.* 20, 1126. Cf. p. 22, nn. 21, 25.

[5] *Christian Answer. C. R.* 92, 819 ff.; *St. L.* 20, 1131 ff.

For this reason I am through with them. I shall write no more to them, lest Satan become still more frantic and spew out still more lies and follies, as he has been doing, besmearing paper uselessly and depriving the reader of time for reading something better. For if with my former book I have been unable to elicit a correct answer, though I specified so often, even with capital letters,[6] what I wish answered, I have no hope of obtaining an answer even if I should write a thousand books. And yet we cannot hold this against Satan, for a liar dare not toy with the truth! May the merciful God convert them and free their minds from the snares of the vicious devil. More than this, however, I cannot do. Alas, I fear I must have been a true prophet when I wrote that no arch-heretic will be converted.[7] So now I will let them go their way, according to the teaching of St. Paul in Titus 3 [:10]: "Shun a heretic, after he has been admonished once or twice." For they will not amend as time goes on. They have shown what they are capable of doing; I for my part shall devote myself to our people and instruct them further in this article as much as I am able through Christ's grace.

Through my two little books, the one against the heavenly prophets, the other against the fanatics,[8] I have written quite enough for all intelligent Christians, so that everyone who wants to avoid error and has not been bitten so far by the fanatical spirit will find help in them to resist the seducers, no matter how much the latter cry victory. Nevertheless, in order to strengthen the weak and better to expound this article, I wish to publish this little book as my last word on this subject. For I see, yes, I must realize that when Satan gives such a clumsy answer and spews out such worthless words, his purpose is to hinder me from dealing with other matters about which he is much more concerned. Therefore it no longer seems fitting for me to waste time with his buffoonery and neglect the Holy Scriptures.[9] Let him continue to spew forth as much as he pleases.

[6] Cf. p. 144.
[7] Cf. pp. 19 ff.
[8] *Against the Heavenly Prophets,* 1524-1525. *LW* 40, 79 ff., especially Part II; and the aforementioned, "*This Is My Body.*"
[9] Luther was currently engaged in translating the Old Testament prophets. See the Introduction. See also p. 101, n. 162.

Three things, however, I propose to do in this little book. First, to warn our people by showing that this fanatical spirit has completely failed to answer my arguments. Secondly, to analyze the scriptural passages which teach of the holy sacrament. Thirdly, to confess all the articles of my faith in opposition to this and every other new heresy, so that neither during my lifetime nor after my death will they be able to claim that Luther agreed with them—as they have already done in certain instances.

In the first place, let every faithful Christian be warned against the enemies of the sacrament, for the reason that this sect from the very beginning has had so many factions and leaders who are at odds among themselves over this text, "This is my body given for you." Such dissension and factionalism cannot and does not come from the Holy Spirit. It certainly comes from the very devil himself, as I have shown in my last treatise.[10] For the text must be quite unambiguous and plain, and must have one single, definite interpretation if it is to form the basis of a clear and definite article of faith. But they have a great diversity of interpretations and texts, each interpretation contradicting the others. Meanwhile, no one is sure of his interpretation, and no one is ever able to prove his interpretation and refute the others. It follows, therefore, that all of them err, and to this very day not one of them has the text in this topic, and thus the whole crowd must celebrate the Supper without a text. For an uncertain text is as bad as no text at all. Now what kind of Supper can that be, in which there is no text or sure word of Scripture? For Christ's words must be sure and clear, otherwise one simply does not have them. We, however, have a text and interpretation that is quite sure, and we take the plain words just as they stand, and we are not at odds over them.

To this they reply:[11] There is no harm if their words or interpretations vary, because they still agree on what matters most, viz. that only bread and wine are present. They offer such comparisons as these: In the Gospels Christ sets forth the essence of

---

[10] Cf. pp. 16 ff. and p. 42, n. 68. Cf. also *Answer to the Christians at Reutlingen,* 1526. *WA* 19, 121 f.

[11] From here to p. 252 Luther follows the sequence of Zwingli's *Christian Answer.* The reference here is to *C. R.* 92, 825 f.; *St. L.* 20, 1135 f.

the gospel in a variety of ways: in John 4 [:14], by the drinking of water; in John 6 [:51], by eating his flesh and drinking his blood; again, by the householder who hires laborers in his vineyard, Matthew 22 [20:1 ff.], etc. By a great variety of parables the one kingdom of God is set forth in the gospel; therefore, they say, it is not improper that the fanatical spirit also should have a variety of interpretations and words about one and the same matter. How does that sound to you? Isn't this admirable consistency? Who does not see here that this miserable spirit either is unwilling to answer, on account of his great arrogance, as if he scorns our question, or else is so completely stark stone blind that he does not see what the question is or what he should answer? Who asked him to come up with such an answer? Who asked him to teach us how one and the same subject may be presented through a variety of interpretations, expressions, illustrations, and figures? All this we knew already, better than he can ever teach us. I am perfectly aware that not only many but indeed all the figures of speech in the Scriptures refer to Christ, the one and only Savior. He is called a lamb, a rock, a cornerstone, sun, morning star, wellspring, bridegroom, householder, teacher, father;[12] indeed, each and every expression points to him and speaks of him, each in its own way. As if we were arguing here how one thing may have many names and signs, or as if there were anyone who doubted it!

This, however, is what he should answer; this is what we have asked: How does it happen among the fanatics that a particular name, term, or meaning, applied to a particular subject, can disagree with itself, so that one says Yes, the other No? Karlstadt says *touto* refers to the body seated there. Zwingli says the same *touto* refers to the bread. Now both cannot be true. One must be a liar and the devil's teacher. For in a single expression it is impossible for a single name or term to have at the same time two contrary interpretations and meanings. In the single passage in John 1 [:29], "Behold, the lamb of God," I cannot say that "lamb" may mean at the same time a sheep and a wolf, or at the same time a sheep and not a sheep. Yet over the single word

[12] John 1:29, I Cor. 10:4, Eph. 2:20, Mal. 4:2, Rev. 22:16, John 4:14, Eph. 5:23, Matt. 20:1, John 13:13, Isa. 9:6.

touto Karlstadt, Oecolampadius, and Zwingli disagree; one says, "It means this," and the other says, "No, it means something else." Again, Zwingli says, " 'Is' means 'represents' or 'signifies' ";[13] Oecolampadius says, "No, it means simply 'is.' " Again, Oecolampadius says, "My body means 'sign of my body.' " Zwingli says, "No, it means simply 'my body.' " Here, here they should answer and reconcile this disunity, so that the devil may not need to be so pilloried and so publicly exposed in his lies. But it is probable that they will never get around to answering this.

Although a passage of Scripture calls Christ a lamb and speaks of him as a lamb, in no passage does it contradict and deny this and repudiate itself. If in one place he is called a lamb, this does not prevent his being called in another place a rock or a stone, nor is there any disagreement there. But here the fanatical spirit slaps his cheeks and gives contradictory interpretations not only to various terms, but also to a single term at one and the same time within a single passage. The lies would not be so crude and the disgrace so great if they gave discordant and dissimilar interpretations to a single word in different passages, or dissimilar interpretations to various words in a single passage. But when they give dissimilar and contrary interpretations to a single word in a single passage, in a single sentence, they are (if you will pardon the expression) soiling themselves and clapping the devil naked into the pillory. For no language speaks in that manner. A child would have to say that it is impossible. For if I say, "Christ is the Lamb of God," it is impossible that one person should understand lamb to mean a wolf, another a sheep; one of the two must be lying, and both opinions cannot come from the Holy Spirit. The fanatics, indeed, have nearly ten different interpretations of the words of the Supper, and no one agrees with the others on what these words mean. Surely we are dealing here with nothing but pure lies and devils and no good spirit.

The false spirit, however, accuses us too of not adhering to the words and to a single interpretation, because we say that the words, "This is my body," are to be interpreted thus: "under the

---

[13] *Deutet* (also *bedeutet*). Cf. p. 34, n. 48.

bread is my body," or "in the bread is my body," etc., and hence we ourselves are also divided. I answer: The lying spirit surely is aware that he is treating us unfairly here, and spewing out such words only to vilify us and to set his lies into a more favorable light in the eyes of his followers. He knows very well what we fight for with all our power: that these words, "This is my body," shall be interpreted as they stand and as they read, in the simplest possible way, and that we shall not make diverse and contradictory texts out of one text, as they do. I have rightly said in my little book[14] that those who say, in common everyday language, "Under the bread is Christ's body," or, "in the bread is Christ's body," are not to be condemned, for with such words they confess their belief that Christ's body is truly present in the Supper. But thereby they make no new text, nor do they intend that these words of theirs should be regarded as the text, but they hold to the single text. Paul says, "Christ is God," Romans 9 [:5], but in II Corinthians 6 [5:19], "God was in Christ," and yet the two Scripture passages are simple and definite, each in its own sense, and not contradictory. But the fanatics' text is discordant within a single passage and a single expression.

If they wish to press us so closely and make so much depend on the expression, or if it be proved that it is incompatible with the text, "This is my body," to say elsewhere, "In the Supper there is Christ's body," then we are ready and willing to retract the expression and say purely and simply, "This is my body," as the words stand. Let them do likewise, and agree on the text. Although no Christian will so constrain us that in all our sermons and discourses, whenever we are speaking about the Supper, we must be limited to saying, "This is my body," provided that in the administration of the Supper we let the text remain as it is and in its place. On other occasions and in other expressions there will surely be no objection to our saying, "Under the bread," or, "in the bread is Christ's body," or, "Christ's body is truly in the Supper," else we should not be permitted to speak about our faith at all. But the fanatics talk drivel to patch up their ragged cloak. They are keenly aware that when it comes to their own

[14] See p. 41, n. 66, and p. 65.

lies concerning a single passage and expression, it is a quite different matter, and thus they try to defend rather than renounce their disunity. But this will not do. Of course we grant them also the right to speak elsewhere about the sacrament in whatever terms they find pleasing or fitting. But we want the text of the Supper to be unambiguous, simple, sure, and certain in every word, syllable, and letter. Since they refuse, I make bold to say that the devil, the father of all dissension, is their teacher. For St. Paul says, "God is not a God of dissension" [I Cor. 14:33]. So also all Christians are of one mind, Ephesians 4 [:3], and do not cause schism, I Corinthians 1 [:10]. Thus you recognize this spirit from the first fruits of their dissension.

Moreover, where Scripture assigns to one object various names or expressions, these are not only in perfect agreement and never contradictory, but also are sure and well-grounded, so that one can take his stand upon them. For example, where Christ is proclaimed as a lamb, there I am certain and sure that he is properly and rightly called a lamb. But none of the fanatics can make his interpretations certain. Karlstadt to this day has not proved that his *touto* may bear the meaning he assigns to it, as they themselves acknowledge. Zwingli and Oecolampadius, however, have never yet undertaken with a single letter to show that they intended to prove how "is" may be the same as "represents," and "body" the same as "sign of the body." They simply assert it as their own word and interpretation, of which they themselves are uncertain, nor do they care enough for anyone else to try to make it certain.

Therefore the fanatical spirit should not teach us here that in the Scriptures the expression, "kingdom of God," may bear diverse interpretations, but should prove that such interpretations are contradictory and uncertain; as we on our part prove our complaint that their erroneous, false interpretations are not only diverse but also contradictory and uncertain. Isn't this a fine answer? If I attack their disunity and uncertainty, he replies in terms of diversity, just as if diversity and disunity were the same thing. I ask: How is it that their interpretations and meanings are not only diverse but also discordant and contradictory? and he answers: It is not wrong for them to be diverse. We are supposed to be satisfied with that, and confess our error, and acknowledge their faith as correct! When will we be given an explanation, how the disunity in such diversity can come from the Holy Spirit? Here no one is at home. If we are to side with them, they must surely remove this stumbling-block of disunity and first reach unity and certainty about the text and interpretation. Otherwise we are quite right in shying away from them, and we say, "The devil is lurking in the hedges!" For to remove such a stumbling-block would be more important than smashing images. Images would not hinder us. But disunity in interpretation and expression—that is the very devil.

Even if they had completely won their point and stopped our mouths, the most they would have accomplished to advance their cause would have been to deprive us of our interpretation of this text, "This is my body." But this would not yet have proved their interpretation, nor can they ever in the future prove it. If there were a right spirit among them, he would not only remove the false interpretation, but would also produce and establish in its place another which is true and irrefutable. Even if St. Paul with all his might had abolished the righteousness of the law or of works, he would have accomplished nothing by it, unless he had also taught and established another righteousness in its place. God did not abrogate the old testament until he instituted in its place the new testament, and made it much more certain than the old. It is no good spirit that teaches and asserts, "This is a lie," but fails to replace it with a sure truth. It is not right to brand something as a lie, and yet have neither the knowledge nor the will to identify the conqueror of the lie, viz. the truth. Whoever wishes to overthrow lies mightily must replace them with totally obvious, certain, and irrefutable truth. For a lie fears not nor flees until the clear, irrefutable truth comes. It gladly remains in darkness, far away from the truth. If then our interpretation of these words, "This is my body," is false, it is Zwingli's obligation to substantiate and prove irrefutably his interpretation and text, viz., "This signifies my body." Likewise Oecolampadius and all the others, each his own. But when will they do that?

Indeed, I wish to say further: Since they cannot substantiate or prove their interpretation and text, it is certain that they have no right positively to decry our interpretation and text as false. For as it is said: who can surely and positively brand something a lie, if he cannot produce the opposite truth? Who can censure the wrong, if he does not on the contrary prove the right? It is ever the light that must reprove the darkness; one darkness does not reprove the other, neither does Beelzebub drive out any devil.[15] Of this the fanatical spirit is well aware, so he runs about, as a cat runs around the hot broth, retorts furiously that our text and interpretation are not correct, and yet shies away from and flees the Word of God like the devil, to avoid being forced to prove that his text and interpretation are correct. For he is well aware that he cannot do it. Therefore he thinks that the subject should be left at this point, where he abolishes the text of the Supper according to our interpretation but produces no other sure one in its place. No! That will not do! If you wish to tear down, then build up again. If you wish to warn of error, then teach the sure truth in its stead, or else quit playing the master and teacher. For thus you admit your own defeat and acknowledge that you are a false lying spirit, because you brand something false whose opposite you cannot and will not establish as true and certain. The Holy Spirit, however, knows quite nicely how to prove and establish the opposite, when he reproves lies or errors.

Let this be written to you as a warning, then, my dear friends and brothers, for you can recognize this spirit by the way he shies away from the light. He is a useless prattler where speaking is not needed, and flits and flutters all around where it is needed. As I have also said in my previous book,[16] you need not expect him to meet you squarely with an open rebuttal or argument. Instead, just as he has done in this first rejoinder, so he does in almost all the others, as we shall hear. Therefore beware of them, or attack them boldly at the point of this disunity and uncertainty in their expression and interpretation, and firmly demand that they furnish you a correct, definite, consistent text with these words, "This is my body." If they do this, then boldly side with them, and I will admit defeat. But since they do not do this, they must be in the wrong, and must be heretics, fanatics, deceivers;

[15] Cf. Matt. 12:25 ff.
[16] E.g. pp. 35 ff.

and further, they must be deemed defeated, no matter how stubborn and proud they are. For even if their main point and their error were right and true, nevertheless one must have a single, correct, definite, consistent text; for upon indefinite, discordant, contradictory texts nothing can be built. Thus my first rebuttal still stands, that this sect has so many conflicting leaders, as a sign that Satan is their master and guiding spirit.

Secondly, I requested[17] that they prove to us out of Scripture that the word "is" means the same as "represents" in the Supper. In my treatise I had shown that the fanatical spirit in previous writings did indeed cite several verses from Scripture in which "is" was said to mean "represents," but that this was his own imagination and he had not yet proved it. Therefore I requested that he should do it now, and prove his silly "representation."[18] His citing of Scripture verses is not particularly necessary for us. We are perfectly familiar with such verses, even without his introducing them, such as, "Christ is the rock" [I Cor. 10:4], etc. But we do not recognize any representation there, and we requested that the examples be produced. So now he continues in the same vein, and cites more verses, such as, "John is Elijah," "Christ is a vine," etc. [Matt. 11:14, John 15:1]. This done, he chatters loud and long, playing with his own words, and draws his conclusion without any Scripture, saying, "Here we have a representation or metaphor, for John is not Elijah, but represents Elijah."[19] There you see again that he does not want to prove how "is" should mean "represents." True, he says it means "represents." But who asks what he says? We already know that he says so. But he should prove from Scripture that he is correct.

He himself is perfectly aware that his chattering is pure twaddle. (He takes great pains to speak bad German, though without such pains his German would be bad enough.) He acknowledges it is not his intention to insist that because "is" has been understood in some passages in the sense of "represents," it must necessarily be so understood here in the Supper. Nevertheless, he argues, since other passages of Scripture and the Creed

---

17 Cf. pp. 30 ff.

18 *Deuteley*. Cf. p. 36, n. 54.

19 *Christian Answer*. *C. R.* 92, 863 ff.; *St. L.* 20, 1157 ff.

do not permit the words of the Supper to bear our old interpretation, they understand the word "is" in the sense of "represents." "For," says he, "the other sense would be absurd even to the believing mind!"[20] Yes, absurd to the fleshly mind! Now, how our interpretation is not consonant with Scripture and the Creed, they have not yet proved. This will become more apparent as we proceed. But it is not right for them to try to make the text of the Supper uncertain, and then steal away secretly like thieves. They should take their stand, and since they have taught that "is" means "signifies," they should prove it beyond question. In place of the former text, the old definite one, which they claim to have undermined and rendered uncertain, they should produce another new and definite one, as I have said above that they are under obligation to do. But since they shy away from this responsibility and do not want to tackle it, they make it quite clear what kind of spirit they have, namely one that wishes only to tear down and not build up, wound and not heal. Such a spirit is the devil. Therefore be warned again of this skittish devil, who so flits and flutters about that he will not answer correctly. Let him go.

But further to instruct you who are on our side: you may be sure that it is pure imagination when anyone says that this word "is" means the same as "represents." No man can ever prove that from a single passage of Scripture. Indeed, I will go further: If the fanatics, in any one of all the languages on earth can produce one saying in which "is" means the same as "represents," then they may claim to have won their case. But they refuse the challenge. These lofty spirits fail to take proper consideration of the art of language, grammar, or as they call it, *tropus,* which is taught in elementary schools. This art teaches how a child may make two or three words out of one, or how he may give to a single word a new application and several meanings. Let me prove this with several examples. The word "flower" according to its primary and original sense means a rose, lily, violet, and the like, which grow out of the earth and bloom. Now if I wish to glorify Christ with an elegant eulogy, seeing that he

[20] *Christian Answer. C. R.* 92, 880; *St. L.* 20, 1169 f. Zwingli inserted this sentence in Latin. His point was that this idea is absurd not so much to reason as to Scripture and the Creed. Cf. p. 156.

is born as a beautiful child of the Virgin Mary, I may take the word "flower" and make a trope, that is, give it a new sense and application by saying, "Christ is a flower."[21] All grammarians say that "flower" here has become a new word and has acquired a new meaning, and now no longer means the flower in the field but the child Jesus. They do not say that the word "is" here has become metaphorical, for Christ does not represent a flower but is a flower, yet a different flower from the natural one.

The poet Horace says, *Dixeris egregie, notum si callida verbum reddiderit iunctura novum,* i.e. "You will have expressed yourself admirably if a clever setting gives the spice of novelty to a familiar word."[22] From this it follows that a single word becomes two or several words, if it acquires in addition to its common meaning other new meanings. So, for example, "flower" is one word when it means Christ, and another when it means a natural rose, etc., and still a different word when it means a golden, silver, or wooden rose. Similarly one may say of a miser: "He is a dog." Here dog means the miserly skinflint, and out of the old word has come a new word according to the teaching of Horace. The word "is" here cannot be metaphorical, for the miser does not represent a dog. This is the way in all languages that men make new words, as when we say, "Mary is the dawn," "Christ is the fruit of the womb," "The devil is the god of this world," "The pope is Judas," "St. Augustine is Paul," "St. Bernard is a dove," "David is a little wood-worm,"[23] and similar expressions which abound in the Scriptures. In grammar one speaks of a trope or metaphor when a single name is given to two different things on account of a similarity in both. Though

---

[21] Luther is apparently thinking of the hymn, "Lo, how a Rose e'er blooming."

[22] *Art of Poetry,* 47 f. Casper J. Kraemer (ed.), *The Complete Works of Horace* (New York, 1936). This thought is quoted also in Luther's *Against Latomus,* 1521. *LW* 32, 195; see Luther's discussion of figurative language in that treatise.

[23] The reference to Christ is based on Luke 1:42; to the devil, on II Cor. 4:4. The curious reference to David is based on the obscure Vulgate text of II Sam. 23:8, which properly describes one of David's "valiant men" (rather than David himself) as "like the most tender little worm of the wood." (Douay version. See R. A. Knox, *The Holy Bible,* 1956, p. 279 n.) The title "dawn" for the Virgin Mary is ancient, cf. the Byzantine *Akathistos Hymn,* in J. B. Carol (ed.), *Mariology* (Milwaukee, 1954), I, 198; the title is based on such passages as Song of Sol. 6:10 and Mal. 4:2. References to Augustine and Bernard are medieval.

in spelling the name is the same, *potestate ac significatione plura:* in force, usage, and meaning there are two words, an old and a new, as Horace says and as children well know.

In fashioning such new words, we Germans customarily prefix "real" or "true" or "a second" or "new," and we say, "You are a real dog," "The monks are real Pharisees," "The nuns are real daughters of the Moabites," "Christ is a real Solomon." Again, "Luther is a second Huss," "Zwingli is a second Korah," "Oecolampadius is a new Abiram."[24] In such expressions all Germans will bear me witness and admit that they are new words. And it is precisely the same if I say, "Luther is Huss," "Luther is a second Huss," "Luther is a real Huss," "Luther is a new Huss." Thus one can readily feel how in such expressions, according to Horace, a new word is coined from one already existing. It does not sound right or ring true if I say, "Luther signifies Huss"; rather, "He is a Huss." In such expressions we are speaking of an essence, what a person is and not what he represents, and we coin a new word to express his new essence. This you will find to be the case in all languages—I am absolutely sure. All grammarians teach this manner of expression, and the boys in school know it, and so you will never find that "is" may mean "represents."

Now when Christ says, "John is Elijah" [Matt. 11:14], no one can prove that John represents Elijah. It would be ridiculous that John should represent Elijah, for Elijah much more fittingly represents John. According to Zwingli's method Christ ought to have transposed the words and said, "Elijah is John," that is, he represents John. But Christ means to say what John is—not what he signifies but what is his nature or office, and he says, "He is Elijah." Here "Elijah" has become a new word, and does not mean the old Elijah but the new Elijah. We Germans would say, "John is the true Elijah," "John is a second Elijah," or "John is a new Elijah." Similarly it is said, "Christ is a rock" [I Cor. 10:4], that is, he

---

[24] Daughters of the Moabites, Num. 25:1. Korah and Abiram, Num. 16:1 ff., 26:9 ff. In Augustine (cf. *City of God*, XVII, 8) and in medieval exegesis Christ was associated with Solomon because of his wisdom and because the king's name means "peace." John Huss, Bohemian theologian and patriot, had been burned at the Council of Constance, 1415; when the indulgence controversy burst out in 1517, Luther was frequently hailed as "the Saxon Huss."

has the nature of a rock and is truly a rock, but a new rock, a second rock, a true rock. Likewise, "Christ is a true vine" [John 15:1].

How does it sound, my friend, when you try to interpret this according to Zwingli's opinion, "Christ signifies the true vine"? Who then is the true vine which Christ signifies? Do I hear correctly that Christ shall be a sign or symbol of the wood in the vineyard? That would be a fine thing! Why would not Christ have said more properly, "The true vine is Christ," that is, the wooden vine signifies Christ? For it is better that Christ should be signified than that he should signify, since that which represents is always inferior to that which is represented; and all signs are inferior to the thing they signify. Even fools and children know that quite well.

But Zwingli overlooks the word *vera,* "true," in this passage, "Christ is the true vine." Had he noticed it, he could never have made a silly representation out of the word "is." For no language or logic permits us to say, "Christ signifies the true vine." In this passage no one can say that the true vine is the wood in the vineyard. Hence the text irresistibly compels us to regard "vine" as a new word, meaning a second, new, real vine, and not the vine in the vineyard. Therefore "is" cannot be metaphorical here, but Christ truly is and has the essence of a real, new vine. Although the text says, "Christ is the vine," it does not warrant my saying, "Christ signifies the vine"; rather I should say, "The vine signifies Christ."

So also this saying, "Christ is the lamb of God" [John 1:29], cannot be understood to mean: Christ signifies the lamb of God, for then Christ as a sign would be inferior to the lamb of God. What then would be the lamb of God which Christ signifies? Shall it be the paschal lamb? Why then does he not transpose the words and say rather, "The lamb of God is Christ," that is, the paschal lamb signifies Christ, as Zwingli interprets it? But since the words "of God" are next to the word "lamb," they irresistibly compel us to regard "lamb" in this instance as a second, new word; it means a second new, and true lamb, which Christ truly is, and not the old paschal lamb.

The same reasoning applies to all the other examples they

produce, as: "The seed is the word of God" [Luke 8:11], "The field is the world" [Matt. 13:38], etc. Here too they cannot produce a sound argument for making a metaphor out of the "is." Even school children say that the seed and field are tropes or words with a new application, according to the nature of a metaphor. For a simple word and a metaphorical word are not one, but two words. Hence, "seed" in this instance does not mean grain or wheat, but the Word of God, and the field means the world. For Christ, as the text says, speaks in parables [Matt. 13:3, 34] and not of natural grain or wheat. But he who speaks in parables makes common words into pure tropes—new and different words. Otherwise they would not be parables, if he used common words in their original sense. What a mad, unreasonable spirit he must be who, contrary to the nature and character of parables, tries to take the words of a parable according to their common signification, and has to resort to this "representation" nonsense and buffoonery.

So also with the passage from Genesis [41:26], "The seven oxen are seven years, and the seven ears are seven years." Since the text itself [41:25] says that it speaks of a dream and of a parable or sign of seven years, the words "seven oxen, seven ears" must be regarded as metaphors and new words, and must mean precisely the same as the words "seven years." Thus those words, "seven years," according to their ordinary sense, and these words, "seven oxen," according to a new sense, mean one and the same thing. For the seven oxen do not signify seven years, but are themselves essentially and truly seven years. For these are not natural oxen grazing in the pasture, which according to the old, ordinary sense are called seven oxen. But here we have a new word; these are seven oxen of famine and of plenty, i.e. seven years of famine and of plenty. In short, they may produce Scripture passages and say, "Here is a representation," but they will never prove it in a single instance, for as yet they have not ventured to furnish the proof for such an interpretation. They think it is enough to cite passages and say: Here is a representation. But this does not satisfy us, for we do not believe in Zwingli or any man; we demand reasons and proofs.

But here, perhaps, the other faction will strut and exclaim,

"Now you are substantiating Oecolampadius' concept of 'sign,' for he, following Horace, also makes a new word or trope out of an ordinary word, and says: 'my body' here means 'the sign of my body.'" This can be quickly answered. The grammarians and all Christian teachers forbid us ever to depart from the old, customary meaning of a word and accept a new meaning, unless the text and the sense require it, or unless it is irrefutably proved by other passages of Scripture. Otherwise no text, meaning, expression, or language would remain definite. For example, when Christ says, "John is Elijah" [Matt. 11:14], the text and the faith compel one to regard "Elijah" as a new word, because it is certain that John neither is nor can be the old Elijah. Similarly, "Christ is a rock" [I Cor. 10:4]: again the text itself and the faith compel one to treat "rock" in this instance as a new word, because Christ neither is nor can be a natural rock.

But when Oecolampadius in this instance makes "sign of the body" out of the word "body"—this we will not grant him, for he does it arbitrarily and cannot prove that the text or the faith require it. Suppose that one arbitrarily decided to allegorize or coin a new word so that "the gospel is the power of God," Romans 1 [:16], should mean the same as "the gospel is the sword of Roland."[25] In this way one might interpret Christ to be Belial and Paul to be Judas, and who could stop him? But no one would admit it unless it were proved and shown that the text required it. Thus Oecolampadius does not carry the debate beyond the point of maintaining that only bread and wine are in the Supper. Even if he won his point (which he cannot do), he still cannot successfully prove that "body" means "sign of the body," as I have shown in my previous treatise.[26] So Oecolampadius also must continue to lack a definite text and interpretation of the Supper. Now, we would have to have a definite text and interpretation in this instance even if there were nothing but straw and chaff in the Supper. But who will furnish such a text? They won't. They don't want to do it, and they cannot do it.

So be it. We shall hold to our own interpretation, and warn all who will heed a warning to beware of these vague, vacillating

---

[25] Cf. p. 226, n. 93; cf. p. 248.
[26] Cf. pp. 30, 40.

tropists and representationists. It is not enough for them to say, "Bread is bread and wine is wine." They are under obligation and pressure to prove how the text, "This is my body," is to be read and interpreted—whether it shall mean "this signifies my body," or "this is the sign of my body," or "this is my body." We do not allow a child's game or a trifle to be made out of this text, as they would like. These are Christ's words. We must know what they contain and what they bestow. In short, it is just as I have said: They are unwilling to answer where an answer is needed, and they prattle meanwhile about their own notions.

In the third place, although by the grace of God I understand, as this fellow knows perfectly well, that one passage of Scripture must be clarified by other passages—after all, I proclaimed this rule before all the world in numerous treatises before the name of Zwingli ever came to the fore—yet he has felt obliged to teach me this on page after page,[27] for other reason than to persuade people that he finally intended to give an answer. Now, God knows, I have requested from him an answer to my objections, and not all this erudition, for which I give him no thanks. But to this very day I would be happy if he would impart his erudition to himself and his followers who need it more than I, and would demonstrate from the text of the Supper what he ought to. He scolds me, indeed, that I have concentrated only on the clause, "This is my body," but have ignored the following one, "which is given for you"; and he prattles on fearfully that the second clause clarifies the first. Well, I understand perfectly that one passage clarifies another. I have just had a bath and have washed my ears; now I am quite able to hear how in the text of the Supper the latter clause, "which is given for you," is supposed to clarify the former, "This is my body." I ask, however, how one may prove or arrive at such an explanation. Now just listen to a master, if you have never heard one before!

Christ's body, says he, was visibly offered on the cross for us. Since we read in the Supper, "This is my body which is given for you," it would also have to be visible in the Supper if it were the same body which was given for us. This is the way the sec-

[27] A section in *Christian Answer* is entitled, "On comparing the Scriptures with one another." *C. R.* 92, 853 ff.; *St. L.* 20, 1152 ff.

ond clause explains the first: since Christ is not visibly present in the Supper, "is" must be metaphorical.[28] Now tell me, dear brethren, whether this spirit is serious in answering us, or whether he is not rather making a mockery of this subject. I thank thee, Jesus Christ my Lord, that thou art so masterful at trapping thine enemies in their own words and putting them to shame, and dost strengthen our faith by thy simple words! This single clause ought truly frighten every one away from this sect, when he sees such monstrous, gross blindness in such a lofty, learned spirit. Schoolboys know that the relative pronoun "which" refers to substance. This spirit says that "which" refers to quality, indeed, to the most common and most variable accident.[29] Let me put this into ordinary language.

Whenever or wherever I can say of Christ's body, "This is Christ's body given for us," then it must be visible, because it was given for us in no other manner than visibly. If it is not visibly present, it is not there at all. If I point toward heaven with my hand and repeat these words, "There at the right hand of God sits the body which was given for us," then it must truly be seated there visibly, or it is not there at all, for the following words, "which is given for you," make this plain, according to this spirit's argument. Likewise, according to John 8 [:59], when Christ hid himself and went out of the temple, I might say, "There goes the body which was given for us." But he was given visibly for us, therefore he must certainly go out visibly, and the Evangelist lies when he says that Christ went out hidden; otherwise he was not there at all. In short, no matter where Christ's body may be, it is the body which was given for us. Because it was visibly given for us, it can be nowhere present unless it is there visibly. What do you think? Now have you heard a master? Here now you have the Scriptures and the Creed, which "cannot tolerate our interpretation." Believe this spirit from now on, and he will instruct you correctly on the Supper! So must the

[28] Cf. *Friendly Rejoinder,* 1527. *C. R.* 92, 775 f.; *St. L.* 20, 1108; *Clear Instruction,* 1526. *LCC* 24, 190 ff. Cf. pp. 46 ff. and 65 ff.

[29] The distinction between relatives which refer to identity of substance and relatives which refer to identity of quality or accident was common knowledge in the schools. Cf. Joseph P. Mullally (ed.), *The Summulae Logicales of Peter of Spain* (Notre Dame, 1945), pp. 20 ff., 34 f.

devil always seal his wisdom with his own dung, and leave his stench behind, so that one may be aware that he has been present.

Since the poor body of Christ was once given for us visibly, then, it is so imprisoned that either it can be invisible nowhere, or if it is invisible it is not present at all. For if being given visibly for us prevents it from being present in the Supper, and if it cannot be present except in a visible mode, because the words read, "This is my body which is given for you," then it surely cannot be present anywhere except in a visible mode; for this is the explanation yielded by these words, "which is given for you." But I ask you, what is the meaning of "which"? This spirit says it is the equivalent of "as" or "in the form in which" the body hung upon the cross. Now it hung there visibly before the eyes of the Jews, amid spears and horses. If the body were now in the Supper, all the Jews, horses, spears, crosses, nails, and everything else would also have to be in the Supper—yes, and at the right of God too, and in every place where Christ's body is.

This is what is meant by expounding the Scriptures and judging one passage by the other! They are angry because I detect the devil speaking through them. My dear friend, can reason itself say that we have here only human error, and not the devil's mockery? Especially since Zwingli develops great learning, ingenuity, and twaddle out of this point as though it were one of his outstanding masterpieces of argument. Münzer[30] was an impudent spirit; but this one is equally impudent and spews out whatever comes into his mouth, never once thinking what he is saying. But this is the way God warns us.

Isn't it a pity that for such flimsy, false reasons the clear words of Christ, "This is my body," should be denied and the Supper profaned? If a boy came up with that kind of syllogism in school, he would receive a good whipping; should a master of the sophists[31] do it, he would be called an ass. Here, in the case of this spirit, it is to be regarded as divine Scripture and truth which they boastfully array against our interpretation! The same kind of ingenuity could also be applied in this way: Christ

---

[30] Cf. p. 70, n. 117, and p. 139.

[31] Scholastic theologians.

at the right hand of God is the son born of Mary; but he was born a mortal being of Mary; therefore he must sit as a mortal at the right of God. Sir Jack the knight does not ride with a cuirass on, therefore he is not a knight. Rachel has no veil on, hence Rachel is no wife. According to the new rule, an accident is a substance and cannot be absent from its subject!

In the fourth place, when he comes to the texts of the Supper, he divides them into two types. Out of some he makes imperatives, which enjoin or command us to do something, e.g. "Take, eat." Out of others he makes declaratives or indicatives, which simply tell us what takes place. But I must use his clumsy, atrocious German, in which he takes more delight than a stork in its own bill-clapping—though a person may sweat a good deal before he understands it. He tries to stammer or cough (I should have said, to state): "Where God commands, we have command-words, e.g. 'Thou shalt have no other gods' [Exod. 20:3]; but where he does something, we have action-words[32] e.g. Genesis 1 [:3], 'Let there be light,' etc." What he would love to say, if he could, is this: "Where action-words occur, nothing happens if I also pronounce the same words myself. For example, if I should quote Genesis 1 [:14], 'Let there be sun and moon,' nothing would come of it.

---

[32] Zwingli's expressions are *heissende wort* and *tätliche wort*. *Christian Answer*. *C. R.* 92, 887 ff.; *St. L.* 20, 1173 ff. In the following discussion Luther ordinarily uses the forms *heissel wort* and *thettel wort*. Luther here ignores the other basic category in Zwingli's mind: words of promise (*verheissende wort*). Zwingli called "take and eat" a command-word, and "This is my body" an example of narrative- or action-words (*gschicht oder tätliche wort*), or indicative words (*zeigwort*), but denied that such a promise is implied as, "Let my body come into existence out of (or in) the bread." In his *Answer to Dr. Strauss' Little Book*, 1527 (*C. R.* 92, 523; *St. L.* 20, 1528 f.) Zwingli drew the following diagram (note that here he included both narrative words and imperatives under "words of action"):

"Words	of promise,	which are	universal, and particular.
	of action. These are	words which narrate the simple event; words which forbid: 'You shall not do this.' Also	universal: 'Be not angry.' And particular: 'You shall not rule.' Concerns only the apostles and persons we call spiritual.
		words which command: 'You shall do this.' We distinguish	words which are only ceremonial; words which concern life and morals."

Therefore, although in the Supper Christ gave his body when he said, 'This is my body,' it does not follow that if I repeat the same words, Christ's body would immediately be present; for Christ nowhere commanded that his body should come into being out of my word."

Oh, this poor, miserable spirit! How he squirms and twists and still cannot get free! Let us take him up on the first point. He admits that Christ did give his body to the disciples in the Supper, for he acknowledges that these words, "This is my body," are action-words, which did take place at that time. We thank them kindly that they have left us the first, original Supper. But if we have this, we shall not lose the others either. Even this first Supper we shall irresistibly wrest from them, through their own words, in the following way.

Let Zwingli regard the words in the Supper as he will, be they command-words or permission-words, action-words or written words;[33] it doesn't matter to me. But I ask this one question: Are these same action-words of Christ false or true words? If they are lying words, let Christ himself be responsible for them; they do not concern us. But if they are true words, then we confidently reply: Even the fanatical spirit must acknowledge that Christ gave his body in the Supper. For they are action-words which Christ spoke at the first administration, and he did not lie, when he said, "Take, eat, this is my body," just as the sun and moon came to be when he said, Genesis 1 [:14], "Let there be a sun and a moon," and it was no lying word. So his word surely is not merely a word of imitation, but a word of power[34] which accomplishes what it expresses, Psalm 33 [:9], "He spoke, and it came to be," especially because it was first spoken here, and was meant to be an action-word. Thus we have retained the first, original Supper, which they themselves grant and acknowledge.

Now we must see how this dainty spirit tries to make out of the action-word "is" a metaphorical word,[35] and so deprive us of our interpretation. Where action-words occur, he says, it does not follow that the action will take place when we speak them, but

[33] *Heisselwort, lasselwort, thettelwort, leselwort.*
[34] *Nachwort . . . machtwort.*
[35] *Deutel wort.*

the words remain a simple description of an action that has taken place. Now although we say in the Supper, "This is my body," Christ's body is not thereby brought forth; therefore, of course, only bread must be present. If only bread is present, then "is" must be metaphorical. Hence our interpretation is nonsense, and the fanatics are right.

All he is doing thereby is to argue that in the first administration of the Supper our interpretation is correct, but not in the subsequent ones. Now if I ask who gave the spirit this power to say, or how will he prove, that the words in the Supper are to be thus divided and separated from one another, some into command-words, some into action-words, the only answer he gives is: He hopes no one will assert that in the Supper there are command-words by which one makes Christ's body. Thus his proof rests upon his hope, although he always boasts that his foundation is the Word of God and clear Scripture. Well, whoever wishes to build upon this spirit's hope may ever hereafter believe that mere bread is present in the Supper, for it serves that kind of faith right to have such a foundation.

To this we reply that this spirit again is teaching us what we already know and neglecting what he ought to teach, and meanwhile playing an outrageous trick in thus dividing and separating the words of the Supper. He ought to prove that they must be thus torn apart, even though they appear in a fine order in a single passage: "Take, eat, this is my body." And after all, they are not our words, but Christ's own words.

Moreover, even though these words, "This is my body," are in themselves action-words, when they are torn out and detached from the others and imprisoned in solitary confinement, nevertheless they are purely and simply command-words, because they are embraced and embodied in command-words. I earnestly hope too, yes, I am sure, that all Christians are bound by the institution and command of Christ to say these words in the Supper, and I do not expect that even the fanatics are so bold that they can omit them with a good conscience. If we must retain and say them in the Supper, they must assuredly be imperatives, because they are embraced in the imperative, and it is not right to separate them from the imperatives as this spirit outrageously does.

Now if the action-words stand in a context of imperatives, they are no longer simple declaratives but imperatives also, for everything that the words declare does take place, by the power of the divine imperative through which they are spoken.

For example, in Matthew 21 [:21] stands an action-word: the disciples were to say, "Be taken up and cast into the sea." If anyone simply said these words, of course nothing would come of it and it would remain simply a declarative. But because Christ embraces it in an imperative, saying, "If you shall say to this mountain in faith, 'Be taken up,' etc.," then truly it is no longer a declarative, but what it declares comes to be, as long as it is spoken in accordance with his command. Likewise, when the priest baptizes and says, "I baptize you," etc. that of course is simply a declarative, but because it stands in the context of an imperative, when Christ says, "Go ye therefore and baptize," it must be nonetheless a baptism in the sight of God. And if Peter or Paul says, "Your sins are forgiven," as Christ said to Mary Magdalene [Luke 7:48]—well, that is simply a declarative, nevertheless the sins are forgiven as the words declare, because it is embraced and commanded in an imperative, since Christ says in the last chapter of John [20:22 f.], "Receive the Holy Spirit. If you forgive the sins of any," etc.

And if the word in Genesis 1 [:14], "Let there be a moon and a sun," stood similarly in the context of an imperative, and we had been commanded to say it, then you would indeed see whether God is a liar, and whether there would not appear another sun were I to say this to a star or to the heavens. But since there is no such imperative here, of course no sun appears.

So, too, if there were an imperative that I should speak to the water these declarative words, "This is wine," [36] you would see indeed whether wine would not appear. Therefore it is nothing but childish dilly-dallying and useless prattle when this spirit separates the action-words from the command-words in the same text, though they are embodied in the imperative words and commanded to be spoken, and when he places them on the same level with other action-words which lack the command and the impera-

[36] Cf. John 2:7 f.

tive words. This is a sophistical and fraudulent treatment of the words of God; but they call it Scripture and the Creed which do not permit our interpretation.

Since in all this he has neither proved any metaphor nor overthrown our interpretation, we now ask further whether Christ has commanded us to speak falsely when he commands and bids us to speak these action-words, "Take, eat, this is my body," since they were spoken entirely in his own person and as his own words? If he commands us to speak falsely, that is his affair; but if he commands us to speak the truth, his body must certainly be present in the Supper by virtue not of our speaking but of his command, bidding, and action. Thus we have maintained not merely the first, original Supper, but all others that are celebrated according to the command and institution of the Lord Christ.

If they now ask: Where is the power that causes Christ's body to be in the Supper when we say, "This is my body"? I answer: Where is the power to cause a mountain to be taken up and cast into the sea when we say, "Be taken up and cast into the sea"? Of course, it does not reside in our speaking but in God's command, who connects his command with our speaking. Likewise, where is the power to cause water to come forth out of the rock, since Moses does nothing but strike it? [Num. 20:11]. If striking were enough we might turn all stones into water. But there is God's command, and Moses has no other power than to speak the action-word, "I strike the rock." This I could say, too, but no water would flow out, for the command was given to Moses and not to me.

Here, too, if I were to say over all the bread there is, "This is the body of Christ," nothing would happen, but when we follow his institution and command in the Supper and say, "This is my body," then it is his body, not because of our speaking or our declarative word, but because of his command in which he has told us so to speak and to do and has attached his own command and deed to our speaking.[37] But if, according to this spirit's celebrated reasoning, it were proper to separate God's command and our speaking, he would not need to teach us that our speak-

[37] This sentence is quoted in the *Formula of Concord,* Solid Declaration, VII, 78.

ing would accomplish nothing. We already know that. But then he should answer and prove his reasoning on this point, that where command and speaking are connected, God must be guilty of falsehood and deception and nothing will take place. The mad spirit always spews out something else than one asks or the subject demands.

Now if I undertook to write against this spirit, I would pose a subtle question just at this point. He argues mightily *quod verbum facti non efficiat factum, sed narret factum*—that an action-word does not effect what it states, but merely relates what has been effected. Thus he acknowledges, of course, that in the first Supper Christ's true body was given at the meal. Otherwise, why should he so torture himself to decide in what way they are action-words, that is, words that narrate an event? Labor on this point would be sheer useless prattle, because he bases everything on the argument that action-words are those which report that an action once took place (else they would not be action-words). Well, then, this spirit acknowledges thereby that in the first Supper Christ's body was given to be eaten, and that this event once took place. But he alleges that for this reason no such result followed when this event was related thereafter, nor did he deny this above.

Now I ask you, where has this spirit left his brains and reason, his sense of modesty and propriety, when he says above that his basic argument why Christ's body is not in the Supper is this that such an understanding of Christ's words neither Scripture nor the Creed permits? "The absurdity of this interpretation is repugnant even to the believing mind." [38] If the body of Christ was present in the first Supper, how can its presence be contrary to Scripture and the Creed? If it is contrary to Scripture and the Creed for Christ's body to be in the Supper, how can it be present in the first Supper? I am not now speaking of unworthy priests, whether they can consecrate or not,[39] but of Christ's words, "This is my body," concerning which they scream and chatter that it is contrary to the Creed and to Scripture for Christ's body to be present, as the words say, even if only saints are present.

[38] Cf. p. 171, n. 20.

[39] The reference is to Donatists, cf. p. 366, n. 285.

But here again this spirit bites his tongue. By his admission it is not contrary to Scripture or the Creed that, as the words say, Christ's body is present in the first Supper; only he claims it does not now follow that it is also present in subsequent celebrations of the Supper. Hence they should not scream and boast that our interpretation is contrary to Scripture and the Creed, as they so arrogantly claim; their objection is against the subsequent celebrations of the Supper. For whether you or I actually receive Christ's body in the Supper, and whether the old interpretation is contrary to Scripture and the Creed, are two very different questions. If it is not contrary to Scripture and the Creed, as the first Supper proves even by this spirit's admission, then we beg them very sincerely to permit us to teach and believe what they acknowledge even in opposition to themselves, that it is not contrary to Scripture or the Creed. But if they have Scripture and the Creed to prove the contrary, we wish they would give their own answer—these people who contend so mightily against their own confession! We are satisfied with their admission that it is not contrary to Scripture and the Creed, as they chatter, whereby they expose themselves as liars, unable to conceal their false opinion.

Since we have caught the lying spirit contradicting himself and admitting that our interpretation—that Christ's body is in the Supper—is not contrary to Scripture or the Creed, as he nevertheless contends, but only contrary to subsequent celebrations, we shall keep our interpretation. For since it is not contrary to Scripture or the Creed that, as we maintain, the words of Christ in the first Supper impart the body of Christ, we see no reason why it should be contrary to Scripture and the Creed in other celebrations. What is not contrary to Scripture and the Creed is not contrary to any subsequent instance either. Isn't he a fine, cautious spirit? Precisely at the point where he intends to prove that our interpretation is contrary to the Creed, he goes to work and proves that there are action-words in the Supper; yet he does not see that by this very argument he proves our interpretation is correct concerning the first Supper and not contrary to the Creed. For action-words on the first occasion impart what they declare, else they are not action-words, as he himself admits. So he demonstrates, in direct opposition to himself, either that there are no action-words in the first Supper, or that our interpretation of the first Supper is right!

If anyone should contend, however, that Christ has not commanded us to say these words, "This is my body," in the Supper, I reply: It is true that the text does not read, "You shall say 'This is my body,'" and there is no printer's index[40] pointing to the command; but I dare them, no matter how bold they may be, to leave these words out as if they were not commanded! We do not read in the text, either, "You shall say, 'take and eat.'" Again, we do not read, "You shall take the bread and bless it," etc. But let us see who would dare to say, "Do not take the bread and bless it," or, "Do not say, 'Take and eat'!" Am I really being told that Christ must spell out these words, "Thus shall you say and do," letter by letter, and that it is not enough that he said in conclusion, "Do this in remembrance of me"? If we are to do what he did, then indeed we must take the bread and bless it, and break and distribute it, saying, "This is my body." For all this is included in the imperative word, "Do this," and we must not leave out these words. For St. Paul also says that he received from the Lord what he delivered to us [I Cor. 11:23]. Surely these are words of command, and they do not permit us to tear out or alter a single point.

Thus it is certainly true that Christ nowhere delivered these words to us letter by letter, "You shall make my body out of the bread." Why should he need to? But when he said, "Do this," by his own command and bidding he directed us to speak these words in his person and name: "This is my body." Further, we do not make Christ's body out of the bread, as this spirit falsely charges us with teaching.[41] Nor do we say that his body comes into existence out of the bread. We say that his body, which long ago was made and came into existence, is present when we say, "This is my body." For Christ commands us to say not, "Let this become my body," or, "Make my body there," but, "This is my body."

---

[40] *Hand dabey gemalet,* i.e. ☞. Cf. pp. 73, 244, n. 123.

[41] *Christian Answer. C. R.* 92, 888, *St. L.* 20, 1174. Cf. *Clear Instruction. LCC* 24, 228.

Now, since we are speaking of these imperatives, we must add one further little detail, to protect our people against these spirits' nonsense. For it is impossible to stop the devil's mouth. He is like the wind which finds its way through even the tiniest chinks, as we say. Imperatives are of two kinds: one kind where faith is presupposed, such as Matthew 21 [:21] on the moving of mountains, and Mark 16 [:17] on the signs that will accompany those who believe. If anyone should speak these words to the mountain without faith, "Be taken up," boasting that he was acting in accordance with the command, the action would not take place, because Christ has expressly bound faith to the command. The other kind comprises the passages where faith is not presupposed, such as these words in the Supper, "Take, eat," for here even the unworthy and unbelieving eat Christ's body, as Judas and many of the Corinthians did.[42] Therefore those who administer the Supper do not necessarily have to have faith, just as faith is not necessarily presupposed in those who baptize. Again, we may say the same of those who preach and of all who hold public office. For Christ has established the validity of all these activities upon his Word and not upon the holiness of men, in order that we might be sure of the Word and the sacraments. This I say because the fanatics take the greatest offense if unworthy men baptize, celebrate mass, preach, etc. They do not see that they themselves may be more offensive before God, or that no man can ever know how good they are, but that they must let the sacraments be grounded and administered simply in God's words and commands.

Next this fellow leads my finger, as if I were a blind man, to the word "Do this,"[43] which St. Paul is said to explain thus: "As often as you eat this bread," etc. [I Cor. 11:26]. From this he attempts to deduce that with the words, "Do this," Christ refers to the eating of the bread and not the eating of his body. Of course, if St. Paul had said, "As often as you eat this bread which is not the body of Christ"—which this spirit has added out of his own head—there would have been no need to lay my finger on it; I would have been able to see it more than five paces

[42] Cf. Matt. 26:25, I Cor. 11:17 ff.

[43] *Christian Answer*. *C. R.* 92, 890 f.; *St. L.* 20, 1175 f.

away. Every time I hope they will produce Scripture, they produce their own dreams. Therefore I repeat, I would like them to lay their finger on the preceding word, where Christ refers to the bread and yet says, "This is my body." Here also stands the word "this," which is waiting to be grasped by the fanatical spirit's fingers. That word exerts a greater and stronger pressure upon me to conclude that Christ's body is eaten in the bread than this fellow's word "this," out of which he would like to make mere bread. For my word "this" and his "this" both refer to one and the same bread, as they admit. And yet, where I cite the word "this" it reads, "It is my body"; but where he cites the word "this" it does not read, "It is not my body," but he must insert it and skip over the whole context in which my word "this" stands. What a faithful, zealous expositor of Scripture!

Now let the whole world be judge between me and this spirit, which bread must yield to the other. My bread has on its side the text, "Eat, this is my body," and explains with emphatic words that this bread is the body of Christ. The spirit's bread has on his side the text, "Do this," or, "As often as you eat this bread," and does not explain that it is mere bread or that it is not the body of Christ. No, the spirit must emend the text and say it is not Christ's body, as he has been commanded to do—yes, by the devil![44] Now if one "this" must yield to the other, then properly his should yield to mine, since his is bare and naked apart from explanations, whereas mine carries its explanation with it. Or else he must sweat still more in order to prove that my "this" must yield to his "this." Finger-pointing doesn't help. If he wished to act fairly and squarely, he should not point out to us with his fingers how his "this" indicates the bread. This indeed we could discover without his spirit, explanations, and arguments. But he should first parry the thrust of this text, "Eat, this is my body." If he could prove that the bread there is not proclaimed as Christ's body, then of course we would know perfectly well ourselves that his "this" does refer to mere bread. However, he does not do this.

[44] An allusion to Zwingli's words: "'Who commanded Zwingli and Oecolampadius to write?' He who commanded us to preach! Do I hear that we should not have written without your permission?" *Christian Answer*. *C. R.* 92, 842; *St. L.* 20, 1144. Cf. p. 24, above.

Thus it is a "begging of the question" and hopeless twaddle, for he does not answer what we ask and beg him to answer, as I continually complain. We say, however, that if the first "this" refers to the body of Christ, then his "this" in the next instance must refer to it also; for "this" in both cases refers to the bread, and yet the first at the same time stands in immediate connection with Christ's body, as the words say, "Eat, this is my body."

Moreover, we do not concede to him that where Christ says, "Thus (or, this) do," it is the same as Paul's expression, "As often as you eat this bread." The spirit says so, of course, but he offers no proof, as usual. For these words, "As often as you eat this bread," speak only of eating and drinking. If there were another spirit as cantankerous as this one, he would probably want to argue from this that we should not take, give thanks, break, distribute, and bless this bread, but should only eat, as the words say, and therefore that we should snatch the bread from the table with our mouth, or bite it out of the oven! But if the words, "As often as you eat this bread," can allow us to take, break, thank, and distribute, then, my friend, they must also allow the one remaining point, viz. the blessing, where Christ says, "This is my body." However, if this one particular part is not allowed to be observed, then I will contend with the same force of argument that according to the letter we must simply eat and not take, nor break, nor bless, nor distribute it. For St. Paul does not say, "As often as you take this bread, or break, or thank, or distribute it," but simply, "As often as you eat." Do you see what a fine thing it is to patch and mend oneself so with letters? And this is to pass for pure Scripture which contradicts our interpretation! Therefore we say that with the word, "Thus (or, this) do," Christ commands not the eating of bread alone but the whole ordinance of the Supper. St. Paul means exactly the same, even though he sets down only the words about eating the bread. Of course he meant to command them to eat the bread as Christ instituted it, and not as the fanatical spirit foolishly pretends, even though in the words, "Eat the bread," he could not express all this; but he had previously taught it with sufficient clarity by many words.

In the fifth place, he tries to prove that our interpretation is contrary to the Creed.[45] Meanwhile he is kept extraordinarily busy teaching us how Christ died for us. This spirit must constantly be teaching me what I have taught so long and so often, all the time skipping over what he should be answering. By God's grace I know well enough what our faith is, that Christ by his suffering redeemed us from sin. All this he did not need to teach us. But how our interpretation in the Supper is contrary to this faith, as he boasts and brags, I would very much like to hear, but my dear spirit is as silent as a mouse; indeed, he leaps over the subject like a deer. But he says, if one teaches that the physical or bodily[46] eating of Christ's body forgives sin, etc., that is contrary to the faith. I reply: I quite agree. Indeed, I have said further that a bodily eating of Christ's body without spirit and faith is poison and death. Then what is this spirit answering, or against whom is he fighting? Do you think that he is in his right mind, when he tries to fight against Luther but actually fights against no man?

Let it even be granted that Christ's body is not eaten in the Supper for the sake of our sin, how will it follow from this that his body is not present in the Supper, or that it is contrary to the faith? If Christ is so to be truncated that the forgiveness of sins is to be ascribed to him solely as the crucified, then by the same method I will also conclude it is contrary to the faith that Christ is in heaven, and I will treat all the passages of this spirit thus: St. Paul says not that Christ ascended to heaven for our sin, but that he was crucified for our sin,[47] *ergo* he is not in heaven and does not forgive sin there. Again, Paul does not say Christ was born and lived for our sin, but that he died for our sin [I Cor. 15:3], *ergo* he was not born nor has he lived. Precisely so this spirit concludes here that Christ's body is not eaten for our sin, but died for our sin, *ergo* he is not to be eaten in the Supper. In this way we would make Christ nothing but a being who suffers on the cross eternally for our sin, in order that we may not act in opposition to the faith by professing in other articles that Christ

---

[45] *Christian Answer*. *C. R.* 92, 895; *St. L.* 20, 1177.

[46] *Leiblich*. Cf. p. 39, n. 62.

[47] Paul does not use this precise expression, but see e.g. Rom. 4:25.

is present and forgives sin, which this spirit insists takes place only on the cross.

The blind fool does not know that the *merit of Christ* and the *distribution of merit* are two different things. And he confuses them like a filthy sow. Christ has once for all merited and won for us the forgiveness of sins on the cross; but this forgiveness he distributes wherever he is, at all times and in all places, as Luke writes, chapter 24 [:46 f.], "Thus it is written, that Christ had to suffer and on the third day rise (in this consists his merit), and that repentance and forgiveness of sins should be preached in his name (here the distribution of his merit comes in)" This is why we say there is forgiveness of sins in the Supper, not on account of the eating, nor because Christ merits or achieves forgiveness of sins there, but on account of the word through which he distributes among us this acquired forgiveness, saying, "This is my body which is given for you." Here you perceive that we eat the body as it was given for us; we hear this and believe it as we eat. Hence there is distributed here the forgiveness of sins, which however was obtained on the cross.

Otherwise, indeed, I would babble as this spirit does, and say: Christ has not redeemed us through our preaching, *ergo* it is contrary to the faith for one to seek forgiveness of sins in preaching. My friend, where else should it be sought, since Christ says that forgiveness of sins shall be preached in his name? Again, Christ has not redeemed us through our faith, *ergo* it is contrary to the faith for one to seek forgiveness of sins through faith. My friend, through what then should it be sought, since Christ says, "He who believes shall be saved"? [Mark 16:16]. Again, Christ has not redeemed us through our baptizing, *ergo* it is contrary to the faith when one seeks pardon of sins in baptism. My friend, why then does Paul call baptism a washing away of sins? [I Cor. 6:11]. Again, Christ has not redeemed us through the Holy Spirit, *ergo* it is contrary to the faith for one to seek forgiveness of sins in the Holy Spirit. Where else, my friend? He who is blind sees nothing. Since this spirit has gone astray and blind over the sacrament, inevitably he fails to understand rightly any article of Christian doctrine. But we know that Christ has died for us once, and that he distributes this death through preaching, baptizing, the Spirit, reading, believing, eating, and in whatever way he wishes, wherever he is, and whatever he is, and whatever he does.

Now, I wrote very carefully in my last treatise[48] that our administration of the Supper consists of two parts, viz. the Word and the eating, and that the Word requires faith and spiritual eating along with the physical; and I begged them to prove that this is contrary to the faith. Nevertheless, this spirit shamelessly dares to bawl out these lies continually in all his books, that I teach no spiritual eating or faith, but only the physical eating.[49] Read my book, and you will be forced to admit that this spirit is an unscrupulous liar. He accuses me of teaching that forgiveness of sins is obtained only through a physical eating of the body of Christ, though he knows the contrary very well through my books. With such lies he is simply trying to babble in order to avoid answering how our interpretation is contrary to the faith. Oh, well! with such sorry tricks they fall far short of overthrowing our interpretation. They rather strengthen us all the more, because they assail us with open lies. For we can never believe that Christian faith and open lies are the same thing.

In the same way I carefully wrote against the heavenly prophets[50] that the fact of Christ's suffering and the use of it are not the same thing: *factum et applicatio facti, seu factum et usus facti*. The passion of Christ occurred but once on the cross. But whom would it benefit if it were not distributed, applied, and put to use? And how could it be put to use and distributed except through Word and sacrament? But why should such great saints read my treatise? They know far better. Well, they have their reward, that they consider the fact and the application to be one and the same, and thereby reduce themselves to folly and shame. They fail to see that in the Supper the application of the passion, and not the fact of it, is concerned. It serves them right for never reading, or for reading superficially—so proud and presumptuous are they—what has been written against them.

This insipid spirit was supposed to prove that Christ's body

48 *"This Is My Body,"* p. 86.
49 *Christian Answer. C. R.* 92, 896 f.; *St. L.* 20, 1179 f.
50 *LW* 40, 213 f.

is not present in the Supper. This he neglects to do, but proves instead that we are not redeemed by the eating of his body but by his suffering. Who would ever have known this new wisdom if this spirit had not brought it to light? It is characteristic of this spirit that he spouts something else than he is asked, and always teaches us what we already know, in order to evade proving what he had undertaken and obliged himself to prove. But by these tactics of a cowardly spirit who dares not look his adversary straight in the eye, he only confirms us in our position all the more. Well do we know that Christ has not redeemed us by our eating. No one has ever heard us say that he has. But that it follows therefrom that there is only bread in the Supper, we would be delighted to hear, and would applaud this spirit if he could prove it.

He is angry, too, because we warn people not to ask how it comes to pass that Christ's body is present in the Supper, but simply to believe the words of God. This advice we have given not for the benefit of common people, for they do not need it, but for the high and mighty, indeed, for the fanatics themselves. Well, let them ascend and speculate all they want, just so long as they satisfy their ambition and prove how our interpretation is contrary to the faith—which they will probably do on the devil's ascension day! One thing is clear: with all their speculation they are becoming open liars and attacking ideas that they have dreamed up, but no one teaches. Obviously they have ascended so high and become so giddy that at last they are mistaking substance for quality, and confusing fact and application, like real filthy cooks. Dissension and uncertainty have developed in all their factions, and they are always falling from one error into another. This is the proper reward for those who do not believe God's Word but want to pry to the bottom of it.

In the sixth place, he wishes to prove that Scripture also is opposed to our interpretation.[51] The first passage is precisely this one: "This is my body which is given for you." It is not true that this is Christ's body in the form in which it was given for us, for it was given visibly for us. This we answered above, showing that this spirit makes a quality out of a substance, by a

[51] *Christian Answer. C. R.* 92, 904 ff.; *St. L.* 20, 1183 ff.

very faulty syllogism in which there are four terms, no universal premise, no essential predication, no distributed middle, and many other faults, for logicians know full well that "an accidental term cannot be subsumed under a substantial term."[52] Such reasoning, however, passes for Scripture and God's Word with this spirit!

In plain language, we do not say that Christ's body is present in the Supper in the same form in which he was given for us—who would say that?—but that it is the same body which was given for us, not in the same form or mode but in the same essence and nature. Now a particular essence can very well be visible at one place and invisible at another. Oh, this is fool's play! No one will answer us. All they want to do is talk twaddle and show off.

Again, it is allegedly opposed to the text, "As often as you eat this bread," etc. [I Cor. 11:26]. Because here the word "this" refers to the bread, therefore in the other expression, "This is my body," it must refer to mere bread, etc. I reply: It is not necessarily so in every instance, nor can this be shown to be a necessary consequence; we have already proved the opposite, that in both places the word "this" refers to the bread, which is the body of Christ, and that neither refers to common bread only.

Again, he cites St. Mark [16:19], "The Lord was taken up into heaven," and, "I am leaving the world and going to the Father" [John 16:28], and, "I am no more in the world, but they are in the world" [John 17:11], and many other passages in which Christ is declared to be in heaven. Well, we also believe and teach all this. We did not need to be taught it. What they do need to teach, however, is that because Christ is in heaven, his body cannot be present in the Supper. This "impossibility" they ought to prove, then we would be convinced that these passages are opposed to our interpretation. But they always teach us with great loquacity what we already know, and meanwhile masterfully keep silent over points about which we are asking. Therefore we must hold on to our interpretation.

Indeed, Christ himself explains what "being in the world" means, in Luke 24 [:44], where he says, "These are the words which I spoke to you, while I was still with you." What! Was

[52] Cf. Mullally (ed.), *Summulae Logicales*, pp. 46 ff.

he not still with them? And did he not eat with them after his resurrection? Certainly he was no longer with them in the manner in which he had once been with them, in mortal form and limited to this life in the present world, as Paul says in I Corinthians 15 [:44] concerning the natural and the spiritual man. But from these expressions it cannot be proved that he cannot be present bodily. For as has been said, he sat and ate and spoke with them —and yet he is not in the world. Thus also, "You always have the poor with you, but you will not always have me with you" [Matt. 26:11]. What is meant here by the expression "with you" is explained by the text itself, and is easy to see, namely he is not with us in the same way as the poor are with us. And so forth. To whatever further passages they may introduce, one may briefly reply: Christ is not with us in mortal and earthly fashion, as the poor are.

Hence they cannot by this method succeed in proving that our interpretation is contrary to Scripture. But it is Zwinglian logic to take substance for accident and "which" for "of what kind," as if I should say, "Christ is not present in the Supper in a certain form, therefore he is not present bodily"; "Christ is not with us in a certain form, therefore he is not with us at all," jumping right from a particular to a universal. "The mayor is not in the bath in his red breeches, therefore he is not in the bath." "The king is not at the table with his crown on, therefore he is not at the table." All this is child's play and buffoonery, as the schools are well aware, but among these spirits it is supposed to pass for Scripture and the Christian faith.

If they insist on the basis of these passages that Christ is no longer with us, they must also conclude that Christ is not with us spiritually either. For the words stand there clearly, "I am no more with you," which declares positively that he is not with us at all. "Yes," they say, "but we have clear passages to the contrary which assert that he is with us spiritually, such as John 16 [14:23], "We will make our home with him," and Paul in Ephesians 3 [:17], "Christ dwells in your hearts," etc. I reply: My friend, if they can find these passages to be opposed to the others, why shouldn't they also find the text in the Supper to be opposed to the same? If Christ can be present with them in a certain form without contradicting the text, "I am not with you," then he can also be present with us in the Supper, notwithstanding the same text, "I am not with you." If that text does not invalidate their passages concerning the spiritual nature of Christ, neither does it invalidate our text concerning the invisible nature of Christ in the Supper.

Thus their objection is as sharply opposed to them as to us, and by whatever means they extricate themselves they extricate us also. And our interpretation remains unimpugned: "This is my body." For if they prove anything with their passages, they prove that Christ is not present in the Supper in a visible, mortal, and earthly mode—a thing which it is not in the least necessary to prove, for we acknowledge it all. But what they ought to prove is that our interpretation is false and that Christ lies when he says, "This is my body." But no one steps forth to prove it, for they are nothing but fickle windbags, soiling a lot of good paper with vain and worthless words and making fools of poor simple Christians.

Next he prattles about the paschal lamb, citing Paul in I Corinthians 5 [:7], who calls Christ a paschal lamb.[53] He tries to infer that just as Christ in this passage is not the natural paschal lamb but, by a figure of speech, a new paschal lamb, so also there is a figure of speech in these words, "This is my body." This is nonsense. For he had previously acknowledged that it does not follow, if a figure of speech occurs at one point, that therefore there is also a figure here; but such a consequence must be proved, and we have written enough already concerning figures of speech. All this spirit cares about is to write a book and flatter his followers, in order to evade answering what he was bound and obliged to answer, but still have the appearance of giving an answer. He is bound to prove that our interpretation is contrary to Scripture. So he teaches us that Christ is a paschal lamb; this he calls a "passing over."[54] Let them use this term and make of it what they will, they do not answer thereby how our interpretation is contrary to Scripture.

[53] *Christian Answer*. *C. R.* 92, 909 f.; *St. L.* 20, 1186.
[54] *Ein uberschritt*. The Vulgate at Exod. 12:11 reads, *Phase* (*id est transitus*) *domini*.

Next the spirit becomes very angry because I have ridiculed their silly "representation" idea so openly, and he scolds me severely.[55] But scolding and raging and raving is not in our view the same as Scripture that is contrary to our interpretation. He who cannot answer finds it easy to rage and rave, as a mother may teach her child, "Dear child, if you can't win, start a quarrel." I have thrown a club among the dogs, and by the yelp I know which one I have hit.

This spirit puts me in mind of a madman with a crossbow, who with great hue and cry seized the winch and bent the bow, boasting with mighty words that he would split the iron nail in the center of the target, but in his great haste and excitement he neglected to insert an arrow. So he shot, and as soon as he heard the string whir, he swung the crossbow around crying, "Bull's-eye! The nail is split in two!" And when others laughed and told him there was no arrow there, he scolded them for not recognizing it as an arrow. This is just what this spirit is doing, too. With great ostentation he announces that he will answer and hit the target, but he always forgets the arrow, so that he has never once answered rightly. Nevertheless, jaw-flapping so delights him that he fancies he has an arrow in the bow and has shot to pieces the nail in the target. But we are accustomed to this silly marksmanship. Indeed, even if they did lay an arrow upon the crossbow, we should still be well assured that they would shoot it into the ashes or three ells over the barrier before they would hit us.

So they quote the word of St. Paul in Colossians 3 [:1 f.], "If you have been raised with Christ, seek the things that are above, where Christ is, seated at the right hand of God. Set your mind on things that are above, not on things that are on earth." "Here, here, you flesh-eaters and blood-drinkers," they exclaim, "listen! Christ's body is not to be sought in the sacrament, for the sacrament is on earth, while Christ is above at the right hand of God."

Now it is not necessary for this spirit to show us what St. Paul means by the expression "on earth," though the force of the passage depends on this expression. But he passes lightly over it, rushing blindly wherever their spirit of vanity drives them.

---

[55] *Christian Answer. C. R.* 92, 911; *St. L.* 20, 1187.

But suppose I ask why they attend preaching and seek the gospel, and why they observe the Lord's Supper? Why do they love and serve their neighbor? Our father, mother, master, servant, and neighbor are all on earth; all right, let us not seek them, nor honor, obey, serve, or love anyone! Wouldn't this be fine? But all this is on earth. And St. Paul says that we must not seek that which is on earth. Indeed, then the apostles were altogether wrong in following Christ, for he was on earth. Christ himself came to earth, and Paul himself preached and visited Christians here and there on earth. What do you think? Haven't they twisted this passage most wonderfully?

We are quite familiar with this devil's custom, however. All he does is ridicule us, haughtily ignoring those whom he is supposed to answer, since he can secure followers enough anyway with his useless spouting. We on our part, however, will endure his mocking and defy him to overthrow our interpretation with ridicule. We regard it as a confirmation of our belief, since he can produce nothing against us but his woeful, miserable mockery.

By the expression, "on earth," St. Paul means this earthly life as the world lives it in fornication and all kinds of unrighteousness. He speaks of putting to death the old Adam, as his words say quite clearly: "If you have died with Christ" [Col. 2:20], and shortly after, "Put to death your members which are on earth: fornication, impurity, uncleanness, covetousness, etc." [Col. 3:5]. There we hear what "on earth" means: the old, earthly life according to the old Adam, as men live in the world without the Spirit of God. This is the way the old Adam lives. This kind of life we should not seek after, says St. Paul, for we should die with Christ to the world and to earthly life, and live henceforth a heavenly life in Christ.

Therefore we say frankly that our sacrament is not on earth, and we do not seek it on earth. But if the devil will prove that we regard our sacrament and the body of Christ as fornication, covetousness, hatred, and sheer unrighteousness, then we shall acknowledge that we are acting wrongly if we seek Christ on earth. But if he cannot do that, we say that he lies in his hellish teeth, and slanders St. Paul by representing that Christ's body is on earth if it is in the sacrament. For this is not what St. Paul means by the expression, "on earth," as we have shown. But here once more you see how nicely the fanatics treat the Scripture, and what spirit it is that speaks through them. For the devil knows perfectly well what St. Paul means by "on earth," yet he drives his blinded fanatics to say that Christ's body in the sacrament is "on earth." With such arguments they wish to establish their Supper and overthrow ours.

The same kind of derision the devil practices also with the passage of St. Paul in II Corinthians 5 [:16 f.], "We regard Christ no longer according to the flesh," and, "If any one is in Christ, he is a new creation": such passages without exception force us to the conclusion that Christ's body is not in the Supper. Oh, well, we gladly submit to ridicule once more; let us see what the devil will gain by it. The fanatics should show here what St. Paul means by the expression, "according to the flesh," on which the force of the argument depends. "Yes," says the devil, "I don't care about you. It is enough that my followers quote it; you must simply accept it." All right, we should like to be just as humble and point out the same. St. Paul also speaks here of slaying the old Adam, and wishes to say that we must no longer live according to the flesh, but as a new creation in Christ. Hear his words yourself: "We are convinced," he says, "that if one has died for all, all have died," etc. [II Cor. 5:14]. What else can this mean than that which he says in the passage we discussed immediately above, Colossians 3 [:3],[56] "We have died with Christ," and in Romans 6 [:6], "Our old man was crucified with Christ"? It follows here: "And he died for all, that those who live might live no longer for themselves but for him who for their sakes died and was raised" [II Cor. 5:15]. What else is this than that we must live a new life in Christ?

It continues, "From now on, therefore, we regard no one according to the flesh" [5:16]. Here let Paul and the fanatic argue with each other. The fanatic says that to know someone according to the flesh means to regard him as physically present—present with his body, as Christ is in the sacrament, and that this is in-

[56] More accurately, Luther's words here reflect Rom. 6:8.

correct and Paul forbids it. My friend, why then does Paul know his Corinthians as living in the body with him? Why does he know his own body? Again, why do the fanatics know their companions in the body among one another? Why do they know their material Supper? Are not all these material or bodily things, present according to the flesh? St. Paul, however, here forbids us to know according to the flesh. But if they can know these things according to the flesh in such a way that St. Paul is not against them, my friend, why should he be against us when we know Christ as bodily present in the sacrament? But let the mockers mock; may the one who mocks the other best be the champion.

By the expression, "according to the flesh," in this passage St. Paul means that which happens in a fleshly manner and not according to the Spirit, or in a spiritual manner, as he says in II Corinthians 10 [:3], "Though we walk in the flesh, we do not war according to the flesh," i.e. not in a fleshly manner. "According to the flesh" does not signify "in the flesh," as they dream, but signifies, with adverbial force, carnally or with the desire and affection of the flesh, or the way in which flesh acts. "In the flesh" and "according to the flesh" are two quite different things. Paul (Galatians 2 [:20]) lives in the flesh—not, however, according to the flesh but by faith in Christ. In Romans 8 [:6, 13] he describes living according to the flesh as death, saying, "If you live according to the flesh you will die."

Therefore the text of St. Paul irresistibly forces us to conclude that this is his meaning: Because we all have died with Christ to the world and the flesh, from now on we should no longer live or think according to the flesh, or in a fleshly manner. So we should know no one in a fleshly but only in a spiritual manner. For to know another in a fleshly manner is to know him no further than the flesh has power to know. Now the flesh has power only to seek its own from everyone else;[57] it hates, envies, and does all manner of evil to its enemy, seeks pleasure, prestige, enjoyment, and friendship from everyone for its own advantage, etc. This is the way men of the world regard one another. But we Christians regard no one so, for we are a new creation in Christ [II Cor. 5:17],

[57] Cf. I Cor. 13:5.

and regard one another according to the Spirit, i.e. each seeks not his own advantage but what is best for others, as Paul teaches also in Romans 14 [:19] and Philippians 2 [:4].

"Even though we once regarded Christ from a fleshly point of view," he says, "we regard him thus no longer" [II Cor. 5:16]. It is well to understand that he does not refer here to Christ's personal flesh, as this spirit foolishly imagines, for that remains Christ's flesh in eternity and all the angels will recognize him in it eternally. But just as we regard our brothers in a spiritual, no longer a fleshly manner, so much the less do we regard Christ in a fleshly manner. Formerly, he means to say, when we were holy in Judaism and in the works of the law—which the false apostles are once again promoting—we knew nothing spiritually about Christ, but what we sought was merely fleshly. For "we had hoped that he would redeem Israel," Luke 24 [:21], and would regard our holiness and glorify us according to the flesh. This was really to know Christ according to the flesh—a real fleshly perception. But all this has now passed away and died with him. We no longer regard him so, for all this has vanished and we are entirely a new creation in Christ. This interpretation is given you by Paul himself; just read and examine the text rightly.

Now, all who regard and know Christ from a fleshly point of view are inevitably offended at him, as was the case with the Jews. For since flesh and blood thinks no further than it sees and feels, and since it sees that Christ was crucified as a mortal man, it inevitably says, "This is the end; neither life nor salvation is to be found here; he is gone; he can help no one; he himself is lost." But he who is not offended at him must rise above the flesh and be raised by the Word so that he may perceive in the Spirit how Christ precisely through his suffering and death has attained true life and glory. And whoever does this properly, whoever is able to do it, is a new creation in Christ, endowed with new spiritual knowledge. Just so, even now, all are offended at Christ if they view his Supper in a fleshly manner, as the fanatics do. They are the ones who regard Christ according to the flesh, as they accuse us of doing. For flesh cannot say or know more than, "Here is bread and wine," therefore it must be offended at Christ when he says, "This is my body," for it is an old creation in Adam. If it is not to become offended, it must rise above this flesh and believe the words, "This is my body"; then it will understand that this bread is not mere bread but the true body of Christ.

It grieves me, indeed, that the devil should thus ridicule God's words. But it moves me to pity that the poor people should not see how the fanatics use these vague ideas as the foundation of their fantasies. They boast, swearing by all they hold dear, that they have learned nothing from us.[58] Really, this is not necessary. Their writings show it all too plainly, without boasting on their part. We would be sorry if they learned such doctrine from us. If this is the way they interpret the Scriptures and preach in Zurich, Basel, and Strassburg[59] and elsewhere, one could wish that they were still papists, for throughout the world the latter are now becoming fully convinced that their teaching is wrong. Good Lord, if such notorious errors and false interpretations of St. Paul do not alarm or stir up the people against these fanatics, what else can arouse them?

Still they introduce other passages in which it is proclaimed that Christ left the world, went to the Father, ascended into heaven, and sits at the right hand of God, etc. But they can make nothing out of this but to teach us what we have known for a long, long time, in order that we may not notice how they have skipped over the point where they were supposed to furnish an answer. They ought to have proved that on this account our interpretation is incorrect and that these words of Christ, "This is my body," are false. They say it is a contradiction that Christ's body is in heaven and in the Supper. But they do not prove it. We say, therefore, on the contrary that it is not a contradiction, for Scripture says both. And our No is as strong as their Yes, for we cannot deny the clear, lucid words merely on account of their plain, bare, simple Yes. For more than a thousand years it has been known that Christ ascended into heaven, without all the teaching of this modern spirit, nevertheless it was not denied for that reason that Christ's body was present in the Supper or that Christ's words

[58] *Christian Answer*. *C. R.* 92, 825, cf. 906 ff.; *St. L.* 20, 1135, cf. 1185 f.
[59] Zwingli preached in Zurich, Oecolampadius in Basel, Bucer in Strassburg.

were true.[60] Now, if this spirit has any objection, it is only fair that he show and teach it to us. But he will never do this.

However, I will tell you the truth, dear friends. If this spirit is really serious and not wilfully lying when he says our interpretation is contrary to Scripture, then I will regard all my arguments as lost. I will prove this as follows: First, he has admitted above that Christ in the first Supper gave his body to be eaten, since he uses action-words in the Supper, as we have already heard sufficiently. Now tell me, how can he seriously say here that the very thing which he himself acknowledged above as correct and as having once taken place, is false and contrary to Scripture? For if he meant it seriously, he would also attack it with Scripture in regard to the first Supper and not invent action-words there. He does not do this, however, but leaves our interpretation intact. Now, if our interpretation remains in the first Supper, there can be no metaphor or representation in the words. What the words say, they mean. Thus all their storming and raging in search of a metaphor is utterly vain.

Secondly, no one can deny that Christ administered the first Supper while he was in the world, before he went to the Father. Tell me, then, how can this spirit seriously contend that the passages which speak of Christ's going to the Father are contrary to the text in the Supper? But he must acknowledge that none of these sayings was yet fulfilled, and Christ was not yet seated in heaven. If Christ had instituted the Supper from heaven after his ascension, the fanatics' position would have plausibility. But in reality Christ has so acted as if to say, "Fanatics will arise, pretending that my Supper is opposed to the passages which say of me that I go to the Father and am no longer in the world. Therefore I will anticipate them and institute my Supper while I am still in the world and upon earth, so that before they expect it they may be trapped in their own words as notorious liars, and so that you, my beloved children, may be strengthened in the true faith."

How can they maintain their position here? They must surrender all these passages on which they have so wilfully prided

[60] Cf. Sasse, *This Is My Body*, Section I, pp. 13 ff.

themselves up to now, and as notorious liars confess that since Christ was not in heaven when he observed the Supper, those passages could not have seriously moved them to deny that Christ's body is present in the Supper. They must admit, rather, that they have been deceived by the devil into imagining that they saw what they did not see. For these passages contribute nothing to determining whether Christ's body is present in the Supper or not, any more than these: "Jesus was born in Bethlehem, and fled into Egypt."

I will give them some good advice, however. They must now think up some other passage of Scripture, such as this one: "When it was evening, Jesus sat at table with the twelve disciples" [Matt. 26:20], and whatever other passages similarly speak of sitting at table. From these they will necessarily deduce: "The Scripture says that Christ sat at table, therefore he cannot be in the bread." If they only say this, it is enough, and they will not have to prove to us how it is contrary to the Scripture, as they have done with the preceding passages. For whatever this spirit says is right—except where he is lying. But we shall answer, "Too late, dear spirit, too late! These passages about sitting at table never led you into your error; you never thought of them, much less did they move you. If these never moved you, and the former have been unable to move you to become serious, please tell us what has moved you? Dear spirit, if you will catch us also in open lies, we shall concede defeat."

But they continue, "Though the first Supper was not opposed to the passages of Scripture we have cited, subsequent administrations of the Supper, after the ascension, are opposed to them." I reply: This is not my question at this point. It is sufficient for me to have upheld the first Supper, that it cannot be opposed to the passages concerning the ascension of Christ. This spirit has manifestly erred, for if I sustain the point that the passages concerning Christ's ascension can induce no one to deny the first Supper according to our interpretation, we shall easily maintain the subsequent administrations of the Supper as well. For who will believe the fanatics, that the Scripture passages on the ascension of Christ seriously impel them to oppose the Supper after the ascension, if they are forced to admit that they are not impelled by the same passages to oppose the Supper before the ascension? If Christ's body can sit at table and still be in the bread, then it can also be in heaven and anywhere else he wishes, and still be in the bread. Whether it is far from the table or near does not at all affect its being at the same time in the bread. Well, here they have been caught in open lies, yet they will not yield or admit their error so as to honor the truth in obedience to God.

Let this suffice to show that our interpretation is not contrary to Scripture or the Creed, as this mad spirit deludes himself into believing. Next he comes to the two principal points at which I have attacked most strongly, viz. that Christ is at the right hand of God, and that the flesh is of no avail,[61] where he was to prove that these two propositions make it impossible for Christ's body to be present in the Supper. I had called attention to these passages with capital letters,[62] so they might not skip over them. Now this dear spirit comes along with his figure, alloeosis,[63] to make everything plain, and teaches us that in the Scriptures one nature in Christ is taken for the other, until he falls into the abyss and concludes that the passage, "The Word became flesh," John 1 [:14], must not be understood as it reads, but thus: "The flesh became Word," or, "Man became God." This is to give the lie to Scripture.

I cannot at this time attack all this spirit's errors. But this I say: Whoever will take a warning, let him beware of Zwingli and shun his books as the prince of hell's poison. For the man is completely perverted and has entirely lost Christ. Other sacramen-

---

[61] *Christian Answer.* *C. R.* 92, 914 ff.; *St. L.* 20, 1189 ff.

[62] See pp. 144 f.

[63] A section in *Friendly Exposition* is entitled, "On the Interchange (*De alloeosibus*) of the two natures in Christ." *C. R.* 92, 679 ff. (see footnotes there). A similar section is found in *Christian Answer.* *C. R.* 92, 922 ff.; *St. L.* 20, 1192 ff., and another in *Concerning Luther's Book Entitled "Confession,"* 1528, as printed in *St. L.* 20, 1309 ff. *Alloiōsis,* a word which in Plato and Aristotle and the Septuagint meant change, alteration, difference, became a technical rhetorical term in Plutarch's *Moralia,* ch. 41. Zwingli defines it as "an exchange [*abtuschen*] or interchange [*gegenwechsslen*] of the two natures which are in one person, by which in naming one nature we mean the other, or name them both but mean only the one." *C. R.* 92, 925 f., *St. L.* 20, 1194 f. Zwingli asserts that the patristic "communication of properties" concept involved just such a rhetorical *alloeosis.* Cf. *Clear Instruction.* *LCC* 24, 212 ff.

tarians settle on one error, but this man never publishes a book without spewing out new errors, more and more all the time. But anyone who rejects this warning may go his way, just so he knows that I warned him, and my conscience is clear.

You must not believe or admit that this figure, alloeosis, is to be found in these passages, or that you can put one nature of Christ in place of the other. The insane spirit dreamed this up in order to rob us of Christ, for he does not prove it to you nor can he do so. And even if this error of his were true and right, it still would not prove that Christ's body cannot be present in the Supper. I have pressed them to show conclusive grounds why these words, "This is my body," just as they read, are false, though Christ is in heaven. For the power of God is not known to us, and he can find a way to make both true, viz. Christ in heaven and his body present in the Supper. That was the principal question. What I demanded, writing in capital letters, was that they should show how the two were contradictory. But he is silent on this point, passes over it without one letter as if it did not concern him, and spouts meanwhile about his alloeosis.

When I proved that Christ's body is everywhere because the right hand of God is everywhere,[64] I did so—as I quite openly explained at the time—in order to show at least in one way how God could bring it about that Christ is in heaven and his body in the Supper at the same time, and that he reserved to his divine wisdom and power many more ways to accomplish the same result, because we do not know the limit or measure of his power.

Now if they had any intention or ability to answer, they should have proved incontrovertibly that there was no way within God's wisdom and power for Christ to be in heaven and at the same time for his body to be present in the Supper. Here is the difficulty over which these good fellows leap. For they did not need to teach us about the visible mode of existence, that according to our eyesight heaven is high above us and the Supper down here on earth. We know perfectly well that, to judge by our sight, what is here below cannot be above, and vice versa; for this is a human, visible mode of existence. But God's Word and works do

[64] See pp. 47 ff., 55 ff.

not proceed according to our eyesight, but in a way incomprehensible to all reason and even to the angels. So Christ is neither in heaven nor in the Supper in a visible manner, nor as fleshly eyes judge a thing to be at this place or that.

It certainly is a pitiful spirit who judges God's Word and works according to the eyes. For in this way God himself is not to be found wherever he may be, whether everywhere or somewhere. My friend, why then does this spirit cling to the one specific mode of existence which I pointed out? In the first place, because he is worried that his stomach may burst with all his cleverness. In the second place, because in this way he can fool the common people so that they will not see how he skips over questions which he ought to answer and starts a different game in order to sidetrack us and make us forget the matters which torment him. If I were to argue with them only over this one mode to which I referred, they would win the game. Why? Because then they would have an excuse to avoid answering the real problem which presses them, and still they would write one book after another to spew their useless chatter into the world. For they regard much spewing and writing of useless books as fitting rebuttal. So they betray the poor people.

This, then, is what you should do to protect yourself against them. If they prove conclusively that God's power and wisdom extend no farther than the range of our sight, and that he is able to do no more than we can physically see and judge with our eyes or touch with our fingers, then you should join their side. Then I too will believe that God knows of no other way whereby Christ can be at the same time in heaven and his body in the Supper. Demand and insist on this. They are bound to do it. Their teaching cannot be established until they have made this clear and certain, for on this their teaching rests.

The devil is well aware that he cannot furnish this proof; therefore he blusters loudly with his useless twaddle so that we may not press him for it. Meanwhile he spreads his cleverness which no one is asking for. Even if he could overthrow the mode to which I have referred—which he cannot—he still would have accomplished nothing by it, because it still would by no means have been proved a contradiction for Christ to be in heaven and his body in the bread. As I demanded in my previous book, he must prove not only that this mode of existence is impossible, but also that God himself cannot know or devise any other.[65] Since he does not do this, we now say: God is omnipotent; he can do more than we see; therefore I believe his words as they stand. See how these matters stand with this spirit and how he makes a fool of himself with all his learning!

To all his worthless spouting against the mode that I have mentioned, I answer with one little word: No! He brings in his alloeosis, which no one concedes him the right to do in this discussion; it is just as much in need of proof as the rest of his system of lies. But if he proved it, one could make further reply. So the mode of existence to which I have referred still stands absolutely firm, in spite of his alloeosis. Though he says it is an example of alloeosis, no one gives a rip about that; he might just as well say it was irony or some other trope. It simply won't do to play around with tropes[66] in the Scriptures. One must first prove that particular passages are tropes before one uses them in controversies. Oh, it is just as I have said: The devil has been hit so that he cannot answer, therefore he lashes about with vain words. God be praised and thanked that he knows how to arm us so well against the devil.

Dear brother, instead of alloeosis you should teach: Because Jesus Christ is true God and man in one person, in no passage of Scripture is one nature taken for the other. For he calls it alloeosis when something is said about the divinity of Christ which after all belongs to his humanity, or vice versa—for example, in Luke 24 [:26], "Was it not necessary that the Christ should suffer and so enter into his glory?" Here he performs a sleight-of-hand trick and substitutes the human nature for Christ. Beware, beware, I say, of this alloeosis, for it is the devil's mask since it will finally construct a kind of Christ after whom I would not want to be a Christian, that is, a Christ who is and does no more in his

---

[65] See pp. 47 ff., 60 ff.

[66] *Troppens odder troppelns.* The four chief kinds of trope were said to be metaphor, metonymy, synecdoche, and irony.

passion and his life than any other ordinary saint. For if I believe that only the human nature suffered for me, then Christ would be a poor Savior for me, in fact, he himself would need a Savior. In short, it is indescribable what the devil attempts with this alloeosis![67]

Indeed, this subject is an article of great importance and calls for a book itself, and should not come up in this matter at all. Briefly, however, a plain Christian should be satisfied with this: that the Holy Spirit knows quite well how to teach us the manner in which we should speak, and we need no trope-makers or crap-shooters.[68] The Holy Spirit speaks as follows, John 3 [:16], "God so loved the world that he gave his only Son"; Romans 8 [:32], "He did not spare his own Son but gave him up for us all." In the same way all his works, words, sufferings, and whatever Christ does, he does, accomplishes, speaks, and suffers as the true Son of God, so that it may properly be said, "The Son of God has died for us," "The Son of God preaches upon earth," "The Son of God washes his disciples' feet"; as the Epistle to the Hebrews says, chapter 6 [:6], "They crucify the Son of God on their own account," or I Corinthians 2: [:8], "If they had known, they would not have crucified the Lord of glory."

Now if the old witch, Lady Reason,[69] alloeosis' grandmother, should say that the Deity surely cannot suffer and die, then you must answer and say: That is true, but since the divinity and humanity are one person in Christ, the Scriptures ascribe to the divinity, because of this personal union, all that happens to humanity, and vice versa. And in reality it is so. Indeed, you must say that the person (pointing to Christ) suffers, and dies. But this person is truly God, and therefore it is correct to say: the Son of God suffers. Although, so to speak, the one part (namely, the divinity) does not suffer, nevertheless the person, who is God, suffers in the other part (namely, in the humanity).[70]

---

[67] Beginning with the second sentence of this paragraph, this passage is quoted in the *Formula of Concord,* Solid Declaration, VIII, 39 f.

[68] *Keiner troppeler noch toppeler.*

[69] Luther often referred to reason as the devil's bride or mother or grandmother, cf. *LW* 40, 174 f.

[70] This paragraph is quoted in the *Formula of Concord,* Solid Declaration, VIII, 41 f.

Just as we say: the king's son is wounded—when actually only his leg is wounded; Solomon is wise—though only his soul is wise; Absalom is handsome—though only his body is handsome; Peter is gray—though only his head is gray. For since body and soul are one person, everything that pertains to the body or the soul, yes, to the least member of the body, is correctly and properly ascribed to the entire person. This is the way people speak throughout the world, not only in Scripture, and it is the truth. For the Son of God truly is crucified for us, i.e. this person who is God. For that is what he is—this person, I say, is crucified according to his humanity.[71]

Thus we should ascribe to the whole person whatever pertains to one part of the person, because both parts constitute one person. This is the way all the ancient teachers speak; so do all modern theologians, all languages, and the whole Scripture. But this damned alloeosis exactly inverts the matter and changes it so that it ascribes to the parts what Scripture assigns to the whole person. He fashions his own tropes to pervert Scripture and divide the person of Christ, as he has also done with the word "is," just so he may bring to light his new teaching and his foolish ideas.

Well, if he is so fond of tropes, why isn't he satisfied with the old trope which Scripture and all teachers up to now have used? viz. *synecdoche*,[72] for example, "Christ died according to his humanity." But that would have been nothing new; no fame could have been won from it, and no new errors could have been produced. Therefore he had to bring forth alloeosis, and teach us that one nature is taken for the other. As if the apostles were so senseless and foolish that they could not speak of the divinity without calling it humanity, and vice versa. If John had wanted to use alloeosis, he could have said, "The flesh became Word," instead of saying, "The Word became flesh" [John 1:14].

Is this not a mischievous spirit, who blurts out his alloeosis in these passages? Who commanded him to do this? How does he prove there is an alloeosis here? No, this proof is not necessary;

[71] These last two sentences are quoted in the *Formula of Concord,* Solid Declaration, VIII, 42.

[72] Zwingli had actually cited the figure synecdoche in *On Baptism. LCC* 24, 147, *Friendly Rejoinder. C. R.* 92, 779; *St. L.* 20, 1111, and *Reply to Billican and Rhegius. C. R.* 91, 920.

it is enough if he says, "I, Zwingli, say there is an alloeosis here, therefore it is so. I was in the bosom of the Godhead yesterday and I have just come from heaven, therefore I must be believed!" He should prove first that there is an alloeosis here. This he fails to do, but assumes it as if he had established it a thousand years ago and no one may doubt it. But that there is an alloeosis here is much more in need of proof than that which he would like to establish with it. This is the principle of Zwinglian logic called "proving an uncertain proposition by something more uncertain, and an unknown by one more unknown." Oh, beautiful learning! The children should pelt it with dung and drive it away!

If it is proper for him to invent tropes and play around with figures as he pleases, and still be right in all he says, is it surprising that he ultimately makes a Belial out of Christ?[73] If anyone dares to assert whatever he pleases without being obliged to show his reasons, my friend, what conclusions may he not draw? It is no different from what I have complained of: this spirit appeals to Scripture to flatter people with fair words, and yet he produces nothing but his own dreams and his foolish imagination in opposition to Scripture. In this passage, however, we condemn and damn alloeosis right down to hell as the devil's own inspiration. We would like to see how he proposes to establish it. For what we want is Scripture and sound reasons, not his snot and slobber.

They raise a hue and cry against us, saying that we mingle the two natures into one essence.[74] This is not true. We do not say that divinity is humanity, or that the divine nature is the human nature, which would be confusing the natures into one essence. Rather, we merge the two distinct natures into one single person, and say: God is man and man is God. We in turn raise a hue and cry against them for separating the person of Christ as though there were two persons.[75] If Zwingli's alloeosis stands, then Christ

---

[73] Cf. II Cor. 6:15.

[74] *Christian Answer. C. R.* 92, 933 f.; *St. L.* 20, 1200. This is to accuse Luther of Monophysitism, which was condemned by the Fourth Ecumenical Council, at Chalcedon, in 451, and subsequently in the Athanasian Creed. For a discussion of the point at issue in another frame of reference see also Luther's *The Three Symbols or Creeds of the Christian Faith*, 1538. *LW* 34, 197 ff.

[75] Luther thus accuses the Zwinglians of Nestorianism, which was condemned by the Third Ecumenical Council, at Ephesus, 431, at Chalcedon as well,

will have to be two persons, one a divine and the other a human person, since Zwingli applies all the texts concerning the passion only to the human nature and completely excludes them from the divine nature. But if the works are divided and separated, the person will also have to be separated, since all the doing and suffering are not ascribed to natures but to persons. It is the person who does and suffers everything, the one thing according to this nature and the other thing according to the other nature, all of which scholars know perfectly well. Therefore we regard our Lord Christ as God and man in one person, "neither confusing the natures nor dividing the person." [76]

Let this suffice as a treatment of an incidental matter which would serve no useful purpose here, except that this spirit is so full of errors that he seeks occasion everywhere to dupe the simple, and meanwhile sidetrack the real issue. We stand firm, because this chatterbox will not and cannot prove that the two propositions, "Christ is in heaven, and his body is in the Supper," are contradictory. So the words, "This is my body," remain to us just as they read, for one letter of them is better and surer to us than the books of all the fanatics, even if they should fill the world with the books they write.

Again, since they do not prove that the right hand of God is a particular place in heaven,[77] the mode of existence of which I

---

and subsequently in the Athanasian Creed. The Chalcedonian Formula carefully steered between Monophysitism, which fused or *confused* the two natures of Christ and *converted* the human nature into the divine, and Nestorianism, which *divided* and *separated* the natures virtually into two persons. Zwingli defended himself at length against the charge of Nestorianizing in the section on Alloeosis in *Christian Answer*. *C. R.* 92, 922 ff.; *St. L.* 20, 1192 ff.

[76] Beginning with "If Zwingli's alloeosis . . .," this passage is quoted in the *Formula of Concord*, Solid Declaration, VIII, 43, which retouches it at two points: (a) in the second from the last sentence the Formula reads ". . . ascribed . . . to the person"; (b) in the last sentence the grammatical form of the Latin expression is emended from *confundens* to *confundendo* (as Luther's manuscript also had read), in better parallelism with *dividendo*.

[77] Zwingli had not argued that "the right hand of God" is a particular place in heaven; he acknowledged that God's right hand is everywhere, but asserted that Christ is not at God's right hand according to his humanity as he is according to his divinity. Zwingli distinguished between "Christ is everywhere" and "Christ's body is everywhere." *Christian Answer*. *C. R.* 92, 929 f.; *St. L.* 20, 1198 f.

have spoken also stands firm, that Christ's body is everywhere because it is at the right hand of God which is everywhere, although we do not know how that occurs. For we also do not know how it occurs that the right hand of God is everywhere. It is certainly not the mode by which we see with our eyes that an object is somewhere, as the fanatics regard the sacrament. But God no doubt has a mode by which it can be somewhere and that's the way it is until the fanatics prove the contrary.

Even if the alloeosis concept were valid, so that one nature could be taken for the other, still it would pertain only to the works or functions of the natures, and not the essence of the natures. For although in reference to his works—as when we say, "Christ preaches, drinks, prays, dies"—Christ might be taken as a designation for the human nature, the same could not be true in reference to his essence—as when we say, "God is man or man is God." Here there can be no alloeosis, indeed no synecdoche or other trope either, for here God must be taken as a designation for God, and man as a designation for man. Now when I write, "Christ's body is everywhere," I am treating not of the works of the natures, of course, but of the essence of the natures. Therefore neither alloeosis nor synecdoche can refute my argument, for essence is essence, each for itself and none for the other. Whoever wishes to refute my argument must not bring forth alloeoses or synecdoches or other tropes—these are good for nothing here—but he must refute my reasons on which my argument is based.

My grounds, on which I rest in this matter, are as follows: The first is this article of our faith, that Jesus Christ is essential, natural, true, complete God and man in one person, undivided and inseparable. The second, that the right hand of God is everywhere. The third, that the Word of God is not false or deceitful. The fourth, that God has and knows various ways to be present at a certain place, not only the single one of which the fanatics prattle, which the philosophers call "local." [78] Of this the sophists[79]

[78] This much of the paragraph is quoted in the *Formula of Concord,* Solid Declaration, VII, 93 ff., and (with an interpolation) Epitome, VII, 11 ff.

[79] Meaning in this case the Occamist Scholastics, from whom Luther adapted this analysis of the modes of existence or presence. Aquinas had recognized the first two modes. See Sasse, *This Is My Body,* pp. 155 ff.

properly say: There are three modes of being present in a given place: locally or circumscriptively, definitively, repletively.

Let me translate this for the sake of clearer understanding. In the first place, an object is circumscriptively or locally in a place, i.e. in a circumscribed manner,[80] if the space and the object occupying it exactly correspond and fit into the same measurements, such as wine or water in a cask, where the wine occupies no more space and the cask yields no more space than the volume of the wine. Or, a piece of wood or a tree in the water takes up no more space and the water yields no more than the size of the tree in it. Again, a man walking in the open air takes up no more space from the air around him, nor does the air yield more, than the size of the man. In this mode, space and object correspond exactly, item by item, just as a pewterer measures, pours off, and molds the tankard in its form.

In the second place, an object is in a place definitively,[81] i.e. in an uncircumscribed manner, if the object or body is not palpably in one place and is not measurable according to the dimensions of the place where it is, but can occupy either more room or less. Thus it is said that angels and spirits are in certain places. For an angel or devil can be present in an entire house or city; again, he can be in a room, a chest or a box, indeed, in a nutshell. The space is really material and circumscribed, and has its own dimensions of length, breadth, and depth; but that which occupies it has not the same length, breadth, or depth as the space which it occupies, indeed, it has no length or breadth at all. Thus we read in the gospel that the devil possesses men and enters them, and they also enter into swine. Indeed, in Matthew 8[82] we read that a whole legion were in one man. That would be about six thousand devils. This I call an uncircumscribed presence in a given place, since we cannot circumscribe or measure it as we measure a body, and yet it is obviously present in the place.

---

[80] *Begreifflich* could also be translated "comprehensible" or "determinate" in the sense of measurable.

[81] This is the more familiar spelling, cf. Aquinas. With the late medieval Occamists, Luther spelled the word *diffinitive*.

[82] Matt. 8:28 ff. relates the incident of the Gadarene (or Gerasene) demoniacs, but Luther's reference is to the parallel in Mark 5:9 ff. The Roman military legion numbered up to six thousand men.

This was the mode in which the body of Christ was present when he came out of the closed grave, and came to the disciples through a closed door, as the gospels show.[83] There was no measuring or defining of the space his head or foot occupied when he passed through the stone, yet he certainly had to pass through it. He took up no space, and the stone yielded him no space, but the stone remained stone, as entire and firm as before, and his body remained as large and thick as it was before. But he also was able, when he wished, to let himself be seen circumscribed in given places where he occupied space and his size could be measured. Just so, Christ can be and is in the bread, even though he can also show himself in circumscribed and visible form wherever he wills. For as the sealed stone and the closed door remained unaltered and unchanged, though his body at the same time was in the space entirely occupied by stone and wood, so he is also at the same time in the sacrament and where the bread and wine are, though the bread and wine in themselves remain unaltered and unchanged.

In the third place, an object occupies places repletively, i.e. supernaturally, if it is simultaneously present in all places whole and entire, and fills all places, yet without being measured or circumscribed by any place, in terms of the space which it occupies. This mode of existence belongs to God alone, as he says in the prophet Jeremiah [23:23 f.], "I am a God at hand and not afar off. I fill heaven and earth." This mode is altogether incomprehensible, beyond our reason, and can be maintained only with faith, in the Word.

All this I have related in order to show that there are more modes whereby an object may exist in a place than the one circumscribed, physical mode on which the fanatics insist. Moreover, Scripture irresistibly forces us to believe that Christ's body does not have to be present in a given place circumscriptively or corporeally, occupying and filling space in proportion to its size. For it was in the stone at the grave, but not in that circumscribed mode; similarly in the closed door, as they cannot deny. If it could be present there without space and place proportionate to

[83] Cf. Matt. 28:2 and John 20:19, 26; cf. p. 66.

its size, my friend, why can't it also be in the bread without space and room proportionate to its size? But if it can be present in this uncircumscribed manner, it is beyond the realm of material creatures and is not grasped or measured in their terms. Who can know how this takes place? Who will prove it false if someone declares that, since Christ's body is outside the realm of creation, it can assuredly be wherever he wishes, and that all creatures are as permeable and present to him as another body's material place or location is to it?

Consider our physical eyes and our power of vision. When we open our eyes, in one moment our sight is five or six miles[84] away, and simultaneously present everywhere within the range of those six miles. Yet this is only a matter of sight, the power of the eye. If physical sight can do this, do you not think that God's power can also find a way by which all creatures can be present and permeable to Christ's body? "Yes," you say, "but by this you do not prove that it is so." Thank you, I prove this much by it, that the fanatics also cannot refute me and prove that this is impossible to the divine power, which they should and must do. They should prove, I say, that God knows no other way by which the body of Christ can exist in a given place than corporeally and circumscriptively. If they cannot do this, their system stands disgraced. Of course, they cannot do it.

Because we prove from Scripture, however, that Christ's body can exist in a given place in other modes than this corporeal one, we have by the same token sufficiently argued that the words, "This is my body," ought to be believed as they read. For it is contrary to no article of faith, and moreover it is scriptural, in that Christ's body is held to have passed through the sealed stone and the closed door. Since we can point out a mode of existence other than the corporeal, circumscribed one, who will be so bold as to measure and span the power of God, as if He knows of no other modes? Yet the position of the fanatics cannot be maintained unless they can prove that the power of God can be thus measured and spanned, for their whole argument rests on the

[84] In terms of today's measurements this would be a distance of approximately twenty to twenty five miles.

assertion that the body of Christ can exist in a given place only in a corporeal and circumscribed manner. But here they are not answering but leaping over the question while they chatter about Lady Alloeosis.

And now to come to my own position: Our faith maintains that Christ is God and man, and the two natures are one person, so that this person may not be divided in two; therefore, he can surely show himself in a corporeal, circumscribed manner at whatever place he will, as he did after the resurrection and will do on the Last Day. But above and beyond this mode he can also use the second, uncircumscribed mode, as we have proved from the gospel[85] that he did at the grave and the closed door.

But now, since he is a man who is supernaturally one person with God, and apart from this man there is no God, it must follow that according to the third supernatural mode, he is and can be wherever God is and that everything is full of Christ through and through, even according to his humanity—not according to the first, corporeal, circumscribed mode, but according to the supernatural, divine mode. Here you must take your stand and say that wherever Christ is according to his divinity, he is there as a natural, divine person and he is also naturally and personally there, as his conception in his mother's womb proves conclusively. For if he was the Son of God, he had to be in his mother's womb naturally and personally and become man. But if he is present naturally and personally wherever he is, then he must be man there, too, since he is not two separate persons but a single person. Wherever this person is, it is the single, indivisible person, and if you can say, "Here is God," then you must also say, "Christ the man is present too."

And if you could show me one place where God is and not the man, then the person is already divided and I could at once say truthfully, "Here is God who is not man and has never become man." But no God like that for me! For it would follow from this that space and place had separated the two natures from one another and thus had divided the person, even though death and all the devils had been unable to separate and tear them apart.

---

[85] Cf. p. 66.

This would leave me a poor sort of Christ, if he were present only at one single place, as a divine and human person, and if at all other places he had to be nothing more than a mere isolated God and a divine person without the humanity. No, comrade, wherever you place God for me, you must also place the humanity for me. They simply will not let themselves be separated and divided from each other. He has become one person and does not separate the humanity from himself[86] as Master Jack takes off his coat and lays it aside when he goes to bed.

Let me give a simple illustration for the common man. The humanity is more closely united with God than our skin with our flesh—yes, more closely than body and soul. Now as long as a man lives and remains in health, his skin and flesh, body and soul are so completely one being, one person, that they cannot be separated; on the contrary, wherever the soul is, there must the body be also, and wherever the flesh is, there must the skin be also. You cannot indicate a special place or space where the soul is present alone without the body, like a kernel without the shell, or where the flesh is without the skin, like a pea without a pod. On the contrary, wherever the one is, there must the other be also. Thus you cannot shell the divinity from the humanity and lay it aside at some place away from the humanity. For thereby you would be dividing the person and making the humanity merely a pod, indeed, a coat which the divinity put on and off according to the availability of place and space. Thus the physical space would have the power to divide the divine person, although neither angels nor all creation can do so.

Here you will say with Nicodemus, "How can this be?" [John 3:9]. Must all places and space now become one space and place? Or, as this dolt dreams according to his crude, fleshly sense, must the humanity of Christ stretch and extend itself like a skin as wide as all creation? I answer: Here you must with Moses take off your old shoes, and with Nicodemus be born anew.[87] According to your old notion, which perceives no more than the first, corporeal, circumscribed mode, you will understand this as little

[86] The entire two paragraphs down to this point are quoted in the *Formula of Concord*, Solid Declaration, VIII, 81 ff.
[87] Cf. Exod. 3:5, John 3:3.

as the fanatics, who cannot think of the Godhead in any other way than existing everywhere in a corporeal, circumscribed mode, as if God were some vast, extended entity that pervades and embraces all creation. This you may gather from their charge that we stretch and extend the humanity and thereby enclose the divinity.[88] Such words obviously apply to the corporeal, circumscribed mode of being, as a peasant stuffs himself into his jacket and trousers, when the jacket and trousers are expanded so that they will go around his body and his legs.

Get out of here, you stupid fanatic, with your worthless ideas! If you cannot think in higher and other terms than this, then sit behind the stove and stew pears and apples, and leave such subjects alone. If Christ passed through the closed door with his body, and the door was not on that account expanded nor his body compressed, why should the humanity here be expanded or the divinity enclosed, where there is a far different and more exalted mode of presence?

"This is a lofty subject," you say, "and I do not understand it." Yes, this is my complaint too, that these fleshly spirits who scarcely know how to crawl on the earth, untested in faith, inexperienced in spiritual matters, wish to fly aloft above the clouds and measure and judge these profound, mysterious, incomprehensible matters not according to God's words but according to their crawling and walking on the earth. They will fare as Icarus did in the poet's story.[89] For they too have stolen others' feathers—i.e. texts of Scripture—and fastened them on with wax—i.e. adjusted them to their own interpretation with reason—and now they fly aloft. But the wax melts, and they fall into the sea and drown in all kinds of errors.

Christ says, "If I have told you earthly things and you do not believe me, how can you believe it if I tell you heavenly things?" [John 3:12]. Behold, this is entirely an earthly and bodily thing, when Christ's body passes through the stone and the door. For his body is an object which can be laid hold of, as much so as the

---

[88] *Christian Answer.* C. R. 92, 935, 918; *St. L.* 20, 1201, 1190. Cf. p. 65, n. 108.

[89] The myth of Daedalus and Icarus is told in Ovid's *Metamorphoses,* II, 1 ff.

stone and the door. Still, no reason can grasp how his body and the stone are in one place at the same time when he passes through it, and yet neither does the stone become larger or expand more, nor Christ's body smaller or more compressed. Here faith must blind reason and lift it out of the physical, circumscribed mode into the second, uncircumscribed mode which it does not understand but cannot deny.

Now if this second mode must be understood by faith, and reason with its first, circumscribed mode must vanish, how much more must faith alone remain here and reason vanish in the case of the heavenly, supernatural mode, where Christ's body is one person with God in the Godhead? For everyone will grant me this, that it is a far different and higher mode when Christ's body is in the sealed stone and the closed door, than when according to the first mode it sits or stands in his clothes or walks in the open air about him. For here the air and the clothes extend and stretch themselves according to the size of his body which the eyes can see and the hands can touch. But in the stone and the door there is no expansion.

Further, everyone will grant me that it is a far more exalted existence and mode when Christ's body is one person with God, than when it is in the stone or the door. For God is no corporeal thing but a Spirit above all things. And Christ is not one person with the stone or the door, as he is with God. Therefore he must be in the Godhead in a greater and more profound manner than he is in the stone or the door, just as he is in the stone and the door more intimately and profoundly than in his clothes or in the open air. And if the stone and the door did not have to extend or expand themselves, nor enclose the body of Christ, much less in this most exalted mode does the humanity extend and expand itself or enclose and compress the divinity, as this fleshly spirit dreams.

The spirit must answer me and acknowledge that Christ's body has a far higher, supernatural existence, since he is one person with God, than he had when he was in the sealed stone and the door, since this is the highest mode and existence there is, and there cannot be anything higher than for a man to be one person with God. For the second mode, in which Christ's body existed in the stone, will also be common to all the saints in heaven; they will pass with their bodies through all the objects of creation, a property which is common even now to angels and devils. For the angel came to Peter in the prison, Acts 12 [:7]. And goblins come daily into closed chambers and storerooms. So he must also grant me that the stone does not extend itself or enclose Christ's body.

Why then does he babble about the highest existence and mode of all, where Christ is one person with God, saying that here the humanity had to expand and enclose God if it were to be omnipresent with God? Simply to flaunt his crude, fat, puffy ideas! He has never thought about God and Christ in any way but the first, corporeal, circumscribed mode. My friend, whether the humanity is in one place or in all places, it does not enclose the divinity; much less did the stone, which was in one place, enclose his body. Rather, it is one person with God, so that wherever God is, there also is the man; what God does, the man also is said to do; what the man suffers, God also is said to suffer.

Thus the one body of Christ has a threefold existence, or all three modes of being at a given place. First, the circumscribed corporeal mode of presence, as when he walked bodily on earth, when he occupied and yielded space according to his size. He can still employ this mode of presence when he wills to do so, as he did after his resurrection and as he will do on the Last Day, as Paul says in I Timothy [6:15], "Whom the blessed God will reveal," and Colossians 3 [:4], "When Christ your life reveals himself." He is not in God or with the Father or in heaven according to this mode, as this mad spirit dreams, for God is not a corporeal space or place. The passages which the spiritualists adduce concerning Christ's leaving the world and going to the Father[90] speak of this mode of presence.

Secondly, the uncircumscribed, spiritual mode of presence according to which he neither occupies nor yields space but passes through everything created as he wills. To use some crude illustrations, my vision passes through and exists in air, light, or water

[90] Especially John 16:28.

and does not occupy or yield any space; a sound or tone passes through and exists in air or water or a board and a wall and neither occupies nor yields space; likewise light and heat go through and exist in air, water, glass, or crystals and the like, but without occupying or yielding space, and many more like these. He employed this mode of presence when he left the closed grave and came through closed doors, in the bread and wine in the Supper, and, as people believe, when he was born in his mother.

Thirdly, since he is one person with God, the divine, heavenly mode, according to which all created things are indeed much more permeable and present to him than they are according to the second mode. For if according to the second mode he can be present in and with created things in such a way that they do not feel, touch, measure, or circumscribe him, how much more marvelously will he be present in all created things according to this exalted third mode, where they cannot measure or circumscribe him but where they are present to him so that he measures and circumscribes them. You must place this existence of Christ, which constitutes him one person with God, far, far beyond things created, as far as God transcends them; and on the other hand, place it as deep in and as near to all created things as God is in them. For he is one indivisible person with God, and wherever God is, he must be also, otherwise our faith is false.

But who can explain or even conceive how this occurs? We know indeed that it is so, that he is in God beyond all created things, and is one person with God. But how this happens, we do not know; it transcends nature and reason, even the comprehension of all the angels in heaven, and is known only to God. Since this is true, even though unknown to us, we should not give the lie to his words until we know how to prove certainly that the body of Christ cannot in any circumstances be where God is and that this mode of being is a fiction. Let the fanatics prove it! They will give it up.

I do not wish to have denied by the foregoing that God may have and know still other modes whereby Christ's body can be in a given place. My only purpose was to show what crass fools our fanatics are when they concede only the first, circumscribed mode of presence to the body of Christ although they are unable to prove that even this mode is contrary to our view. For I do not want to deny in any way that God's power is able to make a body be simultaneously in many places, even in a corporeal and circumscribed manner. For who wants to try to prove that God is unable to do that? Who has seen the limits of his power? The fanatics may indeed think that God is unable to do it, but who will believe their speculations? How will they establish the truth of that kind of speculation?[91]

If speculation is enough, then I too will speculate, better than they, and say: Even if Christ's body were just at one place, in heaven, as they prattle, yet all creatures may be present to him and around him even there, like the clear, transparent air. For, as has been said, a spirit can see, move, and hear through an iron wall as clearly and easily as I can see or hear through the air or through glass. And that which to our sight is solid and opaque, such as wood, stone, and brass, is to a spirit like glass, yes, like the clear air, as is well proved by goblins and angels, and as Christ also proved in the sealed stone and the closed door.

I have seen crystals or jewels within which was a kind of spark or flame, as in an opal, or a little cloud or bubble; and yet this little bubble or cloud shines as if it were at every side of the stone, for whichever way the stone is turned, the bubble can be seen as if it were at the very front of the stone, though it is really in the center of it. I am not speaking now from Scripture. But we must use our reason or else give way to the fanatics. If Christ also sat at one place in the center of the universe, like the bubble or spark in a crystal, and if a certain point in the universe were indicated to me, as the bread and wine are set forth to me by the Word, should I not be able to say, "See, there is the body of Christ actually in the bread," just as I say, when a certain side of the crystal is placed before my eyes, "See, there is the spark in the very front of the crystal"? Do you not suppose that God in a much truer and more miraculous way can set forth Christ's body in the bread, even if he were at a certain place in heaven, than show me the spark in a crystal?

[91] These five paragraphs, beginning with, "Thus the one body . . ." on p. 222, are quoted in the *Formula of Concord,* Solid Declaration, VII, 98 ff., which emends *dreyerley wesen,* "a threefold existence," in the first sentence of the passage, to *dreier* [*lei*] *Weisen,* "three different modes."

Not that I think this is certainly so, but it is not impossible with God. I only wish to give the fanatics something to mock and misinterpret, as they usually do. Yet I also wish to indicate thereby that they cannot maintain their position, or condemn our interpretation, even if it were true, as they say, that Christ is in heaven at a particular place. Of this, however, they too have no certain knowledge or proof. So far are they from demonstrated truth that even if their notions were correct—which they are not—still they cannot thereby prove their view of the Supper (that nothing but bread is there) nor refute ours.

Moreover, in order to show them that it takes no skill at all to speculate without Scripture, I give you the illustration of Lorenzo Valla.[92] A preacher stands and preaches. His voice is a single voice. It proceeds from his mouth, it is formed in his mouth, and it is in his mouth. But the same single voice, which is at one particular place, viz. in his mouth, passes in an instant into four, five, or ten thousand ears. And yet there is no other voice in those many thousand ears than the voice in the preacher's mouth, and it is at the same time, at the same instant, a single voice in the preacher's mouth and in all the people's ears, just as if his mouth and their ears were one point where his voice was located without any intervening space.

My friend, if God can do this with a physical voice, why should he not be able to do it far more easily with the body of Christ, even if it were at a particular place, as they say, and yet at the same time be truly in the bread and wine at many places, as it were in two ears? For his body is much quicker and lighter than any voice, and all creation is more permeable to him than the air is to the voice, as he proved in the ease of the gravestone, inasmuch as no voice can pass through a stone as easily as Christ's body does.

These thoughts, however, I pursue no further than the point of truth in the fanatics' notions, that Christ is bodily and circum-

[92] In Valla's treatise, *On the Mystery of the Eucharist,* published in a Venetian edition of the works of Lactantius, 1521, as cited in *Nachträge* in *WA* 26, 656. Lorenzo Valla, 1405-1457, Italian humanist, Epicurean, and papal secretary, is best known for his demonstration that the "Donation of Constantine," for centuries a bulwark of papal claims to temporal authority, was a forgery.

scriptively at a particular place. Thus you may see, even to superfluity, that even though they contended for this, his body nonetheless can be in the Supper through God's power, because with created things even less significant, such as a voice, a tone, or a sound, it is not only possible but even natural and common, besides being palpable and tangible. Therefore their fancies are untenable that there must be nothing but bread in the Supper since Christ's body is in heaven.

One thing more. It was taught, even under the papacy, that if a mirror were broken into a thousand pieces, nevertheless the same complete image which had appeared previously in the whole mirror would remain in each piece. Here is the face of a man; he stands before the mirror and looks into it, and now in an instant the very same face is present, whole and entire, in every piece of the mirror. What if Christ also were in the bread and wine, and everywhere? For if God can do this with a man's face and a mirror, causing one face instantly to be in a thousand pieces or little mirrors, why should he not also make Christ's body so, that not only his image but he himself may be at many places at the same time, even if he were in heaven at a particular place, because it is much easier for his body to enter into the bread and wine than a face to enter into the mirror, since he passed through stone and iron, through which no image or face can pass?

"O you double papist!" they will shout. Well, let them shout if they please. With shouts they will be far from answering us, and nothing will be refuted; otherwise geese or asses or soused peasants might also become theologians. Nor have I seen any other point which the fanatics, these mighty Rolands[93] and giants, have won from the pope, that they should boast against the papists so loudly or justifiably. They have bared their teeth a little at the images—poor wood and stone!—but they have not bitten them yet. Now they attack baptism and the Supper, but so far they have not successfully carried out their aim.[94]

---

[93] Roland, in legend the nephew of Charlemagne, was the hero of many romantic tales, most famous being "The Song of Roland." Roland and the giants of mythology were favorite epithets of Luther against his ambitious opponents.

[94] Prominent in the overt break from Roman Catholicism in Zurich had been the removal of images from the churches, 1524. Luther implies that Zwingli's

I know very well that they may retort: The images in the mirror are not the face itself but its likeness, as bread and wine are signs of the Lord's body; hence the illustration is more for them than against them. But I also know, on the other hand, that bread and wine are not like the Lord's body, as the image in the mirror is like the face. Therefore the point of my illustration is this: If God can instantaneously make so many images of a face in a mirror, and if so marvelous a thing occurs naturally and visibly, it should be much more credible that he can cause Christ's body to be actually in many places in the bread and wine, even though he were in one physical place, as they dream. I have given this illustration to show how vacuous their notion is, which cannot imagine more than the single, circumscribed mode of existence in reference to Christ. And even if that were true, still what they would like to deduce from it would not follow. Far less will it follow since Christ's body does not exist in heaven in this physical, circumscribed mode, nor can they prove that he exists in heaven so.

Now this spirit rages against me that if Christ's body were everywhere that God is, I would become a Marcionite[95] and make a phantom Christ, because his body could not become so huge or so extended as to encompass the divinity, which is omnipresent. I reply, first: Perhaps this spirit is simply giving vent to his great petulance and rashness, for he does not prove that this follows from my argument, therefore I utterly disregard his prattle.

Secondly, he is well enough aware of the principle that to point out an inconsistency is not to refute arguments. If one inconsistent expression were sufficient, then no article of the Creed, indeed, no system of justice in the world could stand. But this proud, pompous spirit allows himself to imagine that if he simply declares a certain point inconsistent, such and such a consequence will necessarily follow, then it is inevitably so and needs no proof.

Thirdly, he reveals how crude and clumsy his ideas are by his inability to conceive of God's omnipresence except by imagining

---

doctrine would also destroy baptism and the Lord's Supper, cf. p. 16, n. 7, above.

[95] *Christian Answer. C. R.* 92, 937 ff., 918; *St. L.* 20, 1203 ff., 1190. On the charge of Marcionitism, cf. p. 99, n. 159, and pp. 110 ff., above.

God as a vast, immense being that fills the world, pervades it and towers over it, just like a sack full of straw, bulging above and below, precisely according to the first, bodily, circumscribed mode. Then, of course, Christ's body would be a mere phantom and apparition, like an immense straw-sack with God and the heaven and the earth inside. Wouldn't that really be a crude way to think and speak of God?

But this is not the way we speak. We say that God is no such extended, long, broad, thick, high, deep being. He is a supernatural, inscrutable being who exists at the same time in every little seed, whole and entire, and yet also in all and above all and outside all created things. There is no need to enclose him here, as this spirit dreams, for a body is much, much too wide for the Godhead; it could contain many thousand Godheads. On the other hand, it is also far, far too narrow to contain one Godhead. Nothing is so small but God is still smaller, nothing so large but God is still larger, nothing is so short but God is still shorter, nothing so long but God is still longer, nothing is so broad but God is still broader, nothing so narrow but God is still narrower, and so on. He is an inexpressible being, above and beyond all that can be described or imagined.

But this is what this spirit should tell us: First, where there is Scripture or reason to prove that Christ's body has no other way of existing in a given place than the physical, circumscribed mode, like straw in a sack, or like bread in a basket or meat in a pot, especially since I have proved that he does have other modes, such as being in the gravestone. Again, that the right hand of God is a particular place in heaven. How does it happen that this spirit is so silent on this point, where there is the utmost necessity to speak out? Since he is so silent here, he has lost the argument, inasmuch as his belief rests upon this point, that Christ's body can have no other way to exist in heaven than the "local" mode, like straw in a sack, which however I have demonstrated to be obviously false. Here he should show his cleverness and prove his point. But how can he? He has got too deep in the mud and can't get out!

Secondly, the spirit should answer this: Christ is God and man, and his humanity has become one person with God, and is thus wholly and completely drawn into God above all creatures, so that he remains perfectly united with him. How is it possible, then, for God to be somewhere where Christ as man is not? How can it happen, without dividing the person, that God may be here without the humanity and there with the humanity?—especially since we have not two Gods but only one God, and yet this God is wholly and perfectly man according to one person, viz. the Son. What does it mean that he prattles so much at other places, but here where he needs to speaks, he skips over it and remains silent?

If God and man are one person and the two natures are so united that they belong together more intimately than body and soul, then Christ must also be man wherever he is God. If he is both God and man at one place, why should he not also be both man and God at a second place? If he is both man and God at a second place, why not at a third, fourth, or fifth, and so forth, at all places? But if the third, fourth, or fifth places do not permit him to be both man and God at the same time, neither would the first, original place permit him to be both man and God at the same time. For if place or space can divide the person, the first place can do it as well as all the others. Here an answer should have been forthcoming. It was on this point that I insisted when I showed that God and man were one person, and that Christ thereby had acquired a supernatural existence or mode of being whereby he can be everywhere.

If we wish to be Christians and think and speak rightly about Christ, we must regard his divinity as extending beyond and above all creatures. Secondly, we must assert that though his humanity is a created thing, yet since it is the only creature so united with God as to constitute it one person with the divinity, it must be higher than all other creatures and above and beyond them, under God alone. Well, this is our faith. Here we come with a Christ beyond all creatures, both according to his humanity and his divinity; with his humanity we enter a different land from that in which it moved here on earth, viz. beyond and above all creatures and purely in the Godhead. Now let faith be the judge and arbiter here. Beyond the creatures there is only God; accordingly, since this humanity also is beyond the creatures, it must be wherever God is, without fail. In essence, however, it cannot be God, but because it reaches up above all creation to the essential God and is united with him and is wherever God is, it must be at least in person God and thus exist everywhere that God is.

Of course, our reason takes a foolish attitude, since it is accustomed to understanding the word "in" only in a physical, circumscribed sense like straw in a sack and bread in a basket. Consequently, when it hears that God is in this or that object, it always thinks of the straw-sack and the breadbasket. But faith understands that in these matters "in" is equivalent to "above," "beyond," "beneath," "through and through," and "everywhere." Oh, why do I speak of such exalted matters? They are ineffable, and unnecessary for the common man; for the fanatics, though, they are utterly useless and even harmful. They understand the matter as little as an ass does the Psalter, except that they may wrench a little piece from it and abuse and mutilate it, as an excuse for ignoring and skipping over the main subjects. Thus Zwingli plays the fool and deduces from my argument that if Christ is everywhere, he cannot be received by the mouth, unless the mouth is everywhere too. This is plain, malicious perversion in which the devil shows his hand.

Therefore I will stop speaking about this subject here too. If anyone is open to advice, he has had enough; if anyone does not want it, let him go his way. For the common man, the simple words suffice which Christ spoke at the Supper, "This is my body," for the fanatics can produce nothing certain or irrefutable against it, nor do they answer correctly on any point. He who in these important matters is found standing on shaky ground, in even one point, should rightly be held in suspicion and shunned, especially since they boast with such arrogant self-confidence that they have Scripture on their side and everything is settled. How much more should they be regarded as erring, puffed up sectarians, since they are found standing not just upon one but upon a whole host of bad arguments, so frequently do they openly lie and fail to answer any point correctly.

Zwingli particularly is not worth answering further, unless he retracts his blasphemous alloeosis. As the saying goes, a manifest lie does not deserve an answer. Hence, also, one who denies a common article of faith is to be shunned as a manifest heretic. Now Zwingli not only denies this most exalted and necessary article, that the Son of God died for us; he actually blasphemes it, saying it is the most outrageous heresy that ever existed. His imagination and damned alloeosis lead him to divide the person of Christ, and he leaves us no other Christ than a mere man who died for us and redeemed us. But what Christian heart can hear or endure this? This teaching altogether rejects and condemns the entire Christian faith and the whole world's salvation. For whoever is redeemed by the humanity only, is certainly not yet redeemed, nor will he ever be redeemed.

There is neither time nor space to treat this matter further. I testify on my part that I regard Zwingli as un-Christian, with all his teaching, for he holds and teaches no part of the Christian faith rightly. He is seven times worse than when he was a papist, according to the declaration in Matthew 9 [12:45], "The last state of that man becomes worse than the first." I make this testimony in order that I may stand blameless before God and the world as one who never partook of Zwingli's teaching, nor will I ever do so.

The sum of the whole matter is this: we recognize here no alloeosis, no heterosis,[96] no ethopoeia,[97] nor any other trick that Zwingli produces out of his magician's kit. Reasons we demand out of Scripture, and not cleverness out of his imagination. We are not interested in his fearful fuming and foaming as if he were seized with a towering rage. Wrath and rage will not overthrow our interpretation. This wrathful spirit will not produce anything to convince us that Christ's body cannot be at the same time in heaven and in the Supper in accordance with the words, "This is my body." Perhaps in his great wrath, or out of lofty moderation, he is letting this subject rest, meanwhile roaring by and teaching us new tropes needlessly. He recklessly deduces and concludes that were my teaching to prevail, if Christ's body is present

---

96 *Christian Answer.* C. R. 92, 935; *St. L.* 20, 1201. The word is used as a synonym for alloeosis.

97 Zwingli defined *ēthopoiia* (which Luther transliterated *ithipeia*) as "the ascription of a common custom, used when one imputes to a person a character which the person does not by nature possess," e.g. describing God with anthropomorphisms, or Jesus in John 3:13 and Phil. 2:7 as Son of *man.* *Christian Answer.* C. R. 92, 938; *St. L.* 20, 1203.

wherever God is, then Christ's body would be a second infinite category, like God himself.[98] But he could easily see, if his wrath did not blind him, that this does not follow at all. If the world is not infinite in itself, how should it follow that Christ's body is infinite if he is everywhere? Besides this blind spirit draws his conclusion according to the crude, circumscribed mode; and yet we know that God has more than one way of causing a thing to be in a given place, as has been proved above. An angel can be at the same time in heaven and on earth, as Christ shows, Matthew 18 [:10]: "Their angels always behold the face of my Father in heaven." If they serve us, they are with us on earth; still, they always behold the Father's face in heaven. Yet they are not infinite beings.

This clumsy spirit does not yet know what it means to be in heaven, yet he wants to jump to conclusions on the subject. When I said that Christ was in heaven even while he was still walking on earth, as John 3 [:13] says, "The Son of man who is in heaven," God help us, how he jumped to weird conclusions! "How," he declared, "could Christ be in heaven at that time? Is there eating and drinking in heaven? Is there suffering and dying in heaven? Is there sleep and repose in heaven? See what you have got yourself into, you mad Luther? Phooey on you!"[99] What do you think of this spirit's victory? He has conquered Constantinople and devoured the Turks,[100] and his magician's kit full of alloeoses and ethopoeias begins to dance for joy.

Get out of here, you handsome devil! Let any faithful Christian tell me if it is not a higher and greater thing for the humanity to be in God, yes, to be one person with God, than for it merely to be in heaven. Isn't God higher and more glorious than heaven? Now, the humanity of Christ from his mother's womb was more profoundly and deeply in God and in God's presence than any angel, and certainly it was more profoundly in heaven than any angel. For whatever is in God and in God's presence is in heaven,

---

[98] *Christian Answer*. *C. R.* 92, 929 ff.; *St. L.* 20, 1197 ff.

[99] Here, as frequently, Luther is freely paraphrasing Zwingli. *Christian Answer*. *C. R.* 92, 940; *St. L.* 20, 1204.

[100] The fall of Constantinople in 1453 had been a fearful shock to Christendom. The Turks continued their conquests through the Balkans, and even besieged Vienna in 1529.

just as the angels are, even when they are on earth, as it is said in Matthew 18 [:10]. Unless God himself is no longer in heaven! So I might draw a Zwinglian conclusion and babble, "Is there eating and drinking in the Godhead? Is there suffering and dying in the Godhead? See what you have got yourself into, you mad John the Evangelist, who try to teach us that Christ is God and in the Godhead? For if there is no suffering or dying, or eating or drinking with God, the humanity of Christ cannot be with God, much less can it be one person with God." "This is what I was trying to do with my trickery," says the devil, "but, you spiteful Luther, you have ripped the bottom out of my magician's bag!"

Now if Christ can suffer and die on earth, even though he is at the same time in the Godhead and is one person with God, why should he not much more be able to suffer on earth, though he is at the same time in heaven? If heaven prevented it, much more would the Godhead prevent it. Indeed, what if I said that not only Christ was in heaven when he walked on earth, but also the apostles and all the rest of us mortals on earth, insofar as we believe in Christ? That would kick up a rumpus in Zwingli's magician's kit! He would start drawing conclusions and ask, "Is there also sin in heaven? Is there error in heaven? Does the devil assail us in heaven? Does the world persecute us in heaven? Do flesh and blood tempt us in heaven? And so forth. For we sin and err constantly, as we learn from the Lord's Prayer, 'Forgive us our trespasses' [Matt. 6:12], and we are continually being assailed by the devil, the world, and the flesh. In this way you would place the devil and the world and flesh and blood in heaven. See what you have got yourself into, you mad Luther! Phooey! Won't you ever learn that our spirit is no buffoon? Now, there you have it!"

What shall I do with him? St. Paul has misled me when he said, Ephesians 1 [:3], "God has blessed us with every spiritual blessing in the heavenly places," and again, chapter 2 [:5 f.], "He has made us alive together with Christ and raised us up with him, and made us sit with him in the heavenly places," and in Colossians 3 [:3] he says, "Our life is hid with Christ in God," which certainly means in heaven.

But here this spirit can call on his magician's kit to produce an alloeosis or an ethopoeia, which teach us to make an exchange and take one thing for another; so heaven must mean earth, just as he interprets John 6 [:51 ff.] to mean that Christ's flesh must mean his divinity. For alloeosis is the mistress in the Scriptures. And if we don't want to believe it, he will overpower us by logic and say, "But we are not on the Mount of Olives and from thence ascending to heaven, we are here in German countries;[101] therefore by heaven St. Paul must mean the earth." The only way this spirit can conceive of heaven is to point his finger and cast his eyes upward, where sun and moon are. I hold that since these bodies never stand still, they ascribe to Christ such a place in heaven that he can never sit still. For I cannot imagine or elicit from them what sort of place they ascribe to Christ in heaven. But let that go for what it is worth.

Thus, in regard to the text I quoted from Colossians 3 [2:9], "In Christ the whole fulness of deity dwells bodily," he thinks it unnecessary to say more than that "bodily" means "essentially," just as if Christ had not also been essentially God before God came to dwell bodily in Christ.[102] It is marvelous the way this spirit can explain whatever he wishes, with no need of proving it! The same with the passage in Ephesians 4 [:10], "Christ descended and ascended far above all the heavens, that he might fill all things." Here he explains "filling" as fulfilling the holy Scriptures,[103] and exults once more over the mad Luther as if he had stormed hell. But to prove this interpretation is quite unnecessary for him. It is enough that he says so; then the point is sufficiently answered and our interpretation is false.

He does hit Luther squarely for the first time, however, when he proves his powers of deduction on the word of Christ, "Where I am, there shall you be also" [John 14:3]. "You see," he says, "if Christ is everywhere, we must be everywhere also."[104] To my surprise he does not deduce also that because we are where Christ

[101] Cf. Acts 1:12. "German" in the sixteenth century had a linguistic and cultural, rather than a national connotation; Zwingli often referred to himself as a German. Luther here puts words into Zwingli's mouth, however.

[102] *Christian Answer*. *C. R.* 92, 956; *St. L.* 20, 1216.

[103] *Friendly Exposition*. *C. R.* 92, 676, 653, quoting Luther's *The Sacrament—Against the Fanatics*, 1526. *LW* 36, 342 f. Also *Friendly Rejoinder*. *C. R.* 92, 788; *St. L.* 20, 1118 f.

[104] *Christian Answer*. *C. R.* 92, 956; *St. L.* 20, 1216.

is, we must all be God and man also. For where Christ is, he is God and man. Again, Christ passed through the sealed stone and the closed door, therefore we must also pass through them. Again, Christ exists spiritually in us, therefore we also must exist spiritually in ourselves, etc.

Yes, on the other hand he might reasonably conclude that where Christ is, there we cannot be. For it is just as unreasonable for many bodies to be in one place as for one body to be in many places. But since Christ occupies a particular place in heaven, as they say, it must follow that each of us will have his particular place. Now, since this passage, "Where I am, there shall you be also," is contrary to Scripture and the Creed if it is understood literally, Lady Alloeosis, or heterosis, or perhaps the common figure *narrosis*[105] will stand godmother and help us on to a correct interpretation. Am I not clever too at their art of jumping to conclusions?

Now a sow cannot be a dove, nor a cuckoo a nightingale. This proud devil treats Scripture any way he pleases, and shows with his jugglery that since he cannot answer he will resort to ridiculing us. But we know that Scripture sets this man and no other at the right hand of God. Now although we shall be where he is, according to the first or second mode as described above, we shall not be where he is according to the third mode, viz. at the right hand of God as one person with God, according to which mode Christ exists wherever God is.[106] Indeed, since he is everywhere, of course we are wherever he is, for he must be with us if he is everywhere. This our master logician should have confuted, instead of which he confuses it all together, and refuses to recognize any but the one circumscribed mode. Beyond this he can understand nothing at all, and does not even comprehend what he is raving about.

Let this suffice for the first main point. For from this spirit's passages and answers it is clear to everyone that their whole art consists in much babbling and ranting, but no ability to answer or understand. The more Scripture they quote, the more they expose their insanity. We shall now discuss their second passage, "The

[105] A coined word of sarcasm, based on the German word *narr*, "fool."
[106] Cf. pp. 216 ff.

flesh is of no avail" [John 6:63], and hear whether the devil wishes to answer or ridicule.[107]

In the first place, I had written[108] that the flesh of Christ does not belong with the saying in John 3 [:6], "That which is born of the flesh is flesh," but with the other one, "That which is born of the Spirit is spirit." I had proved this quite incontestably from our Creed and from the gospel, where the angel says to Joseph, Matthew 2 [1:20], "That which is conceived in Mary is of the Holy Spirit," and Luke 1 [:35], "The child to be born of you is holy," etc. Against these thunderbolts of Scripture he does nothing but gush his empty, bare drivel, saying that Christ's flesh also is born of the flesh, and that I err in making pure spirit out of it. This, as I understand it, is the same as if the arrogant devil were to say, "You miserable, mad Luther, must I answer you and refute your arguments? Poop on you! I say Christ's flesh is born of the flesh. That settles it. I don't want a word out of you!"

Here perhaps I might reply, "Excuse me, sir, whatever you say is right; you don't have to prove it," if I considered the matter as unimportant as this spirit does, who, whenever he feels that I have refuted him, either skips over the matter or flies into a rage, or stammers a word or two and calls this an answer.

We know, however, that the flesh of Christ does not belong with the saying, "That which is born of the flesh is flesh," even if this were deemed ten times a maxim[109] or if fifteen alloeoses had nothing but exchange banks there. It adds nothing to the argument to call it a maxim; for here Christ is speaking of the new birth, and he curses the fleshly old birth that it cannot see the kingdom of God. Let it be anathema and accursed to say that the flesh of Christ is born of the flesh, since Christ's flesh is not accursed, and did not need to be born again into the kingdom of God, but is holy and has brought us the new birth.

Who will drill this spirit and teach him the meaning of flesh and spirit? He calls flesh a creature which is not spirit as God created it, as Christ says in Luke 24 [:39] that a spirit has not flesh and bones. How is it possible for one with such a mind to

107 A new section in *Christian Answer*. *C. R.* 92, 959 ff.; *St. L.* 20, 1217 ff.
108 See pp. 79 ff., above.
109 "*Gnômē*, that is, a common notion." *Christian Answer*. *C. R.* 92, 957; *St. L.* 20, 1216.

understand such passages as John 3[110] and the like, where flesh and blood are condemned? For we know that all God's creation is good, Genesis 1 [:31], and God does not condemn his creation. In this way Christ's flesh and blood come from Mary's flesh and blood; but because according to John 3 flesh and blood are condemned as being unable to know the kingdom of God, they cannot truly be called creatures of God in the same sense as flesh, bone, skin, and hair, for all these are the good creatures of God.

Consequently, flesh here must mean not only blood, bone, and marrow, in the sense of what God created, but in the sense of being devoid of spirit, existing in its own strength, work, use, wisdom, will, and ability. So, wherever the flesh does anything in divine matters according to its own wisdom and strength, there "the flesh is of no avail," but is condemned. The reason Christ did not wish to be born of the seed of man is that he did not wish to be born of the flesh, i.e. of the work, desire, will, or aid of the flesh, but only from the power and operation of the Holy Spirit. And thus his flesh is pure spirit, pure holiness, absolute purity. For what can holiness, purity, and innocence mean but spirit, pure spirit?

But our fanatics consider spirit nothing more than a being which has neither flesh nor bone; consequently, holiness, purity, and innocence are not spirit to them. They are such clumsy, illiterate fools in these matters! They wish to teach a great deal, but they do not understand the words that they speak. In John 3 [:6] Christ calls all those spirit who are born of the Spirit, who must, it is true, have flesh, bone, marrow, skin, and hair. Of this I have written enough in my former book.[111] Even if I wrote of this a thousand times, my friends the noble fanatics would not read or regard it; so, for my part, I let them go their way too.

Of three great offenses this spirit accuses me in reference to these words, "The flesh is of no avail."[112] Let us hear and see what

---

110 Cf. John 3:3, 5.

111 *"This Is My Body,"* p. 99, cf. pp. 95 ff.

112 *Christian Answer. C. R.* 92, 960 ff.; *St. L.* 20, 1218 ff. Zwingli cites Luther's sermons on John 6:55-58 (Corpus Christi Day, 1522, subsequently published, *WA* 12, 582 f.) and on the epistle for Septuagesima, I Cor. 9:24 ff. (*Church Postil,* 1525. *WA* 17^II^, 132 ff.; *LE* 8, 99 ff.) as evidence that Luther had formerly acknowledged that the flesh is of no avail. Cf. p. 148, n. 259.

poisonous lies the angry devil invents through his blind, miserable fanatics. The first is that I contradict myself because I have repeatedly taught that the physical eating of Christ's body is of no avail, and yet I teach on the other hand that eating Christ's flesh is profitable. My treatises are before the public. From them this liar can be fully convicted of acting toward me as you would expect of such a pupil. My friend, how would it help if I wrote forever against this spirit, since he takes such pains to operate with notorious, shameless lies? Let the devil go!

I have taught and still teach that Christ's flesh is not only of no avail but actually is poison and death if it is eaten without faith and the Word.[113] I have said further that God and the Holy Spirit himself are pure poison and death, and of no avail, if they are received without faith. For Scripture says, "To the impure nothing is pure," Titus 1 [:15], and Psalm 17 [18:26], "With the corrupt thou art perverse." For certainly the Jews did not become holy when they seized Christ and put him to death. But on the other hand, to eat Christ's flesh is salutary, necessary, and useful if it is eaten physically in connection with the Word and with faith. For Scripture says, "To the pure all things are pure" [Titus 1:15]. Read my book, and you will see that this liar did not know how to answer, and therefore has tried to cast suspicion on my book with his coarse, clumsy lies.[114]

A child of seven years can fully understand that these two propositions are not contradictory: "To eat Christ's flesh physically without faith is of no avail," and, "To eat Christ's flesh physically with faith is profitable." Just as these two propositions are not contradictory: "Christ's flesh is of no avail to the godless," and, "Christ's flesh is profitable to the godly," as I have abundantly explained in my last book[115] that in faith even death and all evil are beneficial, not to mention the flesh of Christ, which in itself is holy and beneficial, and full of divinity, etc. Yet the liar dares to assert openly that I said Christ's flesh is beneficially eaten without faith, as he raves with his examples. For the act of touching was not useless when the woman who suffered from a

---

113 See p. 86.

114 For comment on the handwritten text see *WA* 26, 354, n. 1.

115 *"This Is My Body,"* pp. 134 f.

hemorrhage touched the hem of Christ's garment [Matt. 9:20 ff.]. Otherwise we would also have to say that she did not touch Christ's hem because touching is of no avail. Just as they jabber here, "Eating Christ's flesh is of no avail, therefore his flesh is not present." What devilish villainy!

The second offense of which he accuses me is that I have not properly translated the text, "Flesh is of no avail," because in Greek it reads, "The flesh is of no avail," and I have omitted the word "the."[116] Why this spirit stoops to such nonsense I cannot imagine, unless perhaps he wishes to turn himself by magic into another form in the village square and bewitch the people into marveling at the vast knowledge of Greek in his head, though he has hardly forgotten very much of it. If he is aware that such prattle does not contribute a single thing to the discussion, then it is effrontery. If he is not aware, then it is an indication that he still needs a schoolmaster for a while. Those who understand Latin, German, and Greek must acknowledge that this text, *hē sarx ouk ōphelei ouden,* translated into Latin must read, *Caro non prodest quicquam,* i.e. flesh is of no avail, and the word "the" cannot be prefixed in Latin. So Erasmus and all others have translated it.[117]

Further, Germans must agree with me that according to the common use and practice of our language it is quite indifferent whether one adds a *das* or *ein*, or omits it. If we say, "Man and wife are one flesh," that is the same as, "A man and a wife are one flesh." Indeed, it is more elegant to say, "Man and wife are one flesh," than, "A man and a wife are one flesh." Again, "Peter has house and home, wife and child at Bethsaida" is exactly the same as, "Peter has a house and a home, a wife and a child at Bethsaida." Again, "Master and servant are a pair" is exactly the same as, "The master and the servant are a pair." Again, "He gave me dog for dog, old nag for old mare" is exactly the same as, "He gave me a dog for a dog, an old nag for an old mare." Again, "Woman

[116] *Christian Answer. C. R.* 92, 963; *St. L.* 20, 1220 f. Zwingli accused Luther of inconsistency, inasmuch as Luther's translation of the New Testament did not omit the *das.*

[117] Erasmus' *Novum Testamentum Graece,* Basel, 1516, containing the Latin translation from the Greek text and *Annotationes* confirms Luther's assertion. Of course, which edition of Erasmus' text Luther used is a moot point.

should not be master in the house" is exactly the same as, "A woman (or the woman) should not be the master (or a master) in the house."

And many other expressions of this kind are to be found in the German language. Words which can be either omitted or inserted, the scholars call "articles." In the Latin language there is no article. No one can lay down a definite rule when it is to be omitted or inserted, but its use or omission must be learned from the common usage of a language. It sometimes happens that it sounds better if the article is omitted, as when I say of two equals, "It is man against man." This sounds better than, "It is a man against a man." Again, if we say, "Piece for piece, eye for eye, hand for hand, coin for coin, body for body," in these expressions it is better to omit the article than to use it.

On the other hand, it is sometimes more elegant to insert the article than to omit it, as when I say in German, "A man is stronger than a woman," or, "The man is stronger than the woman." It would be exactly the same, however, if I said, "Man is stronger than woman," although it does not sound as well. In German, "*Der Zwingel* is worse than *der Ecolampad*" sounds better than, "*Zwingel* is worse than *Ecolampad.*" "An apostle is greater than a prophet" sounds better than, "Apostle is greater than prophet."

Indeed, it often happens that we Germans must insert articles where they do not appear in Greek, as we see in Matthew 1 [:1]. The original reads, *Biblos geneseōs,* etc., i.e. "Book of birth of Jesus Christ." This does not sound well at all, therefore I must translate it, "The book of the birth," or better yet, "This is the book of the birth of Jesus Christ." Again, "Joseph did as the angel of the Lord commanded him" [Matt. 1:24], when in Greek there is no definite article but simply "the angel of Lord"; but in our language it must be inserted. Again, in Matthew 3 [:3] and Mark 1 [:3] and Luke 3 [:4] we must say, "A voice" or, "The voice of one crying in the wilderness," though in Greek it reads simply, *phōnē boontos,* "Voice of one crying."

On the other hand, we sometimes need not insert an article where it is required in Greek, as in Matthew 1 [:2], "Abraham begat Isaac," where the Greek reads, "Abraham begat the Isaac." Again, "Emmanuel, which means, God with us" [Matt. 1:23];

the Greek reads, "The God with us." Take the Greek Testament yourself and compare it with the German language; you will find, as I have said, that very often the article is used in Greek where it must be omitted in German, and on the other hand, it is not used in Greek where it must be inserted in German.

I say this in order that people may understand what sophistry Zwingli deals in and what empty prattle he has used to undergird his error. For if, as he babbles, the article were so indispensable, and required some special expression on the basis of that which preceded, then it ought properly to stand in Mark 1 [:3], where Mark says, "Voice of one crying," inasmuch as this is a particular voice and a particular crier such as never at any other time appeared on earth. Again, it ought reasonably to stand in John 1 [:6], where he writes, "There was a man sent from God." Now the Greek text does not read, "There was a man sent," but, "There was man sent." And so forth. Zwingli will have to spend five more years studying Greek[118] before he can prove his dream concerning the article, or before he can show where and when it should be omitted or inserted. I know no other proof than the fact that the very same idea can be expressed, as I have said, without the article and with the article, and still convey the same sense; only, the one is more complete or elegant in style than the other, as we learn from the custom and usage of the language.

So in this passage, "Flesh is of no avail," the Greek does read, "The flesh is of no avail." But the one is precisely the same as the other, as I have proved with the examples above, and each one may find for himself plenty of similar passages in the Greek. Therefore I have translated in both ways, and will continue to translate both ways, because both are correct, even if it makes this spirit's belly burst, though it sounds better in German to say, "*Fleisch ist kein nütze,*" than to say, "*Das fleisch ist kein nütze.*" Christ's meaning is the same as if I should say, "Flesh, however, is of no value," or, "Flesh is a useless thing." This meaning may be expressed thus: "Flesh is of no avail," or thus, "The flesh is of no avail." The one is just as good as the other. Otherwise the

[118] Perhaps this gibe clarifies why at the Marburg Colloquy, the following year, Zwingli explained his frequent quoting of Greek by remarking that he had been using the Greek Testament for twelve years, and had read the Latin through only once. Sasse, *This Is My Body*, p. 256.

Latins could never have conceived of the meaning and use of this text, since they must say without any article at all, "Flesh is of no avail," yet they have the correct translation just the same. But Zwingli's appeal to certain scholars[119] who teach such things concerning articles does not help him at all, for these men do not teach as Zwingli does at this point. Nor do their proofs contradict us at all. Besides, he is not really in earnest, for he does not consider them so learned that they should advise and assist him in these matters.

Now he is not satisfied with his sophistry concerning the article, but proceeds to render the definite article in this passage, "The flesh is of no avail," in this fashion: "This very flesh is of no avail." [120] So "the" has the force of "this very"! Thus he corrects the meaning of Christ: "This very flesh" (viz. which I cited above, "My flesh is food indeed" [John 6:55]). Now the whole world knows that in our language "precisely this" is not an article, but a good, strong pronoun, which is both a relative and a demonstrative, like the Latin *idem*. Here the learned will understand what an ass's blunder it is to make a demonstrative and relative pronoun out of an article. This is the way Luther must be taught to translate the text! I am nonplused by these wicked spirits who take substance for quality, article for pronoun, flesh for divinity, and fashion any and every interpretation in Scripture that they dare imagine. If he learned this stuff about the article from Cyril, Chrysostom, and Erasmus, he certainly read it in a dream or somewhere.[121] Not one of them teaches this; he slanders them treacherously.

My friend, there is a great difference between, "The flesh is of no avail," and, "*This* flesh is of no avail," or, "This very flesh," or, "This same flesh," etc. For such words as "this very" or "this" or "this same" may not be omitted like the article, without altering the sense. If I say, "The man should be master in the house, not the woman," I speak of no particular man or woman actually

[119] Citing as a parallel John 1:2, "The same was in the beginning with God," Zwingli claimed the support of Cyril of Alexandria, Chrysostom, and the contemporary Erasmus. *Christian Answer. C. R.* 92, 963 (identifies references); *St. L.* 20, 1220.

[120] *Christian Answer. C. R.* 92, 964; *St. L.* 20, 1220.

[121] *Rauchloch*, i.e. really nowhere.

present, but indefinitely of all men and women in general. But if I say, "This (or, this very) man should be master, not this (or, this very) woman," I point out a particular man and woman in distinction from all others, as being actually present. For a pronoun is a word which specifies a particular object as being actually present, and distinguishes it from all others.

An article, however, specifies nothing particular or present in distinction from others, but has an indefinite reference, without specifying or defining. For example, "This man is upright; this woman is respectable; this bread is fine":[122] here the reference is to particular persons [or objects] as present. If these pronouns or words were omitted and we said, "Man is upright; woman is respectable," the sense would be altogether different from the preceding. But if I say, "The man should be a man; the woman should be a woman," I can easily omit the article and still retain the same sense, for example, "Man should be man; woman should be woman," for the article refers to nothing present and specifies nothing as being present, as the pronoun does.

Now this spirit must acknowledge that in this passage, "The flesh is of no avail," there is no pronoun but an article. Yet he makes a pronoun out of it not only in the translation, where he says *das* is equivalent to *eben das,* "precisely this," but also in his interpretation that in this passage "the same flesh" is referred to as that of which Christ had previously spoken, "My flesh is food indeed" [John 6:55]. Here, then, he demonstrates that he falsifies the Word of God and treats the common people shamelessly. For an article never refers to an antecedent or to particular objects, as a pronoun does, but merely indicates things in general, which could be equally well understood if the article were omitted, though the style would not be so nice and elegant. Therefore it is impossible according to the rules of grammar that "flesh" here should mean Christ's flesh in particular, to which he had previously referred. It must mean flesh in general, and we could with perfect propriety speak of it without the article, namely thus: "Flesh is of no avail."

This distinction of pronoun and article we Germans express

122 Examples chosen to illustrate the three genders in German: *dieser, diese, dis.*

orally by the inflection or tone of voice which the Latins call "accent." The *das* which Christ uses when he says, "This is my body," is altogether different from the one in his saying, "The flesh is of no avail." The first *das* is a pronoun, and the vowel is pronounced strongly and long, as if it were spelled *dahas,* as it sounds in the Swabian dialect, or *daas* in Allgau. When it is pronounced so, it is as if the sign of a finger[123] were pointing out an object to the hearer. The other *das* is cut short so that one hardly hears the vowel and cannot tell whether it is an *a, e,* or *i,* and no sign of a finger is there pointing at anything. So it sounds just the same as when the Bohemians cut short their vowels and say *przikasani;*[124] you cannot tell if they are saying *parzikasani* or *perzikasani* or *pirzikasani,* so quickly is it pronounced. Thus if a German says correctly, "How dear the grain [*das korn*] is," you probably cannot tell whether he is saying *das* or *des* or *dis,* for it sounds as if the word had no vowel, e.g., "How dear th' grain is," or, "How dear's th' grain,"[125] so shortly and quickly is it pronounced. What I say concerning *das* applies also to the other forms of the article: *der, die, das, den, dem.* When the vowel is lengthened, as if it were doubled, we have pronouns; when they are pronounced quickly, as if the vowel had dropped out, we have articles. If you say, "Th' woman, th' man, th' child, th' house," cutting the vowel very short, you have articles, with no sign of a finger pointing out something particular.

From this discussion every German can understand this controversial question, and discern this spirit's treachery and knavery. For in John 6 [:63], "This (*das*) is my flesh," he makes the vowel a long Swabian *dahas,* i.e. a pronoun, though it is really an article, to be cut short and pronounced quickly, so: "Th' flesh–*Dsfleisch*–is of no avail," or even *Sfleisch,* as if only the letter *s* stood before the whole word. Here you see properly and clearly what the text from John 6 means, and what is the function of the article. Now, anyone who knows German, judge between me and this Zwingli! Zwingli says the text should have the same meaning as, "This very flesh is of no avail," or, "This same flesh is of no avail."

123 ☞

124 An Old Bohemian word meaning "commandment."

125 *Wie ist dskorn so theur,* or *wie istds korn so theur.*

Who falsifies the text here? Who is so crude as to be unaware of the great difference between saying, "Th' flesh is of no avail," and, "This very flesh is of no avail?" Are you fairly clear how this rascal operates? Moreover, my friend, if I say at one place, "Flesh is of no avail," and at another, "Th' flesh—*Dsfleisch* or *Sfleisch*—is of no avail," is there any difference between the two? One is pronounced differently from the other, but the sense is exactly the same. It is like saying: This spirit has to serve up a mess of useless chatter in order to butter up the people and make them think he intends to answer, so that they will not notice meanwhile his hopping and flopping about!

Next he proceeds in earnest to the subject at hand. He tries to prove from the text in John 6 [:63] that Christ is speaking of his own flesh when he says, "The flesh is of no avail." [126] Here let us listen to his logic. "In the first place," he says, "the disciples murmured [6:61] because Christ taught that they had to eat his flesh. Now they did not murmur against the spiritual sense, but against the physical eating." There you have it! Tell me, friend, is this a proof that Christ's flesh is of no avail? Or that this passage is to be understood of Christ's flesh? Of course, in Zwingli's logic everything follows from anything, just as he wishes. Oh, it's an annoying thing to discuss the words of God with such rascals!

We say that the disciples murmured both against the spiritual meaning and against the physical eating of Christ's flesh. For they understood neither one aright, because they thought they must rend his flesh with their teeth, as they did with other perishable flesh. But from this it does not follow that Christ's flesh, an imperishable, spiritual flesh, may not be physically eaten with faith in the Supper. That is what this spirit should refute. Instead, he teaches us that the disciples understood Christ's flesh was to be eaten physically, just as if we could not have known this without his magisterial wisdom. He avoids an answer wherever he can.

In the second place, he teaches us that the disciples were offended at this word of Christ concerning the physical eating of his flesh, from which he deduces that Christ in his reply always spoke concerning his own flesh. My friend, why does it follow?

---

[126] *Christian Answer*. *C. R.* 92, 965 ff.; *St. L.* 20, 1221 ff.

Because Zwingli says so! That is enough! Just as if Christ were unable to speak of other flesh, when he wanted to teach a spiritual interpretation of the eating of his flesh! But he could not have expressed himself more precisely than to indicate two kinds of flesh and two kinds of eating and thus to say, "Flesh and blood do not permit you to understand this kind of eating of my flesh; for the former flesh is of no avail, but the latter flesh is life." For "the only and best kind of teaching is to distinguish and to define well."[127] Consequently, it follows with all the greater force that this expression, "The flesh is of no avail," must be understood as referring to other flesh, which Christ distinguishes and sets over against his own flesh, as all correct teachers are accustomed to do, when they are at their best.

"In the third place, Christ says, 'What if you were to see the Son of man ascending where he was before?'" [John 6:62]. What the spirit means by this I cannot imagine, unless he thinks that everything he spouts must serve his lies. Perhaps he wants to sing their old refrain: Christ has ascended into heaven, therefore his body cannot be eaten in the Supper. What this prattle amounts to, we have shown sufficiently above.[128] But his effort to prove that the passage, "The flesh is of no avail," refers to Christ's flesh—this is truly fine logic, a most marvelous deduction! As if I should say, "Christ ascended to heaven, therefore the passage about his body is to be interpreted: All men are liars!"[129] Doesn't this fit and follow beautifully? This, in the Swiss dialect, is called defeating Luther down to his last foot soldier, as this spirit boasts![130]

"In the fourth place, 'it is the Spirit that gives life' [John 6:63]. There! There! This is brief and well put," he says, and makes this passage prove that if the Spirit alone gives life, then Christ's flesh is of no avail, for it is not spirit. To this we must say: If the flesh of Christ is not spirit, and therefore is of no avail since only the Spirit is profitable, how can it be profitable when it was given for us? How can it be useful if it is in heaven

[127] An old Latin maxim.

[128] See pp. 195 ff., 206 ff.

[129] Cf. Ps. 116:11.

[130] Zwingli made this boast in his letter to Andreas Osiander, May, 1527. *C. R.* 96, 129. See the Introduction, p. 154.

and we believe in it? If the reasoning is correct and adequate, that because Christ's flesh is not spirit it must be of no avail, then it can be of no avail on the cross or in heaven either! For it is quite as far from being spirit on the cross and in heaven as in the Supper. But since no spirit was crucified for us, therefore Christ's flesh was crucified for us to no avail. And since no spirit, but Christ's flesh ascended into heaven, we believe in an unprofitable flesh in heaven. For wherever Christ's flesh may be, it is no spirit. If it is no spirit, it is of no avail and does not give life, as Zwingli here concludes. See what the devil is driving at! This is a fine way of driving the mist away from one's eyes![131]

"In the fifth place, 'The words that I speak are spirit and life'" [John 6:63]. From this he concludes that Christ refers to his own flesh when he says, "The flesh is of no avail." Oh, what a marvelous deduction! Just like the one above! I believe this spirit in his enormous arrogance thinks he is the only man on earth, or else regards all men as mere geese and jackdaws. Otherwise how could he be so bold and impudent as to bring such crude foolishness to the light of day? We know very well that Christ's words are spirit and life. But that it follows therefrom that Christ's flesh is of no avail, no man will assert unless he is insane or inane, or haughtily despises the mind and thought of the whole world. This spirit says it follows, but when will he prove that it follows? Certainly these words of Christ, "The flesh is of no avail," are also spirit and life. Thereby he enlightens us and turns us from the flesh to the spirit, which is a salutary spiritual teaching that gives life. Now it is a manifest blasphemy if anyone should say that Christ wishes to turn us away from his own flesh, to which however he does turn us when he says, "My flesh is food indeed" [John 6:55]. Unless Lady Alloeosis once again makes divinity out of flesh! But we do not listen to the witch.

"In the sixth place, Christ says, 'But there are some of you that do not believe' [John 6:64]. Again, Peter says, 'To whom shall we go? You have the words of eternal life'" [6:68]. From these two passages he deduces and prattles once more that since such texts speak of faith and the living Word, the flesh of Christ

---

[131] Here Luther gives Zwingli's statement (*C. R.* 92, 966; *St. L.* 20, 1222) a sarcastic turn.

must be interpreted so in the passage, "The flesh is of no avail," and Christ must not begin anew to speak of some other flesh. I have heard many insane conclusions and deductions in my time, but a more insane and outrageous one I have never heard than this spirit makes, that because Christ speaks of faith and the Word, the passage, "The flesh is of no avail," must refer to his flesh. I honestly believe that this fellow thinks in his heart exactly like this: "We, Zwingli, by the grace of God a giant and a Roland, a hero and conqueror in Italy and Germany, in France and Spain,[132] apostle of all apostles, prophet of all prophets, teacher of all teachers, master of all masters, scholar of all scholars, lord of all lords, genius of all genii, etc., say thus and so. This settles it, it cannot be otherwise!" How could he possibly run on so impudently, drawing conclusions and dealing with the Scriptures and the Word of God everywhere, if he were not possessed by inhuman arrogance and wantonness?

We poor sinners and flesh-eaters have nowhere and never said, as this spirit accuses us, that Christ made a new beginning when he said, "The flesh is of no avail," but we confess even to this day that when Christ begins to speak concerning his flesh, he speaks throughout and constantly, to the end of the chapter, John 6, of the spiritual eating of his flesh. This we say because, in consequence of what he said, there arose two classes of disciples: some were offended, murmured, and left him; some believed, gave praise, and remained with him. So, from this dissension, without a new beginning at all, he could say, "The spirit gives life; the flesh is of no avail." We have interpreted this in no other way than as follows: "My teaching is spiritual. Anyone who understands it in a fleshly manner errs, and his interpretation is of no avail, but whoever understands it spiritually will live." Here nothing new is said concerning the eating of his flesh, but a distinction is made among the disciples who heard him. We have always been ready to change our interpretation if anyone will show a good reason.

Just so, if I preached, "Good works are of no avail for right-

[132] Zwingli boasted to Osiander that within three years Italy, France, Spain, and Germany would come around to his view. May, 1527, letter. *C. R.* 96, 130.

eousness," here I would get two classes of hearers. Some would take offense, murmur, and run away, saying, "What! does this man forbid all good works?" Some however would believe, give praise, and remain. Here, then, I may also say, "My doctrine of good works is spiritual and based on a distinction between good works for righteousness and good works for the glory of God. Whoever interprets them as necessary for righteousness errs; but whoever interprets them as necessary for the glory of God has gotten the point." What I am saying here, I maintain, is no new manner of preaching; it is what is being preached everywhere and constantly concerning good works, even though I am speaking of two classes of disciples.[133]

Christ does the same in John 6. He teaches about the eating of his flesh, and then he treats of the distinction among the disciples who hear his teaching. Some he finds to be fleshly, some spiritual, and he pronounces this judgment upon them: "The flesh is of no avail, the spirit gives life." He explains this himself by adding, "My words are spirit and life." This can only mean, "I must have spiritual disciples of my words; fleshly disciples will not hear, for they are of the flesh, and not disciples of my words. But flesh is of no avail, and deceives them." Just as the Spirit is Christ's word and teaching, so must flesh also be the flesh's word and teaching. Thus the Spirit, i.e. his word and teaching, gives life; and flesh, i.e. the flesh's word and teaching, is of no avail. Of this I have written sufficiently elsewhere.[134]

The third offense I supposedly committed in this passage is that my rule is false when I write: Wherever spirit and flesh are contrasted in Scripture, flesh never means Christ's flesh but the Old Adam.[135] Ah, here the giant Christopher[136] from Zurich pulls

---

133 For the doctrinal controversies to which Luther's views on the relation between faith and works gave rise, see *Formula of Concord,* Art. II-VI, particularly IV. Cf. F. Bente (ed.), *Concordia Triglotta* (St. Louis, 1921), especially pp. 112 ff.; Charles Hay (trans.), R. Seeberg's *Textbook of the History of Doctrines* (2 vols.; Grand Rapids, 1961), II, 362 ff.

134 *"This Is My Body,"* pp. 96 f.

135 *Christian Answer. C. R.* 92, 967; *St. L.* 20, 1223 ff. Cf. *"This Is My Body,"* pp. 95 ff.

136 The legendary giant Christopher was often depicted leaning against an uprooted tree. This is apparently a retort aimed at Zwingli's sarcastic use of the figure of Christopher to represent Luther's alleged extension of the body of Christ, e.g. *Friendly Exposition. C. R.* 92, 686.

up whole trees and hurls hills and dales into a heap. If I understand his muddled, unkempt German aright, which to tell the truth I find very difficult, he makes a distinction between God's spirit and our spirit. This is about as necessary to the subject as a fifth wheel to a wagon, except that it serves to persuade the poor common people that the great giant of Zurich intends to answer, and that there is concealed within him vast, inexhaustible wisdom. But it does not matter to us whether it is God's spirit here or our spirit; my rule still stands, that wherever in Scripture spirit and flesh are set in contrast, there flesh cannot mean Christ's flesh. For his flesh is not contrary to the spirit; much rather, it is born of the Holy Spirit and filled with the Holy Spirit. But since Christ says here, "The spirit gives life, and the flesh is of no avail," it is manifestly clear enough that he means the flesh which is not spirit and has no spirit, but is opposed to spirit. For to give life, and to be of no avail, are as contrary as life and death, as I have explained more fully in my former book.[137]

Zwingli next teaches me how spirit and flesh accord perfectly with each other, as in John 1 [:14], "The Word was made flesh," and I Peter 3 [:18], "Christ died in the flesh but was made alive in the spirit."[138] May the dear God reward him, for who could have discovered this without his aid? My rule reads thus: Where spirit and flesh in Scripture stand in contrast, etc. Thereby I surely acknowledge sufficiently that spirit and flesh are not in contrast everywhere. Here too the question is not whether flesh and spirit sometimes accord with each other in Scripture. The question arises where spirit and flesh do *not* accord with each other, as in this passage, "The flesh is of no avail, the spirit gives life." There, I say, flesh cannot mean Christ's flesh. Here is the point where the dauntless hero should give an answer. Instead, he flutters over it, and meanwhile cuts up with other antics, teaching us that spirit and flesh are not opposed to each other in some passages of Scripture. This is supposed to answer everything, just as in the story where the one fellow asks, "Where does this road lead to?" and the other replies, "I am whittling young woodpeckers!"[139]

---

137 See pp. 95 f.

138 *Christian Answer. C. R.* 92, 969; *St. L.* 20, 1224.

139 In *WA* 38, 117, there is another version of this "moron story."

Satan is certainly a master of gabble, when he does not know how to answer!

I also called attention to the word "my."[140] Christ does not say here, "My flesh is of no avail," as he does above, "My flesh is food indeed" [6:55]. This is the reply he gives me: "Just as Christ does not say, 'My spirit gives life,' though it is his spirit, so he does not say, 'My flesh,' though it is his flesh." Come, now, and turn yourself into another form, little spirit! Christ does not speak here of his own spirit which he has personally, but, as the text reads, of the spirit that gives life, i.e. of the common spirit that is in all believers. Although Christ gives this spirit and it is Christ's spirit, yet it is a common spirit, present everywhere that it gives life, for it does not only make Christ alive. Thus flesh here must also refer to the common flesh which is without spirit and is of no avail.

Accordingly, in regard to the word "my," here, Zwingli has committed a real sophistry and deception, known as "the fallacy of figure of speech."[141] For above, where Christ says, "My flesh is food indeed" [John 6:55], the word "my" signifies his own personal flesh, which is common to no one else. But though spirit here is his spirit, it is not his individual personal spirit, belonging to himself alone, but the common spirit in all to whom he gives it. Hence flesh cannot here mean his flesh as spirit means his spirit, for his flesh is not a common flesh in all. But anyone who does not know how to give an answer must help himself out in this way.

Let this suffice on the second major division, which makes it plain to everyone that the fanatic cannot apply this passage, "The flesh is of no avail," to Christ's flesh, and that this spirit has been put to shame because of it, since he is altogether unable to give an answer. You notice that he silently ignores all the examples where I have so abundantly proved how the flesh of Abraham, Sarah, Isaac, and other saints was profitable to faith, and demonstrated a fortiori that Christ's flesh must be profitable.[142] It is better for him—for this I must give him credit—to keep quiet and rush over the difficulty than to choke on it and publicly be obliged

---

140 See pp. 79 ff.
141 Mullally (ed.), *Summulae Logicales*, pp. 6 f.
142 See pp. 91 f.

to lie down. He certainly feels that it will not help to get angry and abusive.

Then again, you notice he does not answer the quotations from the fathers, but merely says, "Luther, you do not understand them rightly," adding that it would be of little consequence to him if they did not agree with him.[143] Doesn't he handle this beautifully! Why should this important spirit answer such rubbish? Well, let him go his learned way, but my master or assistant he will never be, please God, unless he turns from his blasphemous teaching, not only on this point but on all the others in which he has so deplorably deceived himself and the people. May Christ our Lord help him and all! Amen.

Now let us hear how Oecolampadius answers,[144] for I still have the hope that he does not agree with Zwingli in all points but only in the sacrament [of the altar] and baptism. May God rescue him from these errors! Amen. I have demonstrated above[145] that Oecolampadius' figure or trope cannot and must not be admitted in the Supper, for he cannot prove it. Moreover, it is an inverted, awkward figure, opposed to all the figures of Scripture, so that one must regard it a malicious fabrication. This I must make clear.

Wherever a trope or word with a new sense occurs in Holy Scripture, there two interpretations arise: a new one in addition to the first, old, or previous one, as I said above. For example, the word "vine" in Scripture has two interpretations, one old and one new. According to the first or old sense it means simply the stock or plant in the vineyard. According to the new it means Christ, John 15 [:5]: "I am the vine," or a mother of children, Psalm 128 [:3]: "Your wife will be like a vine," or something else of a similar nature which bears resemblance to the vine on account of

---

[143] *Christian Answer. C. R.* 92, 969 ff.; *St. L.* 20, 1225 ff. Cf. *"This Is My Body,"* pp. 104 ff. Actually Zwingli devotes several paragraphs to a rebuttal. The disclaimer of the importance of patristic support: "Besides, it is of no great importance even if they were not on our side. For God is greater than his apostles, John 13 [:16], not to mention the doctors. Although as a matter of fact they are on our side." *C. R.* 92, 974; *St. L.* 20, 1227.

[144] Now Luther turns to Oecolampadius' works, which he had already treated in *"This Is My Body,"* pp. 104 ff., as he had announced he would do in his letter to Spalatin on March 11, 1527. *WA, Br* 4, 175.

[145] See p. 176.

its fruit, as the grammarians teach: "Transfers of words (i.e. new words or tropes) are produced according to the rules of comparison."[146]

Now these tropes in Scripture are so constituted that the words according to the first or old sense indicate the object which is a likeness of the new; and according to the new sense they indicate the new real object or thing, and not vice versa. For example, in this text, "I am the true vine" [John 15:1], here the word "vine" has become a trope or new word, which cannot refer back to the old vine, which is a likeness of the new, but refers forward to the true, new vine, which is not a likeness. For Christ is not a likeness of the vine, but on the contrary the vine is a likeness of Christ. Again, "The seed is the word of God" [Luke 8:11]. Here the word "seed" does not indicate the grain, which is a simile of the gospel, but as a new word or trope should, signifies the gospel, the true, new seed itself, which is not a likeness. And so forth; all tropes in Scripture signify the true, new object, and not the simile of this new object.

But Oecolampadius reverses this and constructs a trope or new word which refers backward to the likeness of the new object, and says that the word "body" should mean the "sign" or "likeness of the body," in the text, "This is my body"; although, if he wished to follow Scripture, he should rather transfer the word "body" so that it would mean the true, new body, of which the natural body of Christ is a simile. For Scripture does not fabricate backward-referring tropes.[147] Nor would it sound right if I fashioned such tropes: "Christ is a vine, i.e. the sign of a vine," "The gospel is a seed, i.e. the sign of a seed," "Christ is a lamb, i.e. the sign of a lamb," "Christ is a rock, i.e. the sign of a rock," "Christ is our passover, i.e. the sign of our passover," "John is Elijah, i.e. the sign of Elijah." To sum it all up, there are no such tropes in Scripture; they are all worthless. Therefore, Oecolampadius' trope is no good either, when he says, "The bread is my body, i.e. the sign of my body." For it is a backward-pointing, inverted trope;

---

[146] Transfer, or translation or tralation, is the same as metaphor, a change of a word from literal to figurative meaning. Cf. Quintilian, *Institutes of Oratory, VIII*, 6, 4 ff. J. S. Watson (ed.), *Institutes of Oratory*, II, 125 ff.

[147] *Troppet nicht zu rücke.*

it makes of the true substance a likeness or sign, which is not the way it is done in Holy Scripture. Therefore it is pure fancy.

If the text read: "Take, eat, this is my true bread," one could make a proper trope and say quite neatly, "Bread here is a new word; according to its original signification it means simple bread, which is a simile of the body of Christ, and according to its new signification it means the true, new bread itself, which is the body of Christ." But what the text says is, "This is my body," and if he wishes to make a trope there, to be true to Scripture he must say, "The word 'body' according to its old signification means the natural body of Christ, but according to its new signification it must mean a second, new body of Christ, of which his natural body is a likeness." This would be the right and proper way, in the style of Scripture, to give the word a new signification. The new text then would read, "This is my true, new body, which is not a likeness," just as I say in reference to Christ, "This is our vine, i.e. a new, true vine, of which the old vine in the vineyard is the likeness." [148]

Now someone may allege that we find this trope of Oecolampadius in common speech, as when we say of pictures, "This is St. Peter, this is St. Paul, this is Pope Julius,[149] this is the emperor Nero," and so forth; in such expressions the words Peter, Paul, Julius, and Nero are represented by the pictures. I reply, first: This is not the question. Oecolampadius has not undertaken to produce tropes in common speech, but in Scripture. To this he must confine himself and follow the style and character of Scripture. If he can show me a single example of his trope in Scripture, he will have won the argument and I will agree with him in all points. But if he produces no example, he has lost and his trope is nothing but pure fancy.

For Holy Scripture handles its expressions in the same way as God handles his works. Now God always works so that the figure or type appears first, and then the true reality and fulfilment of the type follows. So the Old Testament first comes forth as a type, and the New Testament follows as the true reality. So too

[148] Cf. John 15:5, Luke 8:11, John 1:29, I Cor. 10:4, I. Cor. 5:7, Matt. 11:14. Cf. pp. 70 ff., also pp. 164 ff.

[149] Pope Julius II (1503-1513).

when Scripture makes tropes or new words, it takes the old word, which is the likeness, and gives it a new meaning, which is the true reality.

How would it sound if I should say, "The gospel is a new testament, i.e. a figure of the new testament"? That would be tantamount to saying, "The gospel is the old testament." Again, "Christ is the lamb of God [John 1:29], i.e. an image or figure of the lamb of God." That would be tantamount to, "Christ is the old paschal lamb of Moses." This is exactly what Oecolampadius does with his backward-pointing trope when out of the new word "body" he makes an old word, saying, "It should mean, 'This is the sign of my body,'" which is as much as to say, "This is bread." But "bread" should properly be the old word, and the "body" the new, and the word "bread" should signify the body, not "body" the bread. Thus his trope falls apart and has no place in Scripture.

Secondly, it is even untrue that this trope of Oecolampadius is to be found in any common speech or language in the whole world. If anyone will bring me one incontrovertible example, I will bare my neck to him. They say, of course, that such a trope occurs in the expression, "Here is St. Peter, i.e. a picture of St. Peter." But I say No to this, and they cannot prove it. It is their own false imagination. For it is an infallible rule in all languages that wherever the word "is" occurs in an expression, one is surely speaking of the substance of the said object and not of its representation.[150] This you may see from the following example: If I set before me a wooden or silver rose and ask, "What is this?" someone answers me, "It is a rose." Here I do not ask what it represents but what it is in its essence; so the answer tells me what it is and not what it signifies. These are two quite different questions, if I say, "What does this signify?" and if I say, "What is this?" "Is" always refers to the essence itself; this is beyond question.

"Yes," you say, "but it is not really a rose, but a piece of wood." I answer: All right, but it is a rose just the same. Though it is not a naturally growing rose in a garden, it too is in essence

150 The verb "to be" is designated in grammar the substantive verb. Cf. p. 65, n. 109, p. 331, n. 257.

a rose in its own way. For there are many kinds of roses, such as silver, golden, cloth, paper, stone, wooden, but each one in its own right is a rose essentially, in its essence, and cannot be a mere representation. Indeed, how could it be a representation, if it had no essence before? That which is nothing represents nothing. That which represents something must first have an essence and a figure of another essence.

In reference to a wooden rose, therefore, we must distinguish between the essence and the representation, as we do between *first act* and *second act,* and between a *substantive verb* and an *active verb.*[151] In essence it is truly a rose, viz. a wooden rose. Accordingly, if the essence is so established, one may say, "This represents or is made after another rose." For these are two distinct expressions or propositions: "This is a rose," and, "This represents a rose." Whoever identifies the two expressions virtually regards a hypothetical and a categorical proposition as identical, which is impossible. How absurd this is the scholars know perfectly well.

Now, however, there are different kinds of roses, wooden, silver, golden, etc., and yet each one truly, in its own right, is and bears the name of rose. Just so also does the word "rose" become a new and different word according to its signification (although the spelling remains unchanged) every time the essence or kind of rose changes from one to another. Thus no one needs to use Oecolampadius' tropes and say, "This is the image of a rose." It is not even true, when one says, "This is a rose," that he wishes to be understood as saying, "This is a likeness of a rose." He wishes to say what it is in its essence. And if he wishes to say further what it signifies, he uses two different expressions: "This is a rose, and represents a rose." And everyone must admit that these two expressions are not identical, nor do they refer to the same rose, but each one in its own right expresses something different from the other. I know with certainty that all this is so, and no one can deny it.

[151] Cf. Aquinas, *Summa Theologica,* I, ques. 48, art. 5 c: "Act . . . is twofold; first and second. The first act is the form and integrity of a thing; the second act is its operation." Anton Pegis (ed.), *Basic Writings of St. Thomas Aquinas* (1945), I, 471. The distinction between *substantive verb* (here meaning: used as a gerund) and *active verb* amounts to the same thing.

Therefore Oecolampadius cannot be sustained with his trope, when he wishes to identify these two expressions, "This is my body," and, "This is the likeness of my body." This no tongue or language will permit. Just as little can it mean the same thing if I say of a picture of St. Paul, "This is St. Paul," and, "This represents St. Paul." For the first expression means what the picture is, viz. that it is St. Paul, i.e. a wooden St. Paul, a silver St. Paul, a golden St. Paul, a painted St. Paul. In short, the word "is" refers to essence, whatever kind of essence it may be, and here "St. Paul" has become a new word, not meaning the living St. Paul. Accordingly, if I ask further, "Then what does it represent?" in that moment it is a different expression, referring now not to essence but to signification. Hence, just as essence and signification are not the same, so they must not be expressed with the same words or terms. Each must have its own appropriate expression.

If Oecolampadius wishes to maintain his trope, he must also employ two kinds of expressions in the Supper. The one concerns essence, i.e., "This is my body"; for there stands an "is" in the text, which properly and necessarily refers to essence. Since in the Supper we find no more than one expression, which refers to essence, viz., "This is my body," it must be speaking of the essential body of Christ, whether this body be of wood, silver, or something else. For there stands an "is" in the text, and it demands a body of Christ which is present and is called Christ's body, just as the nature of common speech requires that a Paul be present if one says of a picture, "This is Paul." So Oecolampadius must admit that a body of Christ is present in the Supper, though then he may reflect whether he would make it of bread, wood, clay, or stone. The trope requires a body of Christ, because we do not read the other type of expression, "This represents," or, "This is the sign of my body," but, "This is my body."

In summary, as I have said of the rose, wherever in a sentence the word "rose" is to become a new word or trope, there must be two roses in juxtaposition, both properly bearing the name "rose," one which represents, the other which is represented. Each of the two roses must truly be a rose and be entitled to the name, though each in its own fashion, the one wooden, the other natural. So too, if the word "my body" in the text of the Supper is to become a new word or trope, there must also be two bodies of Christ in juxtaposition, both properly bearing the name "my body," one which represents, the other which is represented. Thus each of the two bodies of Christ really and rightly is called a body of Christ, and is so in essence, whether it is of wood, silver, or bread.

Now if Oecolampadius can prove that bread is in reality a body of Christ, and if he may say it is a body of Christ made of bread, present as a likeness of the natural body of Christ—as the wooden rose is in reality a rose, and a likeness of the natural rose—he will have proved this much, that examples of his trope may be found, and his trope will be similar to that which occurs in common speech concerning pictures: "This is St. Peter, this is St. Paul," etc.—although this is not a trope according to the style of Scripture. But if he cannot, then his trope is good for nothing even apart from Scripture. Now how will he prove that bread is in reality and in name the body of Christ, or that Christ has a body of bread, as St. Paul has a wooden St. Paul? He must do so, or he is off the path. Even if he found the example, how would that help if such a trope had no force in Scripture? Since, then, his trope has no example either in Scripture or outside Scripture, and indeed is contrary to Scripture and the nature of all language, it is easy to see that it is pure, useless fancy.

Oecolampadius has deceived himself over the quotation of Tertullian, "This is the form (*figura*) of my body." [152] He has regarded *figura* or *gestalt* as a trope. It is well to notice that Oecolampadius has not discovered this figure by himself, nor has he taken it from Scripture, for neither Scripture nor any language uses this style. But he has stumbled over Tertullian's expression and come to grief on account of it, falling into error. Tertullian himself does not fashion a trope here. He only gives an explanation or exposition how bread is the body of Christ, viz. it is the form under which the body of Christ is; and he speaks not of words but of realities when he says, "This is the form of my body," for bread is not a figure of speech in grammar but the form of an object in nature. And Tertullian cannot have been so foolish as to imply that Christ made out of the bread a grammatical word,

[152] Cf. pp. 108 ff. Zwingli also defended the figurative interpretation of Tertullian's expression in *Christian Answer*. *C. R.* 92, 973; *St. L.* 20, 1226.

as it would have to follow from Oecolampadius' opinion, thus: "He made bread his body, i.e. a figure of his body, i.e. a grammatical figure." For this figure, viz. that bread is a figure of the body of Christ, is found neither in nature nor in the style of Scripture.[153]

Thus, I think, Oecolampadius' trope and his nonsense about "signs" are as convincingly taken away from him as Zwingli's nonsense about "representation" from him and Karlstadt's *touto* from him. Not one of them has his text, nor can they have any. So they sit naked and bare, altogether lacking a text in the Supper. If they have no text, neither can they have any understanding or interpretation. If they have no interpretation, neither can they know whether they have mere bread and wine or not. For naturally they must first of all arrive at a knowledge of what they have in the Supper. But this they cannot arrive at unless they acquire a sure text and interpretation. And this they can never obtain, as we have proved. We conclude, therefore, that the fanatics themselves do not know what they have in the Supper. O this fine spirit! O this beautiful Supper! This is really and truly what it means to sit and eat in darkness,[154] while one does not know what he is eating or where he is sitting. O friend, for God's sake, give a penny to provide this poor spirit with light!

Not that I mock the fanatics and their god, except in words. I am not Elijah, who dares to mock the most holy prophets of Baal [I Kings 18:27]; especially since they themselves will tell you, even though they sit in darkness, still they have seen that Luther has lost the Spirit and has become a Saul [I Sam. 16:14], and cannot understand that bread is bread, which even dogs and pigs understand. If I wanted to mock them, I would advise them in their misery and distress to follow one of their own disciples who questioned one of our party about the sacrament, and at last, when he had exhausted his arguments, he said, "Ah, my dear brother, but they say truly, very truly, that it reads in Greek, *Hoc est tropus meus,* and not *Hoc est corpus meum.*"[155] This is one

---

[153] In the first edition of Luther's *Confession* this sentence was appended at the end, with a note directing its insertion here. *CL* 3, 515.
[154] Cf. Eccles. 5:17, Ps. 107:10, Isa. 9:2.
[155] Latin: "This is my trope," not, "This is my body."

way they might acquire a sure text and fabricate figures[156] until they finally hit on the right one.

If this annoys them, however—well, they might do like the priest who chanced to meet two other priests and found them profoundly perplexed about this very subject of the sacrament, over the text, *Hoc est corpus meum.* One maintained it must be, *Hoc est corpus meus,* the other that it must be, *Hoc est corpum meum,*[157] in order that the words might agree. Now when they referred the matter to the third for his decision, he said, "You know, this has often bothered me too, but this is the way I get by: whenever I come to this text, I pray an Ave Maria instead!" [158]

Now here is a great question: Which of the three consecrated the elements properly? Let us pass that by for the present. For since our fanatics do not consecrate them,[159] and yet sit in such darkness and doubt and error and disunity as to the text, it would be good if, following this example, they too would pray an Ave Maria in place of the uncertain text; or if they feared becoming old or new papists[160] and were unduly afraid of Mary and the saints, or images, they might sing instead, "Christ has risen," or, "Christ rose to heaven," [161] since these hymns and words espe-

---

[156] *Troppen.*

[157] G. G. Coulton gives other examples of the ignorance of priests even regarding the grammar of the liturgy of the mass. *Medieval Panorama* (Cambridge, England, 1943), pp. 157 ff. See also E. H. Zeydel (trans.), Sebastian Brant's *Ship of Fools* (New York, 1944), pp. 242 ff.; N. Bailey (trans.), Erasmus' *Familiar Colloquies* (Glasgow, 1877), "The Abbot and the Learned Woman," pp. 195 f.

[158] The *Hail, Mary!* originated in the eleventh century as a formula of private devotion. By the fifteenth century it had come to consist of the salutations of Gabriel (Luke 1:28) and Elizabeth (Luke 1:42), and a prayer for the Virgin's intercession. Luther recommended it, purged of the petition for intercession, as a praise to God for Christ's mother, in the *Little Book on Prayer,* 1522. *LW* 43, 39 ff.

[159] Zwingli had eliminated all hints of a consecration of the elements in his Zurich liturgy.

[160] Cf. p. 87, n. 148.

[161] *Christ ist erstanden* was a medieval German hymn based on the twelfth century Easter sequence, "Christians, to the Paschal Victim" (*Victimae paschali*), and related to the Latin hymn *Surrexit Christus hodie.* These were the inspiration for Luther's masterpiece, "Christ Jesus lay in Death's strong bands" (*Christ lag in Todesbanden*), for the hymn by Luther's friend, Michael Weisse, "Christ the Lord is risen again" (*Christus ist erstanden*), and for many others. *Christ fur gen himmel* came from the fourteenth century, associated with the Latin hymn *Coelos ascendit hodie;* it found a place in the Wittenberg "Bapst" hymnal of 1545. Cf. E. Koch, *Geschichte des Kirchenlieds und Kirchengesangs* (Stuttgart, 1866), I, 197, 254.

cially oppose the text in the Lord's Supper and make it so uncertain! A stone should be moved to compassion that those exalted, enlightened spirits, who otherwise have as much sunshine in their minds as hair on their heads, nevertheless on this subject must sit in such darkness that they cannot even see a little star.

If anyone supposes that I attack the fanatics here too severely and deride them unduly, I beg him to consider further that although I am an insignificant Christian, it is not surprising that I feel irritation over this Satan who makes a fickle fool of my Lord and Savior Jesus Christ and ridicules him as if he were a simpleton or a drunkard in the Supper.

In the first place, they so represent Christ in his words and works that there is nothing more to be received in the Supper than mere bread and wine in remembrance of the Lord's death. Therefore they have no need at all of this text, "This is my body; this is my blood." It is an altogether vain, unnecessary, useless text, without which the Supper can still be celebrated properly and completely. For they have text enough and to spare if they read, "Take, eat; take, drink; do this in remembrance of me." In these words they have their Supper whole and complete. Therefore Christ must be a real fool, who at his end was such a useless babbler as to lay down this unnecessary text, "This is my body; this is my blood," etc., which these exalted spirits can dispense with, however, and which they oppose and would like to excise. Let them tell us of what use this text would be, if bread and wine without this text are enough to remind them of the Lord's death—which they make the principal and only purpose of the Supper.

In the second place, if bread and wine represent the Lord's body and blood, why is it necessary for Christ precisely here to teach us this silly "representation"? Though one should not ask why God does anything, nevertheless since he is being made to look like a fool here, I may ask this without being unreasonable. Or what purpose is served if I know that bread represents the Lord's body? How do such allegories help faith, if even the devils and the ungodly can discover them? On the other hand, how harmful or dangerous would it be if I never knew that bread represents the body of Christ but simply regarded bread as bread? Had Christ nothing else to teach than something utterly useless, which, without his teaching we might easily have discovered for ourselves and which the devil and his followers can discover too? Especially because there is no *analogy of faith* here. For all the words of Christ must foster faith and love, and be in accord with faith, Romans 12 [:6]. No, he had to display his folly, and not only burden us with a vain, useless text but also teach us unnecessary, useless knowledge, which without his teaching we could easily find at every table of the godless.

Moreover, suppose he did teach this useless knowledge with such obscure words that the apostles themselves did not understand them with certainty, as we read that they never or seldom understood what he said when he spoke in parables, and he always had to disclose their meaning even to them.[162] Has he now become so niggardly in his last, supreme act of love, that he gives no explanation to the silly, childish disciples, but leaves them entangled in those obscure words which they could not without an explanation understand in any other way than as they read, although on other occasions he was so generous with his explanations? The answer is brief: Christ, like a clown, wished simply for a pastime to fool and tease his disciples with useless obscure words, without which they could have observed the Supper completely with him anyway!

In the third place, it is the greatest foolishness of all when he says, "The bread represents or is a likeness of his body which was given for us, and the cup or wine is a likeness of his blood which was shed for us." My friend, where is this likeness in the bread and the cup of wine? For where there is alleged to be a figure, symbol, or simile, where one thing is asserted to represent another, some similarity must be indicated in both upon which the simile is based. For example, in John 15 [:4], the vine is a likeness or figure of Christ, because, as he says himself, "The branch cannot bear fruit by itself, but withers unless it abides in the vine." Again, Elijah is a figure or type of John, because as the angel Gabriel says, Luke 1 [:17], he will have "the spirit and power of Elijah." The paschal lamb is a type of Christ, because, as the Apocalypse says [Rev. 5:12], he was slain and sacrificed

[162] Cf. Matt. 15:15 f., Matt. 13:36, Mark 4:10 ff., 33 f., etc.

for us. And so forth. In all figures and types there must be some similarity which underlies them and brings the two objects into correspondence. But here in the bread and the cup there is nothing to which Christ's body and blood could bear a similarity.

Now if Christ says, "The bread is a likeness of my body which was given for you; the cup of wine is a likeness of my blood which was poured out for you," this would be exactly the same as saying, "The bread, which has no resemblance whatever to my body which was given for you, is nevertheless a likeness of my body which was given for you." Precisely as if I should say on the basis of St. Paul [II Cor. 6:14 f.], "Belial, who bears no resemblance at all to Christ, is nevertheless a likeness of Christ; the light, which does not correspond to the darkness at all, nevertheless corresponds nicely to the darkness," etc. Everyone knows perfectly well what kind of people they are who talk this way, viz. silly, senseless fools or vagabonds, who tell tales at table about iron birds flying over the sea, or black snow falling in summer, in order to rouse the guests to laughter.[163] Just such a silly fool or vagabond do the fanatics make of Christ, when they impute to him the saying, "This bread is a likeness of my body which was given for you, although there is no such resemblance in the bread at all."

If they allege, however, that the resemblance consists in the fact that, just as the bread is eaten and the cup of wine drunk, so Christ's body is spiritually eaten and his blood spiritually drunk, my friend, this says nothing. For the fanatics locate the trope not in the words, "Take, eat," or, "give thanks," etc., but in these words, "This is my body which was given for you"; therefore no one is asking here about the resemblance in eating, taking, or giving thanks. Here, here in the bread, I say, a resemblance must be shown, how it was given, slain, martyred, and offered up for us for the forgiveness of sins, in order that it may be a figure or likeness of the body of Christ which was given for us for the forgiveness of sins, as the words say. Otherwise Christ is a fool when he calls the bread a likeness, whereas there is not and cannot be any such likeness. So, too, a resemblance must be shown

[163] Probably an allusion to the popular *Lügenmärchen*, "tall tales." *WA* 26, 393, n. 1.

in the cup of wine, that just as it was spilled for our redemption, so Christ's blood also was poured out for the forgiveness of sins.

This is what Moses does with his figures of speech. He shows how the oxen and calves are slain and offered up, and their blood is poured out at the foot of the altar and sprinkled for the forgiveness of sins and the purification of the people, and on the tabernacle and all the vessels, as the Epistle to the Hebrews shows in a masterly manner.[164] Especially the paschal lamb bears a very fine resemblance to the body of Christ which was given for us for the forgiveness of sins, in that it was slain and offered up and its blood was poured and sprinkled and smeared on the door for salvation from the Destroyer [Exod. 12:21 ff.]. Such a correspondence must be shown in the bread and wine, else we must regard anyone a fool who says they resemble the body and blood of Christ given and shed for us for the forgiveness of sins, even though no similarity at all can be found there. For if there is to be a figure of speech, there must be some similarity, otherwise it is a lie and a falsehood to call it a simile.

Now if Christ had intended to institute a Supper in which not his body and blood, but a likeness of his body and blood were present, he would properly have left us the old Mosaic supper with the paschal lamb. Beyond all measure, with absolute conclusiveness, through and through, in every respect, and quite beautifully this represents and prefigures and typifies his body which was given for us and his blood which was shed for us for the forgiveness of sins, as all the world well knows. Why then should he be so foolish as to abolish this fine supper of the Old Testament and substitute a supper which in meaning and in essence is altogether insignificant in comparison with it?

One might fairly reply to this man: The New Testament is to be a fulfilment and a light in relation to the Old Testament, but you reverse it, so that the New Testament is actually an emptying and obscuring of the Old. For in the Old, at least, there is a lamb, a living body, offered up for the people, which represents the body of Christ much more lucidly and clearly than simple bread, which is an obscure simile in comparison with a lamb. And in the Old Testament, there is the blood of the lamb,

[164] Cf. Heb. 9:1 ff., Exod. 24:5 ff., Leviticus 16, etc.

which represents the blood of Christ much more lucidly and clearly than simple wine. In a word, this Supper is in no way comparable to the old one in signification and similarity. Therefore, if in the New Testament everything is supposed to be more perfect than in the Old, even in respect to types, then Christ ought properly to have left us with the old supper, else it is not true that only bread and wine are present in our Supper. For truly it must far excel the supper of Moses, otherwise Christ would not have abrogated the old institution.

Here the fanatics again seek a loophole, pointing out that St. Paul says in his text, I Corinthians 11 [:24], "This is my body which is broken[165] for you." The similarity and signification consist in the breaking. Just as bread is broken at table, so also was Christ martyred for us on the cross, etc. Oh, if the honoring of saints and the possession of images had not been forbidden, one might now fall down before an image of St. Paul and cry, "O holy St. Paul, help us poor, miserable, forsaken fanatics against this furious Luther! See how he drives and chases us until we are exhausted! You alone can help us when you say, 'Christ's body is broken.'" But in short, St. Paul cannot and will not help, for the images of the saints "have ears but do not hear" [Ps. 115:6].

In the first place, that "broken" here is equivalent to "crucified" they may indeed assert out of their own heads,[166] but they can prove it just as little as they can prove a similarity in the bread to the body of Christ. It is sheer, uncertain prattle, establishing the unknown by the unknown. But we demand sure proofs of such a similarity. Since they boast so confidently of their position, they ought to render it indisputable or else stand in the pillory.

Secondly, I have said above that the fanatics do not locate the trope or simile in the words, "Take, eat, give thanks," thus not in these words, "Christ took the bread, broke it, and gave it to his disciples." Here they allow the words, "take," "break," "give," "bread," "disciples," all to remain simply as they stand, without being made figurative. Therefore they may not afterward make the "breaking" into a figure on the pretext that Paul says, "This

[165] Cf. p. 129, n. 224.

[166] Oecolampadius, *Apologetics*. *St. L.* 20, 692 f.

is my body which is broken for you," for this was spoken of the same breaking of which he said above, "He took the bread and broke it" [I Cor. 11:23 f.], until they prove incontestably that it refers to another act of breaking. Meanwhile, we say there is a single breaking indicated in both places, and it may not be understood to refer to Christ's crucifixion and passion. For Christ did not arrest, crucify, and slay himself, as he must have done if "breaking" is equivalent to slaying, for he took the bread himself and broke it with his own hands.

Thirdly, we hold to Scripture when we say that to "break" bread means to distribute bread, as I have proved against the heavenly prophets.[167] And St. Paul says, "The bread which we break is the distribution of the body of Christ" [I Cor. 10:16]. It is altogether vicious to attempt without the authority of Scripture to make "break" equivalent to "crucify" or "slay." Nowhere else, either, is "break" equivalent to "kill" or "slay." Therefore it is pure fancy when the fanatics try to cover their nakedness with this argument. Rather, a manifest similarity should be shown which the bread has with the body of Christ given for us. Moreover, even if the breaking were the similarity (as it is not), nevertheless the main point of the simile is still missing, viz. that the bread was broken and the wine poured out for us, for our redemption. For the bread and wine should and must be a likeness of that body and blood of Christ which was given and shed for us; besides, we are redeemed by them, as the text says, "This is my body and blood, given for you and poured out for the forgiveness of sins."[168] Such a resemblance, however, the word "breaking" cannot convey. But the paschal lamb and the old supper can convey it quite excellently.

Therefore the wine and bread here cannot be the likeness of that body and blood of Christ as the text of the Supper speaks of them. I pass over the fact that John [19:33 ff.] utterly repudiates the application of the word "breaking" to the suffering of Christ, when he writes that not a bone of Christ was broken, "that the Scripture might be fulfilled, 'Not a bone of him shall be broken.'"

167 *LW* 40, 177 f., 208 ff.

168 Here Luther conflates the Pauline and Synoptic texts. Cf. p. 28, n. 36; p. 44, n. 72. He analyzes the four accounts separately on pp. 307 ff.

Scripture therefore does not permit us to refer "breaking" to Christ's suffering or death.

Fourthly, suppose we grant that by virtue of the breaking, the bread resembles the crucified body of Christ (which is not true), what becomes of the cup or chalice of wine in the other part? How will the wine be a likeness of the blood of Christ poured out for our sin? Drinking is a simile not of the shed blood of Christ but of the spiritual drinking, i.e. of faith, as they themselves teach. But here stands the poor cup of wine so naked in its humiliation that it could not be more deeply humiliated, for it possesses in itself not a hair's breath of resemblance, and yet must be a simile of the blood of Christ shed for us.

Where are you now, St. Paul? If only you had said of the cup that Christ's hands trembled and the wine was spilled, we poor fanatics might have enjoyed a little respite with this idea of "spilling," as we now enjoy an hour's peace with the idea of "breaking." Alas, when St. John reclined in Christ's arms [John 13:23], if only he had, perhaps with his head, jostled Christ's elbow when he took the cup and gave it to his disciples, so that even a tiny drop had spilled, we would have had enough to enable us to say, "See, the wine resembles the shed blood of Christ, by virtue of the fact that it was spilled!" Now even if the spilling does not take place for our redemption or benefit, and therefore does not resemble the blood of Christ in this main point of the simile, as the text of the Supper demands, at least it may take place for the redemption of us poor fanatics from our great distress and shame, that otherwise we can point to no simile, although we have noised it abroad for so long and so far and wide and with so many books that the wine resembles and is a figure of the blood of Christ poured out for us for the forgiveness of sin, though not an iota of such a resemblance now appears.

See now what the mockers of our Lord Christ gain, and who is most successful in making the other look like a fool. For their figure can be neither grammatical nor theological nor natural. That is, their figure simply does not hold good in any respect, for such a figure is to be found neither in words nor in Holy Scripture nor in nature. If it were in the words, then the word "body" would have to become two words and yet retain the same spelling but signify the two kinds of body of Christ, as the word "vine" becomes two words, and yet retains the same spelling but signifies the two kinds of vine. But, of course, the bread cannot be or signify Christ's body. If it were in Holy Scripture, the bread must bear such a resemblance that it could manifest Christ's body which was given for us, as is true of all other similes in Holy Scripture. If it were a natural simile, the bread would have to resemble the body as closely as a wooden rose does a natural rose. For it is called a natural simile when everyone naturally perceives the object of reference, without any instruction, as is the case with pictures. For anyone who knows what a rose is need not be told that a painted rose resembles a natural rose. But bread is by no means similar to the body of Christ in this sense, to say nothing of resembling the body as it was given for us.

Thus, whichever way one turns the fanatics' notion, it proves unsound and worthless. We have proved above that they have no sure text at all. However, even if we were willing to accept their text as sure, the rotten thing will not hold together but falls to pieces in our hands. For who can be satisfied with a text that reads, "This bread is a likeness of Christ's body, although it cannot be a likeness of Christ's body"? Who can say No and Yes in the same breath and in the same proposition? They are like the fool who built a mill on a mountain top. When the mill was finished, someone asked where he would get his water to run it. "You know," he said, "I really never thought of that."

In the same way the fanatics are so obsessed with their crazy representations and similes that they can think of nothing else. Even if one would like to concede them the victory and accept their simile, and begged them to teach what constitutes the resemblance of the bread to the body of Christ, they too would have to say, "You know, we really never thought of that! We thought if we only mentioned 'simile,' it would surely be there. For our leader[169] has wanted from the beginning to be God, so that whatever he said should be so!" Behold, this is what you call unhorsing themselves with their own words!

[169] *Geist*.

Although the fanatics' trope now has suffered a sufficiently powerful jolt, they still will not yield and be silent, for who can stop the devil's mouth? Such devils never go out except by fasting and prayer.[170] They urgently crave the sensation of victory for a while. They will say that similes usually do not correspond in every particular, and bread may very well be a likeness of Christ's body in other particulars than that Christ's body was given for us, e.g. in eating, taking, etc. Enough has been said above in answer to the notion that they themselves have not sought or located the resemblance of these words or features in the Supper but in the body which was given for us. They may find similarities in other features, but these do not apply to the Supper and do not give support to their notion. They must stick to this point, namely, "This is a likeness of my body which is given for you." Where they do not show these resemblances and harmonize them, their stand is as firm as a fur coat standing on its sleeves.

Let this suffice for the first point, concerning tropes. Hereby our followers, and everyone who desires to abide by the truth, can successfully defend themselves against the devil's drivel. Further, Oecolampadius complains bitterly against me that I blaspheme, and that my writing takes its start from the devil, as Zwingli also foolishly fusses; and some say that I have mentioned the devil seventy-seven times.[171] This is a laudable, honorable thing to do, and highly necessary for them to write since they have no answers to the real questions. Why don't they also count how often I have mentioned God and Christ, and how I fight for Christ against the devil? Yes, indeed, this would not serve so well to spread the poison with which they strive to impress the common man that Luther's doctrine is of the devil. This brood of vipers[172] wishes to boast of love, peace, and moderation, and yet is as full of poison as a speckled salamander.

---

[170] Cf. Matt. 17:21 (KJV).

[171] From here to p. 288 Luther concentrates on Oecolampadius' most recent treatise, *That Dr. Martin Luther's Misunderstanding . . . is Untenable. The Second Reasonable Answer of John Oecolampadius*, 1527. Oecolampadius charged in chapter 2 that Luther always "starts with the devil and spews out devils in all his words." In the margin: "Someone has counted seventy-seven devils." *WA* 26, 401, nn. 3 and 4. Future citations from this treatise of Oecolampadius are given as quoted in *WA* 26.

[172] Cf. Matt. 23:33.

Well, I have declared that I write not against flesh and blood, as St. Paul teaches [Eph. 6:12], but against the devil and his followers. Therefore I would do well if every other word I write were "devil." Shall I now become so timid for the sake of these delicate, highly spiritual, profoundly holy fanatics, that I must also avoid mentioning my enemy? I am quite willing to be called blasphemous and mad when I attack the devil pungently and pointedly in his messengers. For my frank, public, simple snapping at the devil suits me better than their poisonous, sneaky stabbing, which under the guise of peace and love they practice against the upright, as the Psalter says of these vipers [Ps. 140:3].

In the third place, he writes that this text, "This is my body," is not clear, as I boast, because Christ's body is not visibly present, and that I do not prove my affirmative.[173] The reason is that I produce no Scripture to show that Christ's body is present invisibly. Further, my statement is supposed to be inconsistent, since Christ's body was visibly given for us, and the text says of this body of Christ which was given for us that it will be invisibly present. I answer: To the fanatics, indeed, I have proved nothing nor can I ever do so, for they will neither read nor learn nor understand, as the Psalter says that they stop their ears like an adder, so that it does not hear the voice of the cunning enchanter [Ps. 58:4 f.]. For our own people, I am sure, I have rendered this text clear enough, and have laid down this rule: In Scripture we should let the words retain their natural force, just as they read, and give no other interpretation unless a clear article of faith compels otherwise. This rule is in my book.[174] Still Oecolampadius says I have given no rule. But since these words, "This is my body," according to the nature and style of all languages mean not bread nor sign of the body, but Christ's body, they must be allowed to remain there and not be interpreted differently unless Scripture requires otherwise.

If now we have these words with a sure interpretation known to everyone, and no other interpretation is proved, we can call them clear, lucid, plain words and texts. For no man on earth has ever heard that "body" should mean likeness of a body. This

[173] *Second Reasonable Answer*, chap. 3.
[174] *Against the Heavenly Prophets*. *LW* 40, 157 f.

is an unknown, obscure interpretation, quite new in the world; therefore it requires a good, strong proof. But the first interpretation is clear and certain in itself, as everyone knows. Isn't it a fine thing, then, that Oecolampadius produces a new, unknown, obscure, uncertain interpretation, and tries thereby to make the old interpretation appear obscure and uncertain. In this way no word in Scripture would remain clear, if license were given to every spirit to produce new interpretations and then say the old interpretation is obscure and uncertain. As for the foul deduction which Oecolampadius makes here, viz., "The text says, 'This is my body which was given for you'; now, he was visibly given for us, therefore his body cannot be present invisibly," I have sufficiently shown above in answer to Zwingli how much that argument is worth.[175] It is another case of the mayor without his red trousers in the bath or not in the bath.[176]

I did not know that Oecolampadius was so woefully poor a logician or dialectician that he too would take substance for quality, and syllogize from accident to substance.[177] It is no wonder in the case of Zwingli, one of these self-made doctors who usually turn out this way.[178] Indeed, what good can be expected from a person who wishes to debate, but does not yet know his schoolboy lessons in logic? Oecolampadius disappoints me here so grievously that henceforth I can expect no special degree of clear thinking from him. Even though he need not know the useless hair-splitting and sophistry of the sophists, at least he should know his schoolboy lessons, i.e. common dialectics, such as rules of deduction, forms of syllogism, species of argumentation, etc. Unless I have so confounded him with the truth—as I believe—that he cannot very well see what he is saying!

Tell me, who can imagine any sensible man's saying what Oecolampadius says here, viz. that this text, "This is my body," is not clear because the body of Christ is not visibly present in the sacrament, and only believers understand these words, as Augustine allegedly says.[179] Must a text be unclear if a thing is

[175] See pp. 177 ff. [176] See p. 196. [177] See pp. 178 ff., 194 ff.

[178] Zwingli had received the B.A. (1504) and M.A. (1506) degrees from the University of Basel. He did not have a doctorate in theology.

[179] *On the Trinity*, Book III, chap. 10, par. 21. *MPL* 42, 881. *PNF*[1] 3, 64; Oecolampadius adds: "The instructed know what we are saying."

invisible and none but the believer perceives it? What part of Scripture then would remain clear? If everything that faith teaches is invisible,[180] then this text cannot be clear, "God created heaven and earth" [Gen. 1:1], for God and his creativity are invisible. How will it be made clear, too, that only bread and wine are present in the Supper? Whether more than that is present, is invisible. What advantage is such nonsense to this spirit? They only bring disgrace upon themselves. Honestly, with such silly rubbish it will be a long time before they bring us around to their position and establish their argument.

We know, however, that these words, "This is my body," etc. are clear and lucid. Whether a Christian or a heathen, a Jew or a Turk hears them, he must acknowledge that they speak of the body of Christ which is in the bread. How otherwise could the heathen and the Jews mock us, saying that the Christians eat their God, if they did not understand this text clearly and distinctly? When the believer grasps and the unbeliever despises that which is said, however, this is due not to the obscurity or clarity of the words, but to the hearts that hear it.

The poets are most skilful of all at describing, with perfectly clear words, not only invisible but even insignificant things. How many a man is deceived by fair words of liars, the meaning of which he understands perfectly well! How the people are seduced now when the fanatics speak of insignificant things (to say nothing of invisible things), precisely for the reason that they understand the words clearly and perfectly well! Indeed, the words by which men deceive the people and prattle about trivia are often clearer and more distinct than those which they speak in truth. For if they had not understood clearly and distinctly the meaning of the words, they would never have been deceived. As I have said, however, Oecolampadius and this spirit show a deficiency in elementary dialectics by inferring that because the subject matter is obscure or difficult to understand, the meaning of the words is obscure. This is bad distinguishing, in other words, ignorance of the third part of dialectics.

180 Particularly in his younger days Luther had emphasized that faith is a "knowledge of invisible things" (on the basis of Heb. 11:1, *argumentum non apparentium*), an important idea in the Augustinian and mystical traditions, but also found—with a different epistemological basis—in Occamism.

It shows exactly the same acumen when he alleges[181] that, since the Supper is a sacrament, the words must also be understood sacramentally, "This is my body," i.e. a sign of my body. But what is the purpose of this nonsense? I heartily and gladly admit that the Supper is a sacrament, even though it is not so named in Scripture. But how does it follow that the words must therefore be understood as sacramental, tropical, or (to use their term) figurative? Isn't this a fine conclusion or deduction: Here is a sacrament, therefore the words in it must be taken figuratively? My friend, why then should not the other words also be taken figuratively? And does the trope apply only to the word "is," or to "body"?

Or where is there a rule in this instance to teach us which words must be understood figuratively and which not? On this principle I too will make tropes of the words, "Take, eat, do this in remembrance of me," and say, "Take" means hear, "eat" means believe, "do this" means think in your heart, "memory" means a crucifix or some other symbol. This would be the reason: Here is a sacrament, therefore the words in it must be taken sacramentally or figuratively. I know no reason why these latter words, as well as the former ones, should not be taken as figurative. In this way presumably God himself could not institute a sacrament, for how can he speak of sacraments if one may understand all his words in a sense different from their original? If he spoke of them simply, according to the ordinary nature of words, there would be no sacrament here, for these are not tropes or figurative words; if he used figurative language, no one would know what he was saying.

All this is pure foolishness. When Moses instituted the passover, which of course was a type and figure of Christ, he used not one figurative word, but distinct, clear, simple words, such as were current in ordinary speech. All the figures of the Old Testament were expressed in distinct, simple, clear words, and there is not one in the whole lot which was spoken figuratively. We must reverse Oecolampadius' rule and say: We cannot speak of any sacrament or figure without using distinct, simple, common words.

---

181 *Second Reasonable Answer*, chap. 3.

When Moses says, Exodus 12 [:3], "You shall take a year-old lamb and eat," etc., who would understand it if he did not intend to indicate simply a natural lamb and natural eating, but rather meant, "You shall take a sign of a year-old lamb and eat spiritually"? Again, when John says, John 1 [:26], "I baptize with water," who would understand him if he were not speaking simply of natural water and natural baptism, but rather meant, "I baptize with a sign of water"? Oh, what shall I say? If Oecolampadius, as I hope, does not write this out of pure wickedness, then for a scholar I have never in all my days heard a sillier, simpler, more thoughtless man. Everything he tries to say in favor of his position turns out to be directly opposed to him.

I fear, however, that the devil has another purpose here (for who among us is secure from the devil?). Since he knows that Christ is called a sacrament in Scripture, e.g. in I Timothy 3 [:16],[182] he would infer from this that the words must be figurative also when it is said, "Christ is God and man." For he must have something in mind. He does not play the fool this way for nothing. In a word, Oecolampadius again proves deficient in elementary dialectics, which teach us to distinguish correctly. The sacrament or act, and the words which one speaks concerning it, are two different things. The sacrament or act must indeed be a sign or figure of something else, but the words in their simplicity must signify nothing else than what they say. For example, Moses' paschal lamb must indeed prefigure and signify Christ. But the words which Moses uses in speaking of the paschal lamb must express simply this same paschal lamb, and nothing else.[183] Again, circumcision must indeed prefigure the slaying of [the old] Adam. But the words which Moses uses in speaking of circumcision must refer literally to the physical circumcision.[184] Again, baptism must signify the drowning of sins, but the words used to describe baptism must express simply the plunging into the water.[185]

So, too, the sacrament of the Supper must indeed prefigure

[182] The Vulgate renders *mustērion* as *sacramentum.*
[183] I Cor. 5:7, Exod. 12:3 ff.
[184] Col. 2:11, Gen. 17:10 ff.
[185] Cf. Col. 2:12 f., Rom. 6:3 ff., Acts 8:38.

and signify something, viz. the unity of Christians in one spiritual body of Christ through one spirit, faith, love, and the cross, etc. But the words used in connection with this sacrament shall and must express with simplicity what they say. But my friend Oecolampadius blindly hits upon a true Zwinglian alloeosis, switches madly in the dark to a figurative meaning and makes out of a *form of a thing* a *figure of speech,* in this manner: "The object is figurative, therefore words pertaining to figurative objects are figurative!" You know, this gives all the appearance of a good old simpleton of a priest who has innocently stumbled into this debate, and would better have remained outside!

Since I believe that he does this through sheer lack of judgment, I will excuse him when he wrestles earnestly over the text in Genesis 17 [:10], saying that circumcision is a covenant, though it must mean a sign of the covenant.[186] My Genesis, however, does not say that circumcision is a covenant and a sign, as I could so abundantly prove that it would pain the devil. But because it does not contribute to the matter at hand the least bit, even if his argument were correct, I let it pass. For still it would not be proved that "body" in the Supper must therefore mean "sign of the body." For the same reason I am willing to excuse him when he makes a spiritual rock out of the natural one in the saying of Paul, "The rock was Christ" [I Cor. 10:4], considering that he is talking out of his head and proving nothing. Even if he could prove it tomorrow, it still would not follow that "body" here must mean "sign of the body." So too with the saying in Exodus 12 [:11], "It is the Lord's passover." Enough has been said above concerning such texts and concerning tropes. Now we should like to come to the main point: that Scripture is alleged to be contrary to our interpretation. Perhaps we shall have a display of wisdom here.

"Scripture," he says, "forces us to conclude that Christ is not present in the Supper."[187] What Scripture? Where Christ says, "You always have the poor with you, but you will not always have me" [Matt. 26:11]. Again, Christ does not wish to be sought "here and there" [Matt. 24:23]. So, since "being present" and

[186] *Second Reasonable Answer,* chap. 3.
[187] *Second Reasonable Answer,* chap. 4.

"not being present" are contraries, there must be mere bread in the Supper! On these texts we have already said enough. But I had demanded in my last book[188] that they should not just tell us that these texts are opposed to each other—we have heard this often enough from them, and have known perfectly well that they said so—but that they should prove it. On this point Oecolampadius remains just as silent as Zwingli. Therefore what they say amounts to nothing. For both can be true, that Christ is at the same time present and not present, according to different forms. He has more than one mode of presence, as we have said above.[189]

When I said in reference to the right hand of God that Christ's body must be wherever God is, Oecolampadius infers, just like Zwingli, that Christ cannot have a real body; and he spins the same cheap yarn[190] as Zwingli, viz. that Christ's body would have to be as large as heaven and earth, yet uncircumscribed.[191] This inference he ought to prove, but he is silent again. In short, this spirit will not answer the question being asked. We say No; Christ's body does not therefore need to be as large as heaven and earth. God himself is not so large and broad, yet he is everywhere. Although I have already said a great deal about this question,[192] I must add a bit more against Oecolampadius. Since God can do more than we understand, we must not say without qualification, simply on the basis of our own deduction and opinion, that these two propositions are contrary to each other: Christ's body is in heaven, and in the bread. For both are God's words. Rather, it must be proved with Scripture that they are contrary to each other. As long as this is not done, faith asserts: God can very easily keep Christ's body in heaven in one particular way, and in another way in the bread. If there are two different modes of presence in the two instances, no contradiction is involved, just as it is no contradiction that Christ sat with his disciples after his resurrection, Luke 24 [:44], and yet at the same time was not with them, as he himself says, "These things I spoke to you, while I was still with you." Here we find "with you" and

[188] See pp. 46, 144 f.
[189] See pp. 214 ff.
[190] I.e. he employs the same crude argument.
[191] *Second Reasonable Answer.*, chap. 5.
[192] Cf. pp. 55 ff., 219 ff.

"not with you," and yet there is no contradiction, for elementary dialectics teaches that contradictories must have the same object of reference, in the same terms, in the same context. In other words, these spirits should be sent to school to study Peter of Spain.[193] They need him very badly.

Again I must give a simple comparison. You see the sun shining in a large lake or pond. Naturally there can be no more than one image of the sun in the water, since there is only one sun. How does it happen, then, that if a hundred or two hundred people stand around the lake, each one will have the image of the sun before him at his own vantage point, and no one at another's? And if one walks along the lake, the image of the sun goes with him everywhere he goes. If a thousand eyes look into the water, each one will see the image directly in front of himself and not before someone else. Well, the sun is a created thing, and in a certain way can be in the lake at all points. My friend, who will bid us deny that God can far more readily know and find a way by which Christ's one body may be present according to his will, everywhere or wherever he wishes? Here, here, I say, they must first produce an answer proving that God's power is unable to do this. If this is not proved, it is a fearful blasphemy to denounce the two propositions as contradictory: Christ's body is in heaven and also in the Supper, since they cannot be certain of this, and yet the sure words of God stand there, "This is my body."

These clever spirits, however, will not listen; indeed, they laugh at these comparisons of ours. Therefore I advise our party thus: Let them laugh, let them take substance for quality, flesh for divinity and vice versa, and completely bungle their argument through total ignorance of logic. It is enough for us that they prove nothing. I will offer one more comparison. If a pillar stands in the square and a thousand or more eyes are turned toward it from all directions, each eye has the pillar entirely within its vision, and no eye would obstruct another. The pillar would be entirely within the vision of each observer and each eye, just as if all of them had the same eye and the same vision, for no one would see less or more of the pillar than another. We could point

[193] Petrus Hispanus (Pope John XXI, d. 1277) was the author of widely used elementary textbooks in logic. Cf. p. 178, n. 29.

out many more such comparisons, especially from mathematics, but since they are so common in our experience, no one regards them as marvelous. This is why it is so marvelous to foolish reason that a body should be at several places at the same time, because it does not see this.

Suppose there were no such thing as an eye, and we had only the four senses of touch, smell, taste, and hearing, all of which can perceive things not at a distance but only near at hand. Suppose someone announced that God could create an organ which could instantaneously penetrate and perceive eight, nine, or ten miles or more, viz. an eye. Would this not be a great and incredible wonder too? Even a man born blind would marvel and say, "Ah, friend, how is this possible? My hand cannot feel an object at an ell's distance, my tongue does not taste anything a finger's breadth distant, my nose does not smell anything a span away, my ear hears rather far if it hears something across the street—and yet you tell me of an organ which can perceive things ten miles away!"

We who see at such a distance, however, no longer regard this as marvelous for we can perceive even farther with our eyes, viz. to the sun and the stars, yes, from the rising to the setting of the sun. Now, the eye is a physical, fleshly, mortal thing, yet a single eye can take in half the world in a glance, and be in all places of half the world at the same time by its faculty of vision. Then why should we try to span and measure the power of God, as if he could do no more with the body of Christ than he does with our mortal eye, though our eyes are far more insignificant compared to God's power and works than a blind man's sense of touch and taste compared to our sight?

The clear, distinct words of God, "This is my body," confront us in such a way, then, that neither in Scripture nor in any language has it ever been heard that the expression "my body," was said or understood otherwise than it reads. The power of God is unknown to us. Further, it is nowhere contrary to Scripture, and there are numerous examples of it in the works of nature. Moreover, in this matter the fanatics have been caught in a host of lies and groundless assertions. For all these reasons we would do well to believe God rather than our own notions. If the fanatics have been discovered in a single detail to be manifestly false, we would be sufficiently warned by God not to believe them, but to cling to his words. For the Holy Spirit neither lies nor errs nor doubts. Now by the grace of God we have discovered them guilty of error and falsehood at almost every point, and in other points at least uncertain and doubtful. Consequently, even if I were uncertain of my own interpretation and disposed to yield to them, I could not do so, because I see there so obviously either lies or doubts, and not a single clear-cut or certain argument.

I proved[194] that two bodies can be in the same place at the same time, e.g. when Christ passed through the closed door, which is as great a marvel as that one body may be in two places. He retorts that this is nothing, for there are other ways in which Christ could pass through the closed door, viz. by the extreme tenuity of his body he could have passed through, so that two bodies would not need to be in one place. If I ask, then, "In what ways, and how did this tenuity enter?" silence reigns! I think one way is—*to church,* since, when Oecolampadius should have answered, he had to go and preach; the other way is—*a bad memory,* since he has forgotten ever after to answer the question.

That is the way this spirit acts. He mumbles a word or two. which no one understands, and calls this an answer. If he can discover that the tenuity of the body of Christ here enables Christ to pass into the door without the two bodies being in the same place, my friend, why can't he also discover that this tenuity enables it to be at the same time in the bread, without being obliged to drop from heaven like a tile from the roof? But they will not give me the slip this easily with their "tenuity." It is the very same body of Christ nonetheless, and the door was closed, and Christ did not slip through the cracks or nail holes. He had flesh and bone, as he himself confesses, Luke 24 [:39].

In regard to the appearance of Christ to St. Stephen, Acts 8 [7:55] and to many other saints, and the Father's voice which came from the cloud, Matthew 17 [:5]—examples which I introduced to prove that Christ is not obliged to be in one particular spot in heaven—he demonstrates his wit most ingeniously, saying, "Does this prove there is one body in two places?" What kind of

[194] See p. 66.

reasoning is this for a scholar? I confess my fault, for such examples do not prove also that a wolf likes to eat sheep, or whatever other propositions of this type he may bring up. I submit these examples to show that Christ is near, and not confined to one spot in heaven. He interprets this any way he pleases, and moreover doubts whether St. Stephen saw Christ spiritually or physically; he thinks that Christ was seen in a visual image and not Christ himself. And all this is true solely because Oecolampadius says so out of his own head. So must these clear words of Scripture yield to his fancies. All this is an answer to Luther's book! If I had done this, people would have demanded that I produce Scripture.

But what he says of the passage in John 3 [:13] is not incorrect, and is certainly better than what Zwingli does with it: "The Son of man is in heaven."[195] Oecolampadius admits that in virtue of the person it is rightly said that God was born of Mary and came down from heaven, except that he directs me to the blasphemous exegesis of Zwingli, in which among other abominations alloeosis teaches us to interpret "flesh" as divinity. The best thing about it is that it demonstrates how learned Zwingli is in all branches of knowledge. The real subject, indeed, he treats skimpily enough, being hindered by his vast knowledge.

Besides this, Oecolampadius goes too far at this point when, in contradiction to himself and all Scripture, he locates Christ in heaven according to his divinity, and on earth according to his humanity only. They do not consider my arguments correctly, and what is more, they do not understand their own words. If Christ is one person in his divinity and humanity, the humanity must be simultaneously on earth and in heaven, as I have proved above against Zwingli.[196] For to be one person in God and with God is far more than to be in heaven. Neither is it true that Christ was at that time in heaven according to his divinity. Where was he according to his divinity when he became man in his mother's womb? Was he not in his mother's womb and on earth, in person and essence, even according to his divinity? I have discussed all this abundantly in my last book.[197] But the result is

[195] Zwingli, *Christian Answer*. *C. R.* 92, 937; *St. L.* 20, 1204.

[196] See p. 232 ff.

[197] pp. 61 ff.

that he skips over it, considers nothing correctly, and pays no attention to what he hears or anyone says.

Consequently, his comparison does not hold when he shows that if a person came down from a mountain and donned clothes in the valley, one might say, "No one ascends the mountain but he who descends." For the divinity did not descend from heaven in the same way as the man descended from the mountain, but he is in heaven and remains in heaven, yet he is also at the same time on earth and remains on earth. We also cannot say of the clothed man in the valley, "He is on the mountain, though he is still here below," as Christ says of himself, "The Son of man who is in heaven." Why do we need to multiply words? The kingdom of heaven is upon earth. The angels are simultaneously in heaven and on earth. Christians are at the same time in the kingdom of God and on earth. If one interprets "on earth" as they speak of it, "mathematically or locally," then God's Word is indeed on earth, so was the Spirit given on earth, and Christ the king was on earth and he will have a kingdom on earth as far as the world extends, Psalm 2 [:8], and "he shall execute justice and righteousness on the earth," Jeremiah 31 [33:15]. Oh, they speak childishly and foolishly of heaven, assigning to Christ a particular spot in heaven like a stork with its nest in a tree, and they themselves are not aware what they are saying and how they sound!

Next he contends that Christ has not confined himself to particular places, nor does he wish to be sought here or there, but he must be known in the Spirit. Here again they rush madly about and fail to see what I am writing against them. In short, who confines Christ to a particular place? Is it not the fanatics, who locate Christ in heaven at a particular spot and force us to say, "Look, here is the Christ!" or, "Look, there he is!" [Matt. 24:23]. And what do they do when they direct the people to the gospel and to their neighbors? Are not neighbors and the gospel at particular places on earth? Is not Christ present in believers then? "Spiritually he is there," they say. What does the word "spiritually" mean? Does it mean falsely,[198] or truly? Just as if we said he is present in the sacrament physically or visibly. Is not

[198] Reading with the manuscript *felschlich* instead of the printed *fleischlich*, which would produce: "Does it mean fleshly, or truly?"

Christendom and the kingdom of God on earth extended throughout the world, as the prophets proclaim? Where are they themselves, who wish to be most eminent in Christ's kingdom? If the kingdom of Christ is on earth, then it is also "here and there." This I have maintained against the heavenly prophets.[199] It vexes them sorely that I am always boasting that this book has not been confuted by them. It is still unconfuted by them and it will remain so. Merely to bare one's teeth and babble is not to confute.

Here again this spirit's elementary logic fails him. They do not properly distinguish these words, "To be here and there." Christ himself clearly explained what he refers to by these words and how they are to be understood, when he said previously, "The kingdom of heaven is not coming in an external manner or appearance, nor will they say, 'lo, here it is!' or, 'There!' for behold, the kingdom of God is within you" [Luke 17:20 f.]. How are these words lacking in clarity, except that no fanatic is willing to notice them? "The kingdom of God is within you." Who are these persons designated "you"? Are they not on earth, to speak physically, as they speak of them? Then they are undoubtedly "here and there."

Accordingly, these words "here and there" must be construed in two ways, "in a place" and "according to the custom of a place:" first—essentially, that is—to be "here and there" means that a thing is present and is certainly found in a given place. They must surely grant that God is "here and there" and in all places, and is sought and adored both here and there and everywhere; of this I am certain. Secondly, according to the custom of a place, i.e. when one does not behave and live according to the custom of the place where he is, as Paul says, II Corinthians 10 [:3], "We live in the flesh but we do not war according to the flesh." What does this mean but that we are in the flesh and not in the flesh? If we are in the flesh, then we are indubitably "here and there,"[200] unless it is not conceded that flesh is "here and there." But our warfare is not according to the flesh, i.e. our

[199] *LW* 40, 219 ff.

[200] In print a question mark stands here; the translator has followed the manuscript, which lacks it.

being and behavior do not conform to the usual manner of the flesh.

So I may say: We are on earth and not on earth. We live on earth, but our life is not earthly, i.e. earthly in manner. Again, we are in the world and not in the world. We live indeed in the world, but our life is not worldly, i.e. worldly in manner. For example, in Luke 24 [:44], Christ sits and lives with his disciples after his resurrection, nevertheless he confesses that he is not with them or living with them. "These are the words which I spoke to you, while I was still with you," he asserts. What can this "with you" mean but "in your way of living" or "as you now live"? As to person and essence, he indeed did sit there and spoke and let himself be touched.

A comparison: A traveler may come to Wittenberg and say, "I am at Wittenberg and I am not at Wittenberg. How so? As to body and essence, I am of course here, but I am not here as a Wittenberger, i.e. living in the Wittenberg manner, for I have no citizen's rights here nor do I secure my livelihood and maintenance from the laws and property of the Wittenbergers." So St. Paul writes in Colossians 3 [Phil. 3:20][201] that our *politeuma,* i.e. our citizenship or civil existence is not here but in heaven. When Christ says, "The kingdom of heaven is not coming in an external manner" [Luke 17:20], he manifestly acknowledges that the kingdom of heaven comes to us on earth, as he says, "Repent, for the kingdom of heaven is at hand" [Matt. 4:17]. But it comes not in the same manner as worldly kingdoms come, for its behavior and life are not worldly or according to the human manner. As I have said, it would be highly important for this spirit to go to school and learn his elementary lessons from Peter the Spaniard.[202]

The first time he *really* puts Luther in the wrong is when he cites the passage of John 4 [:20 ff.], that God wills to be worshiped in spirit, not in Jerusalem or on the mountain. "Here now you have a definite answer, that Christ's body is not here and there, hence also not in the Supper!" If only this spirit would answer the question, he would hit the mark very beautifully. But where he leaps over it, he is insufferable. Well, so heaven is spirit, for

[201] Cf. Col. 3:1-4.
[202] Cf. p. 178, n. 29

Christ is to be worshiped in spirit, i.e. in heaven. But how is it possible for him to be at a certain place in heaven? Is "spirit" equivalent to "in a certain place"? Why not? If this spirit says it is, it must certainly be so. But then what would the blind man do who worshiped Christ on earth? John 9 [:38]. Of course he committed an error, and Christ was not serious in accepting such adoration, otherwise "spirit" will mean the same as "on earth." My friend, you must not laugh. This spirit might get angry, for he is serious!

But this is still finer: Christ says of the worshipers that they shall worship neither in Jerusalem nor on the mountain, just as the woman said to him, "Our fathers worshiped on this mountain; and you say that in Jerusalem is the place where men ought to worship" [John 4:20]. These words refer also to the worshipers, for she says not, "God is not on the mountain," and Christ does not say, "God is not in Jerusalem or on this mountain." But this spirit teaches us that this passage refers to God, meaning that he is not here and there, and does not refer to the worshipers.

My friend, what do you think God has in mind by allowing the fanatical spirit to play the fool so outrageously with the Scriptures? Nothing else, surely, than if he should say, "Dear child, there will be no failure on my part; I will faithfully take care of you and not permit these spirits to handle Scripture except in so crude, clumsy, and stupid a manner that if anyone allows himself to be misled, he will have no excuse that he was not sufficiently warned and cautioned by me. He who believes such spirits wilfully plunges into perdition, because he fails even to observe what foolishness they are committing, but swills up everything, as they say, like a filthy pig."

But we believe that to worship in the spirit is to worship spiritually, in a spiritual manner, whether Christ is in heaven, on earth, in the sacrament, or anywhere else. For Christ contrasts this spiritual worship with bodily worship, which the Jews and the hypocrites of our day so bind to given places and times that it must take place in an external manner, as place and time appoint, as if prayer derived its nature and power and life and all its benefit from the place or time. So they teach that obedience is the main concern in such prayers, even though they neither pray for anything nor know what they are prattling about. You see, this is what Christ here calls praying in Jerusalem and at appointed places, and not in spirit and truth.

By now, I hope, a child can understand how forcefully this text opposes the notion that Christ's body cannot be in the bread, and the notion that these words, "This is my body," are to be understood otherwise than as they read. My friend, if they wish to defend their point and confute us, they must certainly change their tactics. As it is now, they will drive us still further from them, and we must say either that they do not take the matter seriously or else that they are stooping to dishonesty, because they build so eagerly on these uncertain, false, shifting foundations.

Thus Oecolampadius stands disgraced over this essential point. He cannot prove that Christ is in heaven only at a particular spot, and he will never find an answer how the two are contradictory, that Christ is in heaven and his body is at the same time in the Supper, upon which I have insisted in my little book. They cannot make it sound convincing. It is impossible, and they feel it keenly. For all their prattle teaches us no more than that Christ has ascended to heaven—something that no one needed to be taught. But how it happens that Christ's body is not present in the Supper, when the words say, "This is my body"—this brings silence, fluttering and skipping about, or self-contradiction and tripping himself with his own words, as we have seen.

What purpose could it serve for me to handle all this devil's dung? I might commit sin by robbing myself and the reader of precious time with these sorry jokes. For even if we marshaled every passage on this subject in the entire Scriptures, we would accomplish nothing more than before, but only give this spirit more excuse to prattle uselessly and expound the Scriptures falsely, so that meanwhile he may forget the main points and flaunt his unnecessary knowledge.

I have said, and I still say, and will continue to say: Their teaching rests on the argument that Christ's body can have no other mode of presence at a given place than like flour in a sack or gold in a purse, that is, "locally."[203] This argument they must prove to us from Scripture. What need is there to write many

[203] Cf. pp. 65 ff., 227 ff.

books? Let them show you this proof, and then concede them the victory gladly. Believe me, if they could have done this, they would not have remained silent so long! They are very patient on this point, like the best of monks, who place a high value on silence[204] where it is most necessary to speak out. And in all the books they strew around, they still have never been willing to treat this boil with a single letter. For these reasons it is good to realize why they boast, bluster, bluff, and brag as if their position were sure. Well, the devil dreads the light, and wishes to silence us by blustering.

Now, I say, since from this tongue-tied goblin no one can obtain this single, necessary proof, I will dismiss Oecolampadius and only examine in conclusion this remaining point: "The flesh is of no avail" [John 6:63].[205] For all of his blasphemy about the external Word may be shown up when I write again on baptism, if God wills.[206]

Well, Oecolampadius wishes to prove from the context of this passage, John 6 [:52 ff.], that flesh here must be construed as Christ's flesh, and he does nothing more than give a comparison of a king dressed in a torn garment which the citizens were obliged to kiss, but they demurred, being offended at it. This he calls answering me and fortifying his iron wall. Behold this fickle spirit once more; he promises to prove his interpretation from the context of the passage, and then gives a comparison of a king! What do we care about the comparison? Even if it were as good and valid as could be, how are we assured that it applies here? We say No, he must prove that it does. Ah, but that is not necessary; you see, "It is enough that we say so, my lord!" There it stands; thus I have my answer!

Next he resorts to this subterfuge: "It is certain that the Jews murmured on account of his flesh, therefore he must have made his reply concerning his own flesh and no other." Isn't this a

---

204 An allusion to "monastic silence," cultivated by all orders but especially by the Cistercians and Carthusians.

205 *Second Reasonable Answer,* chap. 8.

206 Earlier in 1528 Luther had written *Concerning Rebaptism. LW* 40, 225 ff. Besides his catechisms, his next major treatment was the *Sermon on Holy Baptism* (Matt. 3:13 ff.), published in 1535. *WA* 37, 627 ff., where he emphasizes the external Word, but without reference to Oecolampadius.

marvelous deduction, an indubitable conclusion? The Jews murmur about his flesh, therefore Christ must have spoken about his own flesh. This is what is meant by proving from the context of a passage! My friend, why shouldn't any person be able to speak of Christ's flesh, of the Spirit, of the gospel, of faith, or anything he wished, and yet speak immediately thereafter of flesh and blood or of men? Just as Christ does in Matthew 16 [:15 ff.], when speaking with his disciples he asks whom they consider him to be, i.e. he speaks with them of Christ, who was God and man, and yet immediately thereafter says of ordinary flesh, "Flesh and blood have not revealed this to you." And Paul in Galatians 1 [:15 f.], when he writes of his calling, immediately thereafter says, "I did not confer with flesh and blood." If the iron wall does not stand more securely than that, let someone build on it who enjoys falling—not I! It is no better than a paper wall.

The context of the passage supports our interpretation much better, if one examines it simply and impartially as it should be done. I offer no comparisons, but the text says explicitly that the Jews and the disciples alike were offended at the words of Christ about eating his flesh. This is quite certain. Here I can and must say from the context of the passage that Christ has acquired two kinds of disciples: some who are offended and murmur, some who believe and amend their life. When a teacher has pupils who do not rightly understand his position, it is natural that he should turn to this misunderstanding and rebuke it saying, "Ah, blockheads will never get it!" or, "An ass will never be a good scholar," or, "New wine must be put in new bottles,"[207] etc.

Just so can Christ do here. When he finds stupid pupils, he turns to them and says "Does this offend you?" Here he rebukes their false conception, and he may well continue, "Ah, flesh is of no avail; the spirit gives life." Thus "spirit" here must mean spiritual understanding or teaching, for Christ himself so interprets it, saying, "The words that I have spoken to you are spirit and life" [John 6:63]. Therefore, of course, "flesh" must mean, on the contrary, fleshly understanding or teaching. Taking the total context into account and without using any comparison I say

---

[207] Cf. Matt. 9:17.

the text thus yields an interpretation far superior to the gloss of the fanatics.

This too has been said above against Zwingli.[208] Oecolampadius uses exactly the same sophistry as Zwingli on the word "my," and answers nothing. Again, he wishes to invalidate my rule that where flesh and spirit stand in contrast, flesh cannot mean Christ's flesh.[209] He does nothing but quote the passage of I Timothy 3 [:16], "He was manifested in the flesh and justified in the spirit." What shall I say? I speak of spirit and flesh where they are contrasted in Scripture, and he produces a text where flesh and spirit are clearly one! Besides, he does not prove that Christ's flesh is to be understood there. Still, this must pass for a complete answer! Well, my rule still stands, that in the passage we were discussing, flesh cannot mean Christ's flesh. Since it stands, this main argument of theirs must tumble.

In the same way he also treats a quotation from the fathers.[210] I cite their text, whereupon he offers his gloss on it but produces nothing from the text in the way I have done, just as he has emended the text of John 6 out of his own head. Thus they give us to understand how contemptuously they regard mankind, imagining that if they assert something it must forthwith be believed. Well, I have written against the heavenly prophets; I have received no answer except this notion and gloss of theirs. My book against the fanatics[211] has met the same response. Prattle they will, answer they cannot, as I have clearly proved in this little book. Let them go, then, and be holy, spiritual, and learned. I have done all I can. I have followed the teaching of St. Paul and admonished them a second time.[212] May God convert them and protect our people from their poison. Amen.

To clear and free myself completely on these points, however, I must also be mindful of my neighbors,[213] so that they may

[208] See pp. 248 f.
[209] See pp. 249 ff.
[210] Superscription of chap. 11, *Second Reasonable Answer:* "On the doctors, and especially the sayings of St. Augustine."
[211] *"This Is My Body,"* cf. p. 161.
[212] Titus 3:10.
[213] In 1527 Luther had received a long German treatise by Caspar Schwenkfeld, *Ground and Cause of the Error and Controversy Concerning the Lord's Supper* (cf. p. 40, n. 64, above). Having barely noticed it in *"This Is My*

not suppose that I scorn their wisdom and spirit. This spirit writes that neither Zwingli nor Oecolampadius nor Karlstadt nor Luther nor the pope is correct, and he makes the text of the Supper read thus: "My body which is given for you is this." While the evangelists and Paul put the word "this" at the beginning of the sentence, he puts it at the end, insisting that it is equivalent to "a spiritual food." Hence the text reads, "My body which is given for you is this, namely, a spiritual food."

Do you ask why they do this and not adopt the text of Karlstadt, Zwingli, or Oecolampadius, if they uphold the same meaning? A threefold answer may be given: first from the viewpoint of God, viz. that God wishes them to be disunited, at variance with one another, and to contradict one another so that the Holy Spirit may remain above suspicion and manifestly innocent before the whole world of having had anything to do with them, since he is a Spirit of unity and not of disunity, and hereby warns everyone against their lying spirit. Secondly from the human viewpoint: Why should they be so humble as to adopt Karlstadt's, Zwingli's, or Oecolampadius' text, since Karlstadt, Zwingli, and Oecolampadius themselves are so haughty that no one will accept the other's text? Should they not be as ingenious as the others in devising a special text? It would be a great shame if they could not! My friend, honor is as desirable to them as to the other three. Thirdly from the devil's viewpoint, viz. that the evangelists and Paul were drunk or insane so that they walked on their ears or on their heads, and thus turned the text of the Supper upside down and backside forward, therefore this spirit had to come and set the text right and instruct the evangelists.

The argument and reasoning behind this fancy of theirs is in the first place that we must close our eyes to these words, "This

---

Body," though the Silesians urgently requested a reply, Luther now hastily and brusquely attacks the arguments which form the bulk of the second and larger part of the treatise (*Corpus Schwenckfeldianorum* 2, 462, 580). The Silesians' "first argument" appears throughout the pamphlet. The other six arguments are listed in *Corpus Schwenckfeldianorum* 2, 475, developed at length, pp. 475-550, and briefly summarized, pp. 550 f. A compendium of this second part of Schwenkfeld's treatise came into Zwingli's hands in 1528. The Zuricher promptly published it under the title, *An Indication that the Opinion of the Bodily Presence of our Lord Jesus Christ in the Bread or Under the Form of Bread Is Condemned,* 1528. On Schwenkfeld, see George H. Williams, *The Radical Reformation* (Philadelphia, 1963); *LCC* 25, 161 ff.; *S-J* 2, 371.

is my body," and first consider these matters in the spirit. For anyone who begins with these words, "This is my body," cannot arrive at this fancy—I should say, this lofty interpretation—that bread is bread and wine is wine. But he who puts these words out of his sight can very well come to such an interpretation. Here you have a clear rule which will lead you into all truth better than the Holy Spirit himself can do: When the Holy Scriptures mislead or obstruct your fancy, put them out of your sight and first of all follow your own fancy; so you will surely find the right course in all cases, as Moses teaches, Deuteronomy 12 [:8], "You shall not do whatever is right in your own eyes," i.e. you *shall* do whatever is right in your own eyes!

This devil stalks about boldly and without disguise and teaches us openly to disregard Scripture, just as Münzer and Karlstadt also did, who developed their wisdom out of the witness of their "inwardness,"[214] and needed the Holy Scriptures not for themselves but only for the instruction of others, as an external witness to the witness in their inwardness. Whoever believes such a manifest devil, however, will go willingly into the fire of hell. But no answer at all is needed, even for pure fools. This, however, is the sort of ground such blasphemers must have for their faith, since they do not believe Christ.

In the second place, the "impanation"[215] of the body of Christ, as they say, is contrary to the entire Holy Scripture. What do you think of this spirit now? He dares to open his mouth wide enough, all right, for he wishes to be far and away superior to Zwingli and Oecolampadius, who do not cite the entire Scripture against it. Listen to him: "The Old Testament," he says, "says nothing about it, though Christ directs us to the Old Testament, John 5 [:46]. And the New Testament speaks of his coming into the flesh, of which John is a forerunner,[216] and not into the bread.

---

[214] Cf. *LW* 40, 147 ff.

[215] "Impanation" (*Einbrödtung*) is the teaching that Christ's body is *in* the bread. If this term was interpreted to mean a "local" or "circumscribed" presence of Christ's body in the bread, Lutheran theologians rejected it. As early as the summer of 1525, Schwenkfeld had written (but not published) *The Twelve Questions or Arguments Against Impanation.* (Cf. *Corpus Schwenckfeldianorum* 2, 129-140).

[216] Cf. John 1:14 f.; Matt. 11:10.

And Christ himself says, 'No one knows the Father but by me';[217] he does not say 'by the bread.'" Here you see what a mighty aid to truth it is when one dismisses from sight these words, "This is my body." How else could this spirit say that our interpretation is contrary to all Scripture, if he kept these words before his eyes?

Besides, even if someone bound these words before his eyes with iron chains so that he could not remove them, he has still another trick and rule for truth. He says, "These words do not occur in the Old Testament." The fact that St. Luke, St. Matthew, St. Mark, and St. Paul place them in the New Testament means nothing, since he can easily put these out of sight. But God must allow himself to be fettered and prevented from placing his words when and where he pleases, except in the places and in the manner that this spirit directs him. Now this spirit places and seeks them in the Old Testament, and God has not placed them there; therefore the spirit has won again, fairly and squarely.

How can this spirit miss the truth? Indeed, who can pin him down when he has these two neat tricks or rules on his side? One is to dismiss from sight the words of God wherever he finds them written. The second: Wherever he cannot dismiss them from sight, he shifts his eyes from them to some other place where they are not written, and says, "See, these words are not to be found here; prove to me that they are here in this very place, otherwise you have lost. For you must set the words before me in such a way that I cannot put them out of my sight, nor turn my eyes away from them to another place." This is the way we flesh-eaters must be attacked, this is the way to overthrow our impanated God!

Look and see here whether the devil is not mocking us maliciously. It serves, nevertheless, to strengthen and confirm our faith, since this wicked Satan jabbers such preposterous nonsense. He knows that we cannot find Christ's words of institution of the Supper in the Old Testament. Therefore, he pretends that he is willing to be shown where we found them in the Old Testament, and imagines that no one will see his clumsy lies. For since he will not look at the words in the New Testament but dismisses them from sight, what would he do even if we could point them

[217] A conflation of John 14:6 and Matt. 11:27.

out in the Old Testament? Still more would he cast them out of his sight, alleging that the Old Testament is obscure or abrogated, that he should be shown them in the New Testament, which is the fulfilment, etc.

If everything that we are to believe were in the Old Testament, what need would there be of the New? Why should Christ have had to come to earth to teach us? In this way I could also say: Baptism is nothing; the sending of the Holy Spirit is nothing; that the mother of God[218] is Mary is nothing; in short, no article of the Christian faith would stand. For the Old Testament, it is true, speaks of Christ's coming. But that he has now come and has fulfilled all things, instituted baptism, secured the forgiveness of sins, bestowed the Holy Spirit, etc.—of this it contains not a single letter. All these things the New Testament had to explain. But this spirit ought to explain himself and show what grounds he has for his lies, so that we might more surely protect ourselves from him.

His third argument is that this "impanation" is contrary to Christian faith, for faith must have a spiritual object to which to cling, but bread is a material object. From this reasoning one can also conclude that Christ was not man on earth, for his humanity was physical and not a spiritual thing. Therefore no one could have believed in such a man, that he was God, without heresy. Again, no one can believe that a Christian man is our neighbor, that there are such beings as man and wife, our parents, relatives, brothers. Again no one can believe that heaven and earth are God's creation. Why? Because faith can have nothing physical or material as its object, but all these matters are observed physically. So blind is this spirit that he does not know that faith is always offered a physical object under which it understands and perceives something else, as I have proved in my little book with numerous examples,[219] such as Romans 4 [:19], the womb of Sarah, and the like.

The fourth argument: It is contrary to the nature and char-

[218] Condemnation of the liturgical expression *theotokos*, "Mother of God," by Nestorius, archbishop of Constantinople, had sparked a bitter fifth century Christological controversy. With the rejection of Nestorianism came a vindication of the expression. Cf. p. 212, n. 75.
[219] See pp. 91 f., cf. pp. 89 ff.

acter of the Word. For he understands by the Word not a sound or an oral word but the eternal truth of God: this Word cannot bind itself to bread or any mere creature. This article needs to be carefully tested, because they so vehemently blaspheme the external Word as unsuitable for belief. Thus, what they prove thereby is meaningless because the principle itself is not proved. Of this more at another time.[220]

The fifth argument: It is contrary to the priesthood and kingdom of Christ, as the Epistle to the Hebrews teaches. For wherever Christ is, he is a priest and a king [Heb. 6:20]. But in the bread he cannot be king, for bread is a creaturely thing in the world, whereas his kingdom is not of this world. Isn't this wonderful? Christ's kingdom is not of this world, therefore it is not in the world. For this spirit makes "of the world" and "in the world" synonymous. Woe to us poor Christians! We must live in the world, in death, under the devil, and our king is imprisoned in heaven so that he cannot rule and protect us, or help us, or be with us, for his kingdom is in heaven and not in this world. Such mad, senseless teachers this rabble deserves, and no other! God be praised and thanked, we know that Christ said before Pilate not, "My kingdom is not here below," but, "My kingdom is not from here" [John 18:36]. It is and prevails everywhere that he is, in the bread, the world, death, hell, among the devils. But the power of his kingdom consists not in the power of the bread, of the world, of death, hell, and the devils, for he receives nothing from them to strengthen his kingdom, as the world and the devils must do in their kingdom.

The sixth argument: It is contrary to the glory of God. For Christ is in heaven in the glory of the Father, Philippians 2 [:9], and has his throne prepared not in the bread but in heaven. This argument awakens the same impression as the previous one, that Christ is imprisoned in heaven as in a jail or in stocks. For it would be disgraceful if he were with us on earth in all the pangs of sin and death; it is better if he leaves us to the devil here

[220] Luther frequently attacked any disparagement of the external Word, e.g. *Genesis Commentary*, 1535-1545, on Gen. 19:14. *LW* 3, 273. Particularly because of Schwenkfeld he wrote his *Brief Confession Concerning the Holy Sacrament*, 1544.

below and enjoys himself above with the angels! Isn't this priceless? It is not contrary to God's glory that he is everywhere according to his divinity, even in hell, and yet it is allegedly opposed to God's glory for his body to be present in the bread, as if his body were nobler than his divinity! Away! away! What a nice, handsome spirit this is!

Finally, it is also said to be contrary to the institution of Christ and the practice of the primitive church. The words of Christ are declaratives where he says, "This is my body," and are not imperatives. Christ nowhere says, "If you have spoken these words, my body will be present." This argument he has stolen from Zwingli, and it has been abundantly answered above.[221] Thus we have given this mad spirit a hearing also, and have found no new tooth which can bite the words of Christ; none indeed which can assail my little book. I have reread my book against the heavenly prophets, and I find myself astonished at the cowardly devil, that he rages against it with no Scripture at all but only with simple words, and thus has left it altogether unconfuted up to now.

The Law of Identical Predication[222]

There is one most important and troublesome point still in the background of this subject, which it seems to me none of the fanatics understand, for they either do not touch upon it at all or in any case quite awkwardly, and all the fanatics' prattle about it is mere drivel. Yet this subject should properly engage every

[221] See pp. 180 ff.

[222] This section is chiefly an attack on the eucharistic doctrine of John Wycliffe, whose support Zwingli had claimed in *Commentary*, 1525. *LWZ* 3, 224. Luther may have read Wycliffe's *Trialogue*, which had been printed in 1525, but his knowledge of the Englishman's writings was fragmentary. After 1379 Wycliffe had attacked transubstantiation as contrary to reason, the fathers, and Scripture. The bread is not changed; it remains bread. The words of institution are not an "identical predication" affirming an identity between two beings, e.g. "Christ is man," but a "figurative or tropical" or "parabolic" predication, e.g. "John the Baptist is Elijah." Wycliffe wanted to retain the Real Presence, but he insisted that this is not the presence of the true body and blood of Christ. The first of his theses of 1381 asserts that "the consecrated host is neither Christ, nor any part of him, but the effectual sign of him." The fourth states that the eucharist contains "truly and really" the body and blood of Christ; but this means "sacramentally," "intentionally," "mystically:" no unbeliever receives it. Cf. Sasse, *This Is My Body*, pp. 56 ff.

competent thinker. Wycliffe in his writings regards it as the most important of all. Throughout the world universities have long been plagued by it, until they forced themselves to teach that in the sacrament no bread remains in essence, but only its form. This "identical predication of diverse natures" is untenable both in Scripture and in reason, i.e. the idea that two diverse natures should be identical.[223] If the fanatics were not such ignorant logicians, they would have known how to handle this problem. It would have been worth talking about, and they could have left their useless flesh and Christ up in heaven, along with their other childish nonsense. Accordingly, we shall say a few words here on this subject also.

It is undeniably true that two diverse substances cannot be one substance. For example, an ass cannot be an ox, a man cannot be a stone or a piece of wood. It will not do for me to say of St. Paul, "This is a material stone or piece of wood," unless I make "stone" or "wood" new words and give them a new interpretation, as I have said above. All this every rational being in creation must acknowledge; nothing else makes sense. Now, when we approach the Supper with this conception, reason takes offense, for here it discovers that in these words, "This is my body," two distinct substances, bread and body, are spoken of as one object or substance. It shakes its head and exclaims, "Oh, it is quite impossible that bread should be body! If it is bread, it is bread; if it is body, it is body—take your choice."

In this case the sophists have retained the body and let the bread go, saying that the bread disappears and sheds its substance when the words of institution are spoken, and the word "this" indicates not the bread but the body of Christ, since the text says, "This is my body." Wycliffe, on the contrary, opposes this and retains the bread, rejecting the body, and says the word "this" indicates the bread and not the body. These wiseacres have so irritated each other that the sophists have had to invent a miracle to show how the bread disappears and lets its substance be annihilated.

223 Zwingli: "The expression, 'This is bread, and moreover it is my body,' has absolutely no support either in God's Word or in philosophy, for two substances cannot be one thing." *Friendly Rejoinder*. *C. R.* 92, 779. *St. L.* 20, 1111.

Now, I have taught in the past[224] and still teach that this controversy is unnecessary, and that it is of no great consequence whether the bread remains or not. I maintain, however, with Wycliffe that the bread remains; on the other hand, I also maintain with the sophists that the body of Christ is present. So against all reason and hairsplitting logic I hold that two diverse substances may well be, in reality and in name, one substance. These are my reasons: First, when we are dealing with the works and words of God, reason and all human wisdom must submit to being taken captive, as St. Paul teaches in II Corinthians 10 [:5], must allow themselves to be blinded and led, directed, taught, and instructed, lest we presume to be God's judges in his words, for we shall surely lose out when we try to judge him in his words as Psalm 50 [51:4] testifies.

Secondly, if we take ourselves captive to him and confess that we do not comprehend his words and works, we should be satisfied. We should speak of his works simply using his words as he has pronounced them for us and prescribed that we speak them after him, and not presume to use our own words as if they were better than his. For we shall surely go wrong unless we simply repeat his words after him as he pronounces them for us, just as a young child repeats the Creed or the Lord's Prayer after his father. Here we need to walk in the dark and with our eyes closed, and simply cling to the Word and follow. For since we are confronted by God's words, "This is my body"—distinct, clear, common, definite words, which certainly are no trope, either in Scripture or in any language—we must embrace them with faith, and allow our reason to be blinded and taken captive. So, not as hairsplitting sophistry dictates but as God says them for us, we must repeat these words after him and hold to them.

Now what if "identical predication" should interrupt here, saying that it is inadmissible both in Scripture and in reason for two substances to be one, or one substance to be another, as we have said: Stone cannot be wood, water cannot be fire,[225] even in

[224] Cf. *Babylonian Captivity*, 1520. *LW* 36, 28 ff.; *Adoration of the Sacrament*, 1523. *LW* 36, 287.

[225] Cf. Zwingli: "What is the use of calling flesh spiritual, when that would be the same thing as calling fire watery or iron wooden?" *Commentary*. *LWZ* 3, 240.

Scripture? that therefore it would be contrary to God's Word and to the articles of faith if a thing were something else than what it is, and bread must be bread and cannot be body? You should reply: It is not contrary to Scripture, indeed, it is not even contrary to reason or true logic; they only imagine it is contrary to Scripture, reason, and logic, for they do not see these in their proper relation to one another. This we must prove, for the sake of a better understanding, by examples first from Scripture and afterward from common speech.

The sacred article of the holy Trinity teaches us to believe and say that the Father, the Son, and the Holy Spirit are three distinct persons, yet each person is the one God. Here it is said of the one Godhead that it is threefold, being three persons. This is far, far more sublime and uncompromisingly contrary to reason than that wood is stone. Certainly wood in itself has no such unique essence as the Godhead has; and conversely, wood and stone are not so clearly and unconfusedly distinct as the persons are. Now if the union of nature and of substance here can enable us to say that distinct persons are nevertheless one being, one substance, it surely cannot be contrary to Scripture or the articles of faith for us to speak of two distinct objects, such as bread and body as one—one substance. But this article is too sublime; we must set another before us.

I point to the man Christ and say, "This is God's Son," or, "This man is God's Son." It is not necessary here that the humanity vanish or be annihilated in order that the word "this" may refer to God and not to the man, as the sophists imagine concerning the bread in the sacrament. Rather, the humanity must remain. Yet there is a far greater difference between man and God, and a far greater disparity between them than between bread and wine, fire and wood, an ox and an ass. Who brings it about here that two such diverse natures become one substance, and that one may be referred to as the other? Without doubt it is not the substantial union of natures—for there are two distinct natures and substances—but the personal union. For although there is not a single substance according to the natures, yet it is one single substance according to the person. Hence there arise two kinds of union and two kinds of substance, viz. a natural union and a personal union. And so forth. From the personal union is derived such an expression as that God is man and man is God. Similarly, from the natural union in the Godhead is derived the expression that God is the Father, God is the Son, God is the Holy Spirit, and conversely the Father is God, the Son is God, etc.

Thus we have two unions, the one natural and the other personal, which teach us that identical predication is not contrary to Scripture, nor is it contrary for two distinct beings to be called one being. If we need further examples, Psalm 104 [:4] says, "He makes his angels winds and his ministers flames of fire." Here also there are two kinds of being, angels and wind, or angels and flames of fire, just as in the sacrament bread and body. Yet here Scripture makes a single being out of the two, saying, "He makes his angels winds and flames," just as he makes his body bread, so that one must say of these winds and flames, "This is an angel." Scripture thus says that he who sees this wind or flame sees an angel. Now no one can see an angel in his intrinsic nature but only in his form of flame or brightness; moreover, this form of brightness does not have to vanish if one points to it and says, "This is an angel," as the sophists insist that the bread in the sacrament is annihilated; rather, it must remain.

Here, now, we have still another union of two distinct beings, viz. of the angel and of the flame. I do not know how to describe it. It is not a natural union, as in the Godhead Father and Son are one nature; nor again a personal union, as God and man are one person in Christ. Let it simply be called a "union of effect,"[226] in that the angel and his form accomplish one and the same work or effect. Yet Scripture says here that Abraham and Lot saw angels, heard them, fed them, and entertained them overnight. Gideon and Manoah saw and heard angels. David and Daniel saw and heard angels. The two Marys at the grave of Christ saw and heard angels.[227] So also in many other instances, in all of which, meanwhile, the angel was never seen in his own nature but only in his form of brightness or flame. If someone points to him, one

---

[226] *Wirckliche einickeit.* Cf. *Formula of Concord,* Solid Declaration, VIII, 59, which translates *wirklich* with *per modum efficaciae.*

[227] Cf. Gen. 18:2, 19:1; Judg. 6:12, 13:11; I Chron. 21:16, Dan. 6:22, Matt. 28:5.

must say, "This is an angel," yet the word "this" indicates the form of the angel.

Now, the subtle Wycliffe and the sophists may wish to appeal here to the rule of "identical predication," that two distinct beings cannot be one, nor can one being be confused with the other, but either the empty form without the angel must remain, as Wycliffe holds, or a pure angel without a form, as the sophists hold. But we shall not pursue the inquiry. Clear Scripture and the manifest work of God are before us, that God makes his angels flames and the flame is the angel, if one points to it and says, "This is an angel," by virtue of the "union of effect" whereby two kinds of being have become one, just as in Christ by virtue of the personal union God and man are one personal being. So, too, must one say of the sacrament, "This is my body," although the word "this" indicates the bread, for here also a union has taken place out of two distinct substances, as will be seen from the following.

In the fourth place, the evangelists write that the Holy Spirit descended upon Christ in the form of a dove at the river Jordan. Again, he came upon the disciples on the day of Pentecost, in the form of wind and tongues of fire. Again, upon Mt. Tabor in the form of a cloud.[228] Here Wycliffe and the sophists may play wise men and say, "This dove is present without the Holy Spirit," or, "The Holy Spirit is present without the dove." We say, in opposition to both parties, that as one points to the dove, he rightly and properly says, "This is the Holy Spirit," in virtue of the fact that here the two diverse beings, Spirit and dove, in some degree are also a single being, though not naturally or personally. Well, it may be called a "formal union," because the Holy Spirit has deigned to manifest himself in such a form. Here the Scripture says precisely that he who sees this dove sees the Holy Spirit, e.g. John 1 [:33], "He on whom you see the Spirit descend and remain," etc.

Why then should we not much more say in the Supper, "This is my body," even though bread and body are two distinct sub-

[228] Matt. 3:16, Acts 2:2 f., Matt. 17:5. In *On the Trinity*, Books II-III, describing how God works through his creatures, Augustine uses many of the scriptural examples which Luther cites on pp. 298 ff.

stances, and the word "this" indicates the bread? Here, too, out of two kinds of objects a union has taken place, which I shall call a "sacramental union," because Christ's body and the bread are given to us as a sacrament. This is not a natural or personal union, as is the case with God and Christ. It is also perhaps a different union from that which the dove has with the Holy Spirit, and the flame with the angel, but it is also assuredly a sacramental union.

Therefore, it is entirely correct to say, if one points to the bread, "This is Christ's body," and whoever sees the bread sees Christ's body, as John says that he saw the Holy Spirit when he saw the dove, as we have heard. Thus also it is correct to say, "He who takes hold of this bread, takes hold of Christ's body; and he who eats this bread, eats Christ's body; he who crushes this bread with teeth or tongue, crushes with teeth or tongue the body of Christ." And yet it remains absolutely true that no one sees or grasps or eats or chews Christ's body in the way he visibly sees and chews any other flesh. What one does to the bread is rightly and properly attributed to the body of Christ by virtue of the sacramental union.

Therefore, the fanatics are wrong, as well as the gloss in Canon Law, if they criticize Pope Nicolas for having forced Berengar to confess that the true body of Christ is crushed and ground with the teeth."[229] Would to God that all popes had acted in so Christian a fashion in all other matters as this pope

[229] In 1059 Pope Nicolas II forced Berengar of Tours to confess that "after consecration the bread and wine are not only a sacrament but also the true body and blood of Christ, and are *sensibly* . . . handled and broken by the hands of the priests, and *pressed and crushed by the teeth of the faithful*, not only sacramentally but *in reality*. . . ." The Swiss opponents of Luther sharply denounced this recantation, cf. Zwingli, *Commentary*. *LWZ* 3, 210; *Clear Instruction*. *LCC* 24, 193 f. Even the early scholastic theologians found that confession subject to criticism, which is reflected in Canon Law, in the Gloss on the *Decretum of Gratian III, De Consecratione*, dist. II, cap. 42. *Corpus Iuris Canonici*, I, cols. 1328 f. Berengar accordingly was required in 1079 to make another recantation which has become a dogma of the Roman Catholic Church, confessing that "the bread and wine placed on the altar are *substantially changed into* the true and proper and life-giving flesh and blood of our Lord Jesus Christ, and that after consecration they *are* the true body of Christ. . . . and the true blood of Christ, . . . not only through the sign and power of the sacrament, but *in their proper nature and true substance*. . . . Cf. Roy J. Deferrari (trans.), Heinrich Denzinger's *Sources of Catholic Dogma* (St. Louis: Herder, 1957), No. 355. On the whole subject see Sasse, *This Is My Body*, pp. 32 ff.

did with Berengar in forcing this confession. For this is undoubtedly the meaning, that he who eats and chews this bread eats and chews that which is the genuine, true body of Christ and not mere, ordinary bread, as Wycliffe teaches. For this bread is truly the body of Christ, just as the dove is the Holy Spirit and the flame is the angel.

Deceived by a premature application of logic, the subtle Wycliffe and the sophists did not first take into account the rules of grammar or the science of words. If someone wants to know something about logic before he becomes familiar with grammar, and to teach before he listens and judge before he can speak, surely nothing good will come of it. Logic rightly teaches that bread and body, dove and Spirit, God and man are diverse beings. But it should first seek the aid of grammar, which lays down a rule of expression applicable to all languages: when two diverse beings become one being, grammar embraces these two beings in a single expression, and as it views the union of the two beings, it refers to the two in one term.

For example, as in Christ God and man constitute one personal being, grammar speaks thus of the two beings: "He is God; he is man." Likewise of the dove, John 1 [:32 f.], "This is the Holy Spirit; this is a dove." Likewise of the angel, "This is a wind; this is an angel" [Ps. 104:4]. "This is bread; this is my body." On the other hand, occasionally each substance is called the other: "Man is God, God is man"; "The dove is the Holy Spirit, the Holy Spirit is the dove"; "That wind or this flame is the angel, the angel is the flame"; "This bread is my body, my body is the bread." Here one must not speak of the beings as diverse and distinct in themselves, as Wycliffe and the sophists misuse logic, but in terms of the nature of the union, according to the fact that the diverse beings have become one single being, each in its own fashion. It is in truth the case that these diverse natures which thus have united have truly acquired a new, unique being by this convergence, whereby they are rightly and properly called a single being, even though each has its own particular, unique nature. This circumstance has deceived Wycliffe and the sophists, who syllogize on total unity by means of partial unities, and vice versa.

This mode of speaking about diverse beings as one the grammarians call "synecdoche." It is quite common not only in Scripture but also in all languages. For instance, if I point to or hand over a bag or purse and say, "This is a hundred gulden," both the gesture and the word "this" refer to the purse. But since the purse and the money in some degree constitute one object, one lump, my words apply at the same time to the money. In this manner, I lay my hand on a cask and say, "This is Rhine wine; this is Italian wine; this is red wine." Again, I take a glass and say, "This is water; this is beer, this is ointment." In all these expressions you see that the word "this" refers to the container, and yet because the liquid and the container in some degree are one, it applies also and indeed principally to the liquid.

Thus I have given another example above:[230] he who wounds the hand of the king's son is judged as having wounded the king's son, because the hand forms one being, i.e. one body, with the king's son, even though it has in its own right an individuality as a hand, for a hand of course is no body. Here also applies my illustration of the red-hot iron, borrowed from St. Augustine,[231] over which the fanatics have racked their brains all in vain. For whatever fire may be, it is correct to say in any language, "This object is fire, and it is iron."

Now a subtle Wycliffe or a sophist may laugh and say, "You show me a purse, saying, 'This is a hundred gulden'; but how can a purse be a hundred gulden?" Again, he may say, "You show me a cask, saying, 'This is wine'; but my friend, a cask is wood and not wine, a purse is leather and not gold." At such a remark even the children would laugh, as they do at a fool or a jester, for he tears apart the two united substances and tries to speak of each separately, whereas here we have to do with two substances which have become one substance. For the cask here is no longer merely wood or a common cask but a wine cask, wood containing wine; and the purse here is no longer mere leather or a mere purse but a money purse, leather containing money. If you wish

---

[230] See p. 211.

[231] Cf. *Babylonian Captivity*. *LW* 36, 32; *Against the Heavenly Prophets*. *LW* 40, 196. This common patristic illustration goes back to Origen, *First Principles*, II, 6,6. *MPG* 11, 213 f.; *ANF* 4, 283. Why Luther cites Augustine is not apparent. According to ancient science, fire is one of the four elemental substances.

to break down this complex and separate the money from the leather, it is true that each constituent exists in its own right and one must describe the matter differently: "This is money, this is leather; this is wine, this is a cask." But if you retain the wholeness, you must describe the matter in terms of the whole, and point to the cask or purse, saying, "This is money, this is wine," by virtue of the unity of substance. We must pay no attention to the nonsense of these subtle sophists, but examine the mode, use, and custom of language.

Thus, since this mode of speaking is common both in Scripture and in all languages, "identical predication" is no obstacle to us in the Supper. No *identical* predication is even there; Wycliffe and the sophists only dream that it is. For even though body and bread are two distinct substances, each one existing by itself, and though neither is mistaken for the other where they are separated from each other, nevertheless where they are united and become a new, entire substance, they lose their difference so far as this new, unique substance is concerned. As they become one, they are called and designated one object. It is not necessary, meanwhile, that one of the two disappear or be annihilated, but both the bread and the body remain, and by virtue of the sacramental unity it is correct to say, "This is my body," designating the bread with the word "this." For now it is no longer ordinary bread in the oven, but a "flesh-bread" or "body-bread," i.e. a bread which has become one sacramental substance, one with the body of Christ. Likewise with the wine in the cup, "This is my blood," designating the wine with the word "this." For it is no longer ordinary wine in the cellar but "blood-wine," i.e. a wine which has been united with the blood of Christ in one sacramental substance. This may suffice on this subject for our friends; the others are taught by their leaders to heed nothing but what suits their fancy.

The Second Part

Now we shall examine the texts of the evangelists and St. Paul, for the strengthening of our consciences.[232] First you should

[232] Oecolampadius had analyzed the four texts individually in *Apologetics*. *St. L.* 20, 651 ff. Zwingli had done likewise in *Friendly Exposition*. *C. R.* 92, 729 ff.

accept the fanatics' own confession. They acknowledge and must acknowledge that our interpretation takes the words naturally, just as they read, and that if the literal sense of the words is followed, our understanding is correct beyond a doubt. But they contend that the words should not be understood as they read. This confession, I say, you should accept. It means we have won more than half the battle. Since they now acknowledge that if the words were to be understood as they read, our interpretation would be right, they acquit us with their own testimony. First, in proving our interpretation we need not go beyond what the words say as they stand and read. This is one point; mark it well! Secondly, they bind and burden themselves with two immense tasks or duties: (1) They are bound to prove why the words should not be understood as they read, but otherwise; (2) To supply in place of these words a different set of words or a text which is certain and reliable. Neither of these two things have they done as yet. The second in particular they have never undertaken, as we have stated and proved above. Consequently, they compel us to retain the literal sense conveyed by the words, and they bring themselves into disgrace with their indefinite lies.

In the second place, you do know and must know that our text, "This is my body," etc. comes not from men but from God himself, spoken by his own lips and set down in these very letters and words. But the fanatics' text, "This signifies my body," or, "This is the sign of my body," is not from God himself, spoken in these words and letters, but from men only.

Thirdly, you have heard above that they themselves without exception are utterly uncertain of their text, and none of them as yet has irrefutably proved that his text is plausible and necessary, as they allege. Moreover, they never will succeed in producing a certain text. But our text is certain; it is plausible and necessary that it should stand as the words read, for God himself has placed it where it is, and no man dare take away or add a single letter.[233]

Fourthly, you know that they are divided and make many incompatible texts out of the words. These texts are not only uncertain—which of itself would be devilish enough—they also

---

[233] Cf. Deut. 4:2.

contradict one another and denounce one another as false. Not only is our text certain but it is also a single and simple one unanimously accepted by us all.

Fifthly, even supposing that our text and interpretation were uncertain or obscure—which it is not—as well as their text and interpretation, you still have this glorious, reassuring advantage that you can rely upon our text with a good conscience and say, "If I must have an uncertain, obscure text and interpretation, I would rather have the one uttered by the lips of God himself than one uttered by the lips of men. And if I must be deceived, I would rather be deceived by God (if that were possible) than by men. For if God deceives me, he will take the responsibility and make amends to me, but men cannot make amends to me if they have deceived me and led me into hell." Such assurance the fanatics cannot have, for they cannot say, "I would rather rely upon the text which Zwingli and Oecolampadius discordantly express than upon that which Christ himself concordantly proclaims."

Consequently, you can boldly address Christ both in the hour of death and at the Last Judgment: "My dear Lord Jesus Christ, a controversy has arisen over thy words in the Supper. Some want them to be understood differently from their natural sense. But since they teach me nothing certain, but only lead me into confusion and uncertainty, and since they are not willing or able to prove their text in any way, I have remained with thy text as the words read. If there is anything obscure in them, it is because thou didst wish to leave it obscure, for thou hast given no other explanation of them, nor hast thou commanded any to be given. No one finds anywhere in Scripture or in any language that 'is' should mean 'signifies,' or that 'my body' should mean 'sign of my body.'

"Now if there should be anything obscure about these words, thou wilt bear with me if I do not completely understand them, just as thou didst forbear with thine apostles when they did not understand thee in many things—for instance, when thou didst announce thy passion and resurrection.[234] And yet they kept thy words just as they were spoken and did not alter them. Thy beloved mother also did not understand when thou saidst to her, Luke

[234] Cf. Luke 9:45.

2 [:49], 'I must be about my Father's business,' yet with simplicity she kept these words in her heart and did not alter them. So have I also kept to these thy words, 'This is my body,' and I have neither tried nor permitted anyone else to make other words out of them, but have committed and commended to thee anything obscure in them. I have kept them just as they read, especially because I do not find that they conflict with any article of faith." Behold, no fanatic will dare to speak thus with Christ, as I know full well, for they are uncertain and at odds over their text.

Even if nothing but bread and wine were present in the Supper, and yet I tried, simply for my own satisfaction, to express the thought that Christ's body is in the bread, I still could not say anything in a more certain, simpler, and clearer way than, "Take, eat, this is my body." For if the text read, "Take, eat, in the bread is my body," or, "With the bread is my body," or, "Under the bread is my body," it would immediately begin to rain, hail, and snow a storm of fanatics crying, "You see! do you hear that? Christ does not say, 'This bread is my body,' but, 'In the bread, or with the bread, or under the bread is my body!'" And they would cry, "Oh, how gladly would we believe if he had said, 'This is my body'; this would have been distinct and clear. But he actually says, 'In the bread, with the bread, under the bread, so it does not follow that his body is present." Thus a thousand evasions and glosses would have been devised over the words "in, with, and under," no doubt with greater plausibility and less chance of stopping it than now.

Still they dare to say, "Where is it written that the body of Christ is present in the bread?" just as if they were prepared to believe if we could prove it. Yet they are unwilling to believe when we prove more cogently that the bread is the body of Christ, which certainly expresses more forcefully and clearly that his body is present than such a text as, "In the bread is my body." But they lie and pretend that God should establish the text just as they direct him; yet even if he did so, they would not accept it, since they do not accept this one.

Now since we have proved convincingly enough that neither Zwingli's representation-concept nor Oecolampadius' sign-concept holds water, we have also confirmed thereby that in their literal sense all the texts dealing with the Supper yield our interpretation. And although I had sufficiently treated these texts in my book against the heavenly prophets,[235] and even to this day nothing has been produced by the fanatics to refute it except sheer, barren glosses without a single passage of Scripture, invented out of their own heads and built upon their nonsense about representation and sign. Now all this, together with their representation and sign nonsense, has toppled to the ground and my book still stands, as you may read and learn for yourself in sexterns G, H, J, and K.[236] Once more, however, I will discuss these same texts in succession, in order to confirm our interpretation.

St. Matthew's is the first. He says in chapter 26 [26 ff.], "Now as they were eating, Jesus took bread, and gave thanks, and broke it, and gave it to the disciples and said, '*Take, eat; this is my body.*' And he took the cup, and gave thanks and gave it to them, saying, *Drink of it, all of you; for this is my blood of the new testament, which is poured out for many for the forgiveness of sins.*'"

These words were spoken by the mouth of God, although the fanatics regard them no more highly than if they had been spoken by a common vagabond or drunkard. Zwingli in one passage even becomes angry with us, saying that we cling obstinately to five poor, miserable words.[237] He has learned from the art of rhetoric that when one has a bad case and his adversary harasses and harrows him with the clear truth, one should dismiss it with a wave of the hand, make a wry face, and say, "This is nonsense, it does not deserve an answer, these are only five poor, miserable words," etc. But meanwhile, he must imagine nothing less than that God is an idol or an ape and all the world mere stocks and stones who will simply acquiesce in what he says when they hear such ridicule. Thus Zwingli's rhetoric agrees perfectly with the Silesians,[238] that we must put these words out of our sight and disdain them as poor and miserable, and then they will have won

[235] A very brief treatment in *LW* 40, 175 f., and a few other scattered references.

[236] *"This Is My Body"*; the four sexterns cover pp. 56-87.

[237] The words of institution, in Greek and (with *enim*) Latin, number five. Perhaps Luther is paraphrasing a passage in Karlstadt's *Dialogue*. St. L. 20, 2357.

[238] Schwenkfeld and Krautwald, cf. pp. 289 f.

the argument and discovered the indubitable truth. This will be the way to gloss and explain these clear words!

We poor, miserable flesh-eaters, meanwhile, are struck with astonishment that such mighty iron-eaters and hell-stormers[239] can bring absolutely nothing against these five poor, miserable words but a bare, unvarnished, arrogant volley of abuse. If abuse is a match for the truth, then the devil is really God above all gods. With such arguments, however, they reveal against their own intention what kind of spirit they have and how dearly they value God's words, since they abuse these precious words as "five poor, miserable words," that is, they do not believe that they are God's words. For if they believed that these were God's words, they would not call them "poor, miserable words," but would prize a single tittle and letter more highly than the whole world, and would fear and tremble before them as before God himself. For he who despises a single word of God certainly prizes none at all. If they ridiculed our interpretation or any misconception of ours, and not the very words of God, it could be tolerated. But what shall we do with those who regard these miserable words not as miserable but as glorious, mighty, and awesome? What should we do? Why, such people must be regarded as miserable fools, if they cannot despise these words or cast them out of their sight!

Here the word "is" cannot be proved to be figurative, nor "my body" be "the sign of my body"; and neither the text, "The flesh is of no avail" [John 6:63] and "Christ is seated in heaven" [Eph. 1:20], nor any other reasons can be given why the words must be interpreted otherwise than in their natural sense, as we have already heard. Consequently, we must remain content with them and cling to them as the perfectly clear, certain, sure words of God which can never deceive us or allow us to err. For it is said with the utmost possible simplicity, "This is my body"—"This is my blood of the new testament," so that if we brought together all the languages and expressions of the world, it would be impossible to choose a simpler expression. Indeed, Christ cannot speak more simply of his body and blood than to say "My body," or, "This is my body"—"This is my blood."

239 I.e. loudmouths and braggarts.

The fanatics' contention that Christ did not say, "In the bread is my body," or, "If you repeat these words, my body shall be present," is nonsense. Let them take their choice and try to find a simpler expression. If Christ had actually said, "In the bread is my body," they would have a much better case and could claim that Christ is in the bread spiritually or figuratively. For if they have been able to find a figurative expression in the words, "This is my body," how much more would they find the same in these words, "In the bread is my body"?—indeed, with greater plausibility, since the expression, "This is my body," is clearer and simpler than, "In this is my body."

But if Christ had said, "When you recite these words, my body shall be present," they would immediately have objected, "Yes indeed, my friend, Christ did not say, 'This bread is my body,' but, 'My body shall be present.' Now he can surely be present and yet the bread need not be his body." You see how nicely they would have been checked? However, if he had said, "When you recite these words, my body will be present in the bread," then they would have declared, "Yes, Christ's body is certainly present in the bread, but not essentially, only spiritually or figuratively." And if he had said, "when you recite these words, my body will be essentially in the bread," they would have objected again, "Yes, of course, his body is essentially present in the bread, but "essentially" must be understood of Christ's body, viz. Christ has an essential body, and not such a one as Marcion imagined;[240] this same essential body, to be sure, is present in the bread, but as in a sign, not truly present."

In short, if God himself gave them their choice of a text, they would never fix on one as simple as this, and yet they would always be finding more holes and gaps in it than they find in this one. Hence, whoever will not stick to this text according to our interpretation will not stick to any other text either. Now it is quite certain that the fanatics have resolved among themselves that they will not be subjected to it. This is proved by the fact that they pierce and riddle this simple text in so many ways. One makes a hole in it by his *touto,* a second by the "is," a third by

---

[240] Cf. p. 99, n. 159.

"my body," and others by this or that, as the fishes broke St. Peter's net [Luke 5:6], and they advance all kinds of silly, empty arguments which are far more uncertain and obscure than this text is. It is sheer lying and knavery when they demand a surer, simpler, clearer text. For they know that no clearer or simpler text could be framed even if they were given the choice of framing it. But because they feel that this text is too clear and too certain, they would like to decoy us away from it and induce us to frame another, in which they could find many more holes and gaps. In this way they would appear to have demolished a clearer text than the one we find in the gospel, which then would have no validity whatsoever. No, devil! You won't get away with this! You must choke on this text and be overthrown, and nothing can help you.

St. Mark's text is the second. In chapter 14 [:22 ff.] he says, "And as they were eating, Jesus took bread, and blessed, and broke it, and gave it to them, and said, '*This is my body.*' And he took a cup, and gave thanks, and gave it to them, and they all drank of it. And he said to them, '*This is my blood of the new testament, which is poured out for many.*'"

From this text Karlstadt developed his first ideas about *touto*, because Mark here speaks as if the disciples had all drunk from the cup before Christ said, "This is my blood"; immediately afterward, therefore, he would have referred to his own blood as he sat there, because the cup was now empty. This argument, however, was entirely refuted and fell to pieces long ago. Not only do the other evangelists and St. Paul write otherwise, but St. Mark himself, speaking of the second part of the sacrament, does not write that the disciples first ate the bread, after which Christ said, "This is my body." Therefore, the reference to drinking must be construed according to the order which the other evangelists and Paul maintain, and as St. Mark himself does in his reference to eating. For he cannot contradict himself and all the others.

I, too, wonder why only St. Mark records this point, "And they all drank of it" [Mark 14:23], and does it, moreover, precisely where Matthew writes in his text, "Drink of it, all of you" [Matt. 26:27]. It seems extremely probable that the text in St. Mark has been altered from *piete* to *epion*.[241] For if *piete* stood here, the text would be identical with St. Matthew, with whom St. Mark otherwise generally agrees. This I leave to the scholars. I maintain that since Matthew is the only one who writes, "Drink of it, all of you," and since Mark is the only one who writes, "And they all drank of it," these words are written because the two evangelists wished to indicate that the disciples all drank of this cup together, not from thirst as perhaps it was done in other instances when the cup would have had to be filled more than once before it had gone around, but that they had to pass the cup on this round drinking moderately so that they all might receive some. Just so, Luke also writes that when Christ passed around a farewell drink before instituting the sacrament, so that they all drank from one cup, He said, "Divide this cup among yourselves" [Luke 22:17], as if to say that there were actually several cups on the table, and each drank from his own, or one cup was filled more than once, but that this was passed as a cup of parting so that all might drink of it and bid farewell to the old paschal lamb.

In reference to this particular cup, then, Matthew and Mark may be understood as saying that each of the apostles had a cup before him on the table, or at least that there were more cups than one. But now, when Christ gives a new, special drink of his blood, he commands them all to drink out of this single cup. Thus, in proffering it and with a special gesture, Christ takes his own cup and lets them all drink of it, in distinction from all the other ordinary cups on the table, in order that they might better observe that it was a special drink in distinction from the other draughts which had been given them during the meal. The bread he could readily—indeed, he must—have so distributed that each received a piece for himself. But the wine he could not have distributed in this manner, but had to serve it in a cup for them all, indicating verbally that it was to be a drink in common for them all, not offered to and drunk by only one or two or three, as the other cups on the table were available to each as he wished.

Hence with these gestures he doubtless intended to distinguish

[241] *Piete* (drink) is the present imperative and *epion* (they drank) is the aorist of the verb *piein* (to drink).

his Supper conclusively from the old paschal supper. First, by offering the farewell drink, as Luke writes. By this he surely aroused the disciples' minds so that they had to think, "What is his object in giving the farewell drink from his own cup? Never before has he done this at table." Especially because St. Luke writes that he designated this with explicit words a farewell, saying, "I tell you that from now on I shall not drink of the fruit of the vine until the kingdom of God comes" [Luke 22:18], as we shall hear.

Secondly, by taking in his hands a particular loaf, in preference to all other loaves, blessing and breaking it after this farewell drink. This surely caused them to think, "What? Does he intend to eat again, even though he has offered the farewell drink?" Thus, of course, they were induced to watch very closely what he was doing and listen to what he was saying, for he had not acted thus at table with the other bread in celebrating the paschal supper; but now after the farewell drink and the supper he institutes a new one, saying that it is his body. Here they keep silent and simply believe; not one of them asks how bread can be body.

Thirdly, by giving his own cup and commanding all to drink of it he must surely have moved them also, because he had never before done such a thing with any other cup, saying that it was his blood. Once again they keep silent and believe. They doubtless thought that what he said must be true. For they saw from this new gesture following the farewell that he was beginning anew, giving thanks anew, pronouncing the blessing anew; further, that he took a special loaf which he divided among them all and passed his cup among them all, and concluded this supper with one loaf and one cup. They doubtless thought that he knew exactly what he was doing and saying, so there was no need for questions, yet they saw that it was an entirely new and different supper.

In summary, they had eaten the paschal lamb without his having commanded them to eat or drink, nor had he placed or laid it before anyone, but each one had eaten and drunk whatever he wished of that which stood before him, as Matthew and Mark say, "As they were eating, he took bread," etc. [Matt. 26:26, Mark 14:22]. But now the meal proceeds in an entirely new manner.

He takes and chooses a certain, particular loaf, pronounces thanks over it, breaks it, and divides it among them and offers it to them, and commands them to eat. Then he adds, "This is my body which is given for you." In the same way also he took the cup, choosing and giving a special draught for them all. Of other loaves he does not command them to eat, or drink out of other cups, nor does he place or lay anything before anyone as he does here. With all this he doubtless indicated that this bread and wine were not ordinary bread and wine as was customary with the passover, but something quite different, special, nobler, viz. as he says in his own words, it is his body and his blood.

Thus we have seen that Matthew and Mark agree, both speaking with utmost simplicity and with practically the same words, except that Matthew adds this phrase at the end, "for the forgiveness of sins" [26:28]. On the other hand Mark says [14:22], speaking of the bread, *eulogēsas,* i.e. he blessed it, while all[242] the others say *eucharistēsas,* i.e. he gave thanks, as Mark himself also says in referring to the cup. It appears to me that he means to identify "blessing" and "giving thanks." This, however, I leave to those who find pleasure in troubling themselves over such problems.

It is much more useful to observe that since the evangelists all so unanimously record these words in their perfect simplicity, "This is my body," one may conclude that there certainly can be no figure of speech or any trope in them. Had there been a trope there, one of them would certainly have touched on it with at least one letter, so that a different text or interpretation might have resulted. This they do on other occasions when one inserts what the other omits, or expresses it in different words, e.g. Matthew writes that Christ said, "If it is by the finger of God that I cast out demons," etc. [12:28], but Luke writes, "If it is by the Spirit of God that I cast out demons" [11:20].[243] And where Mark says, "Some seed yielded fruit thirtyfold, some sixtyfold, some a hundredfold" [4:8], Luke says simply, "And it yielded a hundred-

[242] The texts of Luke 22:19 consistently read *eucharistēsas;* the text of Matt. 26:26 familiar to Luther read *eucharistēsas,* but modern text critics find *eulogēsas* better attested.

[243] Luther errs in his identification. Matthew's text reads "Spirit," Luke's reads "finger."

fold" [8:8]. There are many other such passages where one writer clarifies what the other says, or expresses himself differently.

Here, however, they are without exception and with perfect simplicity identical. No one of them permits himself to be distinguished from another by a single letter. It is as if they said in concert, "No one can speak differently, more simply, or more surely about this subject than to say, 'This is my body,'" though Luke and Paul express themselves quite differently from Matthew and Mark in regard to the cup, as we shall hear. Since we have four witnesses before us, then, all concurring perfectly in their words, we may boldly and securely rely on their testimony and base our judgment and faith upon it. For if God declares that the evidence of two witnesses shall be true [John 8:17], how much stronger should we regard these four witnesses than all the fanatics' crying and babbling? They dare not assert that Matthew, Mark, Luke, and Paul were less learned, holy, godly, and spiritual than they and their followers are. But if they declare the words of these witnesses dubious, the words of the fanatics must reasonably be considered much more dubious, especially because they disagree among one another; not one of them is sure of his text nor can he become so. But these four witnesses agree on the text down to the last letter. This is the way I speak with our party. For the fanatics can readily answer all questions, since they do not bother with Scripture but rashly produce empty glosses out of their own heads.

St. Luke's text is the third, chapter 22 [:19 f.]: "And he took bread, and when he had given thanks he broke it and gave it to them, saying, '*This is my body which is given for you.* Do this is remembrance of me.' And likewise the cup after supper, saying, '*This cup is the new testament in my blood, which is poured out for you.*'"

Anyone who is willing to be taught should find complete satisfaction on this subject in St. Luke alone, so clearly and well does he speak of the Supper. First he describes Christ's farewell drink, as we have related above, and says, "He took a cup, gave thanks, and said, 'Take this, and divide it among yourselves; for I tell you that from now on I shall not drink of the fruit of the vine until the kingdom of God comes'" [22:17 f.]. Here Christ testifies that this will be his last drink of wine on earth with his disciples. Immediately afterward he gives the cup of wine of the new Supper.[244] If there were nothing but common wine in the new Supper, how is it possible that this should be his farewell drink—that he will drink no more wine? If that was his last drink of wine, then this cannot be wine which he afterward gives them to drink. If it is not wine, it must be what he calls it, viz. his blood, or the new testament in his blood. Thus St. Luke forcefully takes his stand that there cannot be ordinary wine in Christ's Supper.

Here you may say, "Yes, who knows whether Christ spoke these words about the farewell drink before or after his Supper? For Luke writes that he spoke these words before the Supper, but Matthew and Mark write as if he spoke them after the Supper" [Matt. 26:29, Mark 14:25]. Well, the question hinges on which evangelist retains the correct order in his account. If Luke retains it, the matter is simple and our interpretation correct and the fanatics are defeated, beyond a shadow of a doubt. Or, if the fanatics still have doubts about it, we at any rate are certain that we are right, and this is enough for us.

Now let us learn from the evangelists' own words and works which one retains the correct order in his account. At the opening of his gospel [1:3] St. Luke declares his intention to write from the beginning and in order. This he proves in practice; his gospel proceeds in admirable order from beginning to end, as all the world acknowledges. But Matthew and Mark make no such promise, nor do they follow this pattern, as could be proved from many passages. For instance, when Matthew describes the temptation of Christ in chapter 4 [:1 ff.] and the appearances of Christ after the resurrection [28:1 ff.], he does not observe the order of events at all. St. Augustine in his *Harmony of the Gospels*[245] has wrestled considerably with these problems. Mark does not maintain the order either, even in this passage on the Supper, when he places the clause, "And they all drank of it," before these words, "And he said to them, 'This is my blood'" [14:23 f.], though by natural and logical order it ought to follow them.

---

244 Textual evidence now is unclear whether "which is given for you," v. 19, and all of v. 20, should be retained or omitted.

245 IV, 8, 9. *PNF*[1] 6, 230 ff. and *passim.*

Thus, since there is no doubt that Matthew and Mark do not maintain the strict historical order, but Luke obligates himself to maintain it and actually does so, Matthew's and Mark's narratives must be judged according to St. Luke's order and not the other way around. We must say that Matthew and Mark have placed after the new Supper that which occurred and should have been placed after the old supper, for they place no great emphasis upon the order, being satisfied simply to relate what transpired and the truth. Luke, however, who wrote later, declares that one of his motives is to write in historical order, since many others had disregarded the sequence of this history. Hence many are of the opinion, and it is quite credible, that St. Paul had St. Luke in mind when he declares, commending him to the Corinthians, "With him we are sending the brother who is famous among all Christians for his preaching of the gospel" [II Cor. 8:18].

It is also a corroboration of the opinion that Luke zealously intended to maintain the historical order, that he describes not only the farewell drink, but also the entire preceding farewell passover supper, saying, "When the hour came, he sat at table, and the twelve apostles with him. And he said to them, 'I have earnestly desired to eat this passover with you before I suffer; for I tell you I shall never eat it again until it is fulfilled in the kingdom of God.' And he took a cup," etc. [Luke 22:14 ff.] Here you see that everything about this farewell is recorded in orderly sequence in a single text with regard to both the eating and the drinking, which Matthew and Mark do not observe. If, then, so far as the order is concerned, the farewell eating takes place and must take place before the new Supper, then it must be true that the farewell drink must also take place before the new Supper. For the two constitute one farewell act and are not to be separated from each other.

With this we now return to the argument and conclusion mentioned above. If Luke retains the correct order, as has now been proved, then Christ took his farewell drink of wine before the new Supper. But if he took the farewell drink of wine before the new Supper, it is impossible that common, ordinary wine was drunk in the Supper. For his words are clear, when he says that after this drink he will never again drink of the fruit of the vine.

Against this someone will object once more, "But you yourself declare that the wine remains wine in the new Supper. These words of yours make you a good papist who believes that there is no wine in the Supper." I reply: This bothers me very little, for I have often enough asserted that I do not argue whether the wine remains wine or not. It is enough for me that Christ's blood is present; let it be with the wine as God wills. Sooner than have mere wine with the fanatics, I would agree with the pope that there is only blood.

Moreover, I have said above that if the wine has become Christ's blood, it is no longer ordinary wine but a "blood-wine," to which I may point and say, "This is the blood of Christ." This too Christ does not conceal, for he says here, "I shall not drink of the fruit of the vine." Why does he say not "wine" but "fruit of the vine"? Undoubtedly because what is drunk in the Supper does not come from the vine like other ordinary wine. Although it is surely wine also, it has not come by ordinary processes of growth to be what it now is. Just as when malmsey is mixed with a little water, the water is there but it has so completely become malmsey that it can no longer be tasted; as I can say of that drink, "This water was not taken from the spring," so the wine in the Supper is no longer a fruit of the vine, for the fruit of the vine is assuredly nothing but ordinary wine.

"What if Christ did not drink at his Supper, but only the disciples?" I reply: What if a fool can ask more questions than ten wise men can answer? It is not recorded that he partook of the farewell drink, nevertheless he would not have given it only to the disciples but would also have drunk with them. Thus the disciples surely drank nothing after this farewell drink, but refrained as Christ did. Again, if the disciples after the farewell drink drank the blood of the Lord, he undoubtedly drank with them. Oh, why should I play the fool by dealing with such foolish questions? Let this suffice for the first part of St. Luke's account; it is sufficiently clear that what we have in Christ's Supper cannot be the fruit of the vine. If it is not the fruit of the vine, it can be nothing else than the blood of Christ according to his words, "This is my blood."

Secondly, this part of the text, "which is given for you," which only Luke and Paul insert [Luke 22:19, I Cor. 11:24], some other fanatics torture, especially Karlstadt's crowd. They claim that since it reads, "which is given for you," as a present event, the body of Christ cannot be present in the Supper, because neither at that time nor now could it be properly said that his body *is* given or his blood *is* poured out for us. In the first Supper it should have been said, "which *shall be* given for you," and now it should be, "which *has been* given for you." O what clever, lofty spirits! On this point I answered Lady Hulda abundantly in my little book against the heavenly prophets, in quire K.[246]

The spirits do not see that what they are babbling works as strongly against them as against us. Suppose Karlstadt's text were valid: "This is my body which is sitting here; this is my blood which is present here"; how will his body be given and his blood poured out while He is present there as the words read, "which is given for you; which is poured out for you"? Christ cannot lie or speak in vain when he says in the Supper, "This is my body given for you; this is my blood poured out for you." Now it is not given or poured out there, as it must have been if the fanatics' reasoning on these words were to be sustained. If in their version of the Supper they can maintain both propositions, viz. that Christ's body and blood were there at the table *not yet* given and poured out for us, and yet that what he says is true, that this is the body and blood given and poured out for us, then, my friend, our interpretation also will sustain the same words, even though Christ is not now given but *was* given once in the past. Read farther in the same book, if you like.

Thirdly, this text of Luke comes along: "This is the cup, the new testament in my blood, which is poured out for you" [22:20]. It has to knuckle under; they are not agreed even to this day how to torture and mangle it on the wheel. One seizes on the word "new testament," a second the word "in my blood," etc., but no one considers how he may clothe or support his naked ideas and glosses with Scripture and good reason. We would like to be told.

In the first place, Luke and Paul alone record these words,

[246] *LW* 40, 193 f. *Frau Hulda* is a common designation in Luther for "clever Reason."

"Do this in remembrance of me" [Luke 22:19, I Cor. 11:24], and both record them where they speak of the bread and not where they speak of the wine. For they maintain it is enough to mention the words once, and this is quite true, even though they apply to both parts of the sacrament and so to the whole Supper, as Paul further emphasizes: "As often as you eat this bread and drink this cup, you proclaim the Lord's death" [I Cor. 11:26]. This they do in order to indicate the purpose and the fruit of this Supper, viz. that we should praise and thank God for our deliverance from sin and death, as the Jews were bound to thank and praise him for their deliverance from the land of Egypt [Exod. 12:17]. This is the subject on which we should speak and write. Instead the fanatics draw us into these bitter controversies.

Both Luke and Paul also record in connection with the cup these words: "And likewise the cup after supper" [Luke 22:20], or, "After they had eaten supper" [I Cor. 11:25]. Why? I truly believe it was all for the sake of future fanatics, as if with that word as with a finger Luke wished to recall and point back to the farewell drink. As if he should say, "Remember what I said above concerning the farewell drink, that from now on Christ will not drink of the fruit of the vine. I want you to know that I speak here of another drink which took place after the supper, after they had entirely finished drinking of the fruit of the vine, and not to mistake this drink for that farewell drink but regard it as a drink at the commencement of the new Supper." In particular, Luke and Paul say this with reference to the cup and not the bread, because it was more fitting and necessary in connection with the cup, since at a farewell one does not usually eat, but drinks. Thus he did not want it to be understood as a farewell drink, though it applies to both elements and to the entire Supper, just the same as the clause quoted above concerning remembrance.

We let them rant and invent glosses here to their hearts' desire. Of this we are certain, of course, that with the text, "This cup is the new testament in my blood," St. Luke intends to say nothing different but the very same thing that St. Matthew and Mark say with the text, "This is my blood of the new testament." For they cannot contradict one another, but must be of the same opinion. Construe the text of Luke as you will, then, the sense must be that which Mark and Matthew say: "This is my blood of the new testament." If we construe Luke's words so that they give us in the Supper the blood of Christ for the new testament, as Mark and Matthew do, we assuredly have his correct meaning. Anyone who construes differently or twists it does not have it aright, for he would not agree with the others.

Hence it follows that they are great fools who try to conclude from the words of Luke that the cup must consist in the blood, if we wish to follow his words literally, because he says, "The cup is the new testament in my blood." For they imagine that "in blood" must be taken here in the same sense as a peasant in his boots or meat in a pot, even though they have to acknowledge that this cannot be the meaning in Mark and Matthew, and yet the evangelists cannot be at variance with one another.

But Luke, as he often does, is using the Hebrew idiom. We find such expressions in the Hebrew language, e.g. Psalm 78 [:64], "Their priests fell in the sword, i.e. they fell *by* the sword. Again, "Princes are hung up in their hands," i.e. suspended *by* their hands, Lamentations 4 [5:12]. Again, "We drink our water in money" [Lam. 5:4], i.e. *for* money. Again, "The children fell in the wood" [Lam. 5:13], i.e. they fell *under* the wood which they were obliged to carry. Again, in Hosea [12:12], Jacob served in Rachel, i.e. *for* Rachel; and many similar examples. So you see that in Hebrew the word "in" has a very comprehensive meaning, yet it indicates that the object to which it refers must be present.

Here too, then, Luke means: "This cup is the new testament in the blood of Christ," i.e. *through* the blood, or *with* the blood, or *on account of* the blood, etc., just as Matthew says, "This is my blood of the new testament." The cup, of course, cannot be the new testament in silver or by silver or for the sake of silver. Explain these words as you like: "This cup is the new testament in my blood," so long as you do not contradict Matthew and Mark. A patient and uncontentious spirit can easily be told that in plain language the words of Luke mean: "This cup is a new testament, not on account of its fine silver or of its wine, but *on account of* (or *according to,* or *for the sake of*) the blood of Christ. A German might fill in St. Luke's text on his own in this fashion: "This cup is the new testament on account of the blood of Christ," which everyone would interpret thus: "The cup is the new testament because Christ's blood is in it."

This subject I have been obliged to draw out at such length in order to clarify the text of Luke. Apart from the fact that he uses a Hebrew idiom, the text in itself is expressed with perfect clarity and simplicity, and agrees perfectly with Matthew and Mark, except that he arranges the words in the usual Hebrew manner. Where Matthew according to the Greek idiom says, "This is my blood of the new testament," Luke says according to the Hebrew idiom, "This is the new testament in my blood." Now "the new testament in my blood" and "my blood of the new testament" are not conflicting expressions but the very same in terms and meaning; only the word order is different, which results from the nature of the Hebrew language, as scholars well know. In order to avoid all error I would translate the text of Luke in the clearest and briefest manner thus: "This cup is the new testament in my blood," though Luke does not insert the word "is" but says, "This cup the new testament in my blood." If anyone likes, he may use the word "is" twice, viz.: "This is the cup which is the new testament in my blood." But since Paul, who quotes precisely these words of Luke, uses only one "is," saying, "This cup is a new testament in my blood" [I Cor. 11:25], the text of Luke also certainly ought to be translated with one "is."

But Luke and St. Paul, who strictly retain the Hebrew manner of speech at this point, please me better than Matthew and Mark, who expressed it in the Greek idiom, since it enables us to have the words of Christ with greater precision and to check future sects. How powerfully Luke and Paul with their text have overthrown Karlstadt's *touto*, they acknowledge themselves. If anyone is unaware of this, let him read my book against the heavenly prophets, quire K.[247] But as they have overthrown Karlstadt's *touto*, so also have they also overthrown that of the Silesians, who transpose this *touto* and place it near the end, as we heard above:[248] "My body which is given for you is this, viz. a spiritual food."

Well, since St. Luke here inserts the word *touto* in connec-

[247] Cf. *LW* 40, 217 f.

[248] Cf. p. 289, above.

tion with the cup, saying, "this cup," let them also transpose this text thus: "The new testament in my blood which is poured out for you is this cup, viz. a spiritual drink." How does that strike you?—a material cup is a spiritual drink! My friend, what does Luke make of such fanatics when they transpose his language so? He takes them for people who would believe that a silver or golden cup is a spiritual drink. But it would surely seem to me a strange spirit who would quaff and swallow a material, silver or golden cup. Keep him away from me! He would soon drink up all my money and my gold, and I would have more trouble putting up with him than with the entire papacy. He would swallow up more gold, without masses, than the papacy with masses!

Behold, this is the way these thoughtless spirits act, who suppose that if they can apply make-up to their fantasies in one passage, it will do quite well everywhere, and who never take the trouble to consider how it fits with other passages. For since they could say in Mark and Matthew, "My body is this; my blood is this, viz. spiritual food and drink," because they find the *touto* there standing all by itself, they would like to apply this all around, any way they please, like the men described in Daniel with Susanna,[249] perverting and shaming it with a false interpretation. But meanwhile they overlooked the fact that Luke with his text would so turn the tables on them and all their cleverness that they would be trapped and covered with shame for their wickedness.

This means, of course, "with the perverse thou dost show thyself perverse," Psalm 18 [26]. They want to change God's Word from the fleshly into the spiritual, and in so doing they change themselves from the spiritual into the fleshly. For Luke clearly stands there with his *touto* and points to the material cup and says, "This cup," so that it is impossible to refer *touto* here to a spiritual drink. On the contrary, these fanatics stand there with their transposition and say that *touto* should mean a spiritual drink. Then either Luke or the fanatics must clearly be false and fallacious. But if this *touto* in connection with the cup will not

[249] The apocryphal Story of Susanna (in the Vulgate, chapter 13 of the book of Daniel).

permit itself to be thus transposed and turned into a spiritual *touto*, just as little can the *touto* in connection with the bread be so treated. Thus the Silesian *touto* lies as deep in the slop as that of Karlstadt. But when will these sectarians show any signs of shame, after having been caught so often in lies?

Next in order, Oecolampadius must also appear before St. Luke's judgment seat with his "sign-concept." "Body and blood" says he, "are tropes in the Supper, and mean sign of the body, sign of the blood." If this is true, undoubtedly the word "blood" in Luke's text must also be a trope, i.e. sign of the blood. For he is certainly speaking of the same blood that Matthew and Mark speak of, as no one can deny. Well, Luke's text then must contain the following, according to Oecolampadius' opinion: "This cup is a new testament in the sign of my blood, viz. in mere wine." This would be magnificent, if the new testament is nothing more than a drink of wine, or if a drink of wine has the power to make this cup a new testament! For this is the result and intention of Oecolampadius' text.

Take the meaning of testament here as we will, it is certainly set into contrast with the old testament; for Luke calls it the new, therefore it must have spiritual blessings in it, which were signified and promised by the old testament and accomplished and fulfilled in the new. This no one can controvert. But what Christian heart can tolerate the assertion that our new testament is a drink of wine? Or that this cup is a new testament on account of a drink of wine? Oecolampadius lets the word "is" stand as it reads. Therefore, in his reasoning the new testament must be nothing else than the miserable cup, and yet it must be so for no other reason than *in virtue of* and *on account of* the wine as a sign of the blood of Christ. In this way we might reasonably call all the figures of the Old Testament the new testament, since they are all such signs.

If he means to say, however, that the text should be interpreted: "This cup is a sign of the new testament in my blood," so that the trope here would consist not in the blood but in the new testament, why does he not make everything mere signs and tropes and say, "That figure of the cup is a figure of the testament in the figure of my blood," i.e. that painted cup is an image of the new testament through the sign of my blood, i.e. through the wine; "This sign of the cup is a sign of the new testament in the sign of my blood"? What a beautiful idea! Who will show a reason why one word, and not all the others, must be a trope?

But suppose we grant him the right to reduce this text to a trope, thus: "This cup is a sign of the new testament in my blood," so that "blood" here would not be a trope, but real blood. Then he would really be getting somewhere! In the first place, by this construction he acknowledges that in the Supper, as Luke records it, "blood" is not a trope but the true blood of Christ. Here we ask: Why then does he make it a trope in Matthew and Mark? How can one say that Luke mentions a different blood in the Supper from Mark and Matthew? If in Luke it is the true blood of Christ, it must be the same in Matthew and Mark, for they are assuredly speaking of the same Supper, and they must surely be speaking also of the same blood and drink. Squirm as you will, if "blood" in Matthew and Mark is a trope, it must also be a trope in Luke. If it is not so in Luke, it cannot be so in Matthew and Mark either. But if blood is not a trope, body cannot be one either. And if Luke thus abolishes and puts to shame all tropes with a single word, then trope suffers the same fate as *touto*: it destroys itself.

In the second place, here is something still more shameful: the text, "This cup is a sign of the new testament in my blood," admits that Christ's true blood is in the cup, yet it effects nothing more than to make this cup a sign or figure of the new testament. This is no different from saying that the cup with the blood of Christ is a figure of the new testament. Thus the blood of Christ cannot give us the true new testament, but only serves as a sign of the new testament, in no sense better than the paschal lamb's or goat's blood in the old testament, which also is a figure or sign of the new testament. We have heard above[250] that this expression, "in my blood," is equivalent to "by or with my blood," so that it is present in the cup, and the cup therefore is a new testament because it has the blood of Christ in it.

What excellent fashioning of figures this is, and what honor

[250] Cf. pp. 320 f.

it gives to Christ's blood when it is considered equal to the goat's blood and a figure of the new testament! We are supposed to be living in the new testament, yet we have to live in the old testament at the same time. For he who has the figure of the new testament cannot yet have the new testament itself, as the Epistle to the Hebrews [8–10] teaches. But from this text of Oecolampadius, if he really means it, we would at the same time have the new testament and not have it. For we would have at one and the same time the figure of the new testament and the new testament itself, which is the same as saying that we would have at the same time Christ's blood and not his blood.

Besides, it cannot be admitted that "new testament" is a trope. How would one prove this? Where is there a single example of it? Indeed, what would become of the ordinary expressions by which I should like—or perhaps, am obliged—to speak simply of the new testament, if people may understand a sign or figure as often as I mention the new testament? In that way the new testament would not be the gospel or promise of the Spirit or of eternal life, but an old figure or image of a future new testament. In short, a trope is not at all appropriate in the expression "new testament"; much less can it be established by any reason. Thus Oecolampadius must cling to his first text, that "blood" is a trope, and say, "This cup is a new testament in the sign of my blood." That text, however, our faith can never admit—that ordinary wine should make this cup become the new testament.

For the new testament is promise, indeed, much more: the bestowal of grace and the forgiveness of sin, i.e. the true gospel. Although the cup is a material thing, yet because it becomes sacramentally united with the blood of Christ or with the new testament, it is rightly called a new testament or the blood, and one may point to it and say, "This is a new testament; this is the blood of Christ," just as the material flame mentioned above is in reality and in name a spiritual thing, viz. an angel, and the dove is the Holy Spirit.[251] Therefore, he who drinks of this cup really drinks the true blood of Christ and the forgiveness of sins or the Spirit of Christ, for these are received in and with the cup. Here

[251] Cf. pp. 298 ff.

is received no mere figure or sign of the new testament or of the blood of Christ, as would befit the Jews in the old testament.

Suppose someone should resort to a subterfuge, however, alleging that Oecolampadius might construe his text, "This cup is a sign of the new testament in my blood," in such a way that the blood relates not to the cup but to the new testament, with this signification: "The new testament is in the blood of Christ and subsists through the blood of Christ"; not in the sense that the cup through the blood of Christ is a sign or figure, as if his text were so construed: "This cup is a sign of the new testament, but the new testament is something which consists in the blood of Christ." I answer: Oecolampadius knows well that this text cannot be accepted here, for in Greek an article would have to stand after "new testament," so: *kainē diathēkē, hē en tō haimati emou.* This article, however, is lacking, and the text is closely connected as if it were a single indivisible word, just as cup, blood, and new testament also are closely connected as if they were a single indivisible object. Thus the sense must be: "This cup is a new testament in my blood," i.e., "On account of my blood the cup is this, which it would not be without my blood."

As Oecolampadius now is defeated with his trope or sign-concept, so also is Zwingli with his representation-concept. The objections sustained against the sign-concept also stand against the representation-concept, since the two are entirely parallel. For Zwingli's text would have to read, "This cup represents the new testament in my blood," which would be equivalent to saying, "This cup, by virtue of my blood which is in it, has the value of representing the new testament." Christ's blood thus would have to be a representation, nothing more, just as I have proved above in reference to Oecolampadius' sign-concept. For Zwingli cannot even construe the text thus: "This cup represents the new testament which is in my blood," for the pronoun "which" is lacking and the entire text forms as it were a single word, as has been said.

Now isn't St. Luke a nasty man, that with a single word, so to speak, he suddenly fells such mighty giants and heroes, both "*toutists*" and "figurists" and "representationists" and all fanatics in a heap? And how would their signs and representations help, even if their texts were valid? Still they cannot indicate one iota of similarity in which such a sign or figure might consist, as we have shown above with reference to Oecolampadius' trope. For in what respect is the cup through the blood of Christ similar to the new testament? In this, that just as our sins are forgiven us through the testament, so they are forgiven in the blood of Christ? Where else can we find the similarity? Up the flue! Why then do they teach figures where there can be none?

Luke, however, has in this text an expression that no other evangelist uses or Paul either, viz.: in the clause, "which is poured out for you," "which" in Greek refers to the cup and not to the blood, as no one can deny: *touto to potērion . . . . ekchunnomenon,* and not *en tō haimati . . . . ekchunnomenō.* In Latin the distinction cannot be expressed by saying, *Qui pro vobis funditur,* for "cup" and "blood" in Latin are both masculine, but in German it is easily noticed since *blut* is neuter and *becher* masculine. Some three or four years ago a very learned village pastor[252] brought this to my attention, and expounded his opinion to me that Luke should be interpreted thus: "This cup, which is poured out for you, is the new testament in my blood," i.e. the cup which is poured out for you at the table and set before you to drink, as on other occasions one pours wine from a tankard for guests. And one of his reasons was that Luke, as we have said, writes not of the blood as Matthew and Mark do but of the cup: *ekchunnomenon* —"is poured out." And he further cited the text of Paul [I Cor. 11:24], "This is my body, which is *broken*[253] for you," i.e. broken into pieces and set before you on the table.

When I learned that he was not on the fanatics' side but acknowledged that the real body and blood were present in the sac-

[252] Schwenkfeld records that Luther received this suggestion from "someone killed at Frankenhausen." *Corpus Schwenckfeldianorum* 2, 244 f. This couldn't have been Thomas Münzer, however, for Luther describes the pastor as "not on the fanatics' side."

[253] The RSV text of I Cor. 11:24 reads, "This is my body which is for you"; the marginal reading, "broken for you" (*klōmenon*), represents among others the Erasmian text which Luther followed. The Vulgate reads, "which shall be delivered for you" (*tradetur*). It is interesting to note that in this parallel Latin text to the *Novum Testamentum Graece* (Basel, 1516) Erasmus corrects the Vulgate's *tradetur* with *frangitur.* In his *Annotationes* he takes account of the fact that certain Greek codices support the Vulgate's rendering. But then he goes on to say that some authorities have changed the text because to "break the body" appeared absurd to them.

rament, I was happy and pleased with his interpretation, although I deemed it unnecessary because there was nothing dangerous in the old interpretation. It still pleases me to this day, and I sincerely wish that the Greek text would allow for this exegesis. For this would most forcefully stop the mouth of every fanatic. There is not the least doubt in my mind that the text of Paul, "This is my body which is broken for you," is simply to be understood of the breaking and distributing at table, as he also says in I Corinthians 10 [:16], "The bread which we break is the distributed body of Christ."

Because the text in Paul which speaks of the bread or the body of Christ is understood to refer to the distribution at table and not to his sacrifice on the cross, the text concerning the cup undoubtedly admits of a similar interpretation. Matthew and Mark would also become clear, viz., "This is my body," where they say nothing of the giving, since it would be clearly perceived anyway that he gave them his body when he said, "This is my body," i.e. here you have my body. Likewise with the cup: "This is my blood which is poured out for you," i.e. distributed and set before you for the forgiveness of sins. I still see nothing in the words which would effectually oppose this interpretation. For St. Paul also, in connection with the cup, omits "which was shed for you," presuming that if he said the bread was broken for them, they would have sufficient reason to infer that the cup was also distributed for them.

Although this interpretation is not the one traditionally held, but the text has been commonly understood of Christ's delivering himself up to suffering and being poured out on the cross, there would have been no dangerous error in this, nor is there even now. No one does wrong in holding that Christ's body and blood were given and poured out for us on the cross, even though he does it in connection with a passage that makes no mention of it, provided that there is no real contradiction, just as it is not harmful that the ancient fathers often cited Scripture passages inappropriately, yet in a good and useful sense. It appears to me, indeed, that certain of the ancient fathers also had this conception when they said that Christ's blood is poured out as often as the Supper is celebrated. Especially Ambrose, where he says, "If the blood of Christ, as often as it is shed, is shed for sin, then I should properly receive it daily, because I sin daily."[254] For the word *funditur* actually means not only "is shed," but also "is poured out." Again, Gregory: "The blood of Christ is poured into the mouth of believers."[255]

This I do not say in the sense that I stand upon it with firm conviction, for what I am not myself sure of I will teach no one. But I would be happy if it were so, and since I am not an expert in Greek, I urge scholars to investigate the subject and determine whether the Greek language will permit it. Thus the fanatics would have no further subterfuge or excuse whatsoever to oppose our interpretation. They would have to acknowledge that Christ's body and blood are distributed at the table and physically eaten and drunk in the bread and the cup.

Claiming my jester's privilege I say that Luke and Paul strongly convey this impression. Paul, from the fact that he says, as we have observed, "This is my body, which is broken for you," and, "The bread which we break is the distribution of the body of Christ" [I Cor. 10:16]. Thus we find several other passages in which Paul uses *huper humōn*, "for us," for *coram* or *ante*, as in I Corinthians 15 [:29], "Why are they then baptized for the dead?" Luke, from the fact that he also says the cup in the blood is poured out *huper humōn*, i.e. set before you, before your eyes, to drink. Also from the fact that he says the body is given for you, as Paul also relates. Now "to give" certainly means to bestow something, not to deliver up something to death.

Matthew and Mark, however, seem to have a contrary view when they say, "This is my blood which is shed, or poured out, for many." This sounds as if Christ speaks of many who are not present at the table. And they do not say *huper humōn* but *peri pollōn*. This I leave for the Greek experts to settle. Anyone who has a liking for the above-mentioned interpretation may answer in some such manner as this: Luke and Paul speak of the pouring or bestowing at the table, but announce the shedding of blood on the cross

[254] Cf. Ambrose, *Exposition of Psalm 118, Sermon 18*, 26 (119:141). *MPL* 15, 1537.
[255] Cf. Gregory I, *Homily 22 on John*, 7 f., (20:1-9). *MPL* 76, 1178 f.

by saying that we should do this in remembrance of him, or to proclaim his death, therefore they speak in a more orderly and clear fashion than Matthew and Mark. On the other hand, Matthew and Mark speak of the shedding at the cross, and are silent about the pouring at the table, which they considered they had sufficiently expressed by the word "this." We know it is customary among the evangelists for one to treat a particular subject more extensively and frequently than another does, and for one to omit what another reports. Thus the expression, "which is given for you," does not refer so clearly and certainly to the suffering of Christ as Zwingli dreams when he cites it in order to explain the preceding clause, "This is my body," as we have heard above.

If anyone does not like this interpretation, however, he may answer on the basis of Luke's words, "The cup is poured out for us," and therefore may say that since cup and blood and new testament are sacramentally united, the cup is "shed" by virtue of this unity, in the sense of *synecdoche,* whereas only the blood is shed, as we mentioned above[256] that it is proper to say the Son of God died althougn only his humanity died, and that the Holy Spirit is seen although only the dove is seen, and the angel is seen although only his shining form is seen, etc. If anyone regards this explanation as too meager or unconvincing, let him offer a better one, or acknowledge the above-mentioned interpretation as valid. I believe this is a correct and sufficient answer, for thus we see and drink the cup, i.e. Christ's blood. It is no danger for us but indeed a clear advantage, whichever of the two interpretations we adopt. They are both good and correct, for both in fact assert that Christ's body is given both at the table and on the cross; if we do not strike upon the right passage of Scripture, as has happened with many of the holy fathers, nevertheless we miss nothing of the meaning and the truth. For the fanatics, however, it is a very crucial matter; if this interpretation is not correct in this text, they have nothing superior to it in their arguments, but if it is correct, they lie completely prostrate in ashes.

The fourth and last is St. Paul, who says in I Corinthians 11 [:23-25], "I received from the Lord what I also delivered to you,

---

[256] Cf. pp. 298 ff.

that the Lord Jesus on the night when he was betrayed took bread, and when he had given thanks, he broke it, and said, '*This is my body which is broken for you.* Do this in remembrance of me.' In the same way also the cup, after supper, saying, '*This cup is the new testament in my blood.* Do this, as often as you drink it, in remembrance of me.'"

If I were as learned in the Greek language as Karlstadt and Zwingli, I would prove irrefutably from this text that in the bread the true body of Christ is eaten. For Erasmus shows[257] that there is no "is" in connection with "bread," but simply *phagete, touto emou sōma–comedite, hoc meum corpus,* which I would translate, "Take, eat this my body which is broken for you." This would be a correct word-for-word translation, except for the omission of a little punctuation mark which would not affect the meaning. Thus I would have won the argument neatly and completely. However, since I am not so learned, I must let it pass, lest I too take an article to be a pronoun, or invent an alloeosis, or confuse grammatical cases.[258]

It is true, however, that Matthew and Mark have incompletely described the Supper. We must note from this that were it not for Luke and Paul we would not have this sacrament. For Matthew and Mark do not write that Christ commanded us to do this afterward, and so to observe it. Thus we would have had to let it stand like any other story of Christ's dealings with his disciples which we could not and must not repeat. But Luke and Paul write that Christ also commanded us all to do this. Indeed, if it were not for Paul, even Luke would not be sufficient authority for us, for he might be understood to say that the apostles alone were to repeat this in imitation of Christ–unless the last chapter of Matthew [28:20] indicates something to this effect when Christ says, "Teach them to observe all that I have commanded you." But whether this would be sufficient I do not know. Paul is the

[257] In Erasmus' editions of the Greek New Testament the text of I Cor. 11:24 reads *Labete, phagete, touto mou esti to sōma.* It is in the *notes* appended by Erasmus that the omission of *esti* is stated: "*Touto mou sōma: hoc meum corpus,* without the substantive verb *est,* although I find it added in certain texts." *WA* 26, 473, n. 1. Incidentally, the two imperatives are not found in the best New Testament manuscripts.
[258] *Casum pro casu.*

true teacher and apostle sent to us Gentiles. He speaks freely and fully on this subject, saying:

"*Take, eat,* this my body which is broken for you." For he places the word "my" immediately after the word *touto* or "this," which none of the others does. Moreover, as certain texts would read, he omits the word "is," just as Luke also omits it in connection with the cup. These two items the Holy Spirit points out to strengthen us in our assurance that the body of Christ is present in the bread. For though it is all the same to us whether I say, "This is my body," or, "This my body," or, "My body here," yet it is a clearer and surer expression of the presence of the body if I say, "This my body" or, "My body here," and the sectarians with all their raving cannot so casually play tricks with it as with the expression, "This is my body."

Now, there is no doubt that Christ spoke these words in contrast with the old paschal lamb, which he abrogates here, as if to say, "Up to now you have eaten a lamb, the body of an animal. But here in its stead now is *my* body—*mine, mine,* I say with perfect clarity." Paul lays such great emphasis on the word "my" that with a new turn of expression he places it immediately after the word "this," and says, "this my," as if he wanted to join it so closely to the word "this" as to make it a single word, even though "my" and "body" belong far more intimately together. All this he does in order to express the presence of Christ's body in the Supper with all possible clarity.

"Which is broken for you." Of this we have spoken a great deal already,[259] showing that Scripture will not allow the word "broken" to refer to Christ's suffering. The fanatics may make this claim, as they make other claims also, but they can never prove it. For we must not interpret or use the word "break" according to our own fancies but according to scriptural usage. Now in Scripture the word "breaking," especially where it is used in reference to bread or eating, is the equivalent of "dividing into pieces" or "distributing." Thus the word for broken bread in Greek, Latin, and German is *klasma, fragmentum, brocken.* Indeed, in Hebrew also, on account of the breaking, grain is called *sheber,* i.e. bits of food,

[259] Cf. pp. 265 ff.

Genesis 44 [42:1]. Jacob learned that there was grain in Egypt, i.e. food or corn, which is broken into pieces for eating; and accordingly, buying grain is called *shabar,* as we would say, *Wir wöllen gebrockt,* i.e. we shall go for food. But the body of Christ was not broken or divided on the cross. More has been said about this above. So, this text teaches emphatically that Christ's body is broken and divided at the table and bitten, chewed, and swallowed like other bread, though in the form of bread or in the bread.

Even if it could be proved that "breaking" meant Christ's suffering here, my friend, in what will the similarity consist, that in the Supper the bread may be the sign of Christ's body? For I have admitted above that they might make the broken bread into a simile in whatever way they could. But since they separate the breaking even from the bread and refer it to the body of Christ on the cross, tell me in what respect the bread bears a similarity to his body? In no other way than I have said above that the bread must be said to resemble Christ's body, whereas it really does not resemble the body in any respect, in the sense required by the words in the Supper.

Further, "This cup, the new testament, is in my blood." Now it may be that this text is precisely equivalent to saying, "This cup is a new testament," etc. And yet, Paul not without reason has placed the "is" after the words "new testament" and not before. The Holy Spirit wished to anticipate future sectarians. For St. Paul has both words share the position of subject, both "cup" and "testament," as it were, one subject; i.e. his text reads that this cup, which is a new testament, is such precisely in Christ's blood, and thus he expressly calls the cup the new testament. If the fanatics had this much of a text in their favor as we have here in ours, how proudly they would boast! Now, the new testament cannot be simply wine or a cup.

They would like to argue that "new testament" here should mean a sign or figure of the new testament. But to this it is abundantly and cogently answered that they assert it but do not prove it. On their assertion we place no value. For it never happens in Scripture that "new testament" means a sign of the new testament. If they say that the subject itself demands it, I ask:

What subject? "The cup," they say, "must be a material thing, such as silver, wood, gold, or glass. Now, silver surely can never be the new testament, but if it is any part of the same, then it is its sign; more it cannot be."

We have answered this above in commenting upon St. Luke. But since they are so stiff and stubborn, I shall use their sword-play too. Tell me, how can the cup be a sign of the new testament if it is ordinary silver or wood? Is it a sign of the new testament by virtue of its material, or its sound, or its form, or in what respect? Well, in that case every cup, whether in a chest or in a goldsmith's shop or wherever it may be, whether empty or full, is equally a sign of the new testament, for it too is made of silver or wood and has a sound and a form. Why did Christ need to designate this cup at the table for this purpose, as if no other cup in the world possessed these features of silver, sound, and form, i.e. a resemblance to the new testament? "No," they say, "but when that cup is set before you to drink, filled with wine, it then is a sign of the new testament."

Now let me point out two things. First: here they must fashion a new unity and substance out of cup and wine, even though they are two distinct natures. Then they must call this new substance "cup," although they mean not the cup alone but more accurately the wine in it, just as we have said above with respect to the flame and the angel. Now if they allow it to be said in their circles, "The cup is a sign," etc., though they mean not the cup alone but the wine, which has now become one with the cup, and if they cannot permit this unity or substance of the cup and the wine to be separated or the cup to be called a sign without the wine, then we beg them kindly to give the Holy Spirit permission to speak with us too concerning his own interests, so that he may call the cup a "testament," by virtue of the fact that it is now not only a cup but has become one sacramental object with the testament and blood of Christ. Otherwise, they should show us reasons and arguments why they have power to speak thus among themselves, while the Holy Spirit should not have it.

They mock us for calling the cup a new testament, and they separate the cup from the new testament and divide this sacramental unity or substance. We in turn mock their "sign," and separate cup and wine from each other and divide their sign-unity or substance as they divide our sacramental unity. For if the cup and the new testament are separated and each is to be kept distinct in its own peculiar nature, we would be well assured that a cup is nothing else than a cup or a silver object, fully as well as they are assured that if cup and wine are separated from each other, then the cup would not be a sign of the new testament but only an ordinary cup. Such a fallacy the logicians call arguing from a part to the whole in a negative proposition, i.e. from the lesser to the greater in a negative proposition, or from a particular to a universal—a fallacy quite common with the fanatics, as if I should say, "Peter has no ear, therefore Peter has no body," "Gold is not black, therefore gold has no color." But the fanatics do not even understand schoolboy logic.

In the second place, we would like to know how, or by means of what part, the cup along with the wine is supposed to be a sign of the blood of Christ or the new testament, or wherein this resemblance is supposed to consist, as we have already discussed. For the new testament is gospel, spirit, forgiveness of sins in and through the blood of Christ, and whatever else we may add, for it is all one entity, gathered together into one mass or substance, the whole in the blood, the whole in the cup. Where the one is, there the other is also. Whoever names or points to the one, deals with the whole. Now, how can ordinary wine "represent" or "signify" so important a thing, if all the figures of the Old Testament can scarcely signify it? In no other way than as I have said: with them the wine shall and must be called a sign, even though it cannot be such—but this is not the question. Are these not pitiable people, who not only lose the substance, i.e. the body and blood of Christ, in the Supper but also the sign or figure besides, and have nothing more left than peasants have in a common tavern, except that they comfort themselves with words that the figure is there, although they cannot tell in what the figure consists? Thus since they do not want the real kernel and meat, they deserve to lose even the shells and hulls, and while they try to assail and destroy our position, they lose their own and have nothing left.

We proved above in our comments on Luke that these words, "This cup is the new testament in my blood," cannot be a trope, because the expression "in my blood" has the same meaning as "through" or "with" my blood. For Christ's blood cannot be such an insignificant thing that it yields only a sign of the new testament, as the calves' blood did in Moses' time. Neither can "blood" be a trope, for the cup cannot by virtue of a sign of the blood, or ordinary wine, become so important a thing, viz. the new testament.

In summary,[260] if we collate the evangelists and Paul so that they speak as one man, we find that they tolerate no *"toutists,"* "tropists," or "representationists." If the tropists wish to appeal to Matthew and Mark, that "blood" should mean "sign of the blood," then Luke and Paul step forth and utterly overthrow the tropists. For they witness by their texts that blood cannot mean "sign of the blood" or be a trope, because the fanatics themselves have never made nor can they make a trope out of this text, "This cup is the new testament in my blood." Therefore, of course, in Matthew and Mark the very same blood cannot be regarded as a trope, because it is one and the same blood of which all four are speaking.

If they appeal to Luke and Paul, however, and make a trope out of the expression "new testament," i.e. "sign of the new testament," then Matthew and Mark step forth hand in hand with Luke and Paul and overthrow them again, showing that "new testament" cannot be a trope. The fanatics themselves have not made nor can they make a trope out of the words in Matthew and Mark, "new testament," any more than out of the words in Luke and Paul. It is not permissible for me to say in Matthew and Mark, "This is my blood of the figurative new testament," for Christ's blood is not the blood of the figurative testament or old testament, but of the new, which consists in his blood. Yet it must certainly be understood as the very same new testament in Luke and Paul as in Matthew and Mark, because of course all four are speaking of one and the same testament. Thus Matthew and Mark pre-

260 In the first edition of Luther's *Confession* the following two paragraphs were appended at the end, with a note directing their insertion here. Cf. *WA* 26, 477, n. 1; *CL* 3, 515 f.

serve the expression "new testament" in purity and simplicity, without any trope; Luke and Paul preserve the word "blood" in purity and simplicity, without any trope. Here, I am sure, the fanatics must be lying; if they can give you a proper answer to this challenge, you may cheerfully concede them the victory.

Therefore we must hold to the text as it reads. I hope this is irrefutably proved and our conscience is well assured that our interpretation is correct and that that of the fanatics is not only uncertain but actually false.

Where are these little fanatics now who boast passionately that Christ never performed a sign unless it were visibly or tangibly present? Was it not a sign when John saw the Holy Spirit come from heaven? [John 1:32]. Yet the Holy Spirit did not stand there visibly present, but in the form of a dove. Was it not a sign when Zechariah saw the angel Gabriel beside the altar of incense? [Luke 1:11]. Yet the angel did not stand there visibly present, but in the form of a flame of fire. Was it not a sign when God's Son walked on earth in person? Yet God's Son was not visibly present. What is the point of their building upon such empty, unsound arguments, by which the clear words and works of God are denied and blasphemed, except that they are obstinately determined to be lost?

Of course it is a miraculous sign that Christ's body and blood are present in the sacrament, yet they are not visibly there. It is enough for us, however, that we perceive through the Word and faith that he is there. Their "sign" also is not visibly present. For even though they may see the cup of wine visibly, they cannot *see* that it is a sign of the body and blood, but they must say so in words and believe it in their hearts. For it is not painted or depicted on the cup to show that it is a sign of the blood of Christ. What absurdity this is! but the fearful thing is that men will build upon it and defy the Word of God.

Where now are all the others who babble that there is no forgiveness of sins in the Supper? St. Paul and Luke say that the new testament is in the Supper, and not the sign or figure of the new testament. Figures or signs of the new testament belonged to the old testament, among the Jews. He who admits that he has the figure or sign of the new testament admits that he does not yet have the new testament; he has taken a backward step and denied Christ and has become a Jew. Christians ought to have the new testament itself, without figure or sign. They may have it hidden under an alien form, but they must have it truly present. Now if the new testament is present in the Supper, then forgiveness of sins, Spirit, grace, life and salvation must be there. All these are embraced in the Word. For who would know what was in the Supper if the words did not proclaim it?

See, then, what a beautiful, great, marvelous thing this is, how everything meshes together in one sacramental reality. The words are the first thing, for without the words the cup and the bread would be nothing. Further, without bread and cup, the body and blood of Christ would not be there. Without the body and blood of Christ, the new testament would not be there. Without the new testament, forgiveness of sins would not be there. Without forgiveness of sins, life and salvation would not be there. Thus the words first connect the bread and cup to the sacrament; bread and cup embrace the body and blood of Christ; body and blood of Christ embrace the new testament; the new testament embraces the forgiveness of sins; forgiveness of sins embraces eternal life and salvation. See, all this the words of the Supper offer and give us, and we embrace it by faith. Ought not the devil, then, hate such a Supper and rouse fanatics against it?

Now since all this constitutes one sacramental reality, one can truly and properly say of each part, as for example the cup, "This is Christ's blood; this is the new testament; there is forgiveness of sins; there is life and salvation"; just as I point to the man Christ and say, "This is God; this is the truth, the life, salvation, wisdom," etc. Let this suffice for now on this subject. We must hear Paul further.

"As often as you eat this bread and drink the cup, you proclaim the Lord's death until he comes" [I Cor. 11:26]. Observe once more that the cup cannot be understood here as ordinary silver or wood—for who can drink silver or wood?—but since the cup has become one object with the drink, the drink here is also called the cup. Thus you see that this mode of speech is common to all languages. Immediately after this he also says, "Let him eat of this bread and drink of this cup" [11:28]. Who can drink of the cup, i.e. of silver or wood? But as we have said, all languages speak in this way; where two things become one object, this one object retains both names, as the Holy Spirit is the dove and the dove is the Holy Spirit.

Here the fanatics raise a victory shout, "There, there, you hear that St. Paul names the bread and the cup, and does not say, 'As often as you eat the body of Christ and drink the blood of Christ,'" etc. My friend, let us also exclaim: St. Paul does not say, "As often as you drink the wine," but "the cup." Why then do they drink wine and not the cup? Must it not follow that they should swallow the cup if Paul speaks of drinking the cup? But they interpret it as the wine in the cup, because the cup and the wine have become one object. My friend, why then must it follow that we eat mere bread when Paul speaks of eating bread, and why may not the body in the bread also be understood, by virtue of the sacramental union? May the poor flesh-eaters not have such an interpretation, but only the lordly fanatics?

Again I exclaim: St. Paul does not say, "As often as you eat the sign of the body and drink the sign of the blood," etc., therefore bread cannot be a sign of the body, nor wine a sign of the blood. Isn't this wonderful? If this text does not deny the fanatics their "sign," my friend, why should it deny us the assertion that body and blood are present? He mentions "sign" here as little as "body and blood." Therefore he must be as strongly opposed to them as to us, and if he does not strike them, neither does he strike us, however adequate it may be elsewhere to claim, "Paul does not say so here, therefore it is not so!" This is called "syllogizing from pure negatives." What kind of argument this is, especially for establishing articles of faith, even children know quite well.

This, however, is true: according to the Silesian spirit's[261] rule, they are right and I must concede them the victory. For this rule reads that one must put the texts out of sight and simply disregard it when Christ's body and blood are said to be present in the Supper, for they hinder the spirit and a spiritual interpretation.

---

261 Schwenkfeld, cf. pp. 290 f., above.

The second rule is that one should turn his eyes somewhere else where these texts do not stand, and then cry, "See, see, it does not say here that body and blood are present in the Supper!" These rules they follow in this passage, too. For what St. Paul said immediately before this: "This is my body," and "the new testament in my blood"—this is nothing. So they act as if this text were recorded nowhere in the world, and they disregard it. On the other hand, here where the text does not stand, they stare and gape and spread their nostrils and hunt for such a text, just as if St. Paul were obliged in every passage and in every line to write no other words than these: "This is my body," etc., in order that they may see them. But since the purpose of all their exertion is to hunt for this text, "This is my body," etc., at some place where it is not to be found, why don't they look for it also in Morolf or in Dietrich of Bern,[262] where they could be sure not to find it? They must be either rascals or raving maniacs who seek and call for a thing where it is not, and refuse to see it where it is and where it is placed directly under their noses.

However, even though St. Paul had placed this text immediately before, he does not forget it in this passage also, for he speaks not of ordinary bread and cups but says, "*This* bread; *this* cup," undoubtedly referring with the word "this" back to the bread and cup which he had just mentioned. Now if the fanatics would just trace back these two demonstrative pronouns and see to what bread and cup they referred, they would easily discover that this bread is the body of Christ, and this cup is the new testament, for he is certainly speaking of the same bread and cup when he says "this," as even children and fools readily observe.

But the fanatics skip over these words, "this bread and this cup." Indeed, they are following their rule and putting them out of sight, and staring only at the words "bread" and "cup"; yet they are unwilling to have the word "cup" so lightly overlooked as they overlook our word "this." If they exclaim, "St. Paul does not say here, 'As often as you eat the body of Christ,'" etc., you should reply, "Yes, but he does, right here!" "Where? In what text?"

[262] Luther frequently refers to the medieval legends of Solomon and Morolf (Marcolph) and of Dietrich of Bern. Dietrich was another name for Theodoric. *WA* 26, 480, n. 2. Cf. *Large Catechism*, Preface, 11.

Say then, "By the word 'this.' Look at the passage and you will find in it this text: 'This is my body; this is the new testament in my blood.' The word 'this' repeats that text and places it under your nose; but it cannot place it before your eyes, for you turn them away in some other direction."

How seriously this spirit means such questions and boasts, however, you may judge by the fact that above, where we have the clear words, "This is my body; this is my blood," they can discover a little gloss and say, "This is a sign of my body, and a sign of my blood." If Paul had recorded the text in this way, "As often as you eat the body of the Lord and drink his blood," etc., how bitter it would have been to them! They would have done the same thing here also, declaring that it must mean, "As often as you eat the sign of the body and blood," etc. This spirit thinks that his knavery is not understood. My friend, anyone who can gloss this text, "This is my body," which cannot possibly be expressed in more lucid, unambiguous terms, will surely be much more capable of glossing this text, "As often as you eat the Lord's body," which is not so lucid as the other. This spirit, however, must paint and disguise himself to give the impression that he would believe it if Paul had said, "As often as you eat the Lord's body"; as if this would prevent us from seeing how his arrogance despises the text which reads distinctly that we should eat the Lord's body, viz., "Take, eat, this is my body." My friend, let them produce a clear text which they cannot gloss. This I would like to hear! As soon as the word "body" appears, immediately the gloss "sign of the body" can be there. It is a shame, though, to be so silly in these matters. But the fanatics feel no shame at all. Well, its benefits us the most, for we become ever more certain of our interpretation, while they perform their antics so frivolously and childishly against it.

The text continues: *"Whoever, therefore, eats this bread unworthily or drinks the cup of the Lord unworthily will be guilty of profaning the body and blood of the Lord"* [I Cor. 11:27].

Here again stand "bread" and "cup" before the fanatics. Suppose they should construe them to mean mere bread and cup, i.e. wine, and then demand why Paul does not say, "Whoever eats the body of Christ unworthily," etc. The fact that Paul says "this bread," and deliberately refers back to the bread of which he had spoken above—this must not be observed but put out of sight, in order not to hinder their spiritual interpretation! No other thought must be entertained but that Paul said not "*this* bread" but merely "bread," as if his text here read, "Whoever eats bread unworthily," etc., then the truth will surely be discovered! But praise be to God, we see that with the word "this" Paul is constantly repeating and introducing this text, "This is my body," as we said above. Moreover, this is still more clearly confirmed when he says, "Whoever eats this unworthily, let him be guilty of profaning"—not mere bread or the sign of the body of Christ, but—"the body of the Lord."

My friend, let us dispute a little here in their manner. Why doesn't St. Paul say, "He is guilty of profaning the bread, or the sign of the body of Christ, who eats this bread unworthily"? For the text with all possible force insists that this sin is the unworthy eating. And yet they argue that it is mere bread which they are eating. Thus, indeed, according to the nature of words and language, he must be guilty of profaning what he eats. For Paul does not say, "Whoever remembers Christ's suffering unworthily is guilty of profaning the body of the Lord." If they can attack us with such questions as: "Why didn't Paul say, 'Whoever eats Christ's body unworthily,' etc.?" and then claim to have established that Christ's body is not present and unless we prove it, they in turn should answer our question why St. Paul does not say, "Whoever remembers Christ's suffering unworthily, or eats the sign of his body unworthily," etc. Unless they show why Paul does not say this, then by rights they will have lost their gloss, according to the norm and law which they wish to apply to us.

I know full well, however, that they themselves do not believe these glosses, but because they insist that nothing but bread is present, they think that some comment or gloss must be given. If they did not insist on this, they themselves would spit on such a gloss. Indeed, they see Karlstadt's glosses perfectly well, and must admit that they are pure fantasy. For St. Paul reproves the Corinthians not for their unworthy remembrance of the suffering of

Christ, as a child can easily read and prove. He describes in express words what the sin of the Corinthians was [I Cor. 11:20 ff.]: they did not wait for one another, but whoever came early ate early, so that those who came later found nothing and were humiliated, and thus they made a mere feast out of the Supper as if it were nothing but an ordinary meal. This is what he says: "When you meet together, it is not the Lord's Supper that you eat. For each one goes ahead with his own meal." Do you hear this? They did not celebrate the Supper of the Lord but an indulgence of their belly. While others were late in coming, they went ahead, allowed the Lord's Supper to be neglected, and ate their meal, just as Paul says afterward, "When you come together to eat, wait for one another, lest you come together to be condemned" [11:33]. You see then that the sin consisted in the eating.

Therefore, Oecolampadius produces what he thinks is a better gloss, saying, "The Corinthians by their unworthy eating sinned against the sacrament, i.e. the bread and wine, which are signs of the body and blood of Christ. Just as one who dishonors the picture of the emperor dishonors the emperor himself, so whoever eats this bread and wine unworthily, dishonors the body and blood of Christ, whose picture or sign they are." Thus they disagree among themselves over the gloss, just as they do over the text, yet both say the one Holy Spirit teaches this. In particular, the gloss of Oecolampadius is rubbish. First, because we have proved in our claim above that bread and wine are not and cannot be signs or pictures or images of the body and blood of Christ, for no aspect can be pointed out in which such a resemblance may consist. Therefore, this example of the emperor's picture is not valid as an explanation either, until it is made clear how bread and wine are pictures or similes of the body and blood of Christ, as the emperor's picture resembles him.

In the second place, even if this simile were valid here, it would indeed be a fine idea as a gloss, but by no means certain. For who cannot make glosses and then abandon them, saying, "I *was* here." [263] No, since they intend to interpret the text differ-

[263] Possibly an allusion to the legendary prankster, Till Eulenspiegel, who scrawled at the scene of a prank his monogram (owl and mirror) and the words "(Eulenspiegel) was here!" *WA* 26, 483, n. 1.

ently from the natural meaning of the words and overthrow our interpretation, they must not set forth such poor, naked, hungry, thirsty glosses and then discard and forsake them. They must irrefutably prove that these comments are correct and are necessarily appropriate here. Now, Oecolampadius does not for a moment intend to do this, but thinks his bare comment is enough. But what becomes of my conscience, which would like to have a good, sure foundation? Is it supposed to stand on the hungry, thirsty, needy gloss? Oh, but how much does this spirit care what becomes of men's consciences?

In the third place, this gloss, besides being uncertain, can have no plausibility either until it is established and proved that nothing but bread and wine are present in the Supper. For if the real body and blood of Christ are in the Supper, this poor, contemptible gloss lies in ashes. Up to now they have not proved nor can they prove that nothing but bread and wine are present, any more than they have proved or can prove that a sign of the body or sign of the blood is present, even if they could prove that nothing but bread and wine were present. They neither have proved nor can prove either of the two, but we have proved convincingly that as the words read, Christ's body and blood are present. Therefore, if they had first securely established the text in the Supper according to their interpretation, we might in some measure tolerate these glosses at this point for the sake of good fellowship, for intrinsically they are worthless, as we shall hear.

In the fourth place, and the very best of all, Oecolampadius does not regard "body and blood" in this passage as a trope but literally: "He is guilty of profaning the body and blood of the Lord." What is the result? Just this: If body and blood in this passage are to be understood literally, not as a trope, neither can they be a trope in the text of the Supper. For it can in no way be acknowledged that Paul, on the same subject or matter and in the same expression, uses a single word first in one way and then in another, like a double-tongued and crafty deceiver. He must treat "body and blood" simply and precisely in the same way in both places. If "body" in the Supper means "sign of the body" and "blood" means "sign of the blood," they must mean sign of the body and sign of the blood here too. If they mean real body and blood here, they must also mean real body and blood in the Supper, for in both passages he is speaking about the same Supper, hence he must also be speaking about the same body and blood. For there he teaches and institutes it, here he admonishes us to the proper use of it.

Where is this hungry, thirsty gloss now: "Whoever eats unworthily is guilty of profaning the body of the Lord, i.e. whoever ridicules the king's picture derides the king himself"? If "body" is "sign of the body," the gloss must twist itself this way: "Whoever eats this bread unworthily is guilty of profaning the sign of the body, i.e. the bread." For "body" here too must mean sign of the body, or bread; if not, both text and glosses, along with the fanatics and all, lie in a heap in the ditch. See, then, how much toil, danger, and misfortune is his lot who tries to make lies into the truth and lead them to market in opposition to the truth.

If the fanatics are to maintain their position, they have three great tasks to perform: first, to prove in the Supper how body and blood are signs of the body and blood, or mere bread and wine. Second, to prove how such ordinary bread and wine are a sign of the body and sign of the blood. When they have done this—on the devil's ascension day!—they must put forth an effort just as great and even greater, to prove in this passage that body and blood are *not* signs of the body and blood. For they must prove that at one and the same time and in the same expression, blood is not blood and body not body, and yet, on the contrary, that the same blood *is* blood and the same body *is* body, in reality and in name. This will require a great deal of ingenuity, i.e. to make contradictories simultaneously true.

In the fifth place, even if everything else were in order, lacking nothing, still this gloss is inherently unsatisfactory. Paul does not say, "Whoever eats this bread unworthily is guilty of profaning Christ," in Oecolampadius' sense, as one is guilty of dishonoring the king if he jeers at the king's picture. But Paul indicates that the guilt is committed against the members of Christ, of which the bread and wine are analogies or signs; the body and blood, says Paul, are what one is guilty of profaning. Accordingly, Oecolampadius would have to fashion his gloss and illustration in some such way as this: "Whoever dishonors the nose of the picture, dishonors the king's nose; whoever mocks the picture's mouth, mocks the king's own mouth. Thus the dishonor done to the picture affects not the person but the members which are dishonored in the picture. For Paul refers here not to the person of Christ but to the body and blood of Christ, as members of the person."

This I mention in order that you may see that Oecolampadius does not fashion his gloss and illustration properly, and does not bring them into accord with St. Paul's text. If they were to accord, St. Paul would have to say, as we have observed, "Whoever eats this bread is guilty of profaning Christ," just as he is guilty of dishonoring the king who dishonors the king's picture, i.e. he sins not against a member or part of the person but against the majesty and rule of the king—for this is what is meant by such expressions. But here St. Paul says that the sin is against the members of the person, viz. the body and blood of Christ, which is a more intimate and serious offense than against the majesty or rule of Christ. Therefore this gloss is inherently rubbish, because it speaks of the majesty and rule of Christ, where the text speaks of members or parts of the person.

Paul proceeds, "*Let a man examine himself, and so eat of the bread and drink of the cup*" [I Cor. 11:28].

Here again we meet "bread and cup." Thus Paul uses the one for the other. Now he calls them "bread and cup"; then again "body and blood"; then again "bread and cup," and again for the third time, "body and blood," in order to assure us that this sacrament is not mere bread and wine but also the body and blood of Christ. But the fanatics insist on turning away their eyes whenever St. Paul calls them "body and blood," and paying attention only when he calls them "bread and cup," or they insist on turning "body and blood" into glosses and tropes, but not "bread and cup." Thus they play with the text and treat it any way they please.

Especially does this passage strongly favor them, for St. Paul does not say, "And so eat of *this* bread," but simply "of the bread" and "of the cup," not "of *this* cup." Well, we give them the choice whether they will permit St. Paul to speak here of a different bread and cup, or of the same. If he speaks of a different bread and cup, he does not impugn us and we may allow our adversaries to consider them nothing but bread and wine; it does not help them at all, for we are speaking of the bread in the Supper. But if he speaks of the same bread and cup—and there is no doubt about it —we have heard sufficiently what this same cup and bread are in the preceding text. What was said there is relevant here also.

Finally, *"Any one who eats and drinks unworthily, eats and drinks judgment upon himself, as one who does not discern the body of the Lord"* [I Cor. 11:29].

As for Karlstadt's view of "discerning," I have written enough in the treatise against the heavenly prophets.[264] It cannot refer to remembrance of the passion, as Karlstadt's spirit pretends, because the text proves irrefutably that "eating unworthily" and "not discerning the body of Christ" are the same thing, as we understand from the word just as it reads literally, that the Corinthians ate the bread with the misconception and misunderstanding that it was ordinary bread, and discerned no difference between this bread and other bread. This certainly is what is meant by "unworthily eating the body of Christ." This is why Paul admonishes them to examine themselves and perceive who they are and how they regard this bread. If they do not regard it as the body of Christ, or treat it as if it were not the body of Christ, then they do not discern the body of Christ; and this offense will not go unpunished. We know quite well how St. Paul uses the word *diakrinein* for "discern," as in I Corinthians 4 [:7], "Who has *discerned* you?" i.e. who has made you different from others, as if you were something different from or better than the others? And Romans 14 [:23], "He who *discerns* is condemned," i.e. he who considers this to be sin and that to be right, and yet acts contrary to his understanding. And so forth; St. Paul says *diakrinein* where we would say: make a distinction, discern, regard this different from that, etc.

But Oecolampadius makes a better showing, because he relates this discerning to the honor which comes to the king by virtue of the honoring of his picture, as we have seen above in connection with the other verse. But the same defect appears here as there,

[264] *LW* 40, 185 ff.

and everything that I said against him in that verse must also be said against him here. Since we have the simple and literal text and they wish to take it away from us and interpret it differently, it is not enough for them to utter a mere naked gloss and therewith bid us adieu and good night! They must prove it with Scripture and reasons that this gloss is necessarily correct at this point. This he does not and cannot do. Who will believe that "not discerning Christ's body" is nothing more than to dishonor Christ in his sign? Neither has it yet been proved that in the Supper nothing but bread and the sign of the body are present, which is the basis on which this tottering gloss stands.

Besides this, he must take "the Lord's body" here also to mean not the real body of Christ but the sign of his body. For St. Paul cannot be speaking here of any other body than that of which he says, "This is my body." Certainly he is still speaking of the Supper in the same connection, so he must also be speaking in the same words. Now if "body" is not "sign of the body" here, why is it "sign of the body" there? If it is "body" here, why is it not also "body" there? Therefore this gloss must fall to pieces along with their text and all, or else it must be rendered, "who does not discern the sign of the Lord's body." So this argument collapses too, and Paul still stands firmly on our side, for we find his words simply, harmoniously, and unexceptionably consistent with our interpretation, and we have no need at all of glosses or efforts to interpret them differently from what they say.

Now let us also examine the text of St. Paul in the tenth chapter, where he says, "The cup of blessing which we bless, is it not a participation in the blood of Christ? The bread which we break, is it not a participation in the body of Christ?" [I Cor. 10:16]. This text I have extolled, and I do so still, as my heart's joy and crown, for it not only says, "This is Christ's body," as it reads in the Supper, but mentions the bread which was so broken, saying, "The bread is Christ's body," indeed, "The bread which we break is not only the body of Christ but the distributed body of Christ." Here, now, is a text so lucid and clear that the fanatics and the whole world could not desire or demand anything more. Yet it does not help! To this text they give me no further answer than a demonstration of their disunity among themselves. Some say that Paul speaks of representative or figurative participation; some of spiritual participation, bringing in what immediately follows concerning partnership in the altar and partnership with devils [I Cor. 10:18 ff.]. With this they slink away and ignore us as if they have proved it or deduced it from the texts. So I am supposed to be satisfied with their bare words and glosses. They act exactly like a person who, just as I was about to greet him, would turn around and thunder with his backside and then walk away. Well, they will not run off so insolently and leave their stench behind them, if it be God's will!

In the first place, there is no doubt that St. Paul here too is speaking of the Supper, because he speaks of bread, cup, and body and blood of Christ. He must certainly be speaking of the same body and blood, bread and cup, of which the Supper speaks. If not, then this text is irrelevant to our discussion, and whoever wishes may regard it as referring merely to ordinary eating. Hence it follows that according to Oecolampadius' method, this text then must read, "The bread which we break is a participation in bread, which is a sign of the body of Christ. The cup of blessing which we bless is a participation in wine, which is a sign of the blood of Christ." Isn't this a marvelous text? Bread is a participation in bread, cup is a participation in wine! Does this differ at all from saying that the broken bread is a participation or sharing of bread, i.e. the broken bread is a commonly shared bread? Can Paul teach us nothing more here than that distributed bread is distributed bread? Or was he concerned that we might mistake distributed bread for distributed sausages and distributed wine for distributed water? These are actually their own words, that "body" should mean the sign of body, i.e. bread, and "blood" the sign of blood, i.e. wine, as we have heard sufficiently, since all their books are smeared full of such things.

But if the trope is alleged to depend on the word "participation," and to mean a sign of the participation or a figurative participation by which the spiritual participation is represented, then according to this backward-referring and awkward trope Oecolampadius' text must read, "The bread which we break is a figurative participation in the figurative body of Christ, which is bread." My friend, what in the world does this mean: "Bread is a figurative participation in bread"? But this is what they must say if their tropes are to stand. Is one loaf of bread to be a sign or figure of another, as it is distributed and shared? Yet both loaves must be by nature and shape bread, the first because it is broken, the second because it is a sign of the body of Christ.

Since this spirit can do everything, I think he regards the first bread, which is broken, as a bread painted on paper or carved out of wood, which may well be a figure and sign of the other true bread, which represents Christ's body, so that the text would read, "The wooden broken body is a figurative participation in the true bread which is a sign of the body of Christ." All this is necessarily implied by their tropes. Otherwise, it must read thus: "The broken bread, which cannot be a figurative participation in the bread, is nevertheless a figurative participation in the bread." For it is surely impossible for one loaf of bread to be a figurative participation in another loaf.

We have already proved that such a backward-referring and awkward trope cannot exist in Scripture or in any language but is a pure fiction. According to the nature of Scripture and all languages, if the word "*participation*" [or "communion" or "fellowship"][265] is to become a trope, it must point forward to a spiritual participation, or a new and different participation, beyond the old, physical participation, just as "body and blood' must mean a spiritual or different body and blood if they become a trope or if they should not mean the physical blood and body. In this passage, therefore, "participation" must mean simply a physical participation or distribution; or if it is a trope, it must mean a new, spiritual participation, in which case the text would have to read, "The bread which we break is a spiritual participation of the body of Christ." But if "body" here is to be a real trope, it must mean the spiritual body of Christ, which is the church. In brief, the text would read thus: "The bread which we break is a spiritual

[265] All three English words are needed to render *gemeinschafft* or *koinōnia*. "Partaking" also is used in the context of food; cf. I Cor. 10:17, etc. In addition the word "partnership" appears in I Cor. 10:18 ff.; see pp. 355 ff.

distribution of the Christian Church,"[266] with the signification, "Wherever this bread is broken, there the Christian Church is distributed," and then horrors far more horrible would follow.

Let them choose here which alternative they prefer. If "body and blood" in this passage are a trope or "sign of the body and sign of the blood," viz. bread and wine, as their doctrine maintains, they would find it impossible to avert all these horrible consequences to which I have just alluded, as everyone must realize and no one can deny, especially if they are determined to regard "participation" as figurative. If they are not a trope, however, but the true body and blood of Christ, as our doctrine maintains, neither can they be a trope in other passages referring to the Supper. For no one can deny that St. Paul here speaks of the Supper and designates and means the very same blood and body that Matthew, Mark, Luke, and Paul himself in other chapters name and mean when they say, "This is my body, this is my blood." What can they complain against this?

Now their choice will have to be that "blood and body" here are a trope. Their doctrine maintains it because these words refer to the sacrament, and in the sacrament there must be "sacramental or figurative words," as Oecolampadius teaches. Well, then they must draw this consequence, that "the bread is a figurative participation in the bread," i.e. it is a painted bread, or something which it cannot be, as we have seen. For Oecolampadius admits that the word "is" does not mean "represents." Therefore he must admit that the bread is a figurative participation in the bread; and he cannot say that the broken bread is a spiritual participation, for in his view a physical object cannot be in reality or in name a spiritual object.

If, however, he chooses to relate the trope to the word "participation" alone and have his text read thus: "The bread which we break is a sign of the participation in the body of Christ," and if he could prove this, his view would be quite sound; but then the word "body" would not be a trope. But if "body" here is no trope, neither could it be a trope in Matthew, Mark and Luke when they say, "This is my body," because it is the same Supper

[266] *Christenheit.*

and the same body of which they are speaking. Thus, whichever way this spirit turns, he stumbles so badly that he will totter and fall. My advice is that they should say, "The external Word of God is of no avail; we have enough in the internal testimony of the spirit"; they should deride St. Paul's words as "ten poor, miserable letters." Thereafter "body and blood" would have to be a trope or not a trope according to their will. Otherwise I cannot imagine how they can evade Paul here. But they would also have to think that all the world is bound to believe their testimony and their spirit, as if they had won the victory.

All that has been said against Oecolampadius' text applies also against Zwingli's text. For where Oecolampadius fashions a sign, Zwingli constructs a representation; both have the same meaning, though the words are different. Oecolampadius has "figure of the body," Zwingli has "signifying or symbolic body"; these are one and the same thing. Therefore, Zwingli's text must read, "The bread which we break is a participation in the symbolic body of Christ, i.e. of the bread," just like Oecolampadius. However, if he could construe his text so: "The bread which we break represent or signifies a participation in the body of Christ," it would then admirably support his view. However, the text of Matthew, Mark, and Luke would not permit his saying, "This represents or signifies my body." If he has a symbolic body there, he must also allow it to be a symbolic body here, for it is one and the same body, as we have said. Now all the same consequences must follow from assuming a symbolic body as Oecolampadius would deduce from his "significative body," as everyone can easily see for himself; therefore it is not necessary to repeat everything again.

The Silesian fanatic, with his perversion, must also come under consideration. He transposes the text of Matthew, Mark, and Luke thus: "My body is this, viz. a spiritual food," for "this" is supposed to indicate the spirit. Then it must be so here also, and this text, "The cup of blessing which we bless," etc., must also be transposed: "The participation in the body of Christ is the cup of blessing which we bless, viz. a spiritual cup of blessing." Now, this participation is a spiritual thing, yet there must be a material cup of wine here and it must be so designated. Indeed, the material cup must at the same time be a spiritual cup also; in other words, simultaneously spiritual and not spiritual, material and not material! For Paul is speaking of the material cup, but this spirit makes one and the same cup spiritual and not material. Is this not a noble, mighty spiritualizing? Let them go with their foolish antics!

Our text and interpretation stand forth excellently and lucidly, brightly and clearly. "The bread which we break is the participation in the body of Christ." Here you must observe, to begin with, that Paul is speaking of the material bread which we break in the Supper; this no one can well deny. Next, it is also quite certain that at this physical breaking of bread, or Supper, there must be present not only pure saints and worthy recipients but also unworthy ones, such as Judas and others. So, you have heard that "is" neither can nor may mean "represents" in any language on earth, but refers to the substance wherever it stands. Finally, "participation" here means the common possession in which they all participate and share, viz. something which has been given to them all in common. Such a possession may be received in two ways, materially or physically, and spiritually. For a common possession is something which many enjoy in common, such as a common well, common street, common field, meadow, wood, fire, etc. It cannot in this passage mean the fellowship of faith in the heart, for the text speaks here of a common possession which one may receive and enjoy, such as the bread and cup. He says, "The bread which we break, the cup which we bless," and then [10:17], "We all are one body, for we all partake of the same loaf and the same cup." [267] So it is now evident that *koinōnia*, "participation in the body of Christ," is nothing else than the body of Christ as a common possession, distributed among many for them to partake.

Now Paul speaks thus: "The bread which we break is a participation[268] in the body of Christ," i.e. whoever partakes of this broken bread, partakes of the body of Christ as a common possession distributed among many; for the bread is this common body of Christ, says Paul. This is stated in clear and

[267] "And the same cup" does not appear in the best New Testament manuscripts.

[268] *Gemeinschafft.*

distinct terms, which no one can understand differently without altering the words. Now the partakers of this broken bread are not only the worthy, but also Judas and the unworthy, for the breaking of bread takes place among the good and the evil. It is not possible that the latter partake of it spiritually, for they have neither spirit nor faith. Again, Christ has no more than one body.

Thus, if the unworthy partake of it and have it in common among them, it must be physical and not spiritual, since all partaking must be either physical or spiritual. Figurative or symbolic or "representative" partaking cannot take place in the Supper, because there is no representation or symbolization. Therefore the true, real body of Christ must of necessity be physically present in the bread which we break, and the unworthy may partake of it physically, because they cannot partake of it spiritually; as this saying of Paul reads, "The bread which we break is a participation," i.e. the common body of Christ divided among those who receive the broken bread.

Here again the fanatical spirit disputes over the word "participation," wishing to regard it as a spiritual participation among the godly alone, which is to be represented by the breaking of bread, as by a figurative participation. They want Paul's text to have its nose twisted into this shape: "The bread which we break is a sign of the participation in the body of Christ," according to Oecolampadius; or this: "The bread which we break represents a participation in the body of Christ," according to Zwingli. This they prove, first, by the argument, "It seems right to us!" Their own imagination is the strongest argument they have in the whole dispute, except they baptize it and call it Scripture and Creed.

Next, they cite the passage which Paul places after this text, "Because there is one loaf, we who are many are one body, for we all partake of the same loaf" [I Cor. 10:17]. Here some of them once more make a new trope, saying that bread here means a spiritual bread, viz. the body of Christ, and that body is also a trope, viz. the saints alone who partake spiritually of the spiritual bread. And they attack me thus: "Because we are all one body of Christ, the unworthy cannot be in this body, but only the true members; therefore this participation in the body must be of a spiritual kind."

What am I to do with these erring spirits? One moment they make "bread" and "participation" figurative. Then, on the contrary, others make "bread" and "participation" spiritual. They run counter to each other as if they were insane, and no one is certain of his course. We know that St. Paul does not say here, "We who are many are one body of Christ," but simply, "We who are many are one body," i.e. a group, a community, just as every city is a particular body or society in distinction from another city. From this it does not follow that all members of this body are holy, spiritual members and so have only a spiritual fellowship, but it is a physical group or body in which are both holy and unholy people who together partake of the one bread.

Nor can the bread here be spiritual bread. For Paul certainly speaks of the same bread of which he had said before, "The bread which we break." This bread is one and the same bread; therefore it also forms a particular group or body out of those who partake of it. Not a body of Christ, but simply a body; for there is a very great difference between "body" and "Christ's body." Here "body" is a true trope in the scriptural sense: not a figurative body, like the backward-looking trope, but a second, new body, to which a natural body bears a similarity. Such a trope the text demands when it says, "We are one body." Now of course we are not one natural body. This is the way the fanatics ought to construct their tropes also and prove them when they claim that Christ's body and blood are signs of the body and blood.

In summary, St. Paul in this whole passage speaks not of spiritual or figurative, but only of a physical participation or of a common material object which is distributed. This you can see in all the expressions and illustrations which he employs. First, in this: "Because there is one loaf, we who are many are one body, for we all partake of the same loaf" [I Cor. 10:17]. In order that you should understand the participation in a physical sense, he says, "There is one loaf," viz. the bread of which he spoke in the text, "The bread which we break" [I Cor. 10:16], of which we all partake. Now if the broken bread cannot be spiritual bread, so also its distribution or breaking or partaking cannot be spiritual.

The other text: "Consider Israel according to the flesh, are not those who eat the sacrifices partners in the altar?" [I Cor.

10:18]. Here there is certainly no spiritual or figurative partnership. For "to eat the sacrifices" is to eat physically what is on the altar, to be a physical partaker of the altar; moreover, the altar with its sacrifice is certainly one material object, physically shared in common and distributed among those who eat the sacrifices. So our bread also is a bodily participation divided among us. But if the bread is broken, distributed, and received by us in common, so also is the body of Christ physically broken, distributed, and received by us in common, for the broken bread is the common or distributed body of Christ. As Paul says, "The bread which we break is a participation in, or partaking of, the body of Christ" [I Cor. 10:16].

"Yes," they exclaim, "but St. Paul speaks afterward of partnership with demons: 'I do not want you to be partners with demons' [10:20 ff.]. Here there must certainly be a spiritual partnership; for demons have no bodies, therefore the participation in the body of Christ mentioned above may be spiritual too." I reply: It appears to me that the word "participation" or "communion" causes them to err, because they do not understand it aright. It is, of course, true that it is not so idiomatic an expression as I would have liked, for "to have communion or fellowship" is generally understood as having some relationship with another person. But here, as I have explained above, it must mean the same as if many persons share or eat or partake of one common thing. This idea I must translate "communion" or "fellowship" or "participation"; I have been able to find no better word for it.[269]

Well, even if demons have no body, indeed, even if this saying speaks of spiritual partnership, how does it follow that the preceding passage must also be understood as a spiritual participation in the body of Christ? Is it enough simply that one says so? But Paul speaks here of a bodily partnership with demons, as is proved by the words which precede and follow. Just before, he says, "What pagans sacrifice, they offer to demons" [I Cor. 10:20]. You perceive that he speaks of sacrifices to idols, and calls them demon-offerings, and he treats the subject of eating the sacrifices to idols. Whoever eats the sacrifice of demons is in partner-

[269] See Luther's discussion of *gemeinschafft* and *gemeine* (*Gemeinde*) in the *Large Catechism*, Creed, Art. 3, 49 ff. Cf. p. 350, n. 265, above.

ship or communion with the devil. This is certainly a bodily partnership, for it is a devil's sacrifice, a material sacrifice of which many persons partake and eat, and thus they are physically in a bodily partnership with the devil, i.e. with the devil's sacrifice, which is offered to the devil. Just as we might say that both the worthy and the unworthy among us are in communion with God when we physically receive the body of Christ, for we share and partake physically of the body of Christ, which is a divine sacrifice offered to God.

This view is demanded also by the following words: "You cannot drink the cup of the Lord and the cup of the devil at the same time" [I Cor. 10:21]. You perceive why he says that he does not wish us to be in partnership with the devil, viz. that we should not drink the cup of the devil. So the cup of the devil is certainly a material thing. Hence "to drink the cup of the devil" must mean bodily partnership with the devil, just as "to drink the cup of the Lord" means to have bodily partnership with the Lord, or God, i.e. to partake of something which belongs to the Lord, or God, or is offered to God. Now the cup of the Lord is not only a cup but a participation in the blood of Christ, of which we who are many partake.

Paul says further, "You cannot partake of the table of the Lord and the table of the devil at the same time" [I Cor. 10:21]. Is it not sufficiently clear that the devil's table is a material thing? Then certainly the partnership or participation in it is also bodily, just as the Lord's table must be material and its partnership bodily. For we must not be so crude as to understand the partnership with the devil in this passage as if one eats or partakes of the devil himself without any external, physical means. Here both the table and the cup are designated, but one partakes of the thing or object which is the devil's or belongs to the devil. Similarly, one speaks of God's or the Lord's communion or partnership when one partakes of the object or thing which is God's or the Lord's, or belongs to him, as the text clearly expresses it, "You cannot partake of the table of the Lord and the table of the devil at the same time. I do not want you to be partners with the devil" [I Cor. 10:20 f.].

I am using two quite different expressions if I say "the devil's partnership" and "participation in the devil's table," yet both have the same meaning, since it is the same object. "Participation in the devil's table" points to the object or thing in which the partnership consists, but "partnership with the devil" indicates the being to whom this thing or object pertains or belongs, in which the partnership consists. So also, "participation in the Lord's table" is a different expression from "partnership with the Lord." "Participation in the Lord's table" points to the thing or object in which the partnership consists, but "partnership with the Lord" indicates the person to whom this object, in which the partnership consists, belongs.

Similarly, in [I Corinthians] 11 Paul uses two similar expressions in connection with the Supper. At one time he speaks simply of eating the bread, "As often as you eat this bread," and again, "And so let him eat of the bread" [11:26, 28]. But afterward he says, "Whoever eats the bread of the Lord," etc. [11:27]. The first expression designates what it is that is eaten; the second, whose it is and to whom that which is eaten belongs. So this expression, "participation in the body of Christ," indicates simply what it is in which the participation consists, viz. the body of Christ, and not whose this object or thing is, for it belongs to God or the Lord. Therefore no spiritual communion or participation can be understood here, because the broken bread is that participation in the body of Christ, and the body of Christ is the thing or object in which that participation consists, of which both worthy and unworthy may partake, since they partake of the broken bread.

Even if one would like to speak of "the spiritual participation," it would not be necessary to name the two objects, "body and blood of Christ." It would be enough to name Christ alone, as Paul says at another point that we were called into the fellowship of the Son of God [I Cor. 1:9]. Why should he speak so distinctly of body and blood and, as it were, contrast two fellowships or communions as if they were two distinct kinds, the one differing from the other? Since the spiritual communion is only one kind and not two distinct kinds of communion, so also the participation or communion in the body of Christ is not the participation in the blood of Christ, or vice versa. For St. Paul here certainly separates them from each other. Now it is impossible that in a spiritual fellowship the body and the blood of Christ should be separated, and constitute two different fellowships, as is the case here. Therefore the communion or participation in the body and blood here must be bodily and not spiritual.

Thus we have this strong text in our favor, still firm and pure, in opposition to the bare, miserable glosses of the fanatics. Even if they do not accept or believe all this, at least we have shown reasons and arguments enough why we are compelled to maintain our interpretation. For even if I were a Turk, a Jew, or a heathen, who thought nothing of the Christian faith, and yet heard or read this scriptural account of the sacrament, I would still have to say, "I do not believe the Christian doctrine, of course, but this I must admit: if they wish to be Christians and maintain their doctrine, they must believe that Christ's body and blood are physically eaten and drunk in the bread and wine."

The fanatics, moreover, must admit that our interpretation simply and literally follows the words, though they are not satisfied with it and have refused to yield to it. We, on the other hand, are far less satisfied and willing to yield to their hungry, thirsty, naked glosses which they spin out of their heads in opposition to the simple construction of the words. If, indeed, we must cling to naked, bare words, we would rather cling to the naked, bare text which God himself has spoken than to naked, bare glosses devised by men. And even if they baptize these glosses and call them "Scripture and faith," this will not bother us until they also prove that they are Scripture and faith, as they falsely call them. They ought to bear in mind also that we are assuredly as unwilling to teach erroneously as they. To the present time, praise God, we have proved this with facts better and more fully than they, so that they need not haughtily arrogate all this glory to themselves as if they alone have this disposition. But Christ will be the judge of all who are guilty of lying and deceit.

This I will boast before God, that in this little book I have won the victory to the extent of proving that there cannot be any trope in the Supper, but that the words are to be understood just as they read: "This is my body; this is my blood"; this I know to be true. For if there were tropes, they would have to be tropes in all other passages which relate to the Supper. Now we have shown how the fanatics themselves teach and acknowledge that these words are not tropes in the saying of Paul, "Whoever eats and drinks in an unworthy manner will be guilty of profaning the body and blood of the Lord" [I Cor. 11:29]; neither are they tropes, therefore, in this saying, "The cup of blessing which we bless is a participation in the blood of Christ" [I Cor. 10:16]. There is nothing left here that they can answer against us. If there is no trope in the Supper, it is abundantly clear that our interpretation is correct and that of the fanatics is incorrect and erroneous.

Since the sixth chapter of John does not refer at all to the Supper, and since it has already been treated by others such as Philip Melanchthon and John Brenz and many more, I leave it out of account now, although I have in mind to treat this passage also in a treatise, to add my own bit.[270]

The Third Part

I see that schisms and errors are increasing proportionately with the passage of time, and that there is no end to the rage and fury of Satan. Hence lest any persons during my lifetime or after my death appeal to me or misuse my writings to confirm their error, as the sacramentarian and baptist fanatics are already beginning to do, I desire with this treatise to confess my faith before God and all the world, point by point. I am determined to abide by it until my death and (so help me God!) in this faith to depart from this world and to appear before the judgment seat of our Lord Jesus Christ. Hence if any one shall say after my death, "If Luther were living now, he would teach and hold this or that article differently, for he did not consider it sufficiently," etc., let me say once and for all that by the grace of God I have most diligently traced all these articles through the Scriptures, have examined them again and again in the light thereof, and have wanted to defend all of them as certainly as I have now defended the sacrament of the altar. I am not drunk or irresponsible. I know

[270] Luther did not carry out his intention directly, though he did preach on John 6:26-28 in a series of sermons, 1530-1532, transcripts of which were published by Aurifaber in 1565. *LW* 23, 7 ff. Melanchthon's *Annotations on the Gospel of John* had been published in 1523, John Brenz's *Exposition of the Gospel of John* in 1527. *WA* 26, 498, n. 1.

what I am saying, and I well realize what this will mean for me before the Last Judgment at the coming of the Lord Jesus Christ. Let no one make this out to be a joke or idle talk; I am in dead earnest, since by the grace of God I have learned to know a great deal about Satan. If he can twist and pervert the Word of God and the Scriptures, what will he not be able to do with my or someone else's words?[271]

First, I believe with my whole heart the sublime article of the majesty of God, that the Father, Son, and Holy Spirit, three distinct persons, are by nature one true and genuine God, the Maker of heaven and earth; in complete opposition to the Arians, Macedonians, Sabellians,[272] and similar heretics, Genesis 1 [:1]. All this has been maintained up to this time both in the Roman Church and among Christian churches throughout the whole world.

Secondly, I believe and know that Scripture teaches us that the second person in the Godhead, viz. the Son, alone became true man, conceived by the Holy Spirit without the co-operation of man, and was born of the pure, holy Virgin Mary as of a real natural mother, all of which St. Luke clearly describes and the prophets foretold;[273] so that neither the Father nor the Holy Spirit became man, as certain heretics have taught.[274]

---

271 This paragraph is quoted in the *Formula of Concord,* Solid Declaration, VII, 29 ff.

272 Of the heresies listed here only Arianism is mentioned by name in the *Book of Concord,* e.g. *Augsburg Confession,* Art. I. Cf. p. 120, n. 198, above. Macedonianism, named after Macedonius, a fourth century archbishop of Constantinople, affirmed that the Holy Spirit is less than divine, not one of the divine persons; this view was condemned at a council at Alexandria in 362 and subsequently. Sabellianism, a third century form of Modal Monarchianism, treated the terms Father, Son, and Holy Spirit not as distinct divine persons but simply as different modes or even successive phases of the one God. It was Arius' accusation of Sabellianism against his bishop which opened the controversy leading to the Council of Nicaea, 325, where both Arianism and Sabellianism were excluded.

273 Cf. Luke 1:26 ff. With the Middle Ages generally, Luther found the virgin birth foretold in other prophecies besides Isa. 7:14, e.g. Isa. 9:6 (cf. *WA* 40^{III}, 680), but eventually he rejected most of those interpretations as farfetched.

274 The second and third century Patripassians (Monarchians) Noetus and Praxeas, opposed by Tertullian, taught the absolute unity of God in such a way as to affirm that the Father in the person of Jesus suffered on the cross. Montanus, a second century prophet, claimed to be the incarnation of the Holy Spirit.

Also that God the Son assumed not a body without a soul, as certain heretics have taught,[275] but also the soul, i.e. full, complete humanity, and was born the promised true seed or child of Abraham and of David and the son of Mary by nature, in every way and form a true man, as I am myself and every other man, except that he came without sin, by the Holy Spirit of the Virgin Mary alone.

And that this man became true God, as one eternal, indivisible person, of God and man, so that Mary the holy Virgin is a real, true mother not only of the man Christ, as the Nestorians teach,[276] but also of the Son of God, as Luke says [1:35], "The child to be born of you will be called the Son of God," i.e. my Lord and the Lord of all, Jesus Christ, the only, true Son by nature of God and of Mary, true God and true man.

I believe also that this Son of God and of Mary, our Lord Jesus Christ, suffered for us poor sinners, was crucified, dead, and buried, in order that he might redeem us from sin, death, and the eternal wrath of God by his innocent blood; and that on the third day he arose from the dead, ascended into heaven, and sits at the right hand of God the Father almighty, Lord over all lords, King over all kings and over all creatures in heaven, on earth, and under the earth, over death and life, over sin and righteousness.

For I confess and am able to prove from Scripture that all men have descended from one man, Adam; and from this man, through their birth, they acquire and inherit the fall, guilt and sin, which the same Adam, through the wickedness of the devil, committed in paradise; and thus all men along with him are born, live, and die altogether in sin, and would necessarily be guilty of eternal death if Jesus Christ had not come to our aid and taken upon himself this guilt and sin as an innocent lamb, paid for us by his sufferings, and if he did not still intercede and plead for us as a faithful, merciful Mediator, Savior, and the only Priest and Bishop of our souls.

I herewith reject and condemn as sheer error all doctrines

---

275 Apollinaris in the fourth century taught that the Word assumed human flesh and biological life (*psuchē*) but not a human higher soul or mind. Apollinarianism was condemned in the 370's.

276 On Nestorianism see p. 212, n. 75, p. 292, n. 218.

which glorify our free will,[277] as diametrically contrary to the help and grace of our Savior Jesus Christ. Outside of Christ death and sin are our masters and the devil is our god and lord, and there is no power or ability, no cleverness or reason, with which we can prepare ourselves for righteousness and life or seek after it. On the contrary, we must remain the dupes and captives of sin and the property of the devil to do and to think what pleases them and what is contrary to God and his commandments.[278]

Thus I condemn also both the new and the old Pelagians[279] who will not admit original sin to be sin, but make it an infirmity or defect. But since death has passed to all men, original sin must be not merely an infirmity but enormous sin, as St. Paul says, "The wages of sin is death" [Rom. 6:23], and again, "Sin is the sting of death" [I Cor. 15:56]. So also David says in Psalm 51 [:5], "Behold, I was conceived in sin, and in sin did my mother bear me." He does not say, "My mother conceived me with sin," but, "I—I myself—I was conceived in sin, and in sin did my mother bear me," i.e. in my mother's womb I have grown from sinful seed, as the Hebrew text signifies.

Next, I reject and condemn also as sheer deceptions and errors of the devil all monastic orders, rules, cloisters, religious foundations, and all such things devised and instituted by men beyond and apart from Scripture, bound by vows and obligations,[280] although many great saints have lived in them, and as the elect of God are misled by them even at this time, yet finally by faith in Jesus Christ have been redeemed and have escaped. Because these monastic orders, foundations, and sects have been maintained and

---

[277] Luther is thinking particularly of Scotist and Occamist scholasticism, cf. *Disputation Against Scholastic Theology*, 1517. *LW* 31, 9 ff., and Erasmus' humanism, cf. *Bondage of the Will*, 1525. *LCC* 17, 101 ff. Erasmus in turn influenced many of the left-wing reformers.

[278] This paragraph is quoted in the *Formula of Concord*. Solid Declaration, II, 43.

[279] Pelagianism is condemned in the *Augsburg Confession*, Arts. II and XVIII. Pelagius, a fifth century heretic opposed especially by Augustine, taught that man's salvation was due to the faithful exercise of his free will. Though Pelagianism was condemned at councils in Ephesus, 431, and Orange, 529, subtle versions of this doctrine of self-salvation persistently reappeared. Luther objected to Zwingli's conception of original sin, cf. p. 16, n. 7, as well as that of the modernist scholastics and the humanists.

[280] Cf. *Address to the Nobility*, 1520. *LW* 44, 179 ff.; *On Monastic Vows*, 1521. *LW* 44, 251 ff.

perpetuated with the idea that by these ways and works men may seek and win salvation, and escape from sin and death, they are all a notorious, abominable blasphemy and denial of the unique aid and grace of our only Savior and Mediator, Jesus Christ. For "there is no other name given by which we must be saved" than this, which is Jesus Christ [Acts 4:12]. And it is impossible that there should be more saviors, ways, or means to be saved than through the one righteousness which our Savior Jesus Christ is and has bestowed upon us, and has offered to God for us as our one mercy seat, Romans 3 [:25].[281]

It would be a good thing if monasteries and religious foundations were kept for the purpose of teaching young people God's Word, the Scriptures, and Christian morals, so that we might train and prepare fine, capable men to become bishops, pastors, and other servants of the church, as well as competent, learned people for civil government, and fine, respectable, learned women capable of keeping house and rearing children in a Christian way. But as a way of seeking salvation, these institutions are all the devil's doctrine and creed, I Timothy 4 [:1 ff.], etc.

But the holy orders and true religious institutions established by God are these three: the office of priest, the estate of marriage, the civil government.[282] All who are engaged in the clerical office or ministry of the Word are in a holy, proper, good, and God-pleasing order and-estate, such as those who preach, administer sacraments, supervise the common chest, sextons and messengers or servants who serve such persons. These are engaged in works which are altogether holy in God's sight.

Again, all fathers and mothers who regulate their household wisely and bring up their children to the service of God are engaged in pure holiness, in a holy work and a holy order. Similarly, when children and servants show obedience to their elders and masters, here too is pure holiness, and whoever is thus engaged is a living saint on earth.

---

[281] The term "mercy seat," *propitiatorium* (cf. Luther's gloss on Rom. 3:25 in *Commentary on Romans,* 1515-1516. *WA* 56, 37 f.) is more accurately referred to Heb. 9:5, cf. Exod. 25:17 ff.

[282] Luther does not always name the "orders," i.e. the basic social units, in just this fashion. Cf. *Large Catechism,* Fourth Commandment, 158, and Melanchthon's *Augsburg Confession,* Art. XVI.

Moreover, princes and lords, judges, civil officers, state officials, notaries,[283] male and female servants and all who serve such persons, and further, all their obedient subjects—all are engaged in pure holiness and leading a holy life before God. For these three religious institutions or orders are found in God's Word and commandment; and whatever is contained in God's Word must be holy, for God's Word is holy and sanctifies everything connected with it and involved in it.

Above these three institutions and orders is the common order of Christian love, in which one serves not only the three orders, but also serves every needy person in general with all kinds of benevolent deeds, such as feeding the hungry, giving drink to the thirsty, forgiving enemies, praying for all men on earth, suffering all kinds of evil on earth, etc.[284] Behold, all of these are called good and holy works. However, none of these orders is a means of salvation. There remains only one way above them all, viz. faith in Jesus Christ.

For to be holy and to be saved are two entirely different things. We are saved through Christ alone; but we become holy both through this faith and through these divine foundations and orders. Even the godless may have much about them that is holy without being saved thereby. For God wishes us to perform such works to his praise and glory. And all who are saved in the faith of Christ surely do these works and maintain these orders.

What was said about the estate of marriage, however, should also be applied to widows and unmarried women, for they also belong to the domestic sphere. Now if these orders and divine institutions do not save, what can we say about the effects of the devil's institutions and monasteries, which have sprung up entirely without God's Word, and further, rage and contend against the one and only way of faith?

Thirdly, I believe in the Holy Spirit, who with the Father and the Son is one true God and proceeds eternally from the

---

283 *Amptleute* are civil officers in general. The title *Cantzler* not only means "chancellors" at court but also includes many of their underlings in embassies, etc. *Schreiber* (scribes) include prothonotaries, notaries, and other state officials in small localities.

284 The medieval church had commended the "seven acts of mercy," consisting of the six acts mentioned in Matt. 25:35 f., plus burying the dead.

Father and the Son, yet is a distinct person in the one divine essence and nature. By this Holy Spirit, as a living, eternal, divine gift and endowment, all believers are adorned with faith and other spiritual gifts, raised from the dead, freed from sin, and made joyful and confident, free and secure in their conscience. For this is our assurance if we feel this witness of the Spirit in our hearts, that God wishes to be our Father, forgive our sin, and bestow everlasting life on us.

These are the three persons and one God, who has given himself to us all wholly and completely, with all that he is and has. The Father gives himself to us, with heaven and earth and all the creatures, in order that they may serve us and benefit us. But this gift has become obscured and useless through Adam's fall. Therefore the Son himself subsequently gave himself and bestowed all his works, sufferings, wisdom, and righteousness, and reconciled us to the Father, in order that restored to life and righteousness, we might also know and have the Father and his gifts.

But because this grace would benefit no one if it remained so profoundly hidden and could not come to us, the Holy Spirit comes and gives himself to us also, wholly and completely. He teaches us to understand this deed of Christ which has been manifested to us, helps us receive and preserve it, use it to our advantage and impart it to others, increase and extend it. He does this both inwardly and outwardly—inwardly by means of faith and other spiritual gifts, outwardly through the gospel, baptism, and the sacrament of the altar, through which as through three means or methods he comes to us and inculcates the sufferings of Christ for the benefit of our salvation.

Therefore I maintain and know that just as there is no more than one gospel and one Christ, so also there is no more than one baptism. And that baptism in itself is a divine ordinance, as is his gospel also. And just as the gospel is not false or incorrect for the reason that some use it or teach it falsely, or disbelieve it, so also baptism is not false or incorrect even if some have received or administered it without faith, or otherwise misused it. Accordingly, I altogether reject and condemn the teaching of the Anabaptists and Donatists, and all who rebaptize.[285]

[285] Cf. *Babylonian Captivity of the Church,* 1520, *LW* 36, 57 ff., and *On*

In the same way I also say and confess that in the sacrament of the altar the true body and blood of Christ are orally eaten and drunk in the bread and wine, even if the priests who distribute them or those who receive them do not believe or otherwise misuse the sacrament. It does not rest on man's belief or unbelief but on the Word and ordinance of God—unless they first change God's Word and ordinance and misinterpret them, as the enemies of the sacrament do at the present time. They, indeed, have only bread and wine, for they do not also have the words and instituted ordinance of God but have perverted and changed it according to their own imagination.[286]

Next, I believe that there is one holy Christian Church on earth, i.e. the community or number or assembly of all Christians in all the world, the one bride of Christ, and his spiritual body of which he is the only head. The bishops or priests are not her heads or lords or bridegrooms, but servants, friends, and—as the word "bishop" implies—superintendents, guardians, or stewards.[287]

This Christian Church exists not only in the realm of the Roman Church or pope, but in all the world, as the prophets foretold that the gospel of Christ would spread throughout the world, Psalm 2 [:8], Psalm 19 [:4]. Thus this Christian Church is physically dispersed among pope, Turks, Persians, Tartars, but spiritually gathered in one gospel and faith, under one head, i.e. Jesus Christ. For the papacy is assuredly the true realm of Antichrist, the real anti-Christian tyrant, who sits in the temple of God and rules with human commandments, as Christ in Matthew 24 [:24] and Paul in II Thessalonians 2 [:3 f.] declare; although the Turk and

Rebaptism, 1528. *LW* 40, 229 ff., and *Augsburg Confession*, Art. IX. The Donatists were a rigorist sect in North Africa, originating in the fourth century, who insisted that the holiness of the church must be judged in terms of the moral purity of its members, and that the ministerial acts of an unholy priest were invalid. Baptism in the orthodox church therefore was invalid, and converts from that church had to submit to a true baptism. What the Christian Roman empire thus considered "rebaptism" was made punishable by death in the Code of Justinian, as subversive of Christian society itself, and on that basis the sixteenth century "Anabaptists" were persecuted.

[286] This paragraph is quoted in the *Formula of Concord*, Solid Declaration, VII, 32. Cf. also *Augsburg Confession*, Arts. X and VIII.

[287] Cf. *Augsburg Confession*, Art. VII. On the word "bishop," see *Answer to Goat Emser*, 1521. *LW* 39, 154 f.; *Misuse of the Mass*, 1522. *LW* 36, 155 ff.; and *Augsburg Confession*, Art. XXVIII.

all heresies, wherever they may be, are also included in this abomination which according to prophecy will stand in the holy place, but are not to be compared to the papacy.[288]

In this Christian Church, wherever it exists, is to be found the forgiveness of sins, i.e a kingdom of grace and of true pardon. For in it are found the gospel, baptism, and the sacrament of the altar, in which the forgiveness of sins is offered, obtained, and received. Moreover, Christ and his Spirit and God are there. Outside this Christian Church there is no salvation[289] or forgiveness of sins, but everlasting death and damnation; even though there may be a magnificent appearance of holiness and many good works, it is all in vain. But this forgiveness of sins is not to be expected only at one time, as in baptism, as the Novatians teach, but frequently, as often as one needs it, till death.[290]

For this reason I have a high regard for private confession, for here God's word and absolution are spoken privately and individually to each believer for the forgiveness of his sins, and as often as he desires it he may have recourse to it for this forgiveness, and also for comfort, counsel, and guidance. Thus it is a precious, useful thing for souls, as long as no one is driven to it with laws and commandments but sinners are left free to make use of it, each according to his own need, when and where he wishes; just as we are free to obtain counsel and comfort, guidance and instruction when and where our need or our inclination moves us. And as long as one is not forced to enumerate all sins but only those which oppress him most grievously, or those which a person will mention in any case, as I have discussed in my *Little Book on Prayer*.[291]

---

288 From 1520 on (cf. *Address to the Nobility*. *LW* 44, 133) Luther's writings regularly identified the papacy with the Antichrist. On the Turk, see *War Against the Turk*, 1529. *LW* 46, 181, 196.

289 On Luther's understanding of this famous dictum of Cyprian see *Large Catechism*, Creed, Art. III, 56, where Luther closely connects the church with the forgiveness of sins.

290 Novatian, a third century rigorist, insisted that once baptized, a Christian could not be forgiven a grave sin. Some Left-Wing Protestants revived this teaching, cf. *The Keys*, 1530. *LW* 40, 374. The *Augsburg Confession*, Art. XII, condemns Novatianism.

291 This paragraph was added by Luther when Part III of this treatise was issued separately. On private confession see *Babylonian Captivity of the Church*. *LW* 36, 86 ff.; *The Sacrament—Against the Fanatics*, 1526. *LW* 36,

But the pardons or indulgences which the papal church has and dispenses are a blasphemous deception, not only because it invents and devises a special forgiveness beyond the general forgiveness which in the whole Christian Church is bestowed through the gospel and the sacrament and thus desecrates and nullifies the general forgiveness, but also because it establishes and bases satisfaction for sins upon the works of men and the merits of saints, whereas only Christ can make and has made satisfaction for us.[292]

As for the dead, since Scripture gives us no information on the subject, I regard it as no sin to pray with free devotion in this or some similar fashion: "Dear God, if this soul is in a condition accessible to mercy, be thou gracious to it." And when this has been done once or twice, let it suffice. For vigils and requiem masses and yearly celebrations of requiems are useless, and are merely the devil's annual fair.[293]

Nor have we anything in Scripture concerning purgatory. It too was certainly fabricated by goblins. Therefore, I maintain it is not necessary to believe in it; although all things are possible to God, and he could very well allow souls to be tormented after their departure from the body. But he has caused nothing of this to be spoken or written, therefore he does not wish to have it believed, either. I know of a purgatory, however, in another way, but it would not be proper to teach anything about it in the church, nor on the other hand, to deal with it by means of endowments or vigils.[294]

354 ff.; the two *Catechisms*, and *Augsburg Confession*, Arts. XI and XXV.

[292] A full year before posting his *Ninety-five Theses*, Luther had publicly criticized the current indulgence doctrine. In the *Theses*, 1517, and the *Explanations of the Ninety-five Theses*, 1518 (*LW* 31, 25 ff., 83 ff.) Luther questioned the propriety of the practice and the clarity of the doctrine; by late 1520 he rejected indulgences in principle, cf. *Babylonian Captivity of the Church*. *LW* 36, 11; *Defense and Explanation of All the Articles*, 1521. *LW* 32, 33 f., 64 f.

[293] A requiem mass (*seelmesse*) is celebrated on the anniversary of decease; a vigil is a commemoration on the eve of the anniversary. Luther had questioned the celebration of masses for the dead in Thesis 83 of the *Ninety-five Theses*. *LW* 31, 32; he sharply criticized the practice in *Address to the Nobility*, 1520. *LW* 44, 180 f.

[294] On Luther's reinterpretation of purgatory see *Explanations of the Ninety-five Theses*. Thesis 15. *LW* 31, 125 ff., and *Defense and Explanation of All the Articles*, esp. Arts. 4 and 37. *LW* 32, 31 f., 95 ff.

Others before me have attacked the invocation of saints, and this pleases me. I believe, too, that Christ alone should be invoked as our Mediator, a truth which is scriptural and certain. Of the invocation of saints nothing is said in Scripture; therefore it is necessarily uncertain and not to be believed.[295]

If unction were practiced in accordance with the gospel, Mark 6 [:13] and James 5 [:14], I would let it pass. But to make a sacrament out of it is nonsense. Just as, in place of vigils and masses for the dead, one might well deliver a sermon on death and eternal life, and also pray during the obsequies and meditate upon our own end, as it seems was the practice of the ancients, so it would also be good to visit the sick, pray and admonish, and if anyone wished in addition to anoint him with oil, he should be free to do in the name of God.[296]

Neither is there any need to make sacraments out of marriage and the office of the priesthood. These orders are sufficiently holy in themselves.[297] So, too, penance is nothing else than the practice and the power of baptism.[298] Thus two sacraments remain, baptism and the Lord's Supper, along with the gospel, in which the Holy Spirit richly offers, bestows, and accomplishes the forgiveness of sins.

As the greatest of all abominations I regard the mass when it

---

[295] Precursors in criticizing the cult of saints included high ecclesiastics, e.g. Gerson, popular preachers, e.g. Berthold of Regensburg, would-be reformers, e.g. Huss, humanists, e.g. Erasmus. On Luther's critique see *Explanations of the Ninety-five Theses,* Thesis 58. *LW* 31, 212 ff., *Fourteen Consolations,* 1520. *LW* 42, 121 ff. Cf. *Augsburg Confession,* Art. XXI. Matters treated in these four paragraphs above are crisply criticized by Luther as a "vermin-brood and poison of idolatries" begotten by the "dragon's tail," the mass, in *Smalcald Articles,* 1537, II, Art. II, 11 ff.; cf. *Augsburg Confession,* Art. XXIV.

[296] Cf. *Babylonian Captivity of the Church. LW* 36, 118 ff.

[297] Cf. *Babylonian Captivity of the Church. LW* 36, 92 ff., 106 ff. Melanchthon would not have been averse to calling ordination, properly understood, a sacrament. *Apology,* Art. XIII, 11. He was less willing to call marriage a sacrament. *Ibid.,* 14 ff. Cf. Sasse, *This Is My Body,* p. 25, n. 10.

[298] The Wittenbergers wavered for a long time between acknowledging and not acknowledging absolution—part of the Roman Catholic sacrament of penance—as a third sacrament; see the ambiguity on the subject in *Babylonian Captivity of the Church. LW* 36, 18 and 124, and Melanchthon's explicit recognition of it in *Apology,* Art. XIII, 4. Luther preferred to subsume repentance under baptism, *Babylonian Captivity of the Church. LW* 36, 58 f., 61, 69, 81 ff.; *Large Catechism,* Baptism, 74 ff. Cf. *Augsburg Confession,* Art. XII.

is preached or sold as a sacrifice or good work, which is the basis on which all religious foundations and monasteries now stand,[299] but, God willing, they shall soon be overthrown. Although I have been a great, grievous, despicable sinner, and wasted my youth in a thoughtless and damnable manner, yet my greatest sins were that I was so holy a monk, and so horribly angered, tortured, and plagued my dear Lord with so many masses for more than fifteen years.[300] But praise and thanks be to his unspeakable grace in eternity, that he led me out of this abomination, and still continues to sustain and strengthen me daily in the true faith, despite my great ingratitude.

Accordingly, I have advised and still advise people to abandon religious foundations and monasteries and their vows and come forth into the true Christian orders, in order to escape these abominations of the mass and this blasphemous holiness, i.e. "chastity, poverty, and obedience," by which men imagine they are saved.[301] Excellent as it was in the early days of the Christian Church to maintain the state of virginity, so abominable is it now when it is used to deny the aid and grace of Christ. It is entirely possible to live in a state of virginity, widowhood, and chastity without these blasphemous abominations.

Images, bells, eucharistic vestments, church ornaments, altar lights, and the like I regard as things indifferent. Anyone who wishes may omit them. Images or pictures taken from the Scriptures and from good histories, however, I consider very useful yet indifferent and optional. I have no sympathy with the iconoclasts.[302]

---

[299] *Babylonian Captivity of the Church.* *LW* 36, 35 f.; *Treatise on the New Testament,* 1520. *LW* 35, 75 ff. Cf. *Augsburg Confession,* Art. XXIV.

[300] Luther's reminiscences about his life in Roman Catholicism are collected in Scheel, *Dokumente zu Luthers Entwicklung,* (2nd ed.; Tübingen, 1929); cf. also *WA* 58^I^, *Gesamtregister.* Interpretations in Bainton, *Here I Stand* (New York, 1950), esp. chaps. 1-3; Rupp, *Luther's Progress to the Diet of Worms* (Chicago, 1951); Fife, *Revolt of Martin Luther* (New York, 1957), esp. chaps. 6-8, 11.

[301] Luther here lists the traditional monastic vows; "chastity" here means celibacy. Cf. *Babylonian Captivity of the Church.* *LW* 36, 74 ff.; *On Monastic Vows,* 1521. *LW* 44, 251 ff. *Augsburg Confession,* Art. XXVII.

[302] Cf. Luther's *Eight Wittenberg Sermons,* 1522. *LW* 51, 70 ff., and his writings against Karlstadt and Münzer in 1524-1525, *LW* 40; and *Formula of the Mass,* 1523. *LW* 53, 30 ff.

Finally, I believe in the resurrection of all the dead at the Last Day, both the godly and the wicked, that each may receive in his body his reward according to his merits. Thus the godly will live eternally with Christ and the wicked will perish eternally with the devil and his angels. I do not agree with those who teach that the devils also will finally be restored to salvation.[303]

This is my faith, for so all true Christians believe and so the Holy Scriptures teach us. On subjects which I have treated too briefly here, my other writings will testify sufficiently, especially those which have been published during the last four or five years. I pray that all godly hearts will bear me witness of this, and pray for me that I may persevere firmly in this faith to the end of my life. For if in the assault of temptation or the pangs of death I should say something different—which God forbid—let it be disregarded; herewith I declare publicly that it would be incorrect, spoken under the devil's influence. In this may my Lord and Savior Jesus Christ assist me: blessed be he for ever, Amen.

[303] Origen in the third century taught that the devils would ultimately be converted. Though this view was condemned at Constantinople in 553, it was revived in the sixteenth century.

INDEXES

INDEX OF NAMES AND SUBJECTS

INDEX TO SCRIPTURE PASSAGES